The Prentice Hall PTR
ActiveX Series

Vivian Neou

ActiveX
Controls to Go

Gary Cornell and Dave Jezak

ActiveX
Visual Basic 5
Control Creation Edition

ActiveX

Visual Basic 5
Control Creation Edition

GARY CORNELL
DAVE JEZAK

Prentice Hall PTR
Upper Saddle River, NJ 07458
http://www.prenhall.com

Editorial/Production Supervision: Navta Associates, Inc.
Acquisitions Editor: Greg Doench
Manufacturing Manager: Alexis Heydt
Marketing Manager: Stephen Solomon
Cover Design: Anthony Gemmellaro
Cover Design Direction: Jerry Votta
Art Director: Gail Cocker-Bogusz
Series Design: Meg VanArsdale

The publisher offers discounts on this book when ordered in bulk quantities.
For more information, contact:

Corporate Sales Department
Prentice Hall PTR
One Lake Street
Upper Saddle River, NJ 07458
Phone: 800-382-3419; FAX: 201-236-7141
E-mail (Internet): corpsales@prenhall.com

To join a Prentice Hall Internet mailing list
point to: http://www.prenhall.com/register

Printed in the United States of America

10 9 8 7 6 5 4 3 2 1

ISBN 0-13-749185-9

Prentice-Hall International (UK) Limited, **London**
Prentice-Hall of Australia Pty. Limited, **Sydney**
Prentice-Hall Canada Inc., **Toronto**
Prentice-Hall Hispanoamericana, S.A., **Mexico**
Prentice-Hall of India Private Limited, **New Delhi**
Prentice-Hall of Japan, Inc., **Tokyo**
Simon & Schuster Asia Pte. Ltd., **Singapore**
Editora Prentice-Hall do Brasil, Ltda., **Rio de Janeiro**

Dedications

To my mother who taught me to drink so
deeply from the sea of knowledge
—Gary Cornell

To my loving wife Cheryl
—David Jezak

Contents

Tables and Figures

Tables

Figures

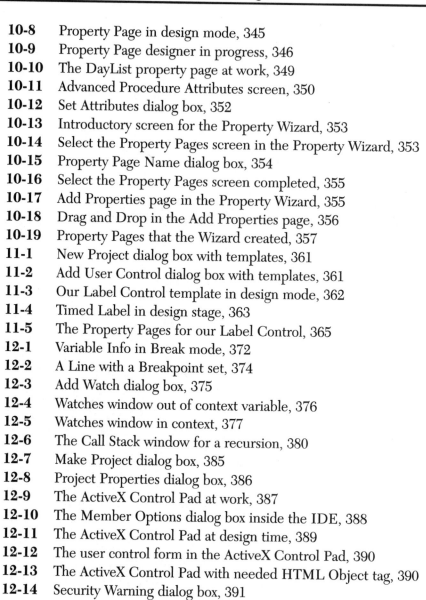

Introduction

With more than 3,000,000 users, Visual Basic is the most popular tool for programming Windows. However, there has always been one thing that Visual Basic couldn't do: make the *controls* that were the foundation of its success. (Control is the term used in Visual Basic for things like the text boxes and command buttons that are the building blocks for graphical user interfaces.) The latest version, called ActiveX Controls, is even more useful than the traditional Visual Basic controls. These controls can be used in standalone application and to make your Web pages come alive. ActiveX Controls are also one of the key building blocks for Microsoft's vision of the desktop and the Internet. Building ActiveX Controls was traditionally the domain of C++; one result was that even with the powerful Wizards available, the construction task was never very pleasant.

In late October 1996, Microsoft astounded the programming community by announcing the Visual Basic 5.0 Control Creation Edition. This extraordinarily powerful version of Visual Basic had the power to take existing controls and make them better—or even make new controls from scratch. Using the familiar Visual Basic model meant that the millions of Visual Basic programmers could finally liberate themselves from the burden of C++ programming. Moreover, the Visual Basic 5.0 Control Creation Edition followed the Visual Basic rule of being powerful, easy to use, and fun!

But that wasn't all. They also said:

"Microsoft is making the Visual Basic 5.0 Control Creation Edition available free."

(Of course, they didn't promise a lot of documentation or hand holding—allowing books like this to get you up to speed on this amazing new product.)

An obvious question is: What is the relationship of the Visual Basic 5.0 Control Creation Edition (or the CCE, as it is usually called) to past and future versions of Visual Basic? The relationship to Visual Basic 4 is easy: the CCE's environment is easier to use, its language far more powerful. The only thing that the CCE can't do in its basic (free) state is make standalone programs or connect to databases.

But what is the connection of the CCE to future versions of Visual Basic? For this, we quote Microsoft's official statement on how the CCE relates to other versions of Visual Basic 5.0:

"Visual Basic 5.0 Control Creation Edition includes the new intelligent code editor, forms engine, and interactive debugger of Visual Basic 5.0. It does not include some of the functionality found in the retail editions of Visual Basic, such as the Jet database engine, report writing, integration with the Visual SourceSafe™ version control system, and other features not required for control creation."

The point is that you have everything you need to build the most amazing controls—and you have it for free. The only limitations remaining are those of your imagination!

About This Book

This book is a complete guide to the Visual Basic 5.0 Control Creation Edition (CCE) for experienced programmers, no matter what language you are coming from. It's filled with what we hope are examples of useful controls. We have also included a set of templates that make it easier to build more powerful controls. We do not assume you have ever programmed in Visual Basic before, and the beginning of this book gives a concise yet complete treatment of the underlying programming language in the CCE. (Of course, if you know an earlier version of Visual Basic, you can skim this material.)

How This Book Is Organized

Programmers familiar with Visual Basic might want to skim the early chapters and spend more time on the later chapters where we cover the details of creating controls. Anyone familiar with Pascal or C but not an event-driven language like Visual Basic might want to spend more time on the early chapters. In any case, no matter what your language background, we suggest looking at all the chapters for information specific to creating controls.

Here are brief descriptions of the chapters:

- Chapter 1 gives an introduction to the CCE and shows how to build a simple but useful extension of the ordinary text box.
- Chapter 2 shows the CCE environment.
- Chapter 3 starts with the notion of a customizable window (called a form) that is the heart of every control. You'll see how to add and manipulate the fundamental Visual Basic objects, such as command buttons, places to enter text, labels, and timers.
- Chapters 4 and 5 survey the underlying programming language in the CCE.
- Chapter 6 goes further into the user interface including a brief but complete treatment of graphics and the mouse.
- Chapter 7 gives the Control Creation Edition's take on object-oriented programming. Object-oriented programming in the CCE is far more sophisticated than in earlier versions of Visual Basic.
- Chapter 8 goes beyond the simple controls you have seen to this point by showing what is needed to make controls full featured. This includes adding custom properties and methods to your controls.
- Chapter 9 covers the Control Interface Wizard which helps automate the routine work needed for creating a control.
- Chapter 10 covers property pages. This is a new feature to Visual Basic that lets you set properties for a control in a much more user-friendly manner.
- Chapter 11 offers a set of powerful templates which you can use to build your own controls.
- Chapter 12 takes up the important issues of testing and debugging along with a short discussion of how to deploy your control.
- Each of chapters 13–17 is devoted to complete coverage of an individual control. These are not toy examples but full-featured controls that you can use immediately or as a foundation for your own controls. Each chapter is self-contained and can be read in any order. (We have tried to place them by what we think of as their increasing level of sophistication.)

- Chapter 13 is a font-friendly label that automatically adjusts itself to the size of the font used.

- Chapter 14 gives all of Visual Basic's powerful financial functions encapsulated in a single ActiveX Control. If you need to do financial calculations on a Web page, you can use our control on your Web and bypass a lot of scripting. This control also serves as a model for encapsulating the functionality of any DLL into an ActiveX Control.

- Chapter 15 gives a full-fledged universal Calendar Control complete with drop-down monthly calendar.

- Chapter 16 is an extension of the ordinary Visual Basic text box that allows both insert and overstrike modes.

- Chapter 17 is a option button group control that lets you simplify the use of many option buttons on a form.

Conventions Used in This Book

Keys are set in small capital letters in the text. For example, keys such as CTRL and ALT appear as shown here. Arrow and other direction keys are spelled out and also appear in small capital letters. For example, if you need to press the right arrow key, you'll see, "Press RIGHT ARROW." Code that is in line appears in `courier typeface`.

When you need to use a combination of keys to activate a menu item, the keys will be separated by addition signs and the entire key combination will appear in small capital letters. For example, "Press CTRL+ALT+DEL" is how we would indicate the "three-fingered salute" that (thankfully) is a lot less common in Windows 95. On the other hand, ALT F, P means press the ALT and F keys, and then the P key—you don't have to hold down the ALT key. Menu choices are indicated with a bar between them, e.g., "Choose Run|Run."

Programs are set in a monospace font, as shown here:

```
Private Sub Form_Click( )
   Message "Hello world!"
End Sub
```

Tips are indicated by the following icon.

Be sure to check out Microsoft's Web site (www.microsoft.com) for updates to the Control Creation Edition. ➲

Notes are indicated by the following icon.

People have asked us about the licensing rules for our code. You may freely use any of our code as the basis for a non-commercial product. You may not post our source code on your Web site without our permission. If you use one of our controls as the basis for a control of your own, then everyone on the development team for the product that is using our code must own a copy of this book. And, obviously, you may not simply repackage our code and sell it! ➲

Caution statements are indicated by the this icon.

Acknowledgments

One of the best parts of writing a book is when the authors get to thank those who have helped them, for rarely (and certainly not in this case) is a book truly the product of the authors' work alone. First and foremost, we have to thank the teams at Prentice Hall and Navta Associates. Their patience, dedication, help, and cheerfulness in producing a book under incredible time pressure went way beyond the call of duty. To Nikki Wise and her team at Navta Associates, to Greg Doench, Mary Treacy and the rest of the Prentice Hall team: thanks! David Holmes, Brad Hoffman, Phil Lee and Ron Bailey went far beyond what authors can expect (or hope) to have from tech reviewers; we are truly grateful.

Gary Cornell would first like to thank Cay Horstmann. Cay's books and conversations taught him most of what he knows about object-oriented programming and, if that was not enough, Cay's friendship has been constant despite the great stress of joint work. He also needs to thank all his other friends. They all put up with his strange ways and, occasionally, short temper for this short but very intense time. In particular, thanks to Bruce, Caroline, and Kurt; without their special friendship and help, his part of the book would have been impossible to write. He also wants to thank Dave's family—their patience with a seemingly endless stream of phone calls was more than anyone could have expected!

Dave Jezak must first thank God for the wisdom and intelligence that enabled him to undertake and complete this book in combination with the rest of his hectic life. Secondly, he thanks his wife Cheryl for her love, patience, and encouragement throughout this project. And to Hannah and Michael, for their unconditional love, support, and sacrifice of their Dad through the many hours of work at home. Finally, to his friends Dave, Brad, Phil, and Ron for their support, encouragement, and accountability, without which he would be lost.

Chapter 1

This chapter will introduce you to the brave new world of ActiveX technologies, in general, and ActiveX Controls, specifically. We briefly explain what the ActiveX technologies are, then move to the ActiveX controls that are one of the cornerstones of the ActiveX technology. We give examples of what existing controls can do, and end by showing how to build a simple yet powerful ActiveX Control of your own using the Visual Basic Control Creation Edition Version 5.0. (That's rather a mouthful. Usually we will just say Visual Basic Control Creation Edition—or "CCE," which is what most people call it.)

Introduction to ActiveX

Introduction

A few years ago in the *New York Times*, Charles Petzold, who wrote two of the standard books on Windows programming, said this about the first version of Visual Basic: "For those of us who make our living explaining the complexities of Windows programming to programmers, Visual Basic poses a real threat to our livelihood." To a large extent, that is true. Visual Basic became so popular because it shields us from most of the complexities of Windows programming. No cryptic hWnd's or event processing loops to worry about. Visual Basic is now, in fact, the world's most popular programming language with more than 3 million users.

However, there has always been one thing Visual Basic couldn't do: it couldn't make the external *controls* (VBXs prior to VB 4.0 and OCXs since 4.0) that were the foundation of its success. (Control is the term used in Visual Basic for things like the text boxes and command buttons that are the building blocks for graphical user interfaces. Other languages may call them something else, for example, *widgets* in X programming)

Visual Basic controls always needed to be built-in languages like C, C++ or, more recently, Delphi. The Visual Basic Control Creation Edition fills this gap. And, hard as it might be to believe, it's *free*. Moreover, the controls you build with it can be used without any royalties in any program that can accept ActiveX controls. This includes ordinary Visual Basic programs, the Internet Explorer (activated via VBScripting), and VBA hosts such as MSWord, Excel, or Access, or any program that supports ActiveX scripting.

By the way, ActiveX have become "magic words" for Microsoft. In October of 1996, Microsoft announced its support for what they called the *Active Platform*. ("The Active Platform is an open platform that enables developers to take full advantage of Microsoft's leading, standard-based implementations of HTML, open scripting, component architecture and underlying operating system services.") Even though this is written in typical Microsoft-speak, it is noteworthy. Why? Well, as Bob Muglia, a Microsoft VP, said, "Keep in mind when we don't use the word platform lightly. Windows 95 is a platform, as is Windows NT. Applications like Office are not platforms." An essential part of the Active Platform is ActiveX technology.

So what is ActiveX? In a nutshell, ActiveX is Microsoft's attempt to come up with a cross platform, language-independent technology to use in networked environments—specifically, the Internet and corporate "intranets." Microsoft has, in fact, made the nearly unprecedented step of releasing control of the standards for ActiveX technology to a third party (the Open Group).

 Even Netscape will provide support for ActiveX in the next version of Netscape Navigator. ⊃

ActiveX is built on a specification for objects called COM, or the common object model. (See Chapter 7 for a short course in Object-Oriented Programming (OOP); see Chapter 8 for a brief introduction to COM.)

ActiveX Controls

ActiveX controls are the most common manifestation of the ActiveX technology. In particular, Microsoft clearly wants to see ActiveX controls everywhere: the desktop, the Internet and the Intranet. ActiveX controls give the developer small footprints, reusable software components. These components can easily be activated through development tools, browsers and applications. In turn, these components can give the user a richer and more rewarding experience than could be hand-coded in a reasonable amount of time by most developers.

Here is the typical situation: you want your user to be able to enter a date. Wouldn't it be nice to click on an icon that pops up to a calendar? Then it would be easy to choose the date. And, wouldn't it be even nicer if the calendar would show weekends and holidays in gray? You wouldn't want to write this from scratch; the rules for leap years are a pain, the GUI needed would be no fun to maintain. However, someone did—we built one, too.

The point is you can drop an ActiveX calendar control into a Web page with a few keystrokes using the ActiveX Control Pad (see Chapter 12). The result is a Web page that is more useful to the browsing public. Using an ActiveX control, you could accomplish this with far less effort than by programming a calendar control in Java, C or C++.

For a more serious example, consider something you would probably never want to program by hand: suppose you want to allow a user to access information from a database on a Web page. Using the appropriate ActiveX control, here's all you have to do:

1. Put a data control and some bound (data-aware) controls on your page;
2. Tell the data control the name of the database via a property setting at design time or via VB Script code that sets a property at run time;
3. Tell the data bound control the name of the table or the query you want it to display, also via a property setting at design time or run time.

The control will then

1. Fetch the data;
2. Resize itself automatically, based on the data it receives (adding scroll bars if necessary); and
3. Display the data.

All this can be done at design time or run time and takes, at most, 5 lines of code for the run-time version.

 The VB Control Creation Edition does not come with the data control needed to bind data-aware controls. You may have purchased one of these controls from Microsoft (in VB4, for example) or from some third party in order to extend them using the VB5 Control Creation Edition. ⊃

By the way, ActiveX controls need not be visible. In Chapter 14, we encapsulate the functionality given by the financial functions supplied with Visual Basic 4.0 and VBA 5.0. The resulting control isn't visible, yet it gives you easy access to some very powerful financial functions—free of charge. This control lets you do complicated calculations like mortgage analysis or net present value on your Web page without programming any of the calculations by hand—no mathematical knowledge is needed at all.

Finally, keep in mind that the controls you build using the Control Creation Edition will most often be based on existing controls. You will rarely be building a control totally from scratch. Since there are more than 2,000 ActiveX controls already available, you have lots of controls to extend. In particular, the controls we wrote and supply on the CD, in source and executable form, are not there only for their instructional value; they can, in many cases, provide the framework for your own controls. (For the third party controls we supply as samples, please check if you are permitted to extend the licensing requirements of the company that supplied them for use in commercial products.)

For those who have worked with OCX controls before: roughly speaking, an ActiveX control is a lightweight OCX. The main difference is that instead of needing to support multiple interfaces, an ActiveX control need only support IUnknown and be self-registering. This makes it much smaller, hence, much easier to deliver via slow network connections. ⊃

The Property/Method/Event Model

Although we will have a lot more to say about objects in Chapter 7, this section explains how most people think about ActiveX controls when they are using them. This, in turn, affects how you program them.

An ActiveX control has properties you can read and write, methods to perform actions, and events that respond to user interaction. The properties can describe how wide or tall it is, what color it is, what font it uses to display information, and so on. You can set the properties of an ActiveX control at design time, run time, or both. You might call a method to add or remove a row or column to a grid control, or add to the list of items in a list box. An event, on the other hand, is something a control can respond to. For example, a button might respond only to a single click but another kind of control would respond (differently) to single and double clicks.

In Visual Basic or VBScript, the code that determines how a control responds to events is contained in an event procedure. For example, in both VBScript and VB code,

```
Sub Command1_Click()
    MsgBox You "clicked me!"
End Sub
```

This is a very simple yet typical event procedure for the Click event attached to a command button.

Building an ActiveX Control

The rest of this chapter will give the steps needed to build a simple ActiveX control.

 We are assuming that you have successfully installed the Visual Basic Control Creation Edition Version 5.0. ⊃

Our simple control will be a text box that accepts only numerals (0–9), i.e., only non-negative integers. Once we build it, we will add an event called BadEntry that is triggered (*raised* is the technical term) whenever the user tries to enter a non-numeral or pastes a non-integer into the box.

Getting Started

When you start the CCE, you see a licensing screen. After that, you are taken to Figure 1-1 which shows the type of projects you can build.

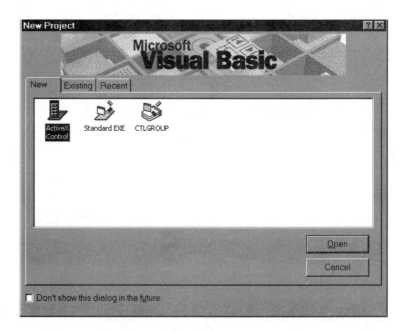

Figure 1-1
The New Project window

Choose ActiveX Control and click on Open. This takes you to the initial screen of the CCE.

We will discuss this screen in the next chapter. The title bar, for example, gives the name of the control you are building (in this case, a rather sterile UserControl1). The left-hand side gives the toolbox which contains the controls you start with. (If it is not visible, choose View|Toolbox from the main menu to make it visible.)

For now, we just want to continue the step-by-step process of building a user control. The window with the grid in Figure 1-2 is called the User Control Object or User Control form. (To anyone familiar with VB, it looks like an ordinary VB form.) What you place or draw in this window is what the user of your control initially sees at design time.

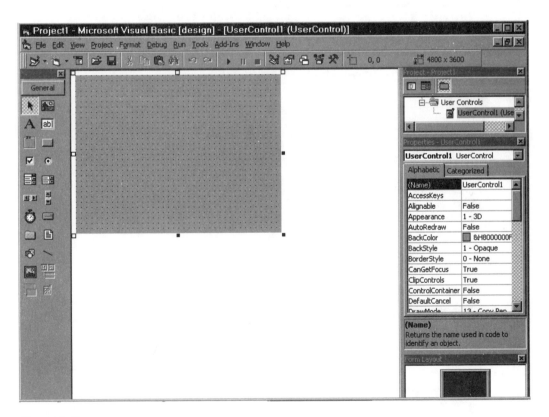

Figure 1-2
The Initial CCE screen

Since UserControl1 is not a very good name for a non-negative integer-only text box, change it to better reflect the object's functionality. For this:

- Go to the Properties window in the right-hand side of the window, as shown here. (If it is not visible, press F4 or choose View|Properties.)

If the Name property isn't highlighted in the Properties window, click in the left-hand column to highlight it. (Notice that the bottom of the Properties window gives you a short description of the property. For example, in Figure 1-3, the Name property is described as "Returns the name used in code to identify an object." Change the name to NonNegativeIntegerTextBox. For this:

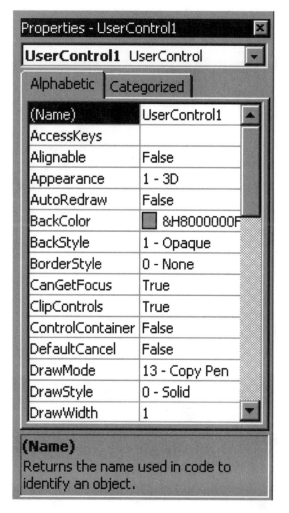

1. Double-click in the right-hand column of the Name property.

2. Enter the term NonNegativeIntegerTextBox.

3. Press ENTER.

Figure 1-3
The Properties window

Notice the tile bar has changed to reflect the new name.

We now want to add the text box that we will customize to the User Control object. For this:

- Double-click on the text box icon in the toolbox. (It is on the second line and says "ab" in it.)

This gives you a text box in the default size and location, as shown in Figure 1-4.

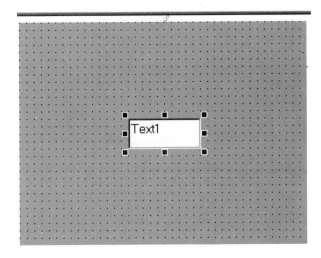

Figure 1-4
A text box in the User
Control object

Make sure the text box is blank. For this:

1. If the Properties window doesn't say Text1 TextBox on the top, click inside the text box.

2. Use the scroll bars to move through the Properties window until you get to the Text property in the left column. (It should say Text1 in the right-hand column.)

3. Erase the value in the right-hand column by double-clicking and then pressing DELETE.

Notice that the text box in the User Control object is now blank. We need to add the code to the text box to reject any non-numerals that are typed. For this:

- Double-click inside the text box. This brings up the Code window, as shown in Figure 1-5 on the next page.

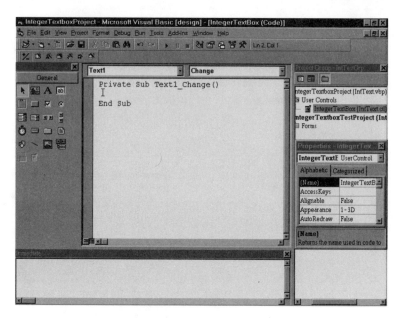

Figure 1-5
The Code window

The Code window shows you an event template for the Change event of the text box. We want to write the code that will make sure the user pastes in only integers. For this:

1. Move the cursor in the blank line between the two lines of the template.

2. Type the following lines before you get to the End Sub. (Don't worry about all the "statement completion boxes" that appear when you press the space bar or a period. These will make your life easier as soon as you become more comfortable with the CCE environment.)

```
If Text1.Text = "" Then Exit Sub
If Not (IsNumeric(Text1.Text)) Or Val(Text1.Text) < 0 _
(Int(Val(Text1.Text)) <> Val(Text1.Text)) Then
    Text1.Text = ""
End If
```

Now we want to make sure the user can only type numerals (0–9). For this, we need to write some code in the KeyPress event procedure. To do this:

1. Click on the DOWN ARROW near the box that currently says Change.

2. Move through the drop-down list box until you get to the KeyPress event. (Pressing "K" twice does this.)

3. Type the following code inside the KeyPress event template.

```
If KeyAscii < Asc("0") Or KeyAscii > Asc("9") Then
    KeyAscii = 0
End If
```

That's it, the control is ready for use. Figure 1-6 shows what your code looks like.

```
UserControl                              Initialize

Private Sub Text1_Change()
   If Text1.Text = "" Then Exit Sub
   If Not (IsNumeric(Text1.Text)) Or _
          (Int(Val(Text1.Text)) <> Val(Text1.Text)) Then
     Text1.Text = ""
   End If
End Sub

Private Sub Text1_KeyPress(KeyAscii As Integer)
   If KeyAscii < Asc("0") Or KeyAscii > Asc("9") Then
      KeyAscii = 0
   End If
End Sub

Private Sub UserControl_Initialize()
```

Figure 1-6
First steps in code

The next section describes the usual way to test a custom control, and the last section shows how to add an event to this control. (We will leave adding custom properties to this control for Chapter 8.)

Testing the Control

The usual way to test a control you have built is to start another project within the CCE environment. (You could compile it and start another environment to test it, but our way is much easier.) Think of this new project as a standalone VB program that would use your control. (Of course, CCE does not have the ability to make standalone VB executables. It can only build ActiveX controls and run them within the environment for testing purposes.) For this:

1. Choose File|Add Project.
2. When you see the Project dialog box, choose Standard EXE and click on Open.

At this point, your Project Explorer window in the top right corner should contain two projects. Figure 1.7 shows an enlarged view of the Project Explorer in this state.

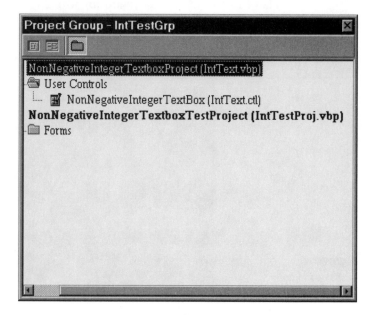

Figure 1-7
Project Explorer with two projects

3. Double-click on Form1 in the Forms folder to bring up the form in this project.

Look where the arrow is pointing in Figure 1-8 (the right corner of the toolbox). You can see a grayed outline of the default icon for a custom control along with a tooltip that describes it. The tooltip is added automatically by the CCE. (You will see how to add meaningful icons for your custom control in Chapter 8.)

Our custom control is currently inactive. This is because the User Control designer is still active and, so to speak, it has control of the control. To activate the control,

1. Double-click on the NonNegativeIntegerTextBox line in the Project Explorer to make the NonNegativeIntegerTextBox designer window active.

2. Close the designer by clicking on the X button in the menu bar (not on the X button in the title bar).

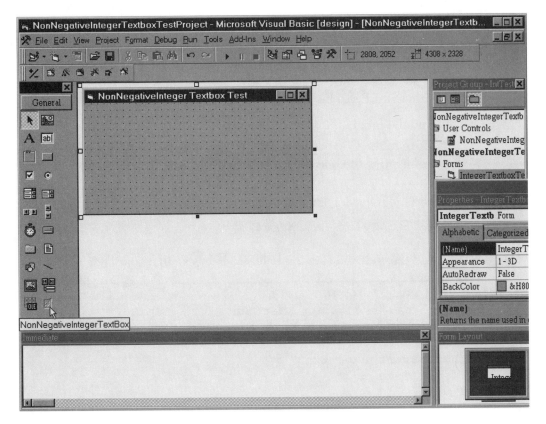

Figure 1-8
Toolbox with grayed custom icon

That's it, the non-negative integer text box is now an active control on the toolbox for Form1. To test it:

1. Double-click on its icon in the bottom right corner of the toolbox—this will place the control on Form1.
2. Press F5 to run Project2.

Try typing in this box. Notice that you can only type non-negative integers in it. If you want to test if you can only cut and paste non-negative integers in it, try cutting and pasting something that isn't one from another Windows application; the box will immediately go blank.

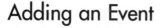

Adding an Event

For our final demonstration of the power you now have at your hands, we want to add a BadEntry event that we can program within the Form window of our Standard EXE. For this:

1. End the program if it is still running.
2. Move to the Code window for the NonNegativeIntegerTextBox by highlighting the line with NonNegativeIntegerTextBox in the Project Explorer and choosing View|Code.
3. Add the following line above the Text1_Change event.

   ```
   Public Event BadEntry()
   ```

4. Add the code indicated in boldface below so that your code reads:

```
Private Sub Text1_Change()
    If Text1.Text = "" Then Exit Sub
    If Not (IsNumeric(Text1.Text)) Or (Int(Val(Text1.Text)) _
    <> Val(Text1.Text)) Or Val(Text1.Text) < 0 Then
        RaiseEvent BadEntry
        Text1.Text = ""
    End If
End Sub

Private Sub Text1_KeyPress(KeyAscii As Integer)
    If KeyAscii < Asc("0") Or KeyAscii > Asc("9") Then
        KeyAscii = 0
        RaiseEvent BadEntry
    End If
End Sub
```

That's it. We have added the code to raise an event whenever the user enters a non-integer. To test it, we need to go back to Form1:

1. Double-click in the Form1 line of the Project Explorer.
2. Double-click on the NonNegativeIntegerTextBox. Notice that this brings up an event procedure for the BadEntry event, as shown in Figure 1-9.

doesn't seem to work in 4.0

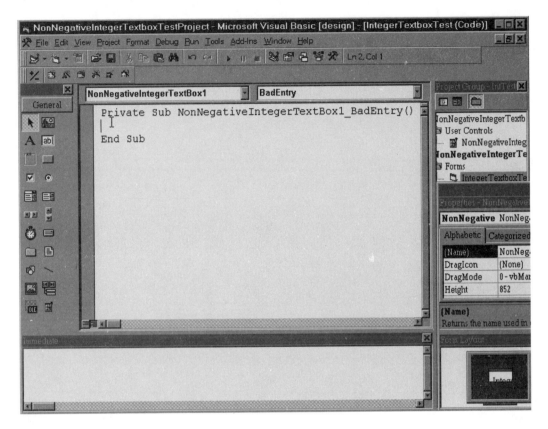

Figure 1-9
The BadEntry event procedure

3. Type the following line of code inside the template.

```
MsgBox "Please enter only non-negative integers!"
```

That's it! If you run the program, you'll see that it accepts only non-negative integers and any attempt to enter anything except a non-negative integer shows the message box (proving that our control does, indeed, respond to a custom event!).

 Obviously, there is a lot more that can be done to this control. In particular, the area for this customized text box is surrounded by a lot of "white space." You will see in Chapter 8 how to make your controls resize themselves automatically. ⊃

Chapter 2

The purpose of this chapter is to show you the Integrated Development Environment (IDE) of the Control Creation Edition, and provide a handy reference that you can return to as needed. Most of the menus and toolbar buttons are fairly self-explanatory, so we suggest skimming the information and returning to this chapter after you get a little further into creating controls.

The Control Creation Edition's Environment

CCE Environment Overview

If you are already familiar with Visual Basic 4.0, then much of the environment will seem familiar. The big difference is that, in earlier versions of Visual Basic, the IDE consisted of a main window made up of a menu and toolbar. All other windows were free-floating on the screen. (This is called single document interface or SDI.) However, the Control Creation Edition gets a new multiple document interface (or MDI) as its default, although the older SDI mode is still available as an option (see below). In MDI, all the windows are child windows of a parent window. With the introduction of the new MDI mode also comes *dockable windows*. Dockable windows enable you to connect child windows into groups of docked windows that can be moved and sized together.

Also new to the IDE is the ability to load multiple projects at the same time, known as *project groups*, which you saw in Chapter 1. This feature allows you to load another project with which to test your control while developing it, which is necessary for the testing of user controls.

The MDI IDE consists of a main window that has a menu and toolbar on top with all other child windows residing somewhere within the MDI space (see Figure 2-1). In SDI mode, the difference is that the child windows float freely and you can see your desktop in between them. See Figure 2-2 for what the default SDI desktop looks like—you will need to make other windows visible via the View menu to get something similar to Figure 2-1.

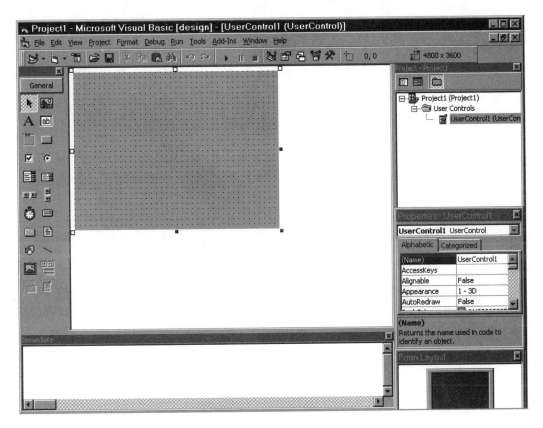

Figure 2-1
MDI mode

The default mode for the CCE is the new MDI mode, but you can change it to SDI using the Tools|Options Advanced tab. The change will take effect the next time you start the CCE. If you are an experienced Visual Basic user with a big screen, try the MDI mode; it is a little uncomfortable at first, but it grows on you.

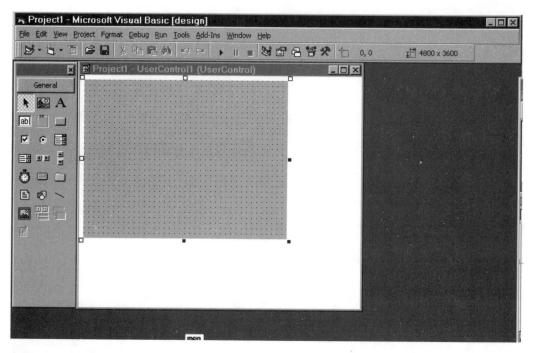

Figure 2-2
SDI mode

 If you are using anything less than 800 × 600 resolution, you will probably want to use SDI mode for coding. The code window in a low resolution MDI is ridiculously small. ⊃

Another new feature is customizable dockable toolbars. The Standard toolbar is visible by default but the other ones (Debug, Edit and Form Editor) are available by choosing View|Toolbars menu and selecting them. (See The Toolbar(s) section later in this chapter.)

If all this were not enough, in addition to the main window, main menu and toolbars, the IDE contains 9 other windows that may be made visible or invisible from the View menu. Finally, there are numerous dialog boxes that pop up when you invoke various commands and operations.

 In the version of the CCE available as we write this, context-sensitive help for the environment is not available. ⊃

An Overview of the Main Window

When you start up the CCE, you see a copyright screen indicating to whom the copy of the program is licensed. After a short delay, a tabbed dialog box appears. The first tab gives you a choice of a new ActiveX control, a Standard EXE, or something called a CTLGROUP (these will be described later). Figure 2-3 illustrates this. Choosing the Existing tab gives you a standard File Open dialog box, as shown in Figure 2-4. Choosing the Recent tab shows a list of your most recent projects. An example of what you will see in this case may be found in Figure 2-5.

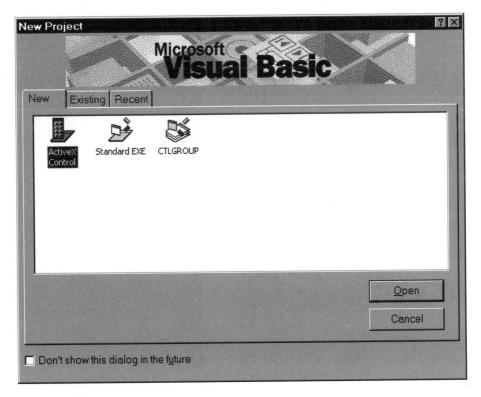

Figure 2-3
The New Project dialog box

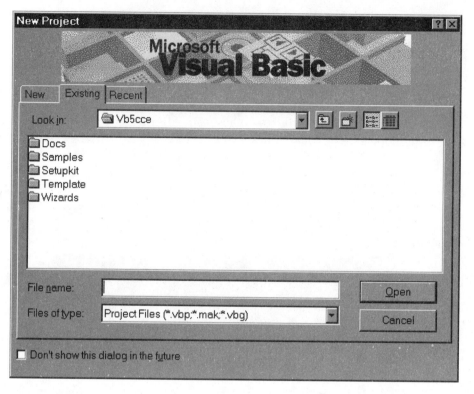

Figure 2-4
The Existing tab in the New Project dialog box

Although the CCE gives you the option of not using this dialog box as your gateway into it, (click off the check box shown in the left corner of Figure 2-3), we don't recommend it. If you want to get it back, select Prompt for Project in the Options dialog, explained later. ⊃

After you choose one of the options, you'll be taken to the main window. As mentioned earlier, this will either be the MDI interface shown in Figure 2-1 or the SDI interface of Figure 2-2.

The CCE remembers your last screen arrangement and reuses it. For this reason, your screen may look different from Figure 2-1 or 2-2. (This information is kept in the Windows Registry.) The CCE also remembers the state of a project and restores the environment as you left it. This information is kept in a file with the same name as your project but with the extension .vbw, which stands for Visual Basic Workspace. ⊃

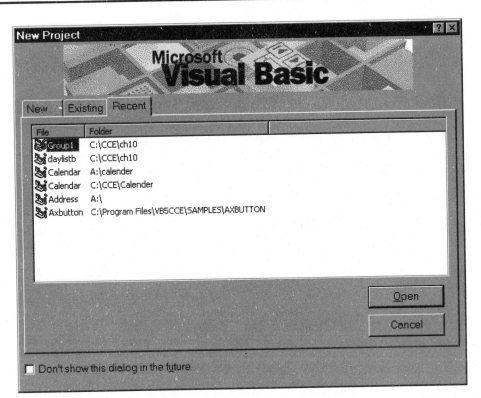

Figure 2-5
The Recent tab in the New Project dialog box

Title Bar

The title bar is the horizontal bar located at the top of the screen; it gives the name of the application and is common to all Microsoft Windows applications. Interactions between the user and the title bar are handled by Windows, not by the application. Everything below the title and menu bar in a Windows application is called the *client area*. Your application is completely responsible for the look, feel, and response of the objects you place in this area.

If you are working with a new user control in the CCE, the title bar starts out by displaying

Project1 - Microsoft Visual Basic [design] - [UserControl1 (UserControl)]

This is typical of Microsoft Windows applications: in sophisticated programs (like the CCE) that have multiple states, the title bar changes to indicate the different states. For example, when you are testing a user control in a Standard EXE, the title bar switches to something like:

Project1 - Microsoft Visual Basic [run]

and when you are debugging and have temporarily stopped the program, the title bar switches to something like

Project1 - Microsoft Visual Basic [break]

The Menu Bar

In the CCE, the menu bar gives you the tools needed to develop, test, and save your application. Most of the options have toolbar equivalents and keystroke shortcuts. For example, the File menu contains the commands for working with the files and projects that go into designing and testing a user control. The Edit menu contains editing tools that will help you write the code to activate the interface you design for your application, including the search-and-replace editing tools. (Only a few are available on the Edit toolbar.) The View menu gives you fast access to the different parts of your program and the CCE environment. The Project menu gives you access for inserting new objects and setting project properties. The Format menu provides tools to arrange the controls on a form. The Debug menu gives you the command you need to operate in a debugging session. The Run menu lets you test your application while developing it. The Tools menu gives you commands to add/modify items in a code module, add/modify menus, and set the options for the IDE. The Add-Ins menu gives you access to tools and Wizards that are added into the Visual Basic environment. The Window menu helps organize your windows. Finally, you use the Help menu to gain access to the (somewhat limited) help system provided with the CCE. This menu also has the very useful Microsoft on the Web option that, if your machine is equipped for it, lets you connect to the World-Wide Web for up-to-the-minute information from Microsoft.

In Windows applications, all the menus have access keys. Pressing ALT and the underlined letter opens that menu. Use the arrow keys to move around the menu bar. Once a menu is open, all you need is a single *accelerator key* (also called an *access* or *hot key*) to select a menu option. For example, if the Help menu is open, pressing L brings up the tutorial. Accelerator keys are not case-sensitive. Some menu items have shortcut keys. For example, as is common in Windows applications, pressing ALT+Q lets you exit the CCE without going through the File menu.

The Toolbar(s)

The CCE contains four toolbars also referred to as command bars since they are based on Office 97 technology. This section describes the toolbars: Standard, Debug, Edit and Form Editor.

Since the toolbars are dockable in the IDE by simply dragging them around, you might want to experiment with their arrangement to have all the toolbars available at one time. The most compact arrangement we have found is to have the Standard and Form toolbars on one line and the Edit and Debug toolbars on the other. ⊃

The toolbars can be customized. See the section on the Context-Sensitive Menus later in this chapter. ⊃

Standard Toolbar

Reading from left to right, here is what the tools on this toolbar do:

Table 2-1:   The Standard Toolbar Icons

Icon	Name	Purpose
	Add Project	Lets you add a new project of type Standard EXE or Control to the IDE. This is the same as File|Add Project. The little down arrow to the right of the button selects a different project type than the one currently shown. The ActiveX EXE and DLL options are not available in the Control Creation Edition version of Visual Basic.
	Add Form	Lets you add a component to the current project. A component can be a Form, MDI form, Module, Class Module, User Control, Property Page, User Document, ActiveX Designer or a file of your choice. The User Document and ActiveX Designer options are not available in the Control Creation Edition version. Clicking the little down arrow to the right of the button opens a dialog that lets you choose a new component template or an existing file of that type. These functions may also be found on the Project menu.

Icon	Name	Purpose
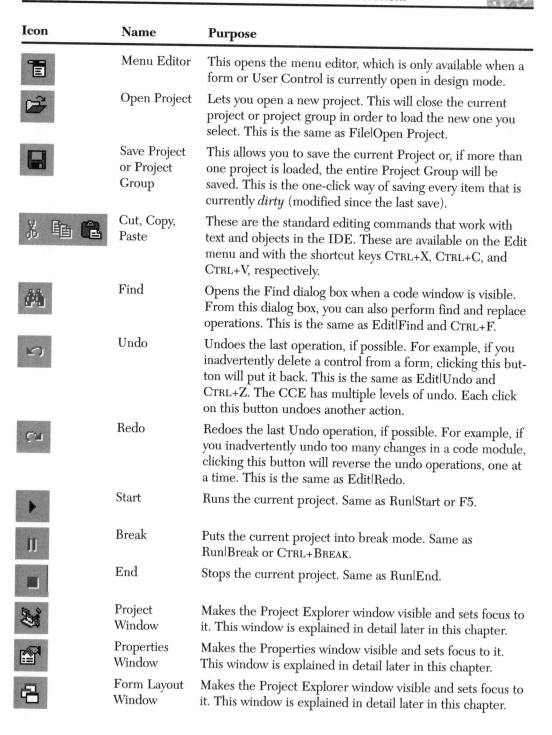	Menu Editor	This opens the menu editor, which is only available when a form or User Control is currently open in design mode.
	Open Project	Lets you open a new project. This will close the current project or project group in order to load the new one you select. This is the same as File|Open Project.
	Save Project or Project Group	This allows you to save the current Project or, if more than one project is loaded, the entire Project Group will be saved. This is the one-click way of saving every item that is currently *dirty* (modified since the last save).
	Cut, Copy, Paste	These are the standard editing commands that work with text and objects in the IDE. These are available on the Edit menu and with the shortcut keys CTRL+X, CTRL+C, and CTRL+V, respectively.
	Find	Opens the Find dialog box when a code window is visible. From this dialog box, you can also perform find and replace operations. This is the same as Edit|Find and CTRL+F.
	Undo	Undoes the last operation, if possible. For example, if you inadvertently delete a control from a form, clicking this button will put it back. This is the same as Edit|Undo and CTRL+Z. The CCE has multiple levels of undo. Each click on this button undoes another action.
	Redo	Redoes the last Undo operation, if possible. For example, if you inadvertently undo too many changes in a code module, clicking this button will reverse the undo operations, one at a time. This is the same as Edit|Redo.
	Start	Runs the current project. Same as Run|Start or F5.
	Break	Puts the current project into break mode. Same as Run|Break or CTRL+BREAK.
	End	Stops the current project. Same as Run|End.
	Project Window	Makes the Project Explorer window visible and sets focus to it. This window is explained in detail later in this chapter.
	Properties Window	Makes the Properties window visible and sets focus to it. This window is explained in detail later in this chapter.
	Form Layout Window	Makes the Project Explorer window visible and sets focus to it. This window is explained in detail later in this chapter.

Icon	Name	Purpose
	Object Browser	Makes the Object Browser window visible and sets focus to it. This window is briefly explained in this chapter and in some detail in Chapter 7.
	Toolbox	Makes the Toolbox window visible and gives it the focus. This window is explained in detail later.
	Current X, Y	Shows the current X and Y position of the current object, whether it is a form or a control on a form.
	Current Width, Height	Shows the current width and height of the current object, whether it is a form or a control on a form.

Debug Toolbar

Reading from left to right, here is what the tools on this toolbar do:

Table 2-2:   The Debug Toolbar

Icon	Name	Purpose
	Start	Runs the current project. Same as Run|Start or F5.
	Break	Puts the current project into break mode. Same as Run|Break or CTRL+BREAK.
	End	Stops the current project. Same as Run|End.
	Toggle Breakpoint	Turns the breakpoint on the current line on or off depending upon its current state. Same as Debug|Toggle Breakpoint and F9.
	Step Into	Executes the next line of code while in break mode, and steps into a sub program if one is called. Same as Debug|Step Into or F8.
	Step Over	Executes the next line of code while in break mode, and steps over a sub program if one is called. Same as Debug|Step Over or SHIFT+F8.
	Step Out	Steps out of a sub program that you entered with Step Into. Same as Debug|Step Out or CTRL+SHIFT+F8.

27

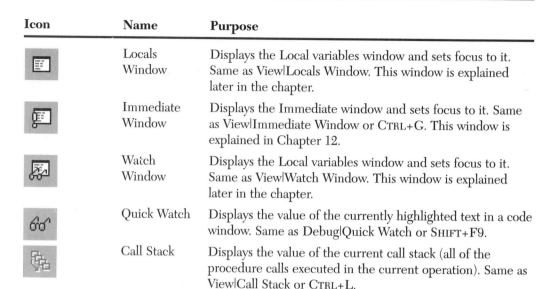

Icon	Name	Purpose
	Locals Window	Displays the Local variables window and sets focus to it. Same as View|Locals Window. This window is explained later in the chapter.
	Immediate Window	Displays the Immediate window and sets focus to it. Same as View|Immediate Window or CTRL+G. This window is explained in Chapter 12.
	Watch Window	Displays the Local variables window and sets focus to it. Same as View|Watch Window. This window is explained later in the chapter.
	Quick Watch	Displays the value of the currently highlighted text in a code window. Same as Debug|Quick Watch or SHIFT+F9.
	Call Stack	Displays the value of the current call stack (all of the procedure calls executed in the current operation). Same as View|Call Stack or CTRL+L.

The functions on this toolbar are discussed in detail in Chapter 12. ⊃

Edit Toolbar

Table 2-3: The Edit Toolbar

Icon	Name	Purpose
	List Properties/ Methods	Displays a pop-up list of the properties and methods for the object preceding the period. CTRL+J is the keyboard equivalent.
	List Constants	Displays a pop-up list of the valid constants after you type an = sign. CTRL+SHIFT+J is the keyboard equivalent.
	Quick Info	Gives the syntax for the procedure or method. CTRL+I is the keyboard equivalent.
	Parameter Info	Provides the parameter list for the current function call. CTRL+SHIFT+I is the keyboard equivalent.
	Complete Word	Completes the keyword or object when enough information is there. CTRL+SPACE is the keyboard equivalent.

Icon	Name	Purpose
	Indent	Indents the selected text one tab stop. TAB is the keyboard equivalent.
	Outdent	Moves the selected text back one tab stop. SHIFT+TAB is the keyboard equivalent.
	Toggle Breakpoint	Used for debugging (see Chapter 12). F9 is the keyboard shortcut.
	Comment Block	There is no default keyboard equivalent for this. (See Chapter 4 for more information on comments.)
	Uncomment Block	There is no default keyboard equivalent for this tool.
	Toggle Bookmark	Bookmarks allows easier navigation between parts of your code.
	Next Bookmark	Jumps to the next saved bookmark.
	Previous Bookmark	Jumps to the previously saved bookmark.
	Clear All Bookmarks	Clears all bookmarks currently saved. Bookmarks do not persist when you exit the IDE so they will be cleared then, as well.

 This toolbar is explained in more detail in Chapter 4. ⊃

Form Editor Toolbar

Reading from left to right, here is what the tools on this toolbar do:

Table 2-4: The Form Editor Toolbar

Icon	Name	Purpose
	Bring to Front	Sets the Zorder of the currently selected control to 0, causing it to display on top of the other controls. (See Chapter 5 for more on Zorder.) Same as Format|Order|Bring to Front or CTRL+J.

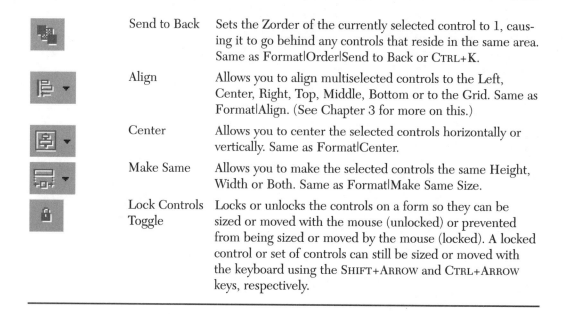

	Send to Back	Sets the Zorder of the currently selected control to 1, causing it to go behind any controls that reside in the same area. Same as Format|Order|Send to Back or CTRL+K.
	Align	Allows you to align multiselected controls to the Left, Center, Right, Top, Middle, Bottom or to the Grid. Same as Format|Align. (See Chapter 3 for more on this.)
	Center	Allows you to center the selected controls horizontally or vertically. Same as Format|Center.
	Make Same	Allows you to make the selected controls the same Height, Width or Both. Same as Format|Make Same Size.
	Lock Controls Toggle	Locks or unlocks the controls on a form so they can be sized or moved with the mouse (unlocked) or prevented from being sized or moved by the mouse (locked). A locked control or set of controls can still be sized or moved with the keyboard using the SHIFT+ARROW and CTRL+ARROW keys, respectively.

The Different Child Windows

This section briefly discusses the nine possible windows in the CCE.

Form Designer

The initial Form Designer window, as shown in Figure 2-6, takes up part of the center window in the MDI. (In Visual Basic programming, the convention is to use the term *form* for a customizable window.) It is simply a window with a grid of dots. (See Chapter 3 for more details on the Form Designer window.)

Form designers are used for user control design, testing form design and Property Page design (Chapter 10). They all use the same designer and, while there are a few subtle differences that we cover later on, they work basically in the same way. ⊃

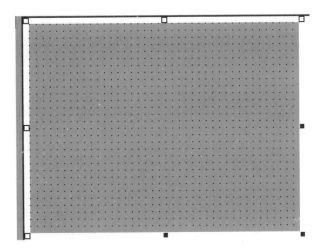

Figure 2-6
Form Designer window

Code Window

Visual Basic comes with a full-screen programming editor. Since it is a programming editor, it lacks features like word wrap and print formatting that even a primitive word processor like WordPad has. On the other hand, it does add features like syntax checking that can spot certain common programming typos, as well as many new features not found in previous versions of Visual Basic such as Quick Info. The Visual Basic program editor also color-codes the various parts of your code. For example, Visual Basic commands can be in one color, comments in another. The colors used are customizable via the Editor page from the Tools menu's Options dialog box. The Visual Basic program editor is activated whenever you are writing or viewing code. The font used in the editor can be changed to suit your needs.

 This window is explained in detail in Chapter 4. ⊃

Object Browser

The Object Browser, shown in the center of Figure 2-7, lets you view properties, methods, events and constants from the object libraries currently loaded in the IDE. By default, the browser loads a few standard libraries such as the one for standard parts of the CCE language. The CCE also loads all the parts of the currently loaded project(s). Whenever you use the Project menu to add a reference to another library or a custom control, that library will appear in the browser as well.

Although we will cover the browser in more detail in Chapter 7, we want to give you a hint of its powers here. It is a great source of information on the available programming resources in the IDE. For example, to see all of the available properties and methods for the App object, load the browser using

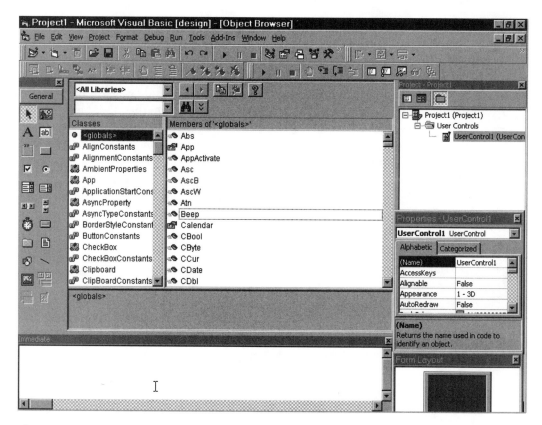

Figure 2-7
The Object Browser at work

the F2 key and choose VB in the top drop-down list. Then click on App in the Classes list. As you can see in Figure 2-8, the browser gives you a short description of the object. (For the App object, this is "Contains general information about an application.") A complete list of the Members of App is shown in the right-hand pane. (*Members* is the standard term in object-oriented programming for everything in that particular object. This includes its properties and methods—see Chapters 7 and 8 if you are not familiar with these terms.)

Playing with the Object Browser is a great way to discover powerful features that would otherwise go unnoticed. As you can see in Figure 2-8, each item will display a short description in the bottom of the window when it is selected.

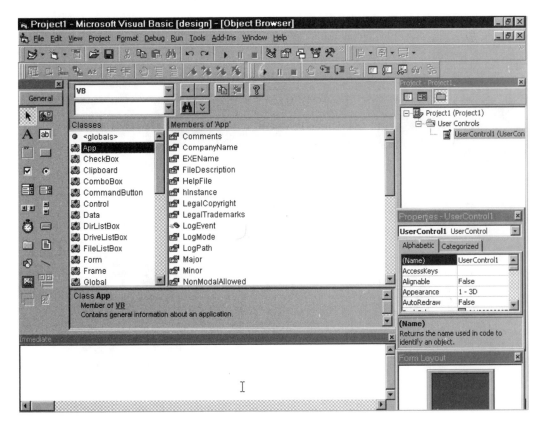

Figure 2-8
The Object Browser for the App object

It is possible to search for a word in a single library or in all the available libraries. Just type in the word in the lower drop-down combo box and click the little binoculars button. For example, let's assume you still have "VB" listed as the object to browser·

1. Type the word "click" in the box.
2. Click the binoculars button.

A new pane will open every occurrence of the word "click" in the VB object, as shown in Figure 2-9. (What you are seeing is the list of all controls built into Visual Basic that have a Click or DblClick event.)

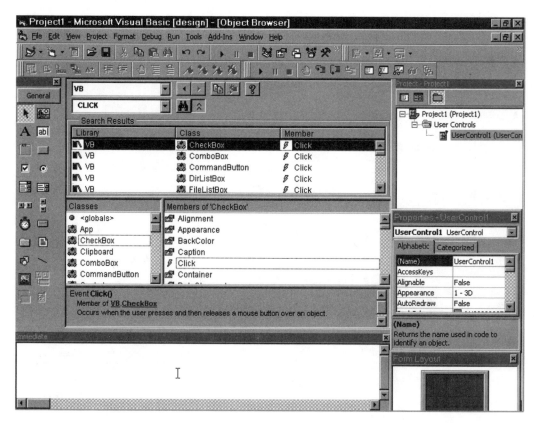

Figure 2-9
Object Browser example screen

For more on the Object Browser, please see Chapter 7. ⊃

Immediate Window (Debug Window)

The Immediate window (or Debug window, as it is commonly called) was a useful tool in earlier versions of VB. It has been made much more powerful in the Control Creation Edition, allowing you to test functions, load forms, evaluate expressions and view the values of objects, variables and properties. It is usually located at the bottom of the screen (see Figure 2-1) and is explained in detail in Chapter 12.

Locals Window

Newly added to Visual Basic is the Locals window. This window is usually hidden; choose View|Locals Window to bring it up. The Locals window displays the names and values of every local variable in the current procedure. It shares similar functionality with the Watch window (explained below). The benefit of the Locals window is that it follows the flow of your program, giving all the values in the current scope. The disadvantage is that you cannot see any values outside of that scope. Of course, that is what the Watch window is for. You can also change the value of any assignable variable. Objects (such as forms and controls) cannot be set, but they may be expanded and their properties can be changed.

Watch Window

This window is used to display the value of variables and expressions for any scope from the current procedure to the entire application. In addition to all of the features available for the Locals window, the Watch window allows you to Add, Edit and Delete items. Edit is the most powerful as it allows you to set the scope of the item and what type of watch statement you want to use for it. This window is also discussed in more detail in Chapter 12 in the section on Advanced Breakpoints. The Watch window allows the same value modification as described above for the Locals window.

Project Explorer

The Project Explorer (or Project Window) lists all projects and their components (forms, modules, user controls property pages) that are currently loaded in the IDE. Figure 2-10 shows one of the samples supplied with the CCE. (If the Project Explorer is not visible, choose View|Project or CTRL+R.)

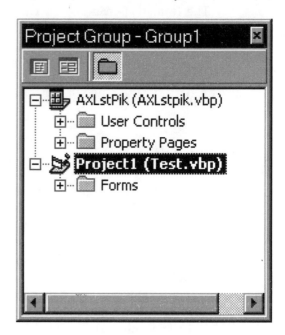

Figure 2-10
Project Explorer in Folder view

There are actually two ways to see the Project Explorer. Figure 2-10 gives the default Folder view where all similar components for each project are kept in a folder and are not visible until you open that folder. This is useful when you have a large number of components of various types and you want to see only certain types at a time.

The other view is a simple hierarchy of projects and components with all components listed alphabetically for each project. An example is shown in Figure 2-11. (Use the last button, Toggle Folders, on the Project Explorer toolbar to change to this view.) This view is better when you want to access any component quickly—you won't have to open a folder. The disadvantage is that it takes more room to display the entire list. Each component type has a specific icon, such as the pencil used for a user control (ctl file), so it is easy to distinguish the different types of components.

Figure 2-11
Project Explorer in Hierarchical view

Figure 2-12 shows what the initial Project window looks like for an ActiveX control project.

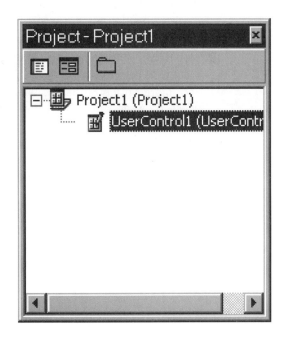

Figure 2-12
Initial Project Explorer for an ActiveX Control

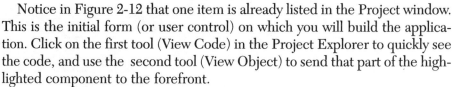

Notice in Figure 2-12 that one item is already listed in the Project window. This is the initial form (or user control) on which you will build the application. Click on the first tool (View Code) in the Project Explorer to quickly see the code, and use the second tool (View Object) to send that part of the highlighted component to the forefront.

Although Visual Basic separately stores all the files that go into making up the project, it keeps track of where they are. It creates a file, called the project file, that tells it (and you, if you look at the file with an editor) where the individual files are located. Visual Basic creates the Project file whenever you choose Save Project from the File menu, or the Save Project tool from the toolbar. It creates a different Project file whenever you choose Save Project As. Project files have the extension .vbp in their filename.

If you have more than one project loaded in the IDE, you have, by default, created a *project group*. Visual Basic saves the information about the group (such as what projects were in it) in a .vbg file. The new project group feature of the CCE makes it easy to create a test project group with designed controls and a Standard EXE project that allows you to test the controls.

Properties Window

The Properties window, shown in Figure 2-13, is where you set and view the properties of the currently selected item in the Project Explorer or the currently selected control on a form or user control. The default view of the Properties window is an alphabetical list of all properties that are available at design time.

For more on the Properties window, see Chapter 3. You can also use the Object Browser discussed previously to see all of the properties of an object. ⊃

The Properties window can also use a Categorized view. In this view, all properties of a control or component fall into categories such as Appearance, Behavior, DDE, Font, Misc, Position, Scale and Text, as shown in Figure 2-14. When you create your own controls, you can place the properties in a category using the Tools|Procedure Attributes dialog box discussed in Chapter 8.

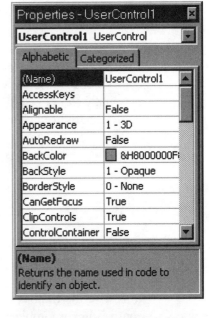

Figure 2-13
The Properties window

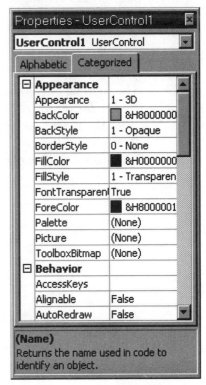

Figure 2-14
The Properties window in Categorized view

Form Layout

The Form Layout window shows you the position and size of your form, relative to the entire screen. This is very helpful for designing forms and user controls that must work well in many resolutions. The Form Layout window optionally shows resolution guides to show how your form fits in various resolutions. (Right-click in the Form Layout window to see this feature at work.)

The Form Layout window default is to be visible directly under the Properties window. It is also available from the View|Form Layout command.

The Toolbox

The toolbox is located at the left of the screen by default, just below the toolbar. It contains the available controls used to develop the UI of your forms and user controls. How many tools are available depends on your custom controls. Use the toolbox to place command buttons, text buttons, and the other controls in your application. See Chapter 3 for more on the toolbox.

Color Palette

The color palette is a handy window that allows you to set the ForeColor and BackColor of any object that exhibits these properties. The window eliminates the need to go to the Properties window to set these color properties. It is not loaded by default, but is available from the View|Color Palette command. See Chapter 3 for more on the Color Palette.

Context Menus

Virtually every window in the IDE has a context menu that pops up when you click the right mouse button, displaying commands that pertain to the object you clicked. (Most are available on the usual menus or via the toolbar.) Once you get comfortable with context menus, they can be one of the most useful features in the IDE. We describe the main features of the most interesting context menus for the different windows in the sections that follow.

Context Menu for the Toolbox

Figure 2-15 shows you the Context menu for the Toolbox.

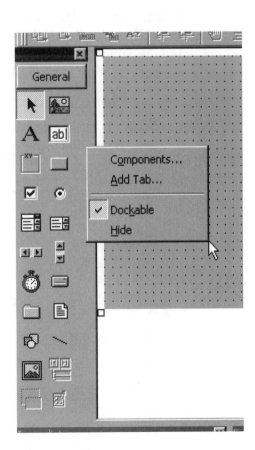

Figure 2-15
The Context-Sensitive menu for the Toolbox

41

Figure 2-16
Toolbox with an additional Tab

Figure 2-16
Toolbox with an additional Tab

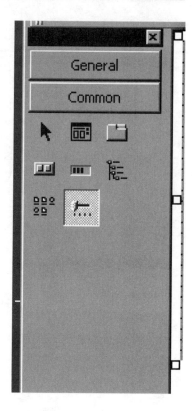

The Components item leads to a dialog box for adding custom controls. The Add Tab item lets you add a new tab to the toolbox when you have too many controls to easily fit. For example, Figure 2-16 shows what you get if you add a Common Controls tab with the usual Windows Common controls.

Context Menu for Toolbars

If you right-click in the toolbar, you'll see a list of all the toolbars (checked ones are visible). Click on any toolbar in the context menu to display or hide it. The last item is, potentially, the most useful. Click on the Customize option and you see a screen like Figure 2-17. Use this dialog box to add your own toolbars or to customize an existing toolbar.

Adding A Custom Toolbar

Custom toolbars can contain items from any of the CCE menus. To build one:

1. Open the Customize toolbar.
2. Choose New.
3. Give your new toolbar a name in the dialog box that pops up and click on OK.

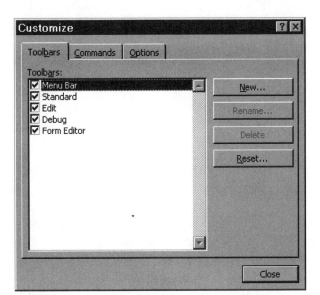

Figure 2-17
Customizing a Toolbar
dialog box

Your screen will now look like Figure 2-18. Notice the toolbar in the center of the Customize dialog box. All you have to do is drag items from the Commands pane (in the Command tab) to the toolbar.

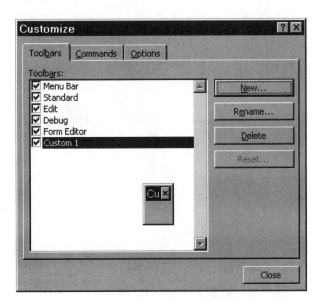

Figure 2-18
Creating a Custom toolbar

Customizing an Existing Tool Button

While you have the Customize dialog box open, the CCE gives you the ability to further customize any of its buttons. For this,

1. Right-click on a command bar and choose Customize.
2. While the Customize Dialog is up, right-click on the button you want to customize. This shows a pop-up menu.

For example, Figure 2-19 is what your screen will look like while you are trying to further customize the comment block tool button.

Since we use this tool a lot, we will give it a keystroke shortcut. For this, go to the pop-up menu and change the name to something like Comment & Block. This will assign the keystroke combination of ALT +B to the Comment Block

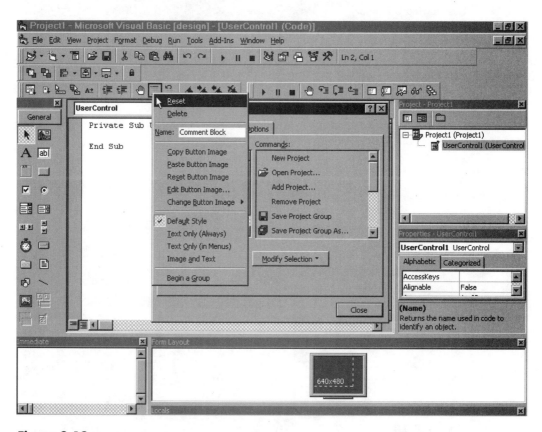

Figure 2-19
Customizing a button

tool. (Note that the Edit toolbar must be active and the text in the caption must be visible for this shortcut to work.) This pop-up menu also gives the option of using the most innovative invention in toolbars since they were first invented—Text. If you are like some people and prefer buttons with textual descriptions to confusing pictures, the Text option shown in Figure 2-19 is ideal.

Context Menu for the Form Designer

Figure 2-20 shows the Context menu for the Form Designer. The options on this menu are discussed in Chapter 3.

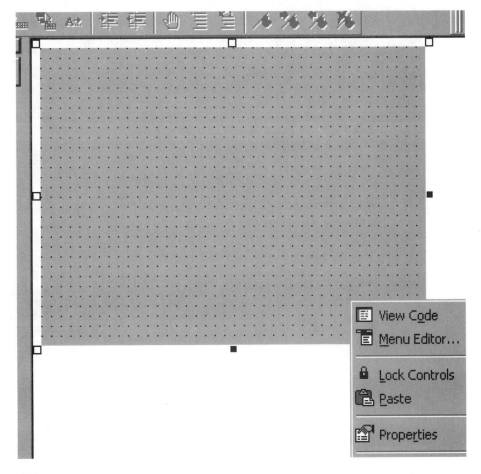

Figure 2-20
Context menu for the Form Designer

Context Menu for the Code Window

Figure 2-21 shows the Context menu for the Code window. The options on this menu are discussed in Chapter 5.

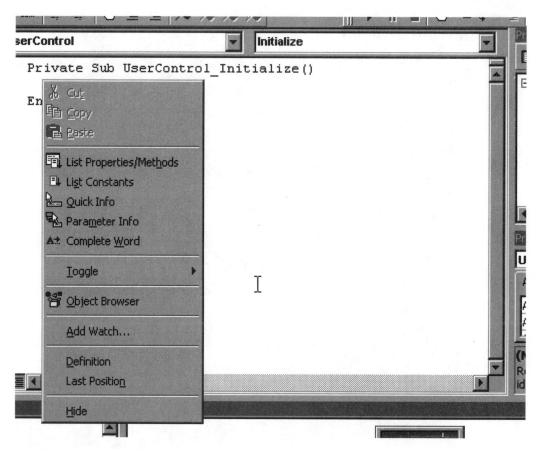

Figure 2-21
Context menu for the Code window

Context Menu for the Project Explorer

There are actually two Context menus available for this window, depending on whether you right-click on a project or one of the objects like a form or control in a project. The functionality of both Context menus is similar. Figure 2-22 shows the Context menu when you click on a user control.

Figure 2-22
Context menu for a user control in the Project Explorer

Miscellaneous Dialog Boxes

Numerous dialog boxes throughout the IDE may not be easily discoverable or intuitive in use. We will explain a few of them here.

Options

The Options dialog box available off the Tools menu is the place to go to change a setting in the IDE. Brief explanations of the six tabs found on this dialog box follow.

Registry Notes

All of the values set here are currently stored in the system registry under the following key:

HKEY_CURRENT_USER\Software\VBA\Microsoft Visual Basic

If you run REGEDIT and look at this key, you will find numerous settings and values, some of which make sense and some that look cryptic. We do not recommend that you change the settings directly in the registry unless absolutely necessary. If you do change a registry entry, the IDE may have problems functioning and issue an error. On the other hand, some entries given here may need to be changed if your IDE gets really confused and you want to bring it back to its defaults. *(This may change in the final release version of the Control Creation Edition.)*

Editor Tab

As its name suggests, the Editor tab (shown in Figure 2-23) affects the way the code editor works. Following are explanations of its options.

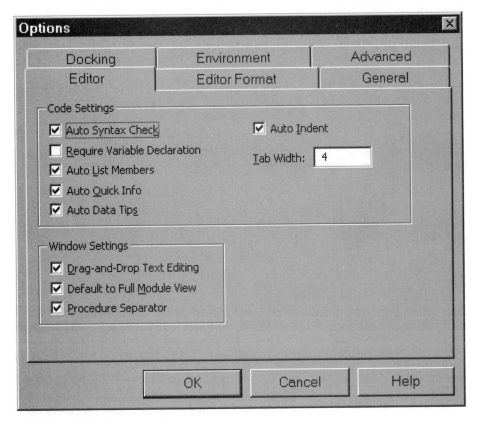

Figure 2-23
The Editor tab

Option	Purpose
Auto Syntax Check	When checked, the editor will issue an error if you move off a line that contains invalid code, such as leaving off the "Then" on an If/Then line.
Require Variable Declaration	Checking this option tells the IDE to add the "Option Explicit" line to the top of every new code module created. We recommend this as a means of preventing misspelled variable names.
Auto List Members	Checking this tells the editor to display a drop-down list of available members of an object whenever you type the Object Name followed by a period.

Option	Purpose
Auto Quick Info	This option tells the editor to list the parameters of the function you are working with. This feature works for VBA functions, other library functions, and even your own user-defined functions.
Auto Data Tips	When activated, this feature lets you see the current value of a variable in break mode. Hold the mouse cursor stationary for a second on the variable you want to examine.
Auto Indent	This option, when checked, will automatically indent the next line of your code to the starting position of the previous line when you press ENTER. If unchecked, the cursor will return to the left margin when you press ENTER.
Tab Width	This is the number of spaces that will be added by the editor when you press the TAB key. It also applies when you use the Indent and Outdent buttons or their TAB and SHIFT+TAB equivalents.
Drag-and-Drop Text Editing	This box enables the type of drag-and-drop editing that is used in Microsoft Word. When you highlight some text, drag it by holding down the left mouse, then drop it in the desired position. This makes moving text fast and easy.
Default to Full Module View	When checked, the editor will display procedures in a streaming fashion. When unchecked, only one procedure will be displayed at a time as it was in earlier versions of Visual Basic.
Procedure Separator	While in full module view, this option tells the editor whether or not to show the separator lines between procedures.

Editor Format Tab

The editor format tab, shown in Figure 2-24, is fairly self-explanatory. It is the place you go to set the colors and font the editor uses for code. Keep in mind that there is no way to set the editor back to default settings from this dialog box except one at a time.

If you really mess up, you can use REGEDIT and delete the CodeForeColor and CodeBackColor values from the Visual Basic key entry. This will force the IDE to return to its defaults. ⊃

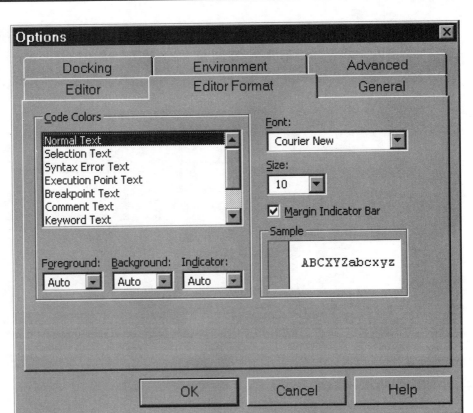

Figure 2-24
Editor Format tab

General

The General tab, shown in Figure 2-25, is used when designing a control or test form. It also controls how the CCE handles errors at design time (see Chapters 6 and 12).

Option	Purpose
Form Grid Settings	If the Show Grid option is checked, all form, user control and Property Page designers will display dots in a grid to help you line up controls. The spacing of the dots is determined by the number of points you enter in the Width and Height fields. The Align to Grid option forces controls to jump to the nearest grid line. See Chapter 3 for more on the grid.

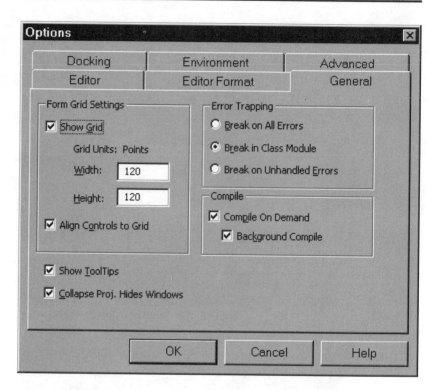

Figure 2-25
General tab

Option	Purpose
Error Trapping	This option has three possible settings. *Break on All Errors* will cause the IDE to break on any error in any code module, regardless if there is an active error handler (Chapter 6 covers error handlers). *Break in Class Modules* causes the IDE to break on any unhandled error in a class module (Chapter 7). This includes the code behind forms, user controls and Property Pages because they are technically class modules. Finally, *Break on Unhandled Error* causes the IDE to break on any error that occurs with no error handler present.
Show ToolTips	When checked, the IDE will display a brief description of the buttons on the toolbars and the items in the toolbox. Let your mouse sit above the button for a second or so and the tooltip text will appear.
Collapse Proj. Hides Windows	This option, when checked, tells the IDE to hide all of the component windows (forms, code, etc.) when you collapse the project in the Project window. This is helpful when you have more than one project loaded and you need a quick way to show only the current projects' windows.

Docking

This tab simply tells the IDE which child windows can be docked. By default, all windows other than the Object Browser are dockable. This is the same as the Dockable item available on the Context menu in each window.

Environment

This tab, shown in Figure 2-26, controls how the IDE works. It includes the very useful options for autosaving your projects.

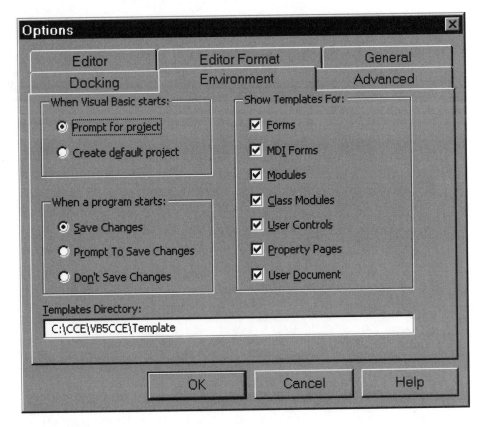

Figure 2-26
Environment tab

Option	Purpose
When Visual Basic starts:	*Prompt for Project* tells the IDE to give you a dialog box that asks you to open a project on startup. If you do not like this dialog box to appear, choose Create Default Project and the CCE will simply create a user control project every time you load the IDE.
When a program starts:	*Save Changes* causes the IDE to automatically save all *dirty* files to disk when you go to run mode. (Dirty is the jargon for any file that has been changed since the last save.) *Prompt To Save Changes* does the same except that it asks you before saving the changes. *Don't Save Changes* leaves you to save your changes before you run. We highly recommended that you either get in the habit of saving your changes regularly, or allow the CCE to do it for you prior to running the application.
Show Templates For:	This option tells the IDE whether or not to display the new object dialog box when you add a new component to your project. If you uncheck a component type, you will get a blank object when you choose Project|New.
Templates Directory:	This tells the IDE where you store your templates. By default, it is in the Template directory directly under the CCE's directory. You may, however, point to a network server or any other location that makes sense. See Chapter 11 for more on templates.

Advanced

The Advanced tab has a few options that are especially useful when working larger projects. It is also where you go to switch between the MDI and SDI environments.

Option	Purpose
Background Project Load	If checked, the CCE will load your project components in the background allowing you to start working right away after loading a large project.
Notify when changing shared project items	This option tells the IDE to let you know when a change you are making will affect more than the current project. It only works for projects currently loaded in the IDE. For example, it is common to have code libraries that you add to

all of your projects. Changing a procedure in such a library can affect the operation of all applications that use that code.

SDI Development Environment	If you prefer to have the old style Visual Basic environment of floating windows and desktop showing through, this option lets you set it. You can start Visual Basic from the command line with a switch telling it which mode to use, CCE /SDI or CCE /MDI. The switch from the command will stick until you change it again from this dialog box or the command line.

Project Properties

The project properties dialog box (Project|Project Properties brings it up) is somewhat limited in the Control Creation Edition; the CCE can only create controls. Therefore, some of the options in this dialog box are disabled. There are four tabs in this dialog box: General, Make, Compile and Component.

General Tab

The General tab, shown in Figure 2-27, controls global properties of your project. The non-disabled parts of this dialog box are described in the table below.

Property	Purpose
Startup Object	For a Standard EXE project, this can be a form or Sub Main. A form name implies that the code project will start by loading the form. Sub Main tells Visual Basic to execute the code in the Main sub procedure. It must be in a standard code module. For a user control, it can be either Sub Main or None. If None is chosen, the control simply goes into run mode without actually executing any basic code.
Project Name	This is the name that will be used to register the user control in the system registry along with the controls class name. It must adhere to the CCE naming convention of no spaces or punctuation (other than an underscore), and must start with a letter.
Help File Name and Context ID	This is the help file and starting context ID that will be used if a user presses F1 while the application is running.

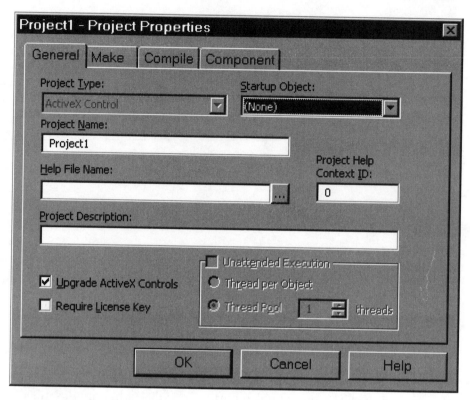

Figure 2-27
General tab in the Properties dialog box

Property	Purpose
Project Description	This is the text that will appear in the Object Browser when this project is chosen from the available libraries.
Upgrade ActiveX Controls	This enables the host application to upgrade your control if a newer version is available.
Require License Key	This tells the CCE to create a VBL (licensing) file when the project is made executable. The information in the VBL must be registered in order for the control to be usable on another system. The Setup Wizard handles this for you. See Chapter 12 for more on the Setup Wizard.

Make tab

This dialog box, shown in Figure 2-28, is especially useful for version control since the CCE has none integrated. The following table describes this tab. This tab is also available when you click the Options button on the Make Project dialog (File|Make Project.ocx).

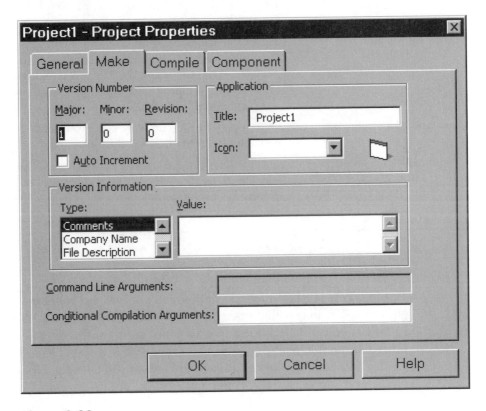

Figure 2-28
The Make tab

Property	Purpose
Version Number	Sets the version number you want placed in the system registry for this project. Checking Auto Increment tells the IDE to increment the revision value each time the application is built.

Property	Purpose
Application Title	This is the title that will be displayed whenever an MsgBox function is used and the title parameter is left off. It is also the value of App.Title at run time.
Application Icon	This is the icon that will be stored in the OCX or EXE for use by the OS in creating shortcuts. It is not the Toolbox Bitmap used for your user control, which is set in the User Control Properties window.
Version Information	This is the data that will be displayed when a user selects Properties from the Win95 Explorer utility. It will also be available at run time from the App object. For example, the value of App.CompanyName will reflect what you enter here as the company name.
Command Line Arguments	Only applies to EXE projects; since you cannot build an executable with the Control Creation Edition, it is disabled.
Conditional Compilation	This is where you enter data such as Debug=1 to cause the compiler to use lines of code that are encased in #IfDef statements. Conditional compilation is explained in Chapter 12.

Compile

The Compile tab has only one option and you will probably never want to change it. The idea is that since a user control is essentially a DLL (Dynamic Linked Library), it is loaded into memory so it can be accessed by other processes running on the system. This property lets you set the address where it will be loaded. This tab is also available when you click the Options button on the Make Project dialog (File|Make Project.ocx).

Component

The Component tab is also somewhat specialized and you will rarely, if ever, need to change the defaults. The following table summarizes the various options on this tab.

Property	Purpose
Remote Server	When checked, the CCE creates a VBR file to make it possible to run this user control from a remote server. This allows you to distribute the processing of your components across servers. It is more applicable to ActiveX DLLs, which the CCE can't build.
Version Compatibility	*No Compatibility* means that compatibility with previously built and registered versions of your project is not enforced. This can lead to numerous entries in your registry for the same object. *Project Compatibility* tells the IDE to maintain compatibility with the project shown in the location field. If you select *Binary Compatibility*, the IDE will enforce that you do not change the interface of the user control from the file shown in the location field. If you do, a dialog will be presented showing the discrepancies between the two at the time of the build. You will be prompted to accept each change one by one, accept them all, or edit the changes before you continue. This helps insure that you do not inadvertently change your interface without warning.

References

The References dialog box available from the Project|References command allows you to view and add object libraries to your application. As shown in Figure 2-29, it consists of a list box of all available libraries. The currently loaded ones have checkmarks next to them. You can check or uncheck libraries, or browse for new libraries not listed because they may not be registered yet.

You may also set the priority order for the checked libraries. Changing the priority is used to resolve conflicts in object models. Say you have the same object name in two loaded libraries. If you do not use the library prefix, the CCE will use the highest library in priority. Therefore, set the library you use the most as the highest priority so you do not have to use the library prefix every time you use members from that object. ⊃

59

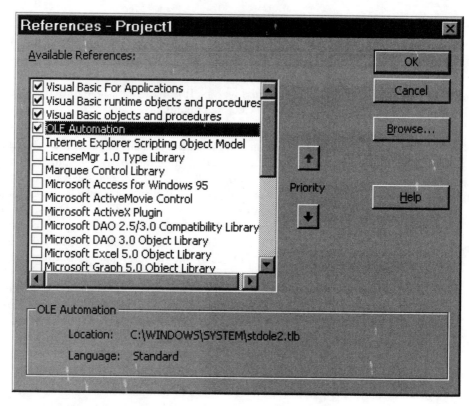

Figure 2-29
The References dialog box

Components

This dialog box, available off the Project menu, displays the Controls and Insertable Objects available to your application. The control list will reflect every OCX that is registered on your system, including the ones you create with the Control Creation Edition. This also includes OCXs in Visual Basic 4.0 and any third-party OCXs you have on your system.

If you see a duplicate entry, this was caused by the same control being built again without any compatibility enforced. The only way to get rid of these orphaned entries is to remove them from the registry yourself. Since this is not an easy process, we recommend that you use project compatibility to avoid it in the first place. ⊃

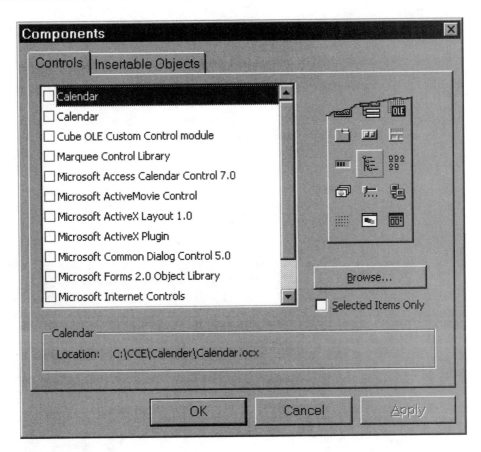

Figure 2-30
The Components dialog box

The Insertable Objects tab list displays objects that are registered as being, you guessed it, insertable. This includes OLE server applications such as MSPAINT, Word and Excel. These cannot be placed on a user control but can be used on a form that is part of a user control project. For example, you could create a form that displays a bitmap using the Bitmap Image object that pops up when the user clicks a button found on your user control.

If an item that you know is on your system is not listed, you can use the Browse function to find it and register it, making it available on the list. ⊃

Print

The Print dialog box, shown in Figure 2-31, is available off the File menu as well as through the Project window context menu. The CCE allows you to print all or part of your project. You may choose whether you want the form image (applies to user control and Property Page as well), the code and/or the entire text of the form (the .frm, .ctl or .pag file).

You can print the *Form Image* (the form as you see it in design mode), the *Code* (only the code portion of the form), and the *Form as Text* (what you would see if you loaded the FRM file into Notepad). The *Print to File* option allows you to send the output to a file of your choice, as opposed to a printer.

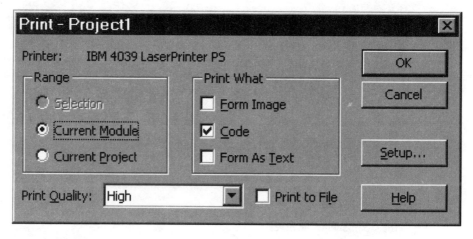

Figure 2-31
The Print dialog box

Chapter 3

Most controls that you build will need to present a winning face to the world. Also, you need to be able to design realistic interfaces in order to test the controls that you build. This chapter will show you how to do both. The test bed for a user control and the control itself are built on a window that is usually called a *form* in all versions of Visual Basic. Changing the appearance of a form or control can be done via the Properties window at design time or by using code at run time. This chapter concentrates on design time and leaves most of the coding tasks to the next chapter.

Included in this chapter is a short introduction to the controls supplied with the CCE, how to use the menu designer, as well as an introduction to the event-driven model of programming that is so important for using ActiveX controls and for VB, in general.

Anyone familiar with early versions of Visual Basic will recognize most of this material. However, the CCE has some neat improvements for laying out controls. There are a few subtleties in how layout and event handling work because of the differences between a user control and a traditional VB project. Therefore, you may want to skim this chapter. ⊃

Building the
User Interface

Properties

Properties affect the appearance of an object, and can be changed at design time or at run time. When they are changed at run time, the syntax takes the form:

```
object.property = new value
```

(For more on coding techniques, see Chapter 4.)

For now, we want to concentrate on the properties you can set at design time using the Properties window. First, press F4 (or View|Properties Window) to bring the Properties window to the top if it is obscured or hidden. Figure 3-1 is a picture of the Properties window.

(If you prefer to see the properties characterized by function, click on the Categorized tab.)

Notice the bottom of the Properties window gives you a short description of the property. The drop-down list box on top shows the object you are working with. When you click on the arrow for the drop-down dialog at the top of the Properties window, the CCE shows all the controls that are currently on the form. If the control (or the form itself) that you want to work with is not shown here, simply drop the list down and choose it.

Figure 3-1
The Properties window

Naming Your Objects

The first property listed in the Properties window is the all-important Name property. The Name property lets you give meaningful names to your CCE objects. The CCE sets up a default name like UserControl1 for the first user control, Form1 for the first form, Form2 for the second, TextBox1 for the first text box, and so on.

Naming conventions for objects have inspired quite a lot of flaming. Most people set the name for their user controls using mixed case, for example, StretchLabel. Many people also add a lowercase prefix that indicates the object, followed by the meaningful name. Examples of this might be frmAbout or frmInitial. Since these are the conventions Microsoft suggests, we use them in this book. ⊃

65

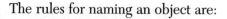

The rules for naming an object are:

- Names can be up to 128 characters.
- The first character must be a letter.
- The rest of the name can include any combination of letters, numbers, and underscores, but no spaces, punctuation marks or non-alphanumeric characters.

The case of the letters in the object name is irrelevant.

Working with the Properties Window

There are various ways of setting properties using the Properties window. For example, the Caption property is an example of the simplest kind of property to set. Just click in the right, or *value*, column and enter the text or the value there. You can use standard Windows editing techniques for cutting and pasting in the value column. The CCE actually checks to make sure that what you entered makes sense. If you enter something that isn't valid, the CCE will pop up an "Invalid property value" message box and reset to its original value. For example, the CCE won't let you enter a string if a number is called for.

For properties like BorderStyle, where you have a finite number of choices, the CCE uses a drop-down list box. You have to click in the row for that item in order to see the drop-down arrow. Figure 3-2 shows what you see for the BorderStyle property of a form, rather than a UserControl.

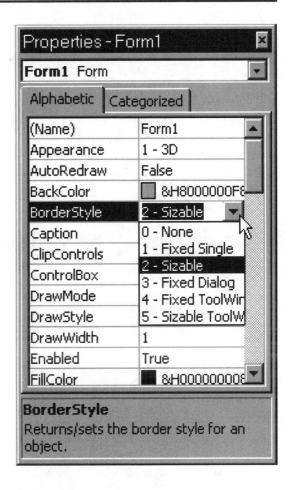

Figure 3-2
BorderStyle properties for a Form

To choose from the drop-down list of properties:

1. Open the list by clicking the down arrow (or with focus on the value box, press ALT+DOWN ARROW). Then select the item you want.

   or

2. If there is a fixed and known set of possible values, repeatedly double-clicking in the value column will cycle through the set. If you know the value you want, you can simply enter it.

When you need to work with a color property like ForeColor, clicking on the arrow brings up a tabbed dialog box. The first tab lists system-supplied colors; the second, a palette. Click on the appropriate-colored box to set the color.

Next, the CCE follows the standard Windows convention where an ellipsis means a dialog box is available. The ellipsis shows up when you click in the value column. Click on the ellipsis to reveal the dialog box, or double-click in the value column. This is usually necessary when the property value type is an object such as a bitmap, icon or font. The typical example is the Font property dialog box, shown here:

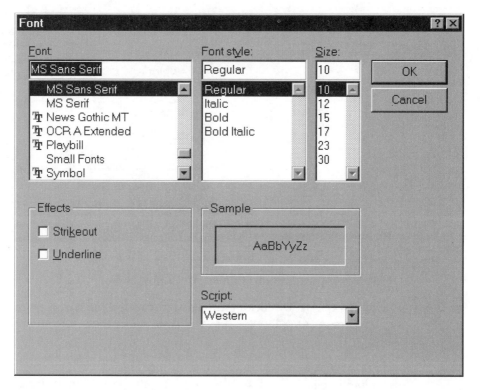

Figure 3-3
The Font dialog box

When you are finished adjusting the settings in the dialog box, click OK and they will go into effect.

Forms

The forms for test projects and the form used for building a control are similar but there are a few properties that they do not share. In a handful of cases, similarly named properties work differently. For example, the BorderStyle property for a form used for an ActiveX control has only two possible values instead of the six for an ordinary form. Forms for user controls have 42 properties you can set at design time; forms used as test beds for your controls in the CCE have 49 properties. Both ordinary forms and user control forms can respond to 31 events, although the sets of events are not precisely the same. The next few sections will introduce you to some of the most important properties and events for both kinds of forms. (The forms that are specialized for use in creating controls are covered in depth in Chapter 8.)

Form Properties

What follows is a short discussion of the most important properties of a form that you can set at design time. We will not bother describing properties which are completely explained by their names or for which the brief description given in the property window is enough. (For example, Caption for an ordinary form is explained here as "resets/sets the text displayed in the object's title bar," which seems sufficient.)

Appearance

Leave this set at the default value of 1–3D to tell the CCE to display controls with a three-dimensional look.

AutoRedraw

This is an extremely important True/False (Boolean) property. It determines whether information displayed on your form persists when the form is repainted. For example, if AutoRedraw is False (the default), then anything on the form will vanish when the form is covered by another form and then uncovered. Of course, setting AutoRedraw to True means more memory is used to save the bitmap. (See Chapter 6 for more on this property.)

BorderStyle

This property determines how the boundary of the form appears. For ordinary forms there are five possible values, as shown in the following table.

Value	Description
0	No border, no system menu, and no min/max or close buttons.
1	*Fixed Single*. The user cannot resize the form with a mouse, but it can still have a control menu box, a title bar, and min/max buttons to minimize or maximize the form.
2	*(Default) Sizable*. The user can resize the form with a mouse.
3	*Fixed Dialog*. Generally used for custom dialog boxes and is not resizable by the user. May have a control box but can't include min/max buttons.
4	*Fixed ToolWindow*. This displays the Close button as well as the title bar text in a smaller font. The form also will not appear in the Windows task bar and will not display an icon.
5	*Sizable ToolWindow*. Does not display min/max buttons but is resizable by the mouse. Gives you a Close button. Displays the title bar text in a smaller font. The form also does not appear in the Windows task bar and will not display an icon.

When you change the setting of the BorderStyle property, you may affect the properties that control the buttons in the title bar. For example, when the BorderStyle property is set to 0 (None), 3 (Fixed Dialog), 4 (Fixed ToolWindow), or 5 (Sizable ToolWindow), the MinButton, MaxButton, and ShowInTaskbar properties are automatically changed to False. The changes you make will not become apparent until the form goes into run mode.

 As mentioned earlier, forms for building user controls have only 0 (None) and 1 (Fixed Single) as possible settings for their BorderStyle. ⊃

ClipControls

This True/False property determines whether the CCE repaints the whole form or just the newly exposed areas. Obviously, it is faster to paint only the newly exposed areas.

ControlBox

The ControlBox property determines whether the CCE puts a control box in the left-hand corner of an ordinary form. It is obviously not an available property for a user control. If this property is set to False, then the form will no longer respond to the ALT+F4 shortcut combination for closing it, nor will an exit button appear on the title bar. (You would have to provide some other method for closing the form or bring up the Close program dialog box via the CTRL+ALT+DEL combination in order to end the task.)

Enabled, Visible

If the Enabled property is changed from the default value of True, the form will no longer respond to any events. Usually this property is manipulated at run time. The Visible property, on the other hand, controls whether the user can even see the form—it is available for user controls in certain hosts such as VB itself.

FontTransparent

This True/False property is used with graphics to determine whether graphics show through text. It is quite useful for special effects.

Height, Width

These properties measure (or set) the height and width of the whole form—including the borders and title bar for a nonuser control form. Both are measured in *twips*. Theoretically, a twip is $\frac{1}{20}$ of a printer point or $\frac{1}{1440}$ inch ($\frac{1}{567}$ of a cm), but how twips translate on a screen depends on the size of the screen. On one 17-inch monitor that we looked at, 4320 twips actually take up five inches and not three. (On the other hand, Windows printer drivers are set up so that when you design an object using twips, you can be sure it will print out at the correct measurement. For example, if you want a form to be three inches high when printed, you should make its height 3*1440 twips (= 4320) and not worry about how it looks on the screen, then let the Windows printer drivers take over.

HelpContextId

This property is only available for ordinary forms, although the components that make up your user control can have individual HelpContextId's. (This should come as no surprise. After all, it is the components in your user control that the user needs help on, not the container. For a form, this property is used when writing a Windows-compatible help system for your application. Normally, you would not be doing this for a test bed form.)

Icon

This property determines the icon used for the control on the toolbox or the form when the form is minimized.

KeyPreview

The default for this property is False. If you change it to True, then most keystrokes are processed by the form's Key events first, rather than the control that has the focus. (See Chapter 5 for more on the Key events.) This property is extremely useful for a user control with controls that can accept keystrokes, but you want to determine which control gets what keystroke.

Left, Top

These properties determine where an ordinary form is, relative to the left top edge of the screen. It is measured in twips. (Determining where a control is relative to the form is, of course, a design-time task, or can be done using code at run time. See Chapter 8 for how to do this for user controls.)

MousePointer, MouseIcon

This property lets you determine the look of the cursor when the mouse is on the form. There are 15 standard shapes, ranging from the usual arrow or hourglass to more exotic shapes. If you set this value to 99 ("Custom"), then you can use the MouseIcon property to assign a custom mouse pointer to your form or control. Regardless of the setting, you can use code to change the mouse pointer.

Picture

This brings up a dialog box that lets you place a picture (bitmap, icon, or Windows metafile) on the form or user control. This is useful for giving your user control a nice window to the world.

ScaleHeight, ScaleWidth

The ScaleHeight and ScaleWidth properties let you set up your own scale for the height and width of the form. For example, if you set the value of each of these properties to 100, the form uses a scale that has point 50, 50 as its center. (Resetting these properties has the side effect of setting the value of the ScaleMode property back to 0.)

 These properties also represent the height and width of the usable part of the form—the part excluding the borders. For user control forms they are interchangeable with height and width. They are commonly used in code to make sure that the components of your control are correctly sized. (See the discussion of the Resize event in Chapter 8.)

ScaleLeft, ScaleTop

The ScaleLeft and ScaleTop properties describe what value the CCE uses for the left and top corner of the form or control. The original (default) value for each of these properties is 0, 0.

ScaleMode

The ScaleMode property allows you to change the units used in the form's internal coordinate system. Tired of twips? There are seven other possibilities. You can create your own units by setting it to 0, keeping the default twips (this value is 1), or using one of the six remaining choices. A useful setting, especially for graphics, is 3 *pixels* (a picture element—the smallest unit of resolution on your monitor, as determined by Windows) as the scale.

Tag

This property isn't used by the CCE. It exists solely to provide programmers a way of attaching information to a control that would otherwise not be available at run time.

WindowState

This property is only available for ordinary forms. There are three values for this property. The default, Normal (0), leaves the form neither maximized nor minimized. You normally use code to change this property to one of the other two values: Minimized (1) or Maximized (2).

Form Events

The ability to recognize events is the key to the CCE's power, but if you do not write the code in the appropriate event handler, nothing will happen. The idea for your user controls, of course, is to take the events recognized by the user control-building components and do more with them. For example, in Chapter 1 we modified the ordinary KeyPress event for a TextBox in order to add new functionality by rejecting non-numeric characters.

The first thing you need to do when writing an event handler is to generate the event procedure template. The general method of generating an event procedure template is to:

1. Bring up the code window by pressing F7 or choosing View|Code.
2. The code window has two drop-down list boxes. The rightmost one, usually called the Procedure box, gives all the events the control or form (selected in the leftmost drop-down list) can recognize. Click on the name of the event procedure you want to work with.

Figure 3-4 is an example of the Code window with the event procedure list box dropped down.

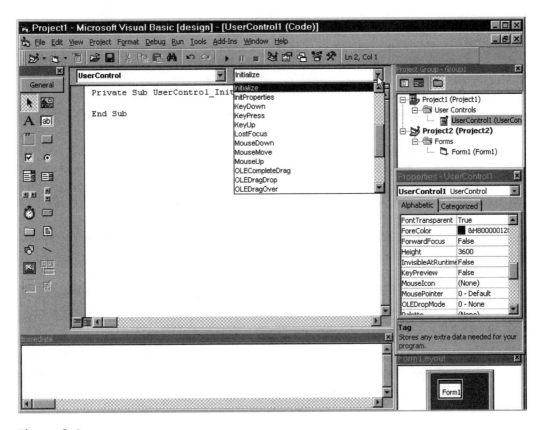

Figure 3-4
The Procedure list box

If you double-click on a user control, a form, or an ordinary control, the CCE pops up the default event procedure template for that object. (For user controls, it is the Initialize event.) ⊃

User Control Life Cycle Events

There are five events that define the life cycle of a user control. In this section, we give a brief overview of them; you'll see a more detailed discussion in Chapter 6. Before we begin, it is important to realize that a user control can come into existence in two ways:

- when you close down the designer of a user control in order to put an instance of the control on a test form ("design time")
- when you run the test bed form or run any code that uses the OCX control you were building ("run time")

The first event for a user control is the Initialize event. This occurs at both run and design time. It is triggered when a control is created. In particular, this event occurs when you switch to your test project and place your user control on the test form, and also when you run the test bed form. Next comes the InitProperties event—you can use this event to give intitial values to your controls. The ReadProperties event occurs next. This lets you read back any properties that were saved about that control, for example, its default property values. This is a design-time event only. Then the Resize event procedure is called, which is both a design-time and run-time event. These four events define the birth of the control.

The death of the control triggers two events. The first is the WriteProperties event. This occurs only when a control is used at design time. It never occurs at run time. This event is triggered when you close the form on which you are testing the control. As you will see in Chapter 8, this gives you a chance to save any properties of the control that were set at design time. The Terminate event, on the other hand, occurs at both design and run time and is the last event triggered by the control's death.

Ordinary Form Life Cycle Events

There are four events that happen when the CCE starts running an ordinary form that you are using for testing: Initialize, Load, Activate, and GotFocus. These events can be confused because they are triggered under similar circumstances. It is important to keep in mind the order in which they are triggered by the CCE.

First is the Initialize event. It is triggered first and only once, when the test form is first created. The Initialize event occurs before the Load event. As its name suggests, the Initialize event is where you place code used for setting initial properties of the form.

The Load event is triggered when a form is loaded into memory; it occurs after the Initialize event. Usually this code is triggered only once. (However, using code, it is possible to unload and then reload a form, so you can have this event triggered more than once.) When you start a program with a single form, it will generally be loaded automatically, thus triggering this event.

The Activate event occurs whenever a form becomes the active window. As such, it can be triggered repeatedly, for example, whenever the user clicks in a previously inactive window.

Finally, after the Activate event is triggered, the CCE will trigger the GotFocus event for the form only if all visible controls on it are disabled. (For this reason, programmers rarely use the GotFocus event for a form and it would certainly be strange in a form used as test bed for a user control.)

Three events occur at the death of a form. The QueryUnload event is triggered when the user tries to close the form, for example, by double-clicking on the control box. You can use this event for clean-up code, or even to prevent the form from closing. The Unload event, on the other hand, is triggered after the form closes. The Terminate event is the last event triggered. It occurs when all references to the form are removed from memory.

Common Form Events

Now we want to discuss some of the most common events that both user controls and ordinary forms can respond to.

Click, DblClick

This event is triggered when the user clicks (double-clicks) in a blank area of the form. (The Click event will always be triggered first, even when the user double-clicks.)

DragDrop, DragOver, MouseDown, MouseMove, MouseUp

These events are used with code to detect mouse movements (see Chapter 6).

KeyDown, KeyPress, KeyUp

You saw one of these events at work in Chapter 1. These events let you determine what the user is doing with the keyboard. (See Chapter 4 for more on this.)

Resize, Paint

The Resize event is triggered whenever the user resizes a form. You usually place code in the Resize event procedure to reposition controls as needed. The Paint event is triggered whenever part of the form is re-exposed or after the form has been enlarged (after the Resize event).

 Both events are triggered when a user control first loads, and the Paint event is fired when a form loads. ⊃

Controls

Ironically, existing controls are the nuts and bolts of your user controls. You will rarely build a control totally from scratch using only the CCE's graphic capabilities. Just as with a form, controls have properties that you can set at design time via the Properties window, or at run time via code. Many properties, such as Height and Width or Name, work essentially the same way for both forms and controls.

 The CCE allows you to add specialized *custom controls* to your project, which you can then (licensing agreements permitting) use as a basis for your user controls. There are custom controls for everything from multimedia to spell-checking to running laboratory equipment. You can use any OCX controls, as they are usually called (named after the extension used for their filenames). If your goal is to use the control in a browser, it is best to get controls that follow the more lightweight ActiveX standard rather than the older OCX standard. (They have the same extension, though, and you will need to check with the vendor to see what standard they follow.) ⊃

To add a custom control, choose Project|Components (CTRL+T). This opens a dialog box like Figure 3-5:

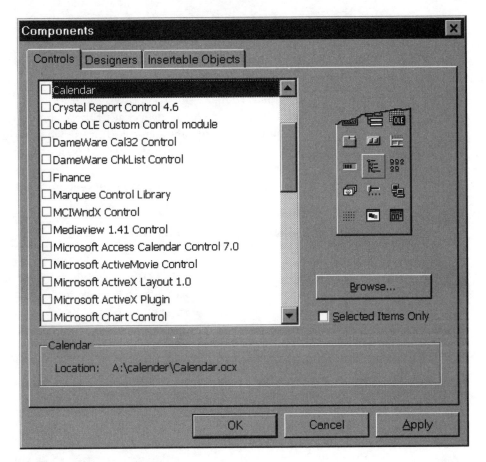

Figure 3-5
The Components dialog box

Now check the control you want to add. (The Windows 95 common controls are quite useful to add.) You can click on the Browse button to search for controls that may exist on your system but aren't registered. Once you add a custom control, the CCE places it on the toolbox along with the standard controls. To remove a custom control, bring up the dialog box and remove the checkmark.

There are many custom controls available on the Net. We give a few samples on the CD. Another good starting point is Microsoft's ActiveX gallery at its Web site. ⊃

An Overview of the Standard Controls

There are 18 controls that are always standard in the CCE Toolbox. The Toolbox itself is usually located to the left of the form but you can drag it around to a new location. (To make the Toolbox visible if it is hidden, choose View|Toolbox.) This section gives you an overview of these standard controls. The following table supplies Microsoft's suggested prefix when writing code for the controls name, for example, cmdButton would be a use suggested by Microsoft.

As always, whether you choose to use Microsoft conventions is up to you. ⊃

	Name (and prefix)	Purpose
	Pointer	Strictly speaking, this isn't a control. It is used to resize or move a control after you have placed it on the form.
	PictureBox (pic)	Used to display graphics. You can both display existing images and draw on picture boxes. Also used as a container for other controls.
	Label (lbl)	Used for text that you don't want the user to change.
	TextBox (txt)	Used for user input.
	Frame (fra)	Used to group controls (both visually and functionally).
	CommandButton (cmd)	Used for buttons that the user can click on.
	CheckBox (chk)	Used for yes/no choices.
	OptionButton (opt)	Used in groups when there is only one possibility from the group.
	ComboBox (cbo)	Used when you need a combination of a list box and a place to enter a choice. The idea is that you can either choose from the list or enter your own choice directly.
	ListBox (lst)	Used when you want to give the user a fixed list of items to choose from.

	Name (and prefix)	Purpose
	HScrollBar (hsb)	This is a horizontal scroll bar. You can use this to give users an analog tool for moving through a list.
	VScrollBar (vsb)	This is a vertical scroll bar.
	Timer (tmr)	Used to trigger events periodically.
	DriveListBox (drv)	Used to display the disk drives available.
	DirListBox (dir)	This is a directory list box.
	FileListBox (fil)	Used to display a list of files.
	Shape (shp)	Used for rectangles, circles, and other shapes. Quite sparing of Windows resources.
	Line (lin)	Used to draw lines on a form—also quite sparing of Windows resources.
	Image (img)	Like a picture box, can be used to display a graphical image from a bitmap, icon, or metafile on your form. You cannot draw on an Image control, however, and Image controls use fewer Windows resources than picture boxes.

Adding Controls to a Form

Once you decide which control you want to add to a form or a user control, there are a couple of ways to place it there. If you double-click on the control, the CCE adds the control in the default size and shape to the middle of the form. (If there are controls already in the center of the form, the new one is placed on top of the previous one.)

If you want to add a control at a specific location:

1. Click on the control.
2. Click and hold down the button at the spot on the form where you want the upper-left corner of the control to appear.

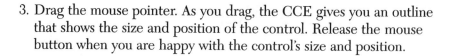
3. Drag the mouse pointer. As you drag, the CCE gives you an outline that shows the size and position of the control. Release the mouse button when you are happy with the control's size and position.

Adding Multiple Controls to a Form

You may want to add multiple controls of the same type to a form, for example, multiple command buttons or edit boxes.

To add multiple controls of the same type:

1. Hold down the CTRL key.

2. Click on the control in the palette. (Release the CTRL key after you select the control.)

3. Click at the place on the form where you want the upper-left corner of each copy of the control to appear, and drag to make it the correct size and shape.

If you use this method, be sure to click on the pointer icon in order to go back to the usual method of working with controls. ⊃

Container Controls

When you use controls like option buttons, keep them in groups. That way, the CCE knows which ones to turn off when one is turned on. Among the standard CCE controls (besides the form itself), both Frames and PictureBoxes can serve as *container* controls. The idea of a container is that all the controls will behave as one—this is sometimes called a *parent-child relationship*. For example, when you move a container control, the child controls move with it, or when you set the Enabled property of the container to false, all of the child controls are disabled as well.

Properties that measure where a control is, such as Left and Top, are always calculated relative to the boundaries of the container control. See Chapter 8 for how to access these properties for the user controls that you write. ⊃

The easiest way to create a container is to add it to the form before you add the child controls. Once you have placed the container on the form, make sure that the container control is selected. Then add controls as you normally would by, for example, clicking inside the container and dragging. (Note that even if the container is in the center of the form, double-clicking on a control will not make it a child of the container control.) You can also set the container property at run time.

You can also add multiple copies of the same control to a container control that is currently active by using the CTRL+CLICK method. ⊃

Working with Existing Controls

Before you can work with a control that is already on a form, you need to select it by simply clicking inside the control. If you are working inside the form's designer window, you can also use the TAB key to move the focus among the controls on the form. When a control is selected on a form, small black squares called *sizing handles* appear on the perimeter. Dragging on them lets you resize the control (see "Resizing and Reshaping Controls" later in the chapter).

Selecting Multiple Controls

You will often need to work with many controls at once, for example, when you have to align them. The easiest way to select multiple controls is:

1. Hold down the SHIFT key.
2. Click on each of the controls.

There is one other method for selecting multiple controls that is occasionally useful.

1. Imagine a rectangle that includes only those controls you want to select. Move to one corner of this imagined rectangle and click the left mouse button.
2. Hold the left mouse button down and drag the dotted rectangle until it includes all (and only) the controls you want to select. Then release the mouse button.

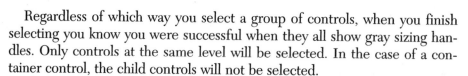

Regardless of which way you select a group of controls, when you finish selecting you know you were successful when they all show gray sizing handles. Only controls at the same level will be selected. In the case of a container control, the child controls will not be selected.

When you have selected multiple controls, the Properties window shows only their common properties. When you change one of the properties listed, all the selected controls are changed accordingly. ⊃

For example, one way to align the edges of a group of controls is to select the controls and set the Left property to the same value; to align the tops, use the Top property.

It is often easier to select the controls and then choose Format I Align or use the equivalent tool on the Form Editor toolbar. You can also use the Format menu to center selected controls on the form, and so on. You can even change the spacing of the controls relative to each other using this menu. ⊃

Moving Controls

To move a control to a different location:

1. Select the control.
2. Place the mouse inside the control, and drag the control to its new location. Be careful not to drag the sizing handles or you will resize it instead of moving it.

Notice that, as you manipulate the control, it seems to move in fits and starts, not smoothly. As the old computer joke goes, this is not a bug, it's a feature. The position of controls on a form defaults so that they are located only at grid points. The General page available on the Tools|Options dialog box lets you control this feature, which is called Align Controls to Grid. You can also make the grid more or less fine by changing options in this dialog box.

When you have selected a group of controls, they all move in tandem. ⊃

Finally, if you want to move a control by only one grid line at a time, select the control and then use CTRL and the appropriate arrow key.

Choosing the Lock Controls item on the Edit menu prevents you from inadvertently moving any control on the form. ⊃

Resizing and Reshaping Controls

The sizing handles are the easiest way to change the shape and size of a control. To resize a single control, first select it. You should be able to see the black sizing handles. Now drag the appropriate sizing handle. If you need to resize multiple controls, first select them. Then you can use the Properties window to change the height and width properties or use other nifty features available either on the Format menu or the Form Editor toolbar. In particular, once you have selected multiple controls, the Format menu makes it easy to make them all the same size and shape. And, if you want to increase or decrease the size by only one grid unit at a time, select the control(s) and then use SHIFT and the appropriate arrow key.

Deleting Controls

If you need to delete controls on the form, first select them. Then press the DELETE key, or choose Edit|Delete. If you delete a container component, all its child components are cut as well.

Cutting, Copying, and Pasting Controls

The CCE lets you cut, copy, and paste controls between forms, or between a form and a user control form or any form and a container control on it, using standard Windows conventions (CTRL+X for cut, CTRL+C for copy, and so on). You can also use the appropriate options on the Edit menu. (Copying a control leads the CCE to think you want to create a control array. Please see Chapter 7 for more on this feature.)

Common Control Properties and Events

This section discusses some common control properties and events that are important when manipulating the focus for controls. We follow this with a discussion of the standard controls.

While we discuss some of the most important properties and events that occur for controls, we will not repeat discussions of the many properties and events (such as Color, Cursor, Enabled, Left, Name, Top, Visible, Width, Click, DblClick, and so on) that work essentially the same for forms and controls.

Properties like Left and Top are always calculated relative to the container component. ⊃

Focus Properties and Events

Only a single control can be active—that is, have the *focus*—at any given time. (The form has the focus only when no control on it can have the focus.) The CCE determines which control to give the initial focus to by first looking at the controls whose TabStop property is set to True, then to the one with the lowest TabIndex value. (If the TabStop property is set to False, the user won't be able to tab to that component; however, this does not prohibit the control from getting focus with the mouse.)

When a project loads, the CCE (and Windows, for that matter) moves the focus to the visible and enabled control with the lowest value for the TabIndex property. The CCE sets the TabIndex property numerically according to the order in which you create the controls. You can change the TabIndex property and the order by using the Properties window.

The two focus events are GotFocus and LostFocus, which are triggered when the control gets or loses the focus, respectively.

Only visible and enabled controls can receive the focus. Frames, labels, menus, lines, shapes, images, and timers can never receive the focus. ⊃

Caption Properties and Accelerator Keys

Many Windows applications use accelerator keys to quickly move the focus or to click a button. These keys are indicated by an underline in the caption. Users can then press ALT and the underlined letter to click the button or move the focus.

To set up an accelerator key for the CCE control, add an ampersand (&) right before the accelerator (underlined letter). For example, if you set the Caption property of a command button to &Quit, the user can then use ALT+Q instead of clicking on the button to activate its Click event procedure.

Command Buttons

Placing buttons on a form so that the user can click on them to do something is very common in Windows applications (although many controls can detect the Click event and, therefore, have a Click event procedure associated to them). Most of the properties of command buttons are already familiar to you. However, even experienced VB users need to be aware of the neat new functionality that has been added to ordinary command buttons.

Cancel

Sometimes you want to press the Esc key to trigger an event. For this to happen, set the Cancel property of the command button to be True. Once you have done this, the CCE triggers the Click event handler for this button whenever the user presses the Esc key. Only one command button can have this property set to True on a form, so setting it True will reset previously set controls to False.

Default

The Click event for a default button (one whose Default property is True) is triggered whenever the user presses the ENTER key. To make a button the default button, set the button's Default property to be True.

 If the user presses ENTER when a button has the focus, then the CCE triggers the Click event for that button. This happens whether or not you have set up a default command button. ⊃

DisabledPicture, DownPicture, Picture, Style

These are new properties for command buttons. As the names suggest, icons can be added to ordinary command buttons. You can have different pictures for when the control is disabled, clicked and not clicked. To place a picture on a command button, set the Style to 1–Graphical.

Text Boxes

Text boxes are the primary method for accepting input and displaying output in the controls you build with the CCE. Extending them is, therefore, among the most common ways to build a useful custom control. (Of course, there are already many custom controls available with fancier forms of text input such as the Microsoft RichTextBox, which allows multiple fonts.)

Text boxes never treat what a user types in as a number; this means that getting numeric information to the CCE program requires transforming a string of digits into a number by using a built-in function or the CCE's built-in automatic conversions (see Chapter 4).

There are more than 40 properties for text boxes, many of which should be familiar to you. As before, the Name property is used only for the code you write; the user never sees it. The Font property gives you a dialog box for setting font properties, and, in this case, they will affect what the user enters or sees. (Unlike RichTextBoxes, which support multiple fonts in the same box, ordinary text boxes allow you only one font for all the text in the box.)

There are three properties you have not seen before and one property that works differently for text boxes than for forms. The three new properties are Text, MultiLine, and ScrollBars. The BorderStyle property also works differently for text boxes than for forms.

Text

The Text property is the analog of the Caption property for a command button or a form. The Text property controls the text the user sees. When you create a text box, the default value for this property is set to the default value for the Name property for that control—Text1, Text2, and so on. If you want a text box to be empty when the application starts up, select the Text property and blank out the original setting.

ScrollBars

The ScrollBars property determines if a text box has horizontal or vertical scroll bars. This is useful because the CCE allows you to accept long or multiple lines of data from a single text box; roughly 32,000 characters is the usual limit. There are four possible settings for the ScrollBars property:

Value	Meaning
0	This is the default value. The text box lacks both vertical and horizontal scroll bars.
1	The text box has horizontal scroll bars only (limits text to 255 characters).
2	The text box has vertical bars only.
3	The text box has both horizontal and vertical bars.

MultiLine

The MultiLine property determines if a text box can accept more than one line of text. (It is usually combined with resetting the value of the ScrollBars property.) When this property is True, the user can always use the standard methods in Microsoft Windows to move through the text box: the arrow keys, HOME, CTRL+HOME, END, and CTRL+END. The CCE automatically word-wraps when a user types more than one line of information into a text box with MultiLine set to be True, unless you've added horizontal scroll bars to the text box.

 Use the ENTER key to separate lines unless you've added a default command button to the form. If you have a default command button, press CTRL+ENTER to break lines. ◗

Finally, we should point out that allowing users to switch between single line and multiline for a custom control is a bit tricky. We provide you with a template to simplify the task for you (see Chapter 11).

BorderStyle

There are only two possible settings for the BorderStyle property for a text box. The default value is 1, which gives you a fixed single border. If you change the value of this property to 0, the border disappears.

MaxLength

This property determines the maximum number of characters the text box will accept. The default value is 0, which (somewhat counter-intuitively) means there is no maximum other than the roughly 32,000-character limit for multiline text boxes. Any setting other than 0 will limit the data to that number of characters entered into that text box.

PasswordChar

As you might expect from the name, this lets you limit what the text box displays (although all characters are accepted and stored). The convention is to use an asterisk (*) for the password character. Once you set this property, all the user sees is a row of asterisks. This property is often combined with the MaxLength property to add a password feature to your programs.

Locked

If this is set to False, the user cannot edit what is displayed in the text box.

Event Procedures for Text Boxes

Text boxes can recognize 17 events. Events like GotFocus and LostFocus work exactly as before. Three others—KeyDown, KeyUp, and KeyPress—are for monitoring exactly what the user types. You saw the KeyPress event in Chapter 1; the rest are covered in Chapter 5. The Change event lacks the flexibility of the key events you'll see in Chapter 4, but it is occasionally useful. The CCE monitors the text box and triggers this event procedure whenever a user makes any changes in the text box. For example, you can warn users that they should not be entering data in a specific text box, since they are blanking out what they typed.

Be very careful not to put any code in the Change event procedure that changes the contents of the text box. This will cause the system to continually trigger the event until the program crashes. (This is usually called an *event cascade*.) ↺

Labels

Labels are used for text that identifies the controls they are next to, for example, you will want to label text boxes. They can also be used to display text that users can't edit.

You can use a label to give an accelerator key for controls that do not have a caption property (like edit boxes). The idea is that when the user uses the accelerator key, the control that follows it in tab order receives the focus. ⊃

Alignment

There are three possible ways to align text. For example, if you set the value of this property to 0 (the default), the CCE will left-justify the text. The other possible values are 1 for right-justified and 2 for centered.

AutoSize, WordWrap

If the AutoSize property is set to True, the label automatically resizes horizontally to fit the text. If WordWrap is True, the label will grow vertically to fit the caption. (We show you a custom control called StretchLabel that goes beyond these capabilities in Chapter 13.)

BorderStyle, BackStyle

The BorderStyle property has two possible values. The default is 0 (no border). Set the value to 1, and the label resembles a text box. This is occasionally useful when your program displays results. The BackStyle property determines whether the label is transparent or opaque.

ListBox and ComboBox Controls

Both the ListBox and ComboBox controls let you display a scrollable list of items that users can select from. The difference is that the user cannot change the entries in a list box. (Combo boxes provide an edit area in which the user can enter information.) You usually use code to enter the items in these controls, but the CCE allows you to enter them directly via the List property in the Properties window at design time. To do this:

1. Choose the List property.
2. Enter the items, pressing CTRL+ENTER after each one. (Not ENTER, which closes the box.)

The most important properties of these controls that you may want to set at design time are discussed next.

Columns and MultiSelect

The Columns property controls the number of columns in a list box. If the value is 0 (the default), you get a normal single-column list box with vertical scrolling. If the value is 1, you get a single-column list box with horizontal scrolling. If the value is greater than 1, you allow (but do not require) multiple columns, which show up only when the items don't fit into the list box. (To force multiple columns, reduce the height of the list box accordingly.) The MultiSelect property controls whether the user can select more than one item from the list. There are three possible values for this property:

Type of Selection	Value	How It Works
No multiselection allowed	0	Click the mouse or press the spacebar.
Simple multiselection	1	SHIFT+CLICK extends the selection to include all list items between the current selection.
Extended multiselection	2	CTRL+CLICK selects or deselects a single item.

Sorted

This property applies to both controls. It determines if the CCE keeps the items sorted as you add more items to the list or combo box.

 An invisible list box with the sorted property set to True is a convenient way to sort small lists. ⊃

Style

This property lets you determine the style of the combo box. There are three possibilities. The default value, 0 (Dropdown Combo), gives you the usual drop-down list with an edit area. If the value of the Style property of a combo box is 1 (Simple Combo), the user sees the combo box with the list already dropped down.

Notice that, in both these cases, the user still has a text area to enter information. On the other hand, the final possible choice for the Style property for combo boxes, a value of 2 (Dropdown List), gives you a drop-down list box with no edit area.

CheckBox and Option Button Controls

Use check boxes when you want to provide nonexclusive options to the user. You then use code to determine if the user checks or unchecks a specific check box (using the value of the Value property). On the other hand, use a group of option buttons when you need to present mutually exclusive choices to the user. Whenever a user clicks on one radio button in a group, the other buttons are switched off. In any case, as one would expect, when the user clicks on a box or button, the CCE also triggers the Click event for that control.

 Since option buttons work as a group, the only way two option buttons on a form can be checked at the same time is if they are in separate container controls. ⊃

Timers

Use a Timer control whenever you want something—or "nothing," such as a pause—to occur periodically. For example, you might want to have a control that "wakes up" at intervals. Timers are not visible to the user; the icon appears only at design time. For this reason, where you place or how you size the timer control at design time is not important.

Enabled

Enabled is a Boolean (True/False) property that determines whether or not the timer should start ticking. If you set this to True at design time, the clock starts ticking when the form loads. (Ticking is meant metaphorically; there's no noise unless you program one.) Also, because timer controls are invisible to the user, he or she may be unaware that a timer has been enabled. For this reason, you may want to notify the user that a timer is working by means of a message box, an image control, or a picture box with a clock icon inside of it.

If you set the Enabled property to False at design time, the timer control starts working only when you switch this property to True in code. Similarly, you can disable a timer inside code by setting its Enabled property to False.

Interval

The Interval property determines how much time the CCE waits before calling the Timer event procedure (see the next section). The interval is measured in milliseconds, and the theoretical limits are between 1 millisecond and 65,535 milliseconds (a little more than one minute and five seconds). The reason these are only theoretical limits is that the underlying hardware reports the passage of only 18 clock ticks per second. Since this is a little less than 56 milliseconds per clock tick, you can't really use an Interval property less than 56, and intervals that don't differ by at least this amount may give the same results. (You can, however, use API functions, described in Chapter 4, for smaller time intervals.)

The smaller you set the Interval property, the more CPU time is spent waking up the Timer event procedure. If you set the Interval property too small, your system performance may slow to a crawl.

An Interval property of 0 disables the timer. ⊃
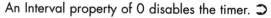

The Timer Event

The CCE tries to trigger the Timer event procedure as often as you have set the Interval property. But since the CPU may be doing something else when the time determined by the interval elapses, you cannot be guaranteed that Windows will call the Timer event procedure exactly when you want it. (Windows will know when the interval has elapsed, but it may need to finish what it is doing before activating the Timer event.) If the time has elapsed, Windows will call the Timer event procedure as soon as it is free to do so. You can use code to determine if more time has elapsed than you planned.

For example, suppose you want to develop a "clock control" with a clock that will update itself every second. It takes about two seconds and one line of code.

1. Add a label and a timer to a blank user control form.

2. Set the BorderStyle property of the label to 1. Set the AutoSize property of the label to be True and the font size to be 18. Set the Interval property of the timer control to be 1,000 (1,000 milliseconds = 1 second).

Now write the following code in the Timer event procedure for the Timer1 control:

```
Private Sub Timer1_Timer()
    Label1.Caption = Now
End Sub
```

The CCE will call this event procedure and update the clock's time roughly every second because the Interval property was set to 1,000. (See Chapter 4 for more on the date/time functions used in this example.) That's it, you now have a "clock control."

 If you want to have a Timer event procedure do something less frequently than about once a minute (the maximum setting for the Interval property), you need to add a static variable to the Timer event procedure. This variable will let you keep track of the number of intervals that has elapsed. (See Chapter 4 for more on these kinds of variables.) ⊃

Designing Menus

Ordinary forms will use menus frequently. Although one rarely thinks of a user control as having menus, add them as pop-ups if the control functionality calls for it.

Think of menu items as specialized controls that you add to your forms. Menu items respond only to a Click event. Designing the right kind of menus will make your applications much more user-friendly. The CCE lets you build multilevel menus and add pop-up menus as well.

Menus that contain submenus are usually called *hierarchical* (or *cascading*) menus. Of course, using too many levels of menus can make the application confusing to the user. Four is certainly too many; two or three levels are what you usually see. The user knows that a submenu lurks below a given menu item when he or she sees an arrow following the menu item.

Instead of using lots of submenus, consider designing a custom dialog box for the options. ⊃

To add a menu to your form, use the Menu Design window available from the Tools menu on the CCE main menu bar. The menu design window looks like the one in Figure 3-6. A short description of each of the components of this dialog box follows.

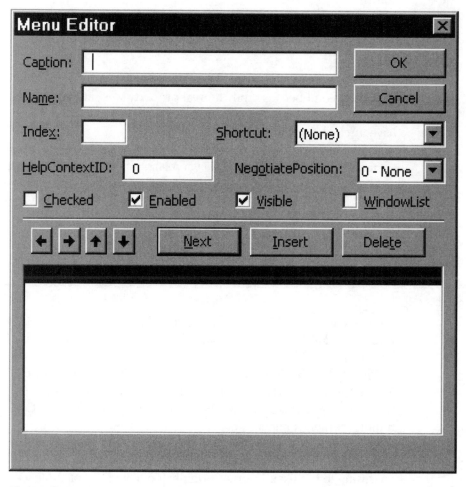

Figure 3-6
The Menu Design window

Caption

What you type in the Caption text box is what the user sees. The caption also shows up in the text area inside the dialog box. Unlike other CCE controls, menu items do not have default captions. As with other controls, use an ampersand (&) in the caption to give the item an access key.

 If you set the Caption property for a non-main menu to a hyphen (-), a separator bar shows up. ⊃

Name

Each menu item must have a control name. Unless the menu items are part of a control array (see Chapter 4 for more on control arrays), they must have different control names. The Microsoft convention is to use a mnu prefix for menu item control names.

The OK and Cancel Buttons

Click the OK button when you are finished designing the menu. Click the Cancel button if you decide not to build the menu. Even after you've finished designing a menu and clicked on the Done button, you can return to the Menu Design window and make changes.

The Index Box

Use the Index box if you want to make a menu item part of a control array (see Chapter 4).

The Shortcut Box

The Shortcut box gives you a drop-down list box from which you can choose accelerator keys to your menu items. Recall that accelerator keys are either function keys or key combinations that activate a menu item without the user having to open the menu at all. (The shortcut key is automatically added to the caption.)

The ALT+F4 shortcut to close a window is not an allowable shortcut key. Response to this key combination is built into the form unless you remove the control box at design time. If you have a File menu and a control box on an ordinary form and want to show ALT+F4 as a shortcut for the Exit item, place this shortcut as part of the caption and use the QueryUnload event to call the Click procedure of the Exit item. ⊃

Window Lists

Window lists are used when you have MDI windows. (MDI forms are not used in creating controls and are rarely needed in forms used as testing ground for controls, so we don't cover them in this book.)

The Checked Check Box

The Checked check box determines whether a checkmark shows up in front of the menu item. It is much more common to switch the Checked property to True when a user selects the item while the program is running than to set it at design time.

The Enabled Check Box

The Enabled check box determines the value of the Enabled property of the menu item. A menu item that is Enabled will respond to the Click event. An item that has this property changed to False—either at design time by toggling the box off or at run time via code—shows up gray.

The Visible Check Box

The Visible check box determines the value of the Visible property of the menu item. If a menu item is made invisible, all its submenus are also invisible and the CCE moves the menu items to fill in the gap.

The Arrow Buttons

The arrow buttons work with the current menu items. The menu item you're currently working with is highlighted in the large text window below the arrow buttons. Submenus are indicated by the indentation level in this text window. The LEFT and RIGHT ARROW buttons control the indentation level. Clicking on the LEFT ARROW button moves the highlighted item in one level; clicking on the RIGHT ARROW button moves it one indentation level deeper. You cannot indent an item more than one level deeper than the item above it. If you try, the CCE will not let you leave the Menu Design window until you fix it.

Clicking on the UP ARROW button interchanges the highlighted menu item with the item above it; clicking on the DOWN ARROW button interchanges the highlighted item with the item below it. The UP and DOWN ARROWS do not change the indentation pattern of an item.

The Next Button

Clicking the NEXT button moves you to the next menu item or inserts a new item if you are at the end of the menu. The indentation of the new item is the same as the indentation of the previous item.

The Insert Button

Clicking the INSERT button inserts a menu item above the currently highlighted menu item.

The Delete Button

Clicking the DELETE button removes the currently highlighted item. You cannot use the DEL key to remove menu items.

Pop-up Menus

One of Windows 95's conventions is that a right mouse-click brings up a context-sensitive menu. In order for a pop-up menu to exist, you must first

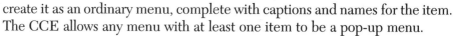

create it as an ordinary menu, complete with captions and names for the item. The CCE allows any menu with at least one item to be a pop-up menu.

If you don't want the user to see it on the main menu bar, set the Visible property of the top level menu item to be False. (For more on pop-up menus, see the section on Mouse events in Chapter 6.) ⊃

The Text Representation of a Form or User Control

The text file that contains an ASCII representation of a form or control is an extremely useful debugging tool, and is often an excellent way to get a sense for how the control was made. Using it, you can easily make sure the properties of the container form and its component controls are exactly what you want and that the code is correct relative to the interface. For this reason, every sample control chapter in the second half of this book ends with the ASCII representation of the control. (The files used for controls have a ctl extension; those used for ordinary forms have an frm extension.)

We suggest not modifying the properties of a form or a control using an ordinary text editor, .ctl in this file, although you may want to do this in unusual circumstances when you are globally changing the names for components. ⊃

Here is the .ctl file for the simple NonNegativeIntegerTextBox control we built in Chapter 1. First comes the version of Visual Basic you are working with. Next are descriptions of the controls we placed on the form, along with any properties not set at their default values. The text about attributes describes certain global properties of the user control, but you don't need to be concerned about them.

```
VERSION 5.00
Begin VB.UserControl NonNegativeIntegerTextBox
   ClientHeight    =    3600
   ClientLeft      =    0
   ClientTop       =    0
   ClientWidth     =    4800
   PropertyPages   =    "IntegerTextBox.ctx":0000
   ScaleHeight     =    3600
   ScaleWidth      =    4800
   Begin VB.TextBox Text1
      Height       =       495
```

```
        Left            =    1800
        TabIndex        =    0
        Top             =    1560
        Width           =    1215
    End
End
Attribute VB_Name = "NonNegative IntegerTextBox"
Attribute VB_GlobalNameSpace = False
Attribute VB_Creatable = True
Attribute VB_PredeclaredId = False
Attribute VB_Exposed = True
Public Event BadEntry()

Private Sub Text1_Change()
    If Text1.Text = "" Then Exit Sub
    If Not (IsNumeric(Text1.Text)) Or (Int(Val(Text1.Text)) _
    <> Val(Text1.Text)) or Val(Text1.Text) < 0
        RaiseEvent BadEntry
        Text1.Text = ""
    End If
End Sub

Private Sub Text1_KeyPress(KeyAscii As Integer)
  If KeyAscii < Asc("0") Or KeyAscii > Asc("9") Then
    KeyAscii = 0
    RaiseEvent BadEntry
  End If

End Sub
```

Chapter 4

This chapter has two purposes:

- To show the mechanics of writing code in the CCE.
- To show the fundamentals (variables, data types and control structures) of the programming language built into the CCE.

Before we begin, we want to stress that the key to creating a control (and for Visual Basic programming, in general) is recognizing the importance of event handling. If you think of the code in a control or a Visual Basic program as a set of independent parts that "wake up" only in response to events they have been told to recognize, you won't be wrong, but if you think of the code as having a starting line and an ending line and moving from top to bottom, you will. In fact, unlike some programming languages, executable lines in a Visual Basic program must be inside procedures or functions. (For illustration purposes, we may show you fragments of a program, but they are not meant to, nor can they, work independently.)

Except for the mechanics of entering code, which have gotten even easier, programmers coming from earlier versions of VB4 can skim or even skip most of this chapter; the only new feature described here is the decimal type. ⊃

Programming Basics

Mechanics of Entering Code

First off, as you have already seen, you always write code in a Code window. The editor built into the CCE automatically color-codes the elements of your program. For example, the default is that keywords are in blue, names of objects and methods are in red. You can change the defaults with the Editor page on the Tools|Options dialog box. The editor is also tied into the compiler. For this reason, you will see an error message box if what you type doesn't make sense to the compiler. (Usually what you see is a message box with "compiler error" after you move off the current line.)

The editor has lots of nifty features to make writing code easier. (Microsoft calls this *IntelliSense*.) For example, when you enter a keyword followed by a space or opening parenthesis, a tip appears that gives the syntax for that element. Figure 4-1 shows an example of this QuickInfo feature at work.

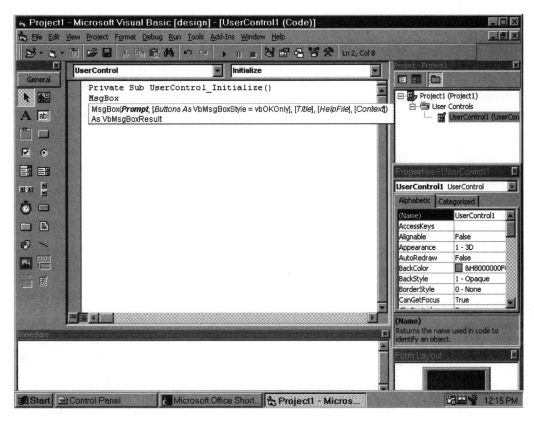

Figure 4-1
QuickInfo at work

We will explain the syntax for these QuickInfo tips a little later. (You can turn this off by using the Editor page on the Options dialog box. In this case, you can use CTRL+I to access QuickInfo for a specific procedure or method.)

The next nifty feature is called List Properties/Methods. It gives you a list of the properties and methods of an object right after you type the period. For example, if you have a TextBox named Text1 and you type `Text1.`, you will immediately see something like the screen shown in Figure 4-2 on the next page.

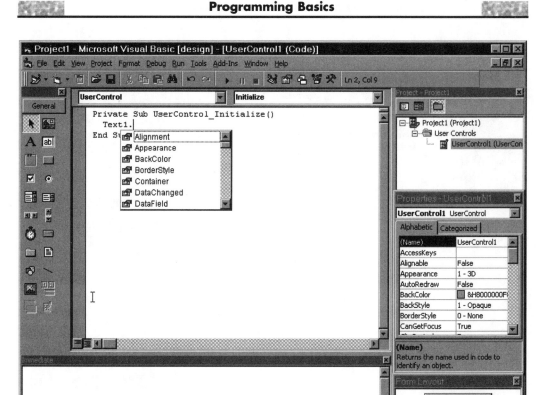

Figure 4-2
List Properties/Methods at work

(CTRL+J is the keyboard shortcut.) Select the item you want and then press the TAB key to insert the item.

The final nifty feature gives you a list of available constants. For example, if you had a text box named Text1 on your control and entered

```
Text1.Enabled =
```

you would see a pop-up box listing True or False. (Again, select the one you want and press TAB to complete it.)

If you have IntelliSense turned off, its features are part of the right click menu in the Code window. ⊃

In general, the Code window has two list boxes, and an area for editing your code. The left list box, usually called the Object list box, lists all the controls on the control or form, plus an object called General that holds common code used by all the procedures attached to the control or form. The right-hand list box is usually called the Procedure list box. As you have seen, this list box shows all the events recognized by the object selected in the Object list box. If you have already written an event procedure, it shows up in bold-face in the Procedure list box. User-defined functions and procedures will show up in the right-hand list box as well.

Advanced Editing Features

The Visual Basic editor follows the standard Windows conventions such as CTRL+X for cut and CTRL+V for paste. The Edit menu, as discussed in Chapter 2, gives you access to most of the editing features, although the Edit toolbar described in Table 4-1 is also useful. The search/replace feature is quite powerful and includes the ability to search:

- selected text
- current procedure
- current module
- current project

You can search up or down or in both directions, find whole words, match case, or use pattern matching. (Make sure the Use Pattern Matching box is checked in the Search or Replace dialog box.)

The following table summarizes the wildcard characters you can use for pattern matching.

Pattern Used	Matches
?	Any single character
*	Zero or more characters
#	Any single digit (0–9)
[charlist]	Any single character in the charlist
[!charlist]	Any single character not in the charlist

For example, with the "Find Whole Words Only" and the "Use Pattern Matching" boxes checked, Count* would match Count, Counts, Counter, but Count? would not match Counter. As another example: you can use [AEIOU] to find vowels.

To match the opening bracket ([ ), question mark (?), pound sign (#), and asterisk (*), enclose them in brackets. The closing bracket ( ]) can't be used inside brackets to match itself, but it can be used outside a group as an individual character. ⊃

Finally, in addition to using the braces for a simple list of characters, you can specify a range of characters by using a hyphen (-) to separate the upper and lower bounds of the range. For example, using [A-Z] lets you search for any alphabetical character. You can even use multiple ranges inside the brackets: [a-zA-Z0-9] matches any alphanumeric character.

Edit Toolbar

Many useful editing features have button equivalents on the Edit toolbar. However, as we write this, some of them, unfortunately, do not have keyboard equivalents. For this reason, you might want to choose View|Toolbars and add the Edit toolbar to your environment. (The Edit Toolbar is also a way to quickly get at the IntelliSense features if you have disabled them from automatically popping up.) The following table summarizes the tools available on this toolbar.

Tool	Function	Keyboard equivalent, if any	Description
	List Properties/Methods	CTRL +J	Displays a pop-up with a list of the properties and methods for the object preceding the period.
	List Constants	CTRL+SHIFT+J	Displays a pop-up with a list of the valid constants after you type an = sign.
	Quick Info	CTRL+I	Gives the syntax for the procedure or method.
	Parameter Info	CTRL+SHIFT+I	Provides the parameter list for the current function call.
	Complete Word	CTRL+SPACE	Completes the keyword or object when enough information is there. (For example, msg would complete to MsgBox.)

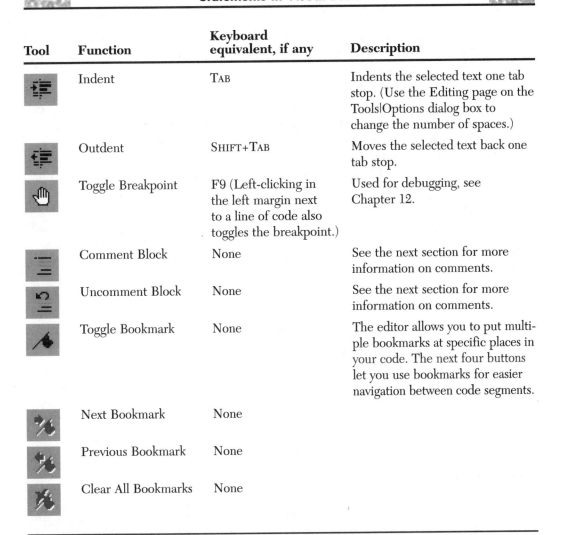

Tool	Function	Keyboard equivalent, if any	Description
	Indent	TAB	Indents the selected text one tab stop. (Use the Editing page on the Tools|Options dialog box to change the number of spaces.)
	Outdent	SHIFT+TAB	Moves the selected text back one tab stop.
	Toggle Breakpoint	F9 (Left-clicking in the left margin next to a line of code also toggles the breakpoint.)	Used for debugging, see Chapter 12.
	Comment Block	None	See the next section for more information on comments.
	Uncomment Block	None	See the next section for more information on comments.
	Toggle Bookmark	None	The editor allows you to put multiple bookmarks at specific places in your code. The next four buttons let you use bookmarks for easier navigation between code segments.
	Next Bookmark	None	
	Previous Bookmark	None	
	Clear All Bookmarks	None	

Statements in Visual Basic

When you enter a statement in the Code window, Visual Basic analyzes it. Many typos are detected by Visual Basic at this stage. The editor can actually correct some common typos like leaving off a closing " on a string.

Unless they are within quotation marks, Visual Basic is not case sensitive nor is spacing relevant to Visual Basic. ⊃

Nonetheless, Visual Basic does try to impose its own conventions. It capitalizes the first letter of command words and often adds extra spaces for readability. For example, no matter how you capitalize the command word `Print`—`PRint`, `Print`, `print`, and so on—moving off of the line will change it to `Print`.

Statements in Visual Basic rarely use line numbers, and each statement generally occurs on its own line. Lines are limited to 1023 characters but can be extended to the next line by using the underscore character (_) preceded by a space as the end of the line. Thus, unless a line ends with an underscore, pressing the ENTER key indicates a line is done. (There's no semicolon statement separator like in some languages.) You can combine statements on one line by placing a colon (:) between them. If you use a line with more characters than can fit in the window, Visual Basic scrolls the window to the right, as needed.

Sometimes in this book you'll see lines that easily fit this limit but are longer than can fit on one line of a printed page. We will use the underscore as the line continuation character whenever possible. Since the underscore does not work as a line continuation character inside quotes, in this case, look for the closing quote.

```
MsgBox "Please click a button" vbOKCancel _
+vbExclamation, "Test Button"
Print "This is an example of text inside quotes
   that won't fit on a single line of the printed
   page."
```

Comments

As with any programming language, commenting your code is up to you. Comment statements are neither executed nor processed by Visual Basic. As a result, they do not take up any room in your OCX file. There are two ways to indicate a comment. The usual way is with a single quote.

```
Sub Command1_Click ()
   'A comment describing the procedure would go here
   '

End Sub
```

(You can also use the older Rem keyword.)

You can add comments to the ends of lines. In this case, it is easier to use the single quotation mark because the Rem form requires a colon before it.

For example:

```
Print "Hello world" 'every one uses this
```

or

```
Print "Hello world" :Rem A bit more cumbersome
```

Everything on a line following a Rem statement is ignored, regardless of whether or not it is an executable Visual Basic statement.

Although the CCE has conditional compilation (see Chapter 12), commenting out executable statements is still a common technique to help debug your programs. This is especially true because the Edit toolbar has the neat Comment/Uncomment Block tools. ⊃

The End Statement

When Visual Basic processes an End statement, the program stops. The various Unload events are not triggered, and if you are developing a program, you are dumped back into the development environment. The effect is exactly the same as choosing the End option on the Run menu. While you may have an End statement in a project used for a test bed, you cannot place End statements in any code for a user control.

Assignment and Property Setting

Giving values to variables and resetting properties are two of the most common tasks in Visual Basic code. Visual Basic uses an equal sign for both these operations, for example,

```
Count = 1
```

You can also use the optional keyword Let that was common in earlier versions of BASIC:

Let *Variable*Name = *value*

If you want to change a property setting for a Visual Basic object, place the object's name followed by a period and then the name of the property on the left side of the equal sign, and put the new value on the right-hand side:

object.*property* = *value*

111

For example, suppose you have a text button (control name of TextBox1) and want to blank it out in code rather than use the properties bar:

```
Text1.Text = ""
```

Since there is nothing between the quotation marks, the text assigned to this property is blank. Similarly, a line like

```
Text1.Text = "Hello world"
```

in an event procedure changes the setting for the text property to the text in the quotation marks.

 Every Visual Basic object has a default property (for example, text boxes have the Text property). When referring to the default property, you don't need to use the property name. For example, you can enter

```
TextBox1 = "This is new text"
```

However, this approach can lead to less readable code and requires you to remember what the default property of the control is. Thus, in spite of the very small gain in speed this approach yields, this book doesn't emphasize this feature of Visual Basic. In addition, the default property may change in future versions of the object, which would cause the program to fail. ⊃

Boolean Properties

Properties that take only the value true or false are usually Boolean properties, after the English logician George Boole. Boolean properties specify whether a command button is visible, enabled, or is the default for cancel or command button. Visual Basic has built-in constants for true and false. For example,

```
Command1.Visible = False   'false works too of course
```

hides the command button. The control stays hidden until Visual Basic processes the statement

```
Command1.Visible = True
```

As another example, to have the TAB key skip over a control while a program is running, change the TabStop property to False:

```
Control.TabStop = False
```

Internally, Visual Basic uses the values 0 for False and –1 for True (actually, any nonzero value will work for True) . The Not operator lets you toggle between Boolean properties. For example,

```
Command1.Visible = Not(Command1.Visible)
```

switches the state of the command button.

For the Not operator to work properly in toggling a Boolean property between on and off, you must use the built-in True constant or a value of –1 for True. ⊃

An Example: Setting Fonts

Which fonts and font sizes you can use depends on what kind of hardware is available to the system in which you run the application. Visual Basic lets you find out this information by analyzing the Fonts property of the Screen or Printer objects. In this case, you should think of the Font object as being a "sub-object" of an existing VB object.

For example, to assign a font name in code, use the Name property of the Font object and place the name in quotation marks on the right-hand side of an assignment statement:

```
ObjectName.Font.Name = "Modern"
ObjectName.Font.Name = "Helv" 'Helvetica
```

All objects that display text let you set these properties. These include forms, command buttons, labels, and text boxes. Of these, only forms (and picture boxes) let you combine different fonts. If you change these properties at run time for any other control, all the old text switches to the new font as well. The rule is that if text is specified by a property (like the Caption property for command buttons), changing a font changes the previous text. On the other hand, if you display text by using the Print method, the changes are not retroactive and, therefore, go into effect only for subsequent Print statements.

You can change all the font properties via code. Except for `Font.Size`, they are all Boolean properties. As with `Font.Name`, any control that displays text lets you set these properties of the Font object. For example:

```
Screen.Font.Size = 24              '24 point type
Screen.Font.Bold = False
Screen.Font.Italic = True
Screen.Font.Strikethru = True
Printer.Font.Underline = True
```

As with changing fonts, only forms (and picture boxes) let you mix these font properties.

Forms, picture boxes, and the printer have one other font property you may occasionally find useful: `FontTransparent`. If you set this to True, background graphics and background text will show through the text displayed in the transparent font.

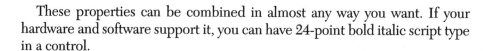

These properties can be combined in almost any way you want. If your hardware and software support it, you can have 24-point bold italic script type in a control.

Method Calls

If you want your Visual Basic objects to actually do something, you will need to work with built-in methods. For example, if you want to set the focus to a specific control at run time, you need to use the SetFocus method:

```
TextBox1.SetFocus
```

In general, of course, the syntax for a method is

```
Object.NameOfMethod ListOfWhatToUse
```

The ListOfWhatToUse (more correctly called the *argument* or *parameter* list) would contain a list of items separated by commas. For example, the Move method, which can be used to move a control around inside its current container, has the following syntax:

```
Object.Move left, top, width, height
```

so

```
TextBox1.Move Screen.Width/2, Screen.Height/2, _
25*Screen.Width, .25*Screen.Height
```

would move a text box to roughly halfway inside the usable area and make its width and height ¼ of the usable area.

Variables

Variable names in Visual Basic can be up to 255 characters long and, provided the first character is a letter, can include any combination of letters, numbers, and underscores. All characters in a variable name are significant, but, as with most things in Visual Basic, case is irrelevant. BASE is the same variable as base. On the other hand, Base is a different variable from Base1, and both are different from Base_1.

The Visual Basic editor always changes the form of the names of your variables to reflect the capitalization pattern you last used if you didn't explicitly declare the variable. If the variable was explicitly declared, the VB editor always converts it to the case which was declared. If you use `Yearlyinterest`, `yearlyinterest`, and `YearlyInterest` successively as variable names, when you move off the line, Visual Basic will automatically change all occurrences to `YearlyInterest` because this was the last one you used. However, if you had originally declared it with `Dim Yearlyinterest As Single`, then it would retain that case no matter how you used it in the following code.

This feature is occasionally useful in detecting typos in variable names. If you think a misspelled variable name is causing a problem, change one occurrence to all caps, move off the line, and scan the program to see if all the occurrences of the variable name have been changed. If you find one that wasn't changed, you will know that variable name contains a typo. Correct the error and then change the variable name back to the form you want; all occurrences of the name will change as well.

For a better method of finding misspelled variables, see the section on "Declaring Variables." ⊃

You can't use names reserved by Visual Basic for variable names. For example, Print is not acceptable as a variable name. Visual Basic will present an error message if you try to use a reserved word as a variable name, usually immediately after you move off of the line. However, you can embed reserved words within a variable's name. For example, PrintIt is a perfectly acceptable variable name.

The most common convention in Visual Basic for variable names is to use capitals only at the beginning of the words that make up the parts of it (for example, `YearlyInterest`, not `Yearlyinterest`).

Variable Types

Visual Basic handles 12 standard types of variables. It is also possible to define your own variable types, as you will see in the next chapter. Many of these types have special identifiers for variables that will hold information of that type. This was more common in earlier versions of BASIC and most people don't use them very much now. (See the section on "Declaring Variables" later in this chapter for more information on this.)

Boolean

Boolean variables are stored as 2-byte numbers, but can only hold the value True or False. Boolean variables have no type-declaration character.

Byte

Byte variables hold (unsigned) integer values between 0 and 255. The Byte data type has no type-declaration character.

Currency

The currency type is designed to avoid certain problems inherent in switching from binary fractions to decimal fractions. (It's impossible to make $\frac{1}{10}$ out of combinations of $\frac{1}{2}$, $\frac{1}{4}$, $\frac{1}{8}$, $\frac{1}{16}$, and so on.) The currency type can have 4 digits to the right of the decimal place and up to 14 to the left of the decimal point. Arithmetic will be exact within this range. The identifier is an "at" sign (@)—not the dollar sign, which identifies strings. While calculations other than addition and subtraction are about as slow as for double-precision numbers, this is the preferred type for financial calculations of reasonable size. (For those who are interested, this type uses 19-digit integers, which are then scaled by a factor of 10,000. This gives you 15 places to the left of the decimal point and 4 places to the right.)

Date

Date variables are stored as 8-byte numbers with possible values in the range January 1, 100 to December 31, 9999. Date has no type-declaration character. Dates are indicated by surrounding the date by #'s, for example:

```
Millenium = #1/1/2000#
```

Essentially, the CCE will accept whatever standard formats for dates that your locale uses.

You can do ordinary arithmetic on Date variables and the results are what you might expect:

```
Tomorrow =  Now + 1
```

Generally, adding or subtracting integers affects the day; adding or subtracting fractions will also affect the hour.

Decimal

A type new to VB, this is currently a subtype of the Variant data type described later. Decimal variables are stored as roughly 29-digit (actually 96-bit unsigned) integers. They are then scalable by a variable power of 10 that specifies the number of digits to the right of the decimal point, and ranges from 0 to 28.

Integer

Integer variables hold relatively small integer values, between –32,768 and +32,767. Integer arithmetic is very fast but is restricted to these ranges. The identifier that can be used is the percent sign (%):

```
AnIntegerVariable% = 37
```

Long Integers

This type holds integers between –2,147,483,648 and +2,147,483,647. The identifier used is the ampersand (&). Long integer arithmetic is also fast, and there is very little performance penalty on 486DX, or Pentium class machines for using long integers rather than ordinary integers.

```
ALongIntegerVariable& = 99999789
```

Object

Object variables hold address information that refers to objects. (See Chapter 7 for more on objects.)

Single Precision

For single-precision numbers, the identifier is an exclamation point (!). These variables hold numbers that are approximations. You can be sure of the accuracy of only seven digits. This means that if an answer comes out as 12,345,678.97, the answer could just as likely be 12,345,670.01. The range for

these numbers is up to 38 digits. Calculations will always be approximate. Moreover, arithmetic with these numbers is slower than with integer or long integer variables.

Double Precision

Double-precision variables hold numbers with 16 places of accuracy and allow more than 300 digits. The identifier used is a pound sign (#). Calculations are also approximate for these variables. You can rely only on the first 16 digits. Calculations are relatively slow with double-precision numbers. Double-precision variables are mainly used in scientific calculations in Visual Basic because of the Currency and Decimal data types described earlier.

String

String variables hold characters. The older (but still accepted) method to identify string variables is to use a dollar sign ($) at the end of the variable name:

```
AStringVariable$
```

String variables can theoretically hold up to 32k characters, although a specific machine may hold less due to memory constraints, overhead requirements for Windows, or the number of strings used in the form. For example, since the information in a text box is stored as a string, you would use a string variable to pick up the text contained in a text box. For example,

```
ContentOfTextBox1$ = TextBox1.Text
```

assigns the string contained in the text box to the variable named on the left-hand side.

The Variant Type

The variant data type is designed to store all the different possible Visual Basic data received in one place. It doesn't matter whether the information is numeric, date/time, string, or an object; the variant type can hold it all. Visual Basic automatically performs any necessary conversions so you don't (usually) have to worry about what type of data is being stored in the variant data type. The built-in VarType function lets you determine whether data stored in the variant type is numeric, date/time, or string. Using variants rather than the specific type is a little slower because of the conversions needed, and some programmers feel relying on automatic type conversions leads to sloppy programming. Variants can also hold two special values "empty" which means nothing is being stored and the special Null value is used. (Using a Null variant in an expression will always give you Null as the value of the expression.)

Declaring Variables

One of the most common bugs in programs is the misspelled variable name. Most versions of BASIC allow you to create variables "on the fly" by merely using the variable name in your program. (And, unfortunately, the CCE kept this "feature.") This is not permitted, for good reason, in strongly typed languages such as Java or Pascal. Obviously, if you create variables on the fly, you can easily misspell a variable name, and a misspelled variable name will almost certainly yield a default value that causes your program to behave incorrectly. Such an error is among the most difficult to eradicate, because you need to find the misspelled variable name.

One way to avoid this problem is to force all variables to be declared. Then you will be notified if a variable name is spelled incorrectly in a procedure. The designers of Visual Basic give you this option but do not force you to use it. To turn on this option, add the command Option Explicit in the General code section. After Visual Basic processes this command, it will no longer allow you to use a variable unless you declare it first.

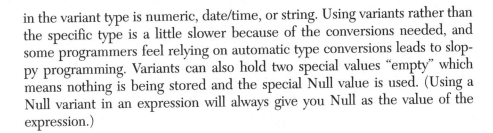

You can also use the Editor page of the Options dialog box on the Tools menu to require variable declaration. ⊃

The most common way to declare a variable inside an event procedure is with the Dim keyword. Here are some examples:

```
Sub Command1_Click()
    Dim I As Integer
    Dim InfoInTextBox As String
    Dim Interest As Currency
End Sub
```

You can combine multiple declarations on a single line but you must include the type with each variable.

```
Dim Year as Integer, Rate As Currency, Name as _
String
```

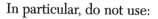

In particular, do not use:

```
Dim I, J, K As Integer
```

since this will only make K an integer variable. The other two are variant variables.

You can use the type identifier instead of the "As"

```
Dim I%, MyName$
```

If a variable is declared in a Dim statement, then trying to use variables with the same name but a different type identifier at the end of the variable will cause a "Duplicate definition" error when the program is run. ⊃

To give a variable the variant data type, just use the Dim statement without any As clause or identifier:

```
Dim Foo        'makes Foo have the variant data type
```

You can also use

```
Dim Foo As Variant
```

You can not currently declare a variable as being of the decimal type. Instead, you must store the information in a variant and either rely on Visual Basic to make the conversion or use a conversion function. ⊃

Finally, as with naming conventions for objects, naming conventions for variables have also inspired quite a lot of flaming. Many complicated systems of prefixes exist that indicate, at a glance, the type of a variable. In this book, we use prefixes only in a very limited way: we try to indicate the scope of a variable (see later in this chapter and also in the next chapter) by a prefix. Also, when the routine is complicated and it is not obvious what type a variable is, we will usually use a prefix like "s" for string or "n" for integer. (Except, we, like almost everyone else, often use a simple "I" or "J" for integer counters—go figure.)

Default Values

The first time you use a variant variable temporarily assigns it a default value of "empty" and gives it the variant type. The "empty" value disappears the moment you assign a value to the variable. Every other type of variable also has a default value. For string variables, this is the null (empty) string—the one you get by assigning " " to a string variable. For numeric variables, the default value is zero.

Scope of Variables

Visual Basic is not like the BASIC of old; it has true local and global variables so that you can isolate variables within procedures. (See the next chapter for more on procedures.) Unless you specifically arrange it, changing the value of a variable named Total in one procedure will not affect another variable with the same name in another procedure.

Of course, occasionally you will want to share the values of variables across event procedures. For example, if an application is designed to perform a calculation involving one interest rate at a time, that rate should be available to all the procedures in the form for the control or the test form. Variables that allow such sharing among all the code in a form (including the form used for a control) are called, naturally enough, *form-level variables*. (You can also have true global variables when you have a multiform application—see the Global Variables section in the next chapter for more on this.)

Put the Dim statements for form-level variables in the General section of the code. For example, if you open the Code window, select Declarations for the General object, and enter

```
Dim InterestRate As Currency
```

then the following is true:

- The value of the variable named `InterestRate` will be visible to all the procedures attached to the form.
- Any changes made to this variable in one event procedure will persist.

Obviously, the last point means you have to be careful when assigning values to form-level variables. Any information passed between event procedures is a breeding ground for programming bugs. Moreover, these errors are often hard to pinpoint.

You can use the same variable name as both a local and a form-level variable. Any Dim statements contained in a procedure take precedence over form-level declarations—they force a variable to be local. Therefore, you lose the ability to use the information contained in the form-level variable. Duplicating the names makes the form-level variable invisible to the procedure. Visual Basic doesn't tell you whether a form-level variable has been defined with the same name as a local variable. This is one more reason to make sure that variables you want to be local really are local by dimensioning them inside the procedure. This forces the variable to be local to that procedure.

As mentioned, we like to prefix form-level variables with the letter "f" (for example, fInterest) and global variables with the letter "g" (for example, gInterest). ⊃

 Visual Basic also has Private/Public and Friend identifiers that can be used to scope variables or procedures. Private, in fact, works just like Dim for form-level variables. (For more on these keywords, please see the next chapter.) ⊃

Static Variables—Having Values Persist

When Visual Basic invokes an event procedure, the old values of local variables are wiped out and they go back to their default values. These kinds of dynamic variables are not enough for all programming situations. For example, suppose you need to keep track of how many times a command button has been clicked. If the counter is always set back to zero, you're in trouble. You could have the values persist by using a form-level variable, but most programmers reserve form-level variables for sharing information among procedures. The solution is to use *static variables*. Static variables are not reinitialized each time Visual Basic invokes a procedure. Besides being ideal for counters, static variables are useful for making controls alternately visible or invisible (or for switching between any Boolean properties, for that matter), and as a debugging tool.

To make a variable static within a procedure, replace the keyword Dim in the declaration with the keyword Static:

```
Static Counter As Integer, IsVisible As Boolean
```

Here is an example of an event procedure for a command button that counts the clicks and displays the number:

```
Sub Command1_Click()
   'This procedure uses a static variable to count
   'clicks
   Static Counter As Integer     ' Counter starts at 0
   Counter = Counter + 1
   MsgBox Counter
End Sub
```

The first time you click, the counter starts out with its default value of 0. Visual Basic then adds 1 to it and prints the result. Notice that by placing the Print statement after the addition, you are not off by 1 in the count.

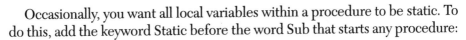

Occasionally, you want all local variables within a procedure to be static. To do this, add the keyword Static before the word Sub that starts any procedure:

```
Static Sub Command1_Click()
```

Strings

As you have seen, strings are indicated by double quotes. To put two strings together (*concatenate* them), use a plus sign (+) or an ampersand (&). The recommended method is to always use the ampersand. For example, if

```
Language = "Visual Basic"
Version = "5.0"
```

then

```
LanguageVersion = Language & Version
LanguageVersion = "Visual Basic 5.0"
```

have the same effect.

The & (or the +) joins strings in the order in which you present them. Thus, unlike when you add numbers together, order is important when you use the + sign to join two strings together.

 The ampersand (&), unlike the + sign, lets you combine numbers and strings into a string equivalent. For example, C=A% & B$ concatenates an integer variable and a string variable by changing them both to variants. ⊃

ANSI Codes

Windows (hence, Visual Basic) uses the ANSI character set. The control characters and such special keys as TAB and line feed have numbers less than 32. The value of the function Chr (n) is the string consisting of the character of ASCII value n in the current font. For instance, the statement

```
Print Chr(169)
```

prints the copyright symbol (©) on the screen if you are using the Courier font.

123

Given the special nature of quotes for Visual Basic strings, you can use the ANSI value for the quotation mark, 34, to display a sentence surrounded with quotation marks.

```
Print Chr(34)& "Necessity is the mother of
    invention." & Chr(34)
```

This gives

```
"Necessity is the mother of invention."
```

(You can also use

```
Print """Necessity is the mother of invention."""
```

since Visual Basic treats `"""` as the literal quotation mark inside Print statements.)

Many common strings have constant equivalents built into Visual Basic. For example, vbCrLf gives you the Chr(13)+Chr(10) carriage return/line feed combination and vbTab gives you the tab character. ⊃

Visual Basic has a function called Asc that takes a string expression and returns the ANSI value of the first character. If the string is empty (the null string), using this function generates a run-time error.

ANSI order is what Visual Basic uses, by default, to compare strings when you use relational operators like < or >. ⊃

Fixed-Length Strings

A fixed-length string is created with a Dim statement. Here is an example:

```
Dim ZipPlusFour As String * 10
```

This variable will always hold strings of length 10. If you assign a longer string to a fixed-length string, the right part will be cut off. If you assign a shorter string to ShortString, like this:

```
ZipPlusFour="11234"
```

then you still get a string of length 10. Only this time, the variable is padded on the right with spaces.

Example: Strings at Work: Input Boxes

Text boxes are the normal way for a Visual Basic application (and, especially, a control) to accept data. There is one other method that is occasionally useful. The InputBox function displays a modal dialog box on the screen. This is the principal advantage of input boxes; it is sometimes necessary to insist that a user supply some necessary data before letting him or her move on. (We also use them frequently when writing a quick and dirty test bed.) The disadvantages are that the dimensions of the input box are fixed beforehand and you lose the flexibility that text boxes provide. Figure 4-3 shows an example of an input box:

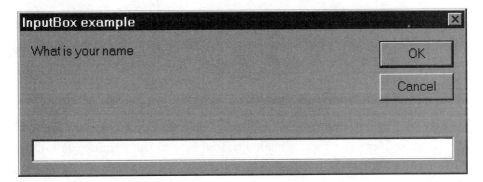

Figure 4-3
An input box

As you can see, input boxes have a title bar and four components, three of which are controls. The first is the prompt, "Please enter your name." There are always two command buttons labeled OK and Cancel. Finally, there is a text box at the bottom. Visual Basic always places the focus here when it processes a statement containing an InputBox function. The simplest syntax for the InputBox function is

```
StringVariable = InputBox(prompt)
```

where the prompt is a string or string variable. This gives a dialog box that is roughly centered horizontally and one-third of the way down the screen.

Now the user types whatever he or she wants in the text box. Pressing ENTER or clicking the OK button makes whatever is in the text box become the value of the string variable. Pressing ESC or clicking the Cancel box causes Visual Basic to assign the null string to the variable.

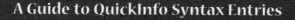

A Guide to QuickInfo Syntax Entries

If you enabled the QuickInfo feature, you can see that the full syntax for the InputBox function is:

InputBox(***Prompt [, Title] [, Default] [, Xpos] [, Ypos]**[, Helpfile, Context])*

This is pretty typical of a QuickInfo help item: optional parameters are indicated by enclosing them in square brackets. In this case, only the Prompt parameter is required. If you use an optional parameter, you must separate it with commas. If you skip a parameter, you must still use the extra comma.

In certain cases, including the InputBox function, you can use what are called *named arguments* to avoid dealing with the commas for optional arguments. Named arguments show up in bold italic when using the QuickInfo feature. For example, all parameters in the InputBox function can use named arguments. (See the next chapter for more on named arguments.)

Here is a more detailed description of the parameters for the InputBox function:

Prompt	This is the string or string variable whose value Visual Basic displays in the dialog box. It is limited to roughly 255 characters. The prompt doesn't wrap, and you have to explicitly add line separators (use vbCrLf).
Title	The title parameter is optional and gives the caption used in the title bar. There is no default value; if you leave this out, nothing is displayed in the title bar.
Default	The default parameter is also optional. It lets you display default text in the Edit box, where the user will enter information.
xpos,ypos	This parameter is also optional. Both xpos and ypos are integral numeric expressions: xpos is the distance in twips between the left edge of the input box and the left edge of the screen, and ypos is the distance in twips between the top of the box and the top of the screen.
Helpfile	The helpfile parameter is also optional. It is a string value to identify the help file to use. If a helpfile parameter is specified, then the context parameter must also be specified.
Context	The context parameter is a numeric expression that is the help context identification number assigned to a help topic. If context is specified, then the helpfile parameter must also be specified.

Numbers

Numbers in Visual Basic cannot use commas to delineate thousands. They can use a decimal point, unless they are integers. They will be displayed in scientific notation if they are very large.

If you need to give a numeric value to a variable, place the number or numeric expression on the right-hand side of the assignment statement. If you assign a number with a decimal point to an integer variable, it is automatically rounded off. If you assign a number larger than the limits for the given variable, Visual Basic gives you an error message at run time. To change a string of digits to a number, use the built-in function Val:

```
Val("3001") = 3001
```

The Val function reads through the string until it encounters a non-numeric character (or a second period). The number you get from it is determined by where it stopped searching:

```
Val ("30Something") = 30
```

Similarly, you will want to change a number back to a string of digits when you display it in a text box. There are many ways to do this, depending on the form you want the number to take. The function Str is the simplest. It converts a number to a string but doesn't clean it up in any way. It also leaves a space in front of positive numbers.

To polish the display, the Str function is often replaced by the Format function described in the next section.

Another possibility to store information is the variant data type. If you assign a variable that holds numeric information currently stored in the variant data type to a numeric variable, then Visual Basic will perform the conversion automatically. However (unlike when you use the Val command, for example), you must be careful that the variable of the variant data type holds something with no extraneous characters or extra periods beyond the one allowed, otherwise, you'll get a run-time error. ⊃

The Format Function

The Format function gives you complete control over how a string or number will be displayed. The Format function returns a new string in the given format. The basic syntax for the Format function is:

Format(expression[, format[, firstdayofweek[, firstweekofyear]]])

For example,

```
WeeklySalary = Format(1000000/52,"Currency")
```

gives the WeeklySalary variable a value which is the string equivalent of 1,000,000/2 using a standard currency (in the U.S., a $ sign, two decimal points and commas) format. Thus, this line of code is equivalent to:

```
WeeklySalary = "$1,923.08"
```

In general, the expression parameter is what you want to format. The format parameter describes the format to be used. As in the example above, many common formats have names, for example,

```
Print Format(Now, "Long Date")
```

might give

```
Saturday, November 23, 1996
```

The following table identifies the predefined date, time and numeric format names, which, as the examples above indicate, must be enclosed in quotes.

Format Name	Description
General Date	Displays a date and/or time in m/d/y format using a 24-hour clock.
Long Date	Displays a date according to your system's long date format.
Medium Date	Displays a date using the medium date format (23-Nov-96, for example).
Short Date	Displays a date using your system's short date format (m/d/y).
Long Time	Displays hours, minutes and seconds using your system's long time format (2:40:23 A.M., for example).
Medium Time	Displays time in 12-hour notation using hours and minutes with an A.M./P.M. designator.
Short Time	Displays a time using 24-hour notation, for example, 17:45.
General Number	Displays number with no thousand separator.
Currency	Displays number with thousand separator, if appropriate, and also displays two digits to the right of the decimal point.
Fixed	Displays at least one digit to the left and two digits to the right of the decimal point.
Standard	Displays number with a thousand separator, at least one digit to the left and two digits to the right of the decimal point.
Percent	Converts and displays number to a percent by multiplying by 100; always displays two digits to the right of the decimal point.

Format Name	Description
Scientific	Uses standard scientific notation.
Yes/No	Displays No if number is 0; otherwise, displays Yes.
True/False	Displays False if number is 0; otherwise, displays True.
On/Off	Displays Off if number is 0; otherwise, displays On.

You can also make your own number formats by using the following special format characters in the form of a format string. For example,

```
Print Format(987.654321,"###.##")
```

yields 987.65. Visual Basic rounds the number off so there are only two digits after the decimal point.

The Format function, unlike the Str function, does not leave room for an implied + sign. This means that in a statement like

```
Print "Your salary is ";Format(Payment,"####.##")
```

the extra space after the word "is" is essential.

In general, a # is the placeholder for a digit, except that leading and trailing zeros are ignored and you don't have to worry about having too few #s before the decimal point in the format string. Visual Basic will always give all the digits to the left of the decimal point.

If you want to have Visual Basic keep leading and trailing zeros, use a zero in place of the # in the format string. For example,

```
Print Format(987.6500,"000.000")
```

yields 987.650.

To display numbers with commas every three digits, place a comma between any two-digit placeholders. For example,

```
Print Format(123456789.991,"#,#.##")
```

gives 123,456,789.99.

If you place the comma immediately to the left of the decimal point (or use two commas), Visual Basic interprets this to mean it should skip the three digits that fall between the comma and the decimal point (or between the two commas). This is occasionally useful in scaling numbers. If your program deals with Japanese yen and you need to display one hundred million yen, you might want to write 100 million yen rather than 100,000,000 yen. To do this, use the following statement:

```
Print Format(100000000,"#00,,");" million yen"
```

Combining the # with the zero in the format string ensures that trailing zeros aren't suppressed. ↄ

129

Finally, if you need to display a −, +, $, (,), or spaces, use them in the format string exactly in the place you want them to occur. For example, if you want to have a dollar sign in front of a value, use this:

```
Print Format(YourSalary,"$#,##.##")
```

You can use Format in any Visual Basic statement that expects a string, not only with the Print method. For example,

```
M$ = "Your balance is " & Format(CurrentBalance, _
"$###.##")
MsgBox M$
```

⊃

The following table summarizes the format characters you can use in your format strings.

Format character	Use
(0)	Always uses a digit.
(#)	Digit placeholder, but if the digit isn't there displays nothing.
(.)	Decimal placeholder. (In some locales, a comma is used as the decimal separator.)
(%)	Percentage placeholder. The expression is multiplied by 100. The percent character (%) is inserted in the position where it appears in the format string.
(,)	Thousand separator.
(:)	Time separator.
(/)	Date separator.
(E− E+ e− e+)	Scientific format.
− + $ ( )	Displays the indicated character. To display a character other than one of these, precede it with a backslash (\) or use double quotes.
(\)	Displays the next character in the format string.

Arithmetic Operators

The following table gives you the symbols for the five fundamental arithmetic operations.

Operator	Operation
+	Addition
–	Subtraction (and to denote negative numbers)
/	Division
*	Multiplication
^	Exponentiation

For integers and long integers, there is one symbol and one keyword for the arithmetic operations unique to numbers of these types:

Operator	Operation
\	Integer division (this symbol is a backslash)
Mod	The remainder after integer division

The ordinary division symbol (/) gives you a value that is a single-precision, double-precision, or currency answer, depending on the objects involved. The backslash (\), on the other hand, throws away the remainder in order to give you an integer. For example, 7\3 = 2. Since a / gives either a single- or double-precision answer, use a \ or the Mod operator if you really want to work with integers or long integers.

The Mod operator is the other half of integer division. This operator gives you the remainder after integer division. For example, 7 Mod 3 = 1. When one integer perfectly divides another, there is no remainder, so the Mod operator gives zero: 8 Mod 4 = 0.

Parentheses and Precedence

To do calculations, you have two ways to indicate the order in which you want operations to occur. The first way is by using parentheses, and you may prefer this method. Parentheses let you easily specify the order in which operations occur. Something like 3 + (4 * 5) gives 23 because Visual Basic does the operation within the parentheses (4 times 5) first and then adds the 3. On the other hand, (3 + 4) * 5 gives 35 because Visual Basic adds the 3 and the 4 first to get 7 and then multiplies by 5.

Visual Basic allows you to avoid parentheses, provided you follow rules that determine the precedence of the mathematical operations. For example, multiplication has higher precedence than addition. This means 3 + 4 * 5 is 23 rather than 35 because the multiplication (4 * 5) is done before the addition.

The following list gives the order (hierarchy) of operations:

1. exponentiation (^)
2. negation (making a number negative)
3. multiplication and division
4. integer division
5. remainder (Mod) function
6. addition and subtraction

For example, –4 ^ 2 gives –16 because Visual Basic first does the exponentiation (4 ^ 2 = 4 * 4 = 16) and only then makes the number negative.

Operations are done in order of precedence and then from left to right when two operators have the same precedence. For example:

96 / 4 * 2

is 48. On the other hand, 96 / 4 ^ 2 is 6. This is because the exponentiation is done first, yielding 16, and only then is the division done.

Number Defaults and Conversions

When you use numbers in your program and do not assign them to a variable of the variant type, Visual Basic assumes the following:

- If a number has no decimal point and is in the range –32768 to 32767, it's an integer.
- If a number has no decimal point and is in the range for a long integer (–2,147,483,648 to 2,147,483,647), it's a long integer.
- If a number has a decimal point and is in the range for a single-precision number, it is assumed to be single precision.
- If a number has a decimal point and is outside the range for a single-precision number, it is assumed to be double precision.

These built-in assumptions occasionally lead to problems. This is because the realm in which an answer lives is determined by where the questions live. If you start out with two integers, Visual Basic assumes the answer is also an integer. For example, a statement like

```
Print 19999*6789
```

starts with two integers, so the answer is also assumed to be an integer. But the answer is too large for an integer, so you would get an overflow error. The

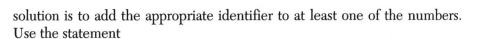

solution is to add the appropriate identifier to at least one of the numbers. Use the statement

```
Print 19999&*6789
```

and Visual Basic treats both 19999 and the answer as long integers.

You can also use a built-in function to force a type conversion.

Conversion Function	What It Does
CBool	Makes an expression a Boolean
CByte	Makes an expression a byte
CInt	Makes a numeric expression an integer by rounding
CLng	Makes a numeric expression a long integer by rounding
CSng	Makes a numeric expression single precision
CDate	Makes a date expression a date
CDbl	Makes a numeric expression double precision
CCur	Makes a numeric expression of the currency type
CStr	Makes any expression a string
CVar	Makes any expression a variant
CDec	Specifies that the value held in a variant is to be treated as being of the decimal type

Conversions will be performed only if the numbers you're trying to convert are in the range of the new type; otherwise, Visual Basic generates an error message.

If possible, Visual Basic will automatically coerce the contents of a numeric variable from one type to another after an assignment statement (using rounding, if necessary). For example,

```
Dim AnInteger As Integer
Dim ADecimal As Single
ADecimal = 1.3
AnInteger = ADecimal
```

gives `AnInteger` the value 1.

(In fact, using the numeric conversion function has the same effect as assigning the numeric expression to a variable of the type specified.)

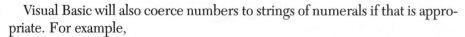
Visual Basic will also coerce numbers to strings of numerals if that is appropriate. For example,

```
Dim I As Integer
I = 37
TextBox1.Text = I
I = TextBox1.Text + 1
Print I
```

works just fine, and prints 38. (In theory, the Text property uses strings. We find this disconcerting and tend to use the Str and Val functions in these situations.)

Constants

Visual Basic has built-in predefined global constants to use in your programs. They are usually given a prefix of vb (lowercase). For example, when you use the MsgBox function you can use built-in constants like vbOKOnly to get only an OK button. You can use the Object Browser discussed in Chapter 8 to examine all the built-in constants.

Visual Basic also has *named constants* to allow you to use mnemonic names for values that never change. Constants are declared just like variables, and the rules for their names are also the same: 255 characters, first character a letter, and then any combination of letters, underscores, and numerals. Our convention is to use all capitals for constants.

If you have only one form or want the constants visible to the event procedures for only one form (as would be the case in a user control), put them in the Declarations section for the General object. You can also define a constant within a procedure, but this is less common, and only that procedure would have access to the constant. Set up a constant by using the keyword Const, followed by the name of the constant, an equal sign, and then the value:

```
Const PIE = 3.14159
```

You can set up string constants:

```
Const USERNAME = "Bill Smith"
Const LANGUAGE = "Visual Basic Version 5.0"
```

You can even use numeric expressions for constants, or define new constants in terms of previously defined constants:

```
Const PIEOVER2 = PIE/2
```

Visual Basic uses the simplest type it can for a constant, but you can override this by adding a type identifier to a constant. For example,

```
Const THISWILLBEALONGINTEGER& = 37
```

or

```
Const THISWILLBEALONGINTEGER As Long = 37
```

forces Visual Basic to treat the constant 37 as a long integer instead of an ordinary integer. Even if you use a type identifier at the end of the constant when you define it, you don't need to use the identifier in the program. Using the preceding example, all subsequent occurrences of this constant can be

```
THISWILLBEALONGINTEGER
```

As mentioned, our convention is to use all caps for constants, but this is not required. Moreover, references to constants don't depend on the case.

Repeating Operations—Loops

Visual Basic, like most programming languages, has language constructs for loops that repeat operations a fixed number of times, for continuing until a specific predetermined goal is reached, or until certain initial conditions have changed.

Determinate Loops

Use the keywords For and Next to set up a loop to repeat a fixed number of times. For example, the following code

```
Dim I As Integer
For I = 1 To 10
   Print I
Next I
```

prints the numbers 1 to 10 on the current form.

For and Next are keywords that must always be used together. The statements between the For and the Next are usually called the *body* of the loop, and the whole control structure is called, naturally enough, a For-Next loop.

135

The keyword For sets up a counter variable. In the preceding example, the counter is an integer variable I whose initial value is 1. The ending value is set to 10.

In general, Visual Basic first sets the counter variable to the starting value. Then it checks whether the value for the counter is less than the ending value. If the value is greater than the ending value, nothing is done. If the starting value is less than the ending value, Visual Basic processes subsequent statements until it comes to the keyword Next. (The variable name is optional.) At that point, it defaults to adding 1 to the counter variable and starts the process again. This process continues until the counter variable is larger than the ending value. At that point, the loop is finished, and Visual Basic moves past it.

Although you can use variables of any numeric type for the counters, choose integer variables whenever possible. This allows Visual Basic to spend as little time as possible on the arithmetic needed to change the counter and, thus, speed up the loop. ⊃

Finally, you may have noticed that the body of the For-Next loop is indented. As always, the purpose of the spacing in a program is to make the program more readable and, therefore, easier to debug. The designers of Visual Basic made it easy to consistently indent code. The Visual Basic editor remembers the indentation of the previous line, and every time you press ENTER, the cursor returns to the spot directly below where the previous line started. To move the cursor back, you can use the LEFT ARROW key. Or if you get into the habit of using the TAB key to start each level of indentation, you can use the SHIFT+TAB combination to move backward one tab stop. (If you've used the TAB key, you can undo the indentation pattern for a block that you've used by selecting the block of text and then pressing SHIFT+TAB or the equivalent toolbar tools.)

More on For-Next Loops

You don't always count by ones. Sometimes it's necessary to count by twos, by fractions, or backward. You do this by adding the Step keyword to a For-Next loop. The Step keyword tells Visual Basic to change the counter by the specified amount rather than by 1, which is the default. For example, a space simulation program would not be complete without the inclusion, somewhere in the program, of the fragment

```
Dim I As Integer
For I = 10 To 1 Step -1
  Print "It's t minus "; I; " and counting."
Next I
Print "Blastoff!"
```

When you use a negative step, the body of the For-Next loop is bypassed if the starting value for the counter is smaller than the ending value. This is most useful when performing an operation such as deleting items from a list. If you went from 0 to ListCount, at the midpoint, you would run out of items while going from ListCount to 0 while step –1 removes the highest item to the lowest item correctly.

You can use any numeric type for the Step value. For example,

```
For YearlyInterest = .07 To .09 Step .0125
```

begins a loop that moves from 7% to 9% by ⅛% increments.

Nested For-Next Loops

Visual Basic allows you to nest loops essentially to unlimited depths. A fragment such as

```
For J = 2 To 12
  For I = 2 To 12
    Print I%*J%,
  Next I
  Print
Next J
```

gives an entire multiplication table.

The rule for nesting For-Next loops is simple: the inner loop must be completed before the Next statement for the outer loop is encountered.

An Example: The Screen Object and Available Fonts

You can find out the fonts available to the system using a simple For-Next loop to analyze a property of the Screen object. To analyze available fonts, you need two properties of the Screen object. The first is the FontCount property,

137

which gives you the number of available fonts that the printer or screen has available:

```
NumberOfScreenFonts = Screen.FontCount
NumberOfPrinterFonts = Printer.FontCount
```

The second is the Fonts property. Screen.Fonts(0) is the first font for your display, Screen.Fonts(1) is the second, and so on, up to Screen.Fonts (Screen.FontCount –1), which is the last. To run this program, create a new project with a blank form. Add the Click procedure given here, press F5, and then click anywhere in the form.

```
Sub Form_Click()
  Dim I As Integer

  Print "Here is a list of the fonts for your display."
  For I = 1 To Screen.FontCount - 1
    Font.Name = Screen.Fonts(I)
    Print "This is displayed in ";Screen.Fonts(I)
  Next I
End Sub
```

To report on the fonts that Windows can pull out of your printer, change the keyword Screen to the keyword Printer.

Indeterminate Loops

Loops often need to either keep on repeating an operation or not, depending on the results obtained within the loop. Such loops are indeterminate—that is, not executed a fixed number of times—by their very nature. Use the following pattern when you write this type of loop in Visual Basic:

```
Do
   Visual Basic statements
Until condition is met
```

A simple example of this is a password fragment in a user control:

```
Dim Password As String
Do
  Password = InputBox("Password please?")
  Loop Until Password = "YOUR PASSWORD"
End Sub
```

It's important to remember that the test for equality is strict: typing **your password** would not work. Another point to keep in mind is that the test is done only at the end of the loop, when Visual Basic processes the Until statement.

When you write an indeterminate loop, something must change; otherwise, the test will always fail and you'll be stuck in an infinite loop. To stop an infinite loop during design time, you can use the CTRL+BREAK combination or choose Run|End or use the End tool on the toolbar.

The Relational Operators

Of course, you will usually need ways to check for something besides equality. You do this by means of the *relational operators.* The relational operators are listed here.

Symbol	Checks (Tests For)
< >	Not equal to
<	Less than
<=	Less than or equal to
>	Greater than
>=	Greater than or equal to

For strings, these operators test for ANSI order. This means that "A" comes before "B," but "B" comes before "a" (and a space comes before any typewriter character). The string "aBCD" comes after the string "CDE" because uppercase letters come before lowercase letters. The ANSI codes from 0 to 31 are for control combinations and include the BACKSPACE and ENTER keys.

You can make all comparisons in the code attached to a form or control case insensitive by putting the statement `Option Compare Text` in the Declarations section of the form. Use `Option Compare Binary` to return to the default method of comparing strings by ANSI order. The `Option Compare Text` uses an order determined by the country that was set when you install Windows. ⊃

The Do While Loop

You can replace the keyword Until with the keyword While in a loop. (You can always change a Do Until into a Do While by reversing the relational operator.) For example,

```
Do
Loop Until X <> " "
```

is the same as

```
Do
Loop While X = " "
```

These loops test at the bottom so they are executed at least once. To do the test at the top (so the loop may not be executed at all), move the While or Until keyword to the top. For example,

```
Do While Text1.Text <> " "
    'process the non empty text
Loop
```

will not even start working unless the TextBox is non-empty.

 There is also a While/WEnd construct that is equivalent to the Do While/Loop form. ⊃

Loops with And, Or, Not

When you have to combine conditions in a loop, use the Or, Not, and And keywords. These three keywords work just like they do in English. You can continue a process as long as both conditions are True or stop it when one turns False. However, it becomes increasingly confusing to try to force a combination of the And, Or, and Not operators into loops that they don't seem to fit. For example, suppose you want to continue a process while a number is greater than zero and a text box is empty. It is much easier to say

```
Do While Number > 0 And Text1.Text = " "
```

than to say

```
Do Until Number <=0 Or Text1.Text <> " "
```

although they both mean the same thing.

Conditionals—Making Decisions

Obviously, Visual Basic has a way of choosing which statements to process depending on what the state of the program is. This is done with the If-Then-Else construct. For example, to warn a user that a number must be positive, use a line like this:

```
If X < 0 Then MsgBox "Number must be positive!"
```

You can also use the keywords And, Or, and Not in an If-Then. These let you check two conditions at once.

More often than not, you will want to process multiple statements if a condition is True or False. For this you need the most powerful form of the If-Then-Else, called the Block If-Then. This lets you process as many statements as you like in response to a True condition. The Block If-Then looks like this:

```
If thing to test Then
  lots of statements
Else
  more statements
End If
```

For example, consider the code from the IntegerTextBox form in Chapter 1:

```
If KeyAscii < Asc("0") Or KeyAscii > Asc("9") Then
    KeyAscii = 0
    RaiseEvent BadEntry
End If
```

which did two things in response to a bad key press.

When you use the Block If-Then you do not put anything on the line following the keyword Then; press ENTER immediately after typing it. This bare Then is how Visual Basic knows it's beginning a block. The Else is optional; putting it there (again, alone on a line) means that another block will follow, to be processed only if the If clause is False. However, whether the Else is there or not, the Block If must end with the keywords End If.

Example: What is It?

You can easily use If-Then to determine whether the user has entered a string in the form of a date or a number. The procedure depends on the variant data type combined with two Boolean functions. For example, the built-in function IsDate, which is a Boolean function, tells you whether an expression can be converted to a date. Consider the following code that checks whether the contents of a text box are in the right form to be used as a date:

```
Dim DT      ' DT is a variant
DT = Text1.Text
If IsDate(DT) Then
  ' do whatever you want with the date
Else
  MsgBox "Please enter the text in the form of a
    date!"
End If
```

Similarly, you can use the IsNumeric function to determine whether a variable can be converted to a number. This gives you a quick way of checking for extraneous characters in a string of digits.

 There are also IsNull and IsEmpty functions to completely determine the state of a variant variable. ⊃

Finishing Up with the If-Then

You often need to continue testing within the confines of the original If-Then. This is done with the keywords ElseIf-Then. For example,

```
If Income > 1000000 Then
   Print "Lots of income this year."
ElseIf (Assets + Income) > 2000000
  Print "Income is irrelevant-you're rich."
ElseIf Assets + Income > 1000000 Then
  Print "Need to analyze your income."
Else
  Print "Not rich in any financial way."
End If
```

Now everything is tied together. And just like in the If-Then-Else, Visual Basic activates, at most, one clause and the final Else clause is only activated when all the other cases fail.

A Block If-Then can have essentially as many ElseIf's as you like but only one Else—as the last clause. ⊃

Combining the If-Then with Loops

You can use the If-Then to give you a way to write a loop that tests in the middle. For this, you combine the If-Then with a new statement, the Exit Do. Whenever Visual Basic processes the Exit Do statement, it pops you out of the loop, directly to the statement following the keyword Loop.

More generally, Visual Basic allows you to set up a potentially infinite loop at any time; just leave off the tests in a Do loop, an unadorned Do at the top and an equally unadorned Loop at the bottom. Once you've done this, the loop will end only when Visual Basic processes an Exit Do statement. (During program development, you can always end the program prematurely from the Run menu, and you can also use the toolbar or CTRL+BREAK combination.)

There is a version of the Exit command for leaving a For-Next loop as well; in this case, it takes the form Exit For.

Select Case

Suppose you were designing a program to compute grades based on the average of four exams. If the average was 90 or higher, the student should get an A; 80 to 89, a B; and so on. This is such a common situation that Visual Basic has another control structure designed exactly for it. It's called the Select Case and is much more flexible than the C/Java equivalent. To use this command, start with something you want to test.

```
Select Case Average
   Case > 90
      Print "A"
   Case > 80
      Print "B"
   Case > 70
      Print "C"
   Case Else
      Print "You fail"
End Select
```

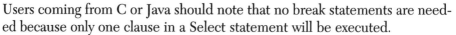

Users coming from C or Java should note that no break statements are needed because only one clause in a Select statement will be executed.

Using commas allows you give a discrete set of variables and using the keyword To allows you to give a range of values.

```
Select Case YourChoice
   Case 1 To 9
      MsgBox("Usable choice")
   Case -1, 0
      MsgBox("Illegal choice")
End Select
```

The GoTo

The final control structure is, of course, the GoTo. To paraphrase the old joke about split infinitives—modern programmers may be divided into three groups: those who neither know nor care about when they should use the GoTo, those who do not know but seem to care very much, and those who know when to use it.

The most common use of the GoTo statement is for error handling. This is discussed in detail in the section on Error Trapping in Chapter 5.

Routine use of the GoTo leads to spaghetti code: code that is hard to read and harder to debug. On the other hand, there are times when using the GoTo actually makes your code cleaner and easier to understand. In Visual Basic, this situation typically comes up when you are deep inside a nested loop and some condition forces you to leave all the loops simultaneously. You can't use the various forms of the Exit statement because all that does is get you out of the loop you are currently in.

To use a GoTo in Visual Basic, you must label a line. Labels must begin with a letter and end with a colon. They must also start in the first column. You should use as descriptive a label as possible. Here's an example:

```
BadInput:
   'Code we want to process can GoTo here
```

For example, suppose we are using a nested For loop to input data and want to leave the loop if the user enters a 'I am done'.

```
For I = 1 to 10
    For J = 1 to 100
        GetData := InputBox("Data Input", "Enter data,
            ZZZ to end", "")
        If GetData =  "I am done" then
            GoTo BadInput
        Else
            'Process data
        End If
    Next J

Next I
Exit Sub
BadInput:
    MsgBox("Data entry ended at user request");
```

Notice how using an Exit For keyword would be cumbersome here. For example, it would require extra code in order to break completely out of the nested loop. Also notice the Exit Sub statement then prevents us from "falling into" the labeled code.

Chapter 5

Chapter 4 showed you the basics of Visual Basic's built-in programming language. This chapter shows you the remaining non-object oriented features of Visual Basic's language that are necessary to create a control. See Chapter 7 for Visual Basic's take on object-oriented programming.

First, you'll see a bit more on the type and scope of variables, then a discussion of Visual Basic arrays, and a short treatment of one way to mimic pointers via arrays of data structures. (Chapter 7 shows you another method to mimic pointers.) Next, there's a brief look at Visual Basic's built-in functions and procedures, including an introduction to using Windows API functions. Following that, there's a section on writing your own functions and procedures. We'll then go a little deeper into the anatomy of a project, illustrating, for example, how to add modules for code alone and true global (Public) code. We end this chapter by showing you how error trapping is done in Visual Basic.

More on Visual Basic's Programming Language

Arrays

Elements in arrays in Visual Basic are identified by

1. The name of the array
2. The position of the item in the array

In Visual Basic, the name of an array must follow the rules for variable names. For an item in the array, the notation is simply the name of the array followed by a number in parentheses that indicates the position. Array indexes are zero-based by default (the section on Arrays with Index Ranges shows how to set this). For example, the third entry in a string array is accessed via `StringList(2)`.

Arrays can't be open-ended in Visual Basic. While the limits are quite large, you must tell Visual Basic how much memory to set aside for the array before you use it. There are two kinds of arrays in Visual Basic: *fixed arrays*, where the memory allocation never changes; and *dynamic arrays*, where you can change size on the fly. The advantage of a fixed array is that memory is set aside at the beginning of the program; you run a much smaller risk of running out of memory while the program is running. The advantage of dynamic arrays is the flexibility they give. You can change the size in response to what the program has encountered.

Both kinds of arrays may be made visible to the whole application, to a specific form or module, or only within an event procedure. To set up a fixed array in the form that will be available to all the procedures in the form or control, place a statement like

```
Dim Presidents(42) As String
```

in the Declarations section of the form. By default in Visual Basic, this actually sets up a 43-element array for strings visible to every procedure on that form or control. The items would be stored in

```
Presidents(0), Presidents(1), …, Presidents(42).
```

To set up a dynamic array in a form, place a statement like

```
Dim Presidents() As String
```

in the Declarations section of the form or control. You then use the ReDim statement inside a procedure to allocate the space:

```
Sub ElectionResults()
'.Clinton won so
' set the value of Number
  ReDim Presidents(42) As String
End Sub
```

You can also use the ReDim statement in a procedure without needing a Dim statement in the Declarations section of the form or module first. In this case, the array becomes local to the procedure and space is allocated for that array only while the procedure is active; it disappears as soon as the procedure is exited. ⊃

Each time Visual Basic processes a ReDim statement, the information in the array is lost. However, a variation of the ReDim statement can be used to increase the size of a dynamic array while retaining any information already stored in the array. For example, the statement

```
ReDim Preserve NameOfArray(NewSize) As String
```

can be placed in a procedure to increase the number of entries in the array to NewSize + 1 without losing data already stored in the array.

Finally, you can set up a local array whose values will be preserved between procedure calls by using the Static keyword. You cannot use a variable inside the parentheses when you do static dimensioning.

Visual Basic has a feature called *collections* that can be used as a replacement (and often, an improvement) on arrays. See Chapter 7 for more on the pros and cons of collections. ⊃

Arrays with Index Ranges

There are two ways to change the bounds used in Visual Basic's arrays:

- The `Option Base 1` statement used in the Declarations section of a form (or Standard module; see below) affects all arrays in the form or module. All new arrays dimensioned in that form or module now begin with item number 1. After `Option Base 1, Dim Presidents(42)` sets aside 42 spots rather than 43.

- Next, Visual Basic allows index ranges in arrays. For example:

  ```
  Dim SalesOfMicrosoft(1986 To 1996)
  ```

  would allow you to store the information about Microsoft's amazing sales growth in an easily accessible form by making the index of the array the same as the year's information being stored. In general, the keyword To marks the range, smaller number first (from 1980 to 1995, in this case), for this way of declaring an array. You can use the To keyword with any statement that declares an array (Dim, ReDim, Static, Private, ReDim Preserve, and so on).

Arrays with More than One Dimension

You can also have arrays with more than one dimension; they're usually called *multidimensional arrays*. Just as lists of data lead to a single subscript (one-dimensional arrays), tables of data lead to double subscripts (two-dimensional arrays). For example, suppose you want to store a multiplication table in memory—as a table. You could do this as:

```
Static MultTable(1 To 12,1 To 12) As Integer
Dim I As Integer, J As Integer
For I = 1 To 12
  For J = 1 To 12
    MultTable(I, J) = I*J
  Next J
Next I
```

Visual Basic allows up to 60 dimensions with the Dim statement and 8 with the ReDim statement.

Only the last dimension in a multidimensional array can be changed with Redim Preserve. ⊃

Although you normally use a For-Next loop to iterate through the elements in an array, you can also use the For Each construct whose syntax takes the form:

```
For Each element In the array
     [statements]
     [Exit For]
     [statements]
Next [element]
```

The advantage is that you need not know the index range for the array. The disadvantage is that this is slightly slower than using the index and you can't be sure of the order in which elements will be accessed. Also, it seems that in the current version of VB you cannot set an array element using the For Each construct but you can read them. Finally, keep in mind when you use this syntax, VB requires the "element" used to iterate in the For Each be a variant even if the array type is not a variant. ⊃

Variants and Arrays

Variants add a powerful tool to array handling in Visual Basic because you can store an array in a variable of variant type. Some people regard this as a little less than elegant, but since you can't assign one array to another, this technique can be very useful. For instance, it gives you a very quick way to swap the contents of two arrays, as the following example shows.

```
Dim I As Integer
ReDim A(1 To 10000) As Long
ReDim B(1 To 10000) As Long
For I = 1 To 10000
  A(I) = I
  B(I) = 5 * I
Next I
Dim Array1 As Variant, Array2 As Variant, Temp As Variant
Array1 = A(): Erase A()
Array2 = B(): Erase B()
Temp = Array1
Array1 = Array2
Array2 = Temp
```

At this point, the variants `Array1` and `Array2` contain the original arrays in reverse order, and the memory for the original arrays has been reclaimed. Since, momentarily, you have two objects instead of one, this technique can be a bit memory-hungry. On the other hand, if you need to swap two arrays, this is a whole lot faster than copying the 10,000 entries one by one!

 If you store an array in a variant, use the ordinary index to get it. For example, after you run the above, `Array1(5)` would have the value 10. ↄ

Occasionally, you need to create an array directly in a variant. Use the Array function whose syntax is

```
Array(arglist)
```

where the arglist argument consists of an arbitrary list of items separated by commas.

Finally, by using an array of variants you can create the equivalent of non-rectangular arrays or build arrays that combine strings in one row and numbers in another. For example, to build a triangular array of numbers,

```
Dim TriangularArray(1 To 5) As Variant
Dim Row1(1 To 1) As Integer
Dim Row2(1 To 2) As Integer
Dim Row3(1 To 3) As Integer
Dim Row4(1 To 4) As Integer
TriangularArray(1) = Row1()
TriangularArray(2) = Row2()
'and so on
```

The Erase Statement

As your programs grow longer, the possibility that you'll run out of space increases. (Given Visual Basic's rather large limits and Windows 95 memory management, it's not likely.) Visual Basic allows you to reclaim the space used by a dynamically dimensioned array. You do this with the Erase command. For example,

```
Erase Presidents
```

would erase the Presidents array and free up the space it occupied. (Note the lack of parenthesis.)

If an array was not dimensioned dynamically (that is, was not dimensioned using the ReDim statement inside a procedure), then the Erase command simply resets all the entries back to zero for numeric arrays, and to the null string for string arrays, or to null for variants. Using the Erase command on a fixed (static) array gives a fast method to "zero out" the entries. (It sets them to the null string for string arrays.) ⊃

Types Revisited

Since variant variables make it easy to avoid dealing with explicit variable types, some programmers, reveling in their freedom from strongly typed languages, are tempted to use them for everything. Most experienced Visual Basic programmers feel this should be avoided. Using variant variables when their special properties are not needed often exacts a performance penalty and will, occasionally, lead to subtle bugs. (For example, any variant takes 16 bytes to store—regardless of the type of the data.) It is usually better for the programmer to be in control of the type of his or her variables.

There are, of course, times when variants are useful. You saw how they can be used with arrays to quickly swap the contents of two arrays, and you have seen how useful the built-in IsDate and IsNumeric functions are.

Using the VarType function combined with an If-Then gives you a way to go beyond the built-in IsDate, IsNumeric functions to build your own IsCurrency function, IsBoolean function, and so on. (Variants can hold any Standard data type except fixed-length strings.) ⊃

User-Defined Types

Suppose you want to have a three-dimensional array for employees in a company. The first column is for names, the second for salaries, and the third for social security numbers. This common situation can't be programmed in a multidimensional array except using the variant data type. The problem is that variants use more memory and are slower. For both speed and memory reasons, one (non-object oriented) idea is to set up three parallel lists—the first for names, the second for salaries, and the third for social security numbers. Having done this, you now would use the same pointer (that is, the row number) to extract information from the three lists.

Traditionally, structured data is not stored in parallel lists but rather in a *user-defined type*. (These are sometimes called *records* or *UDTs*.) Essentially, a record is a type of mixed variable that you create as needed. It usually mixes different kinds of numbers and strings.

Here's the first step: In the Declarations section of the form, enter

```
Type  EmployeeInfo
    Name As String
    Salary As Long
    SocialSecNumber as String
End Type
```

This defines the type. Each of the different parts of the record is called a *field*. From this point on, EmployeeInfo can be treated like any other data type such as single-precision, double-precision, variants, and so on.

 User-defined types must be declared Private in all Visual Basic component types except code modules. To do this, prefix your declaration with the word "Private." ⊃

Now, to set up a variable of "type" EmployeeInfo, all you have to do is declare it using one of Dim, Private, Static ReDim, and so on.

```
Dim YourName As EmployeeInfo
Static YourFriend As EmployeeInfo
ReDim MyNames(1 To 100) As EmployeeInfo 'array of
                                        '100 records
```

To fill the type, you assign values to the various fields using the '.' you have seen for properties:

```
YourName.Name = "Howard"
YourName.Salary = 100000
YourName.SocSecNumber = "036-78-9987"
```

 Because user-defined types are restricted in what they can do in the construction of Visual Basic objects (see Chapter 7), they are often replaced by a user-defined object in the CCE. ⊃

The With Statement

You can use the With statement as a convenient method for quickly getting at the parts of a user-defined type. For example,

```
With YourName
   .Name = "Howard"
   .Salary = 100000
   .SocSecNumber = "036-78-9987"
End With
```

lets you avoid some typing and is more efficient.

You can also use the With statement to get at the properties of objects. For example:

```
With txtBox
   .Height = 2000
   .Width = 2000
   .Text = "This is a text box"
End With
```

With statements can be nested if an object has a sub-object as a property. For example:

```
With txtBox
   .Height = 200
   With .Font
      .Bold = True
      .Italic = False
   End With
End With
```

Enums

The newest data type in Visual Basic is the *enum,* which stands for enumerated type. An enum is useful when you want a way to associate constants to a set of related data. For example, it might be convenient to have Sunday associated to 1, Monday to 2, and so on. Enums are also necessary when giving your control properties analogous to BorderStyle—that is, properties with only a fixed number of possibilities. Here's an example of how to declare an enum.

```
Private Enum DaysOfTheWeek
   Sunday = 1
   Monday
   Tuesday
   Wednesday
   Thursday
   Friday
   Saturday
End Enum
```

This would associate the number 1 to Sunday, the number 2 (automatically) to Monday, and so on. You could use this enum in code like this:

```
Dim ComdexWeek As DaysOfTheWeek
ArrivalDate =Tuesday
If ArrivalDate < Monday Then MsgBox("You missed the
    first day.")
```

The point is that Visual Basic automatically and transparently makes the conversion of a variable declared to be an enum of type DaysOfTheWeek to a value, so the If-Then in the above code makes perfect sense. (By the way, once you set up an enum and a variable of that type, Visual Basic automatically (!) displays the constants used in the enum in the IntelliSense List members box.)

 The starting value for an enum can be any long integer. If you leave out the starting value, it defaults to 0. ⊃

Pointers

There aren't any pointers in the traditional sense of getting directly at memory locations where data is stored. So the question is how to imitate them if you need to create data structures like linked lists or trees that use them. There is no perfect solution because you will need to go through some contortions to dispose of the memory allocated.

One way to create analogues to pointers in Visual Basic is to create an array of records and use one or more of the fields in the record to hold the row of the next item. (See the chapter on objects for another way that is a bit slicker and ultimately more powerful.)

If you choose this approach, you need to keep on using ReDim Preserve to build up the object and assign the memory. For example, if you wanted to create a binary tree,

```
Type DataInBinaryTree
   Data As String
   LeftChild As Integer     'row where left child is
   RightChild As Integer    'row where right child is
End Type
```

In this example, the two fields LeftChild and RightChild act as pointers to the row containing the child. To build the tree, for example, you start with an array of records of this type of size 1.

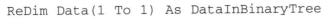

```
ReDim Data(1 To 1) As DataInBinaryTree
```

Each time you need to enter the next item, you have to:

1. Update the counter of the number of items.
2. Use ReDim Preserve to enlarge the array of records.
3. Fill in the "pointer" rows as needed (use a –1 for a pointer to Null.)

The only way to reclaim memory from these imitation pointers is to copy the array of records to a new array of records (or a variant)—after eliminating the entry you want to remove. ⊃

Built-In Functions

There are hundreds of functions built into Visual Basic. The information about the most common functions is summarized in the three tables that follow. Table 5-1 gives short descriptions of the most common functions that do not have to do with date, time, or string information. Table 5-2 provides short descriptions about the date/time functions, and Table 5-3 provides information about the string functions.

Table 5-1: Common Functions

Function	Purpose
Abs	Finds the absolute value of a number
Atn	Finds the arctangent
Cos	Finds the cosine
Exp	Raises e (2.7182 . . .) to the given power
Fix	Returns the integer part of a number
FV	Future value
Hex	Gives the hex equivalent
Int	Returns the integer portion of a number
Ipmt	Interest paid over time
IRR	Internal rate of return
Log	Common logarithm
MIRR	Modified internal rate of return
Nper	Time to accumulate (disburse) an annuity

Function	Purpose
NPV	Net present value
Pmt	Pay out for annuity
Ppmt	Returns the principal paid out in an annuity payment
PV	Present value
Rate	Interest rate per period for an annuity
Rnd	Calls the random number generator
Sgn	Returns an integer indicating the sign of a number
Sin	Returns the sine of the number
SLN	Straight-line depreciation
Sqr	The square root function
SYD	Sum of years depreciation
Tan	The tangent of an angle in radians
Timer	Returns the number of seconds since midnight

Table 5-2: The Most Common String Functions

Function	Description
Asc	Returns the character code corresponding to the first letter in a string
InStr	Returns the position of the first occurrence of one string within another
Lcase	Converts a string to lowercase
Left	Finds or removes a specified number of characters from the beginning of a string
Len	Gives the length of a string
Ltrim	Removes spaces from the beginning of a string
Mid	Finds or removes characters from a string
Right	Finds or removes a specified number of characters from the end of a string
Rtrim	Removes spaces from the end of a string
Str	Returns the string equivalent of a number (the numeral)
StrComp	Another way to do string comparisons
StrConv	Converts a string from one form to another
String	Returns a repeated string of identical characters
Trim	Trims spaces from both the beginning and end of a string
Ucase	Converts a string to uppercase

 Most of the string functions have a form with the $ (for example Mid$, Left$). These versions return true strings rather than strings inside variants as the ones in Table 5-2 would. For this reason, they will often run faster. ⊃

Table 5-3 gives you the functions for handling date and times.

Table 5-3: The Date/Time Functions

Function	Description
Date	Returns the current date (what is shown in the system clock)
DateAdd	Lets you add a specified interval to a date
DateDiff	Lets you subtract a specified interval from a date
DateSerial	Returns a date corresponding to the specified day, month, and year
DateValue	Takes a string and returns a date
Day	Tells you what day a string or number represents
Hour	Tells you what hour a string or number represents
Minute	Tells you what minute a string or number represents
Month	Tells you what month a string or number represents
Now	Returns the current time and date
Second	Tells you what second a string or number represents
Time	Tells you the current time in the system clock
TimeSerial	Returns a variable of date type for the given time
Weekday	Tells you what day of the week a date corresponds to
Year	Tells you what year a date corresponds to

The Logical Operators on the Bit Level

The logical operators (Not, And, Or, and so on) are really functions that work on the bit (binary-digit) level. Suppose you are given two integers, X and Y. Then X And Y make a binary digit 1 only if both binary digits are 1; otherwise, the result is zero. For example, if

X = 7 in decimal = 0111 in binary
Y = 12 in decimal = 1100 in binary

then X And Y = 0100 in binary (4 in decimal) because only in the third position are both bits 1. Because And gives a 1 only if both digits are 1, Anding with a number whose binary digit is a single 1 and whose remaining digits are all zero lets you isolate the binary digits of any integer.

For example,

X And 1   Tells you whether the least significant (right-most) binary digit is on. You get a zero if it is not on.

X And 2   Since 2 in decimal is 10 in binary, a zero tells you that the next significant (second from the right) binary digit is off.

X And 255   Since 255 = 11111111, this gives you the low order byte.

X And 65280 =   Since 65280 = 1111111100000000, this would give you the high order bit.

X And $(2^{\wedge}32 - 1 - 255)$

This process is usually called *masking* and is often needed when using the KeyUp, KeyDown event procedures for a control on a form or user control.

User-Defined Functions and Procedures

In Visual Basic, the distinction is that functions can return values and procedures cannot. (We, like many people, use the term *subprogram* if we want to refer to both at the same time.) To add a user-defined subprogram to the current form:

1. Open the Code window by double-clicking anywhere in the form or by pressing F7.
2. Choose Tools|Add Procedure.

The Add Procedure dialog box will pop up, as shown in Figure 5-1.

Set the option button to the type of procedure you want. (For Property procedures, see Chapter 7; for Event procedures, see Chapters 7 and 8.) The Public/Private buttons control the scope of the subprogram—see the section on Standard modules that follows. Once you enter the name, click on OK, and a template for the procedure or function pops up.

 You can also start a new procedure by typing the keyword Function or the keyword Sub followed by the name of the procedure anywhere in the code window and then pressing ENTER or the DOWN ARROW. (Obviously, do this outide an existing Sub or Function.) ⊃

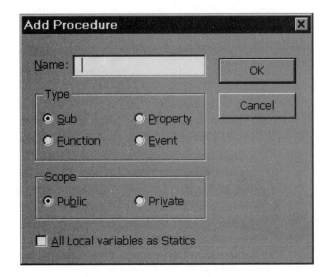

Figure 5-1
The Add Procedure
dialog box

Functions

Suppose you want to write a function that would allow you to chop out any substring. To do this, we use Instr to find out where the string is and then use Right, Left, and Mid to do the cutting. Here's the function:

```
Function sCutItOut (sTarget As String, sWhatToCut As _
String) As String
   'local variables
   Dim nPlace As Integer, nLength As Integer

   nPlace = Instr(sTarget, sWhatTOCut)
   nLength = Len(sWhatToCut)
   If nPlace = 0 Then
     sCutItOut = sTarget
   Else
     sCutItOut = Left(sTarget, nPlace-1)+Mid(sTarget, _
     nPlace+nLength)
   End If
End Function
```

The general form of a Function definition is as follows:

```
Function FunctionName (argument1, argument2, ...)
   statements
   FunctionName = expression
End Function
```

where argument1, argument2 are variables (usually declared as being of a certain type, as in this example). The first line is usually called the *function header*. Function names must follow the same rules as variable names. Visual Basic defaults to sending a memory location, and not a value (passing by reference); any changes you make to the arguments inside the body of the function will persist.

When you use a function, Visual Basic executes the statements in the function definition; the last value assigned to FunctionName inside the body of the function definition is the one used for the statement involving the FunctionName (argument1, argument2, . . .). The argument entries argument1, argument2, and so on, can be constants, variables, or expressions.

Although you usually use the return value of a function, Visual Basic allows you to simply call a function for its side effects with a statement like: ↻

```
FunctionName (arg1, arg2, arg3)
```

You can usually call a function only when you use the same number of arguments as there are parameters in the function definition. The types must be compatible as well. Visual Basic allows you to create your own subprograms with optional, or a varying number of, arguments. More information is given later in the chapter.

Sub Procedures

The tradition is to use a Sub procedure when you do not want to return a single value. A Sub procedure must have a header that gives its arguments and takes the form

```
Sub SubprocedureName(argument1, argument2, ...)
   statement(s)
End Sub
```

When Visual Basic executes statements of the form

```
SubprocedureName argument1, argument2,...
```

or

```
Call SubprocedureName (argument1, argument2, ...)
```

it passes the memory locations of the data stored in the arguments and executes the code in the body of the procedure. (By the way, these two different conventions for calling procedures can be very frustrating for people coming from other languages. A C programmer, by nature, uses parens and forgets to use a call (or forgets to not use parens), and then beats his or her head against the wall trying to figure out why there are errors calling the sub.)

Since Visual Basic defaults to sending a memory location and not a value (passing by reference), any changes you make to the parameters inside the body of the procedure will be preserved. ⊃

When the End Sub statement is reached, execution continues with the line following the call to the Sub procedure.

Passing by Reference/Passing by Value

There are two ways to pass a variable argument to a procedure or function: passing by value and passing by reference. The default in Visual Basic is to pass information by reference. When an argument variable in a subprogram is passed by reference, any changes to the corresponding parameter inside the procedure will change the value of the original argument when the procedure finishes. When passed by value, the argument variable retains its original value after the procedure terminates—regardless of what was done to the corresponding parameter inside the procedure. Arguments to functions and procedures are always passed by reference unless they are surrounded by an extra pair of parentheses or the ByVal keyword is used in declaring the function or subprogram.

Some programmers like to use the ByRef keyword to indicate that a variable is being passed by reference; however, this is the default behavior and ByRef isn't needed. ⊃

Leaving Functions or Procedures Prematurely

You don't have to give every function an explicit value. Sometimes you are forced to exit a function prematurely.

```
Function BailOut (X) As Single
   If X < 0 Then
    Exit Function
   Else
  .
  .
   End If
End Function
```

Use Exit Sub to leave a procedure prematurely. When you leave a function prematurely, it has the last assigned value or the appropriate default value as its return value.

Using Arrays with Procedures

Visual Basic has an extraordinary facility to use both one and multidimensional arrays in procedures and functions. It's easy to send any size array to a subprogram. To send an array parameter to a procedure or function, type the name of the array and include the open parenthesis. For example, assume that DoubleList is a one-dimensional array of double-precision variables. StringArray is a two-dimensional string array, and BigIntegerArray is a three-dimensional array of integers. Then,

```
Sub Example(DoubleList(), StringArray(), _
BigIntegerArray(), X As Integer)
```

would allow this Example procedure to use (and change) an array of double-precision variables, an array of strings, a three-dimensional array of integers, and a final integer variable. Note that just as with variable parameters, array parameters are placeholders; they have no independent existence.

Visual Basic makes this process of dealing with arrays as parameters more practical by including the functions LBound and UBound. LBound gives the lowest possible index and UBound, the highest in an array. For example, you can easily write the following function to find the maximum element in an array.

```
Function FindMax(A() As Integer)
  ' local variables nStart, nFinish, I
  Dim nStart As Integer, nFinish As Integer
  Dim nMax As Integer, I As Integer

  nStart = LBound(A)
  nFinish = UBound(A)
  nMax = A(nStart)
  For I = nStart  To nFinish
    If A(I) > nMax Then nMax = A(I)
  Next I
  FindMax = nMax
End Function
```

In general, LBound(*NameOfArray*, *I*), UBound(*NameOfArray*, *I*) gives the lower and upper bound for the I'th dimension. For a list (one-dimensional array), the I is optional, as in the preceding example.

For a more serious example of using arrays in procedures, here is the code for a Shell sort which is one of the best general purpose sorts for medium-sized arrays.

```
Public Sub ShellSort(AnArray() As Variant)
  'LOCAL variables are NumOfEntries, Increm, J, Temp
  Dim NumOfEntries As Integer, Increm As Integer, J, Temp
  Dim I As Integer, J As Integer
  Dim BotIndex As Integer, TopIndex As Integer
  BotIndex = LBound(AnArray)
  TopIndex = UBound(AnArray)
  NumOfEntries = TopIndex - BotIndex + 1
  Increm = NumOfEntries \ 2
  Do Until Increm < 1
    For i = Increm + BotIndex To TopIndex
      Temp = AnArray(i)
      For J = i - Increm To BotIndex Step -Increm
        If Temp >= AnArray(J) Then Exit For
        AnArray(J + Increm) = AnArray(J)
      Next J
      AnArray(J + Increm) = Temp
    Next i
    Increm = Increm \ 2
  Loop
End Sub
```

Subprograms with a Variable or Optional Number of Arguments

Visual Basic permits you to have optional arguments in functions and procedures you define yourself. Unlike in Visual Basic 4, optional arguments can be of any type. They still must be the last arguments in a function or procedure. For example, you might have a Sub procedure whose header looks like this:

```
Sub ProcessAddress(Name As String, Address As _
String, City As String, _State As String, ZipCode _
As String, Option ZipPlus4 As String)
```

In this case, the last argument (for a ZipPlus4 code) is optional.

You can have as many optional arguments as you want. They simply must be listed after all the required arguments in the procedure (or function) declaration. ⊃

You can also specify a default value for any optional argument, as in the following example:

```
Sub ProcessAddress(Name As String, Address As _
String, City As String, _State As String, ZipCode _
As String, Option ZipPlus4 As String = "0000")
```

which makes the default ZipPlus4 value equal to "0000".

You can also have procedures and functions that accept an arbitrary number of arguments. For this, use the ParamArray keyword with an array of variants, as in the following example:

```
Function AddThemUp(ParamArray VariantNumbers()) As Single
   Dim Total As Single
   Dim Number As Variant
   For Each Number in VariantNumbers()
      Total = Total + Number
   Next
   AddThemUp = Total
End Function
```

Named Arguments

The InputBox function that you have already seen is one of the many Visual Basic built-in functions that supports something called *named arguments*. Named arguments give you a more elegant way of dealing with functions that have many parameters.

Only functions from the Visual Basic for Applications library and user-defined functions support named arguments. As mentioned previously, arguments that can be named show up in bold italic in IntelliSense's QuickInfo feature. ⊃

Here's an example of using an InputBox function with named arguments:

```
MyInput  = InputBox(prompt:="Example", _
Default:= "Default string", xpos:=100, ypos:=200)
```

In general, as this example shows, named arguments use a := (colon plus an equal sign), together with the name of the argument. (While the spelling of the argument must match perfectly, case is irrelevant.) Like any argument, you separate named arguments from each other by a comma.

The neat thing about VB5 is that any functions or procedures you create automatically have named arguments. If you are careful when selecting parameter names, using named arguments can be a useful tool to make your code easier to read. This is especially true if you use optional arguments a lot.

 Even with named arguments, you can still only omit optional arguments. ➲

Recursion

Recursion is a general method of solving problems by reducing them to simpler problems of a similar type. The general framework for a recursive solution to a problem looks like this:

```
Solve recursively (problem)
  If the problem is trivial, do the obvious
  Simplify the problem
 Solve recursively (simpler problem)
  (Possibly) combine the solution to the simpler
      problem(s) into a solution of the original
      problem
```

A recursive subprogram constantly calls itself, each time in a simpler situation, until it gets to the trivial case, at which point it stops. For the experienced programmer, thinking recursively presents a unique perspective on certain problems, often leading to particularly elegant solutions and, therefore, equally elegant programs. (For example, most fast sorts such as QuickSort are recursive.)

For Visual Basic programmers, besides sorting routines, one common use of recursion is when you need to deal with the subdirectory structure of a disk. For example, if you wanted to delete a file but didn't know where it was,

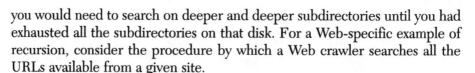

you would need to search on deeper and deeper subdirectories until you had exhausted all the subdirectories on that disk. For a Web-specific example of recursion, consider the procedure by which a Web crawler searches all the URLs available from a given site.

There are actually two types of recursion possible and both are supported in Visual Basic. The first is where the subprogram only calls itself. This is called *direct recursion*. Using direct recursion in Visual Basic is simple. Call the subprogram the way you would call any subprogram. The second type is called, naturally enough, *indirect recursion*. This occurs, for example, when a subprogram calls another subprogram, which, in turn, calls the first subprogram.

As an example, let's look at the greatest common divisor (GCD) of two integers. (For those who have forgotten their high school mathematics, this is defined as the largest number that divides both of them. It's used when you need to add fractions.) Therefore:

- GCD(4,6) = 2 (because 2 is the largest number that divides both 4 and 6)
- GCD(12,7) = 1 (because no integer greater than 1 divides both 12 and 7)

Around 2,000 years ago, Euclid gave the following method of computing the GCD of two integers, a and b:

- If b divides a, then the GCD is b. Otherwise, GCD(a,b) = GCD(b, a mod b)

(Recall that the mod function gives the remainder after integer division.) For example,

GCD(126, 12) = GCD(12, 126 mod 12) = GCD(12, 6) = 6

Here's the code for a recursive GCD function:

```
Function GCD (P as Long, Q As Long) As Long
  If Q mod P = 0 Then
    GCD = P
  else
    GCD = GCD(Q, P mod Q)
  End If
End Function
```

Here, the pattern is to first take care of the trivial case. If you are not in the trivial case, then the code reduces it to a simpler case, because the mod function leads to smaller numbers. (In this example, there is no need to combine results as there would be in, say, a sorting routine.)

Here's the code for a recursive QuickSort that works with variant arrays. Like most naïve versions of QuickSort, the one we give you here doesn't work very well with arrays that are not randomly arranged.

```
Sub QuickSort (AnArray(), Start As Integer, Finish As Integer)
   'Local variable PosOfSplitter
   Dim PosOfSplitter As Integer

   If finish > Start Then
      Partition AnArray(), Start, Finish, PosOfSplitter
      QuickSort AnArray(), Start, PosOfSplitter - 1
      QuickSort AnArray(), PosOfSplitter + 1, Finish
   End If
End Sub

Sub Partition (AnArray(), Start As Integer, Finish As Integer,_
LocOfSplitter As Integer)
' LOCAL variables are: SplitPos,NewStart,I,Splitter
Dim SplitPos As Integer, NewStart As Integer
Dim I As Integer, Splitter

   SplitPos = (start + finish) \ 2
   Splitter = AnArray(SplitPos)
   SWAP AnArray(SplitPos), AnArray(start) 'get it out of the way
   LeftPos = start                        'needs to be written!
      For I = start + 1 To finish
         If AnArray(i) < Splitter Then
            LeftPos = LeftPos + 1
            SWAP AnArray(LeftPos), AnArray(i)
         End If
      Next i
   SWAP AnArray(start), AnArray(LeftPos) ' LeftPos marks the
                                         'hole
   LocOfSplitter = LeftPos            'This gets passed
End Sub                               'to the original procedure

Sub SWAP(foo,bar)
   temp = foo
   foo = bar
   bar = temp
End Sub
```

Standard (Code) Modules

A Standard (code) module is the place where you put code that you want to be accessible to all code in a project. Standard modules have no visual components. Add a new Standard module by choosing Project|Add Module; add an existing one by using Project|Add File. The convention is that Standard modules have a .bas extension.

The Code window for a Standard module looks much like the Code window attached to a form or control. You can have two types of declarations for variables in the General section of a Standard module:

- For variables visible only to procedures in the Standard module.
- For variables you want visible everywhere in the project.

For the former, use the Private keyword; for the latter, the Public keyword.

```
Private LocalToStandardModule As Integer
Public GlobalToProject As Integer
```

Of course, just as form-level declarations can be superseded by declarations in procedures, public (global) declarations will be superseded by declaring a form- or procedural-level variable.

The Sub and Function procedures in code modules default so that they are available to the whole project. For example, a Standard module attached to the user control form would be usable by all the code in the control. A Standard module attached to a test project could be used by all the forms in the test project. To make subprogram code available only to the code in the Standard module, you must use the Private keyword before the subprogram header. (It is a good idea to use the Public keyword even if, strictly speaking, it isn't needed.) For example:

```
Private ALocalProcedure (Foo As Variant)
Public AGlobalProcedure(Foo As Variant)
```

When you use a Sub or Function procedure inside another procedure, Visual Basic follows very simple steps to determine where to look for it.

1. Visual Basic first looks at procedures attached to the current form or module.
2. If the procedure is not found in the current form or module, Visual Basic looks at all code modules attached to the project.

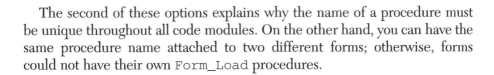

The second of these options explains why the name of a procedure must be unique throughout all code modules. On the other hand, you can have the same procedure name attached to two different forms; otherwise, forms could not have their own `Form_Load` procedures.

The DoEvents Function

Usually, you want Windows (and Visual Basic) to constantly monitor the environment for events to respond to. On the other hand, there can be a lot of idle time that you can use, for example, to do time-consuming numeric calculations or sorts. However, you don't want a Visual Basic application to stop responding to events completely. This is something you may want to do when you write a procedure that wastes time, as you saw earlier in this chapter. Obviously, you need a way to tell Visual Basic to periodically respond to events in the environment and return to the calculation when nothing else needs to be done.

The function that does this is called DoEvents. Whenever Visual Basic processes a statement containing this function, it releases control to the Windows operating system to process all the events that have occurred. (Windows keeps track of events in an events queue, and keypresses in the SendKeys queue.) Obviously, you should not use the DoEvents function inside an event procedure if it is possible to re-enter the same event procedure again. For example, a Click event procedure may be called again by the user's clicking the mouse. If you forget about this possibility, your program may be caught in an infinite regression.

The DoEvents function actually gives you the number of forms loaded for the application. ⊃

Using the Windows API

Microsoft Windows consists of libraries of many hundreds of specialized functions. These are called Application Programming Interface (API) functions. Most of the time, Visual Basic is rich enough in functionality that you don't need to bother with API functions. But some tasks, like rebooting the user's computer, cannot be done with Visual Basic code.

If you use API functions carelessly, your system may lock up and require you to reboot. You should have the "Save before run" option set when experimenting with API functions. ⊃

Another problem is that API functions are cumbersome to use and often require a fair amount of work before the information is usable by your Visual Basic program.

Before using a DLL function within a Visual Basic program, you must add a special declaration to the Declarations section of your code window. For example, if you need to put a control to "sleep" for a while, you would use the Windows API Sleep function. To use this, place the following statement in the Declarations section.

```
Private Declare Sub Sleep Lib "kernel32" _
(ByVal dwMilliseconds As Long)
```

This tells Visual Basic that you will be using the Windows API function Sleep, which is contained in the kernel32 library (Lib stands for library). Since this is a Sub, it doesn't return a value; all you need to do is give it the time to sleep in milliseconds (so 1 second requires passing this API function a value of 1000).

Here's an amusing (if potentially nasty) example of using this API function in a control. Simply add a text box to a user control and use the following code:

```
Private Declare Sub Sleep Lib "kernel32" _
(ByVal dwMilliseconds As Long)

Private Sub Text1_KeyPress(KeyAscii As Integer)
   Sleep (1000) 'wait one second to process keystroke
End Sub
```

This control is guaranteed to drive your users nuts. It will look like an ordinary text box, but every time the user types there will be an agonizing wait of one second before the character appears!

Many of the Windows APIs are functions that return values, using bit masking to tease out the needed information. An example of this is the GetVersion API that returns a long integer that contains information about what version of Windows the user is running.

```
Declare Function GetVersion Lib "kernel32" () As Long
```

The low order byte (i.e., use And with 255) gives the version number as the following amusing example shows (using a Standard EXE).

```
Private Declare Function GetVersion Lib "kernel32" _
() As Long
Private Sub Form_Click()
  Dim WinVersion As Long
  WinVersion = GetVersion() And 255
  Print "Did you know that Microsoft's API says
    Windows 95 is really Windows " & WinVersion
End Sub
```

It is extremely important that the Declare statement for an API function be exactly as Windows expects. Leaving off a ByVal keyword will almost certainly lock your system. Also, names of functions in a 32-bit dynamic-link library (DLL) are case-sensitive, unlike those in the 16-bit version. ⊃

Teaching you all the ins and outs of the Windows API is a task beyond the scope of this book. Most controls you create will never need the special effects that API calls can give. However, the standard reference (which we recommend very highly) is Daniel Appleman's, *Visual Basic Programmer's Guide to the Windows 32 API,* Ziff-Davis Press, 1996. (Of course, being absolutely definitive, it is 1518 pages; you might prefer the shorter survey in our forthcoming "Core Visual Basic" that should be out in late March.)

Using an API call means you will have compatibility problems whenever platforms differ in their support for that API function. ⊃

Using the techniques in Chapter 14, you can wrap any number of Windows API functions into an ActiveX Control for access from VBScript. ⊃

Mixed-Language Programming

Using a DLL created with another language such as C is similar to using one of the Windows DLLs. You will need to use a Declare statement to tell Visual Basic about the function you want to use.

Most DLLs expect the values to be passed by value (ByVal) rather than by reference (ByRef). The one usual exception is arrays that are passed by reference. ⊃

The full syntax for the Declare statement looks like this for a Sub program in a DLL (one that doesn't return a value):

```
[Public | Private ] Declare Sub name Lib "libname" [Alias " _
aliasname" ][([arglist])]
```

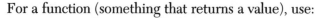

For a function (something that returns a value), use:

```
[Public | Private ] Declare Function name Lib "libname" [Alias " _
aliasname" ] [([arglist])][As type]
```

Most of the elements in a Declare statement (Public, Private, and so on) should be familiar to you. For the new ones, the Lib argument is just book-keeping—it tells Visual Basic that a DLL is being called. The Libname argument is the name of the DLL that contains the procedure you will be calling. The Alias keyword is used when the procedure has another name in the DLL but you don't (or can't) use it (probably because it conflicts with some reserved word in Visual Basic itself). The Aliasname argument is then the name of the procedure in the DLL. The Alias is what you will call it in Visual Basic.

Table 5-4 gives a list of the most common C types, their Windows equivalent, and what you would use in a Visual Basic Declare statement.

Table 5-4: Visual Basic Equivalents for C Types in Declare Statements

Window Type	C Type	Visual Basic Declare Type
BOOL	int	ByVal Boolean
BYTE	unsigned char	ByVal Byte
WORD	unsigned int	ByVal Integer
DWORD	unsigned long	ByVal Long
LPSTR	char far*	ByVal String
HANDLE	WORD	ByVal Long
HWND	HANDLE	ByVal Long
HDC	HANDLE	ByVal Long

Resource Files

Although the CCE does not include the ability to build resource files, it does have the ability to use one resource file per project. Resource files are used for storing strings, pictures, and other data that you need in the project. They are useful for internationalizing your project, or for increasing performance or the information your project can hold. This is because data stored in a resource file is loaded only when needed.

When you create the EXE file, the resource file is linked into the EXE. You access the information in a resource file with the resource functions described in the following table.

`LoadResString`	Loads a string
`LoadResPicture`	Loads a bitmap, icon, or cursor
`LoadResData`	Loads data and returns a Byte array

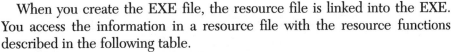

For information on how to create a resource file, consult the Windows SDK or the documentation supplied with the resource compiler in Visual C++. ⊃

To add a resource file to your project:

1. Choose Project|File Add.
2. Select Resource Files (*.RES) in the List Files of Type box.
3. Select the resource file you want to add to the project, and choose OK to close the Add File dialog box.

Error Trapping

Regardless of how carefully you debug your own program, it's impossible to anticipate what an inexperienced user may do. If you want your program to "degrade gracefully" and not just roll over after an error, you'll want to prevent fatal errors. The command that activates error trapping is:

```
On Error GoTo...
```

where the three dots stand for the label (line number) that defines the error trap. (See the section on the GoTo in the previous chapter for more on labels.) The labeled code must be in the current procedure. You cannot jump out of a procedure using an On Error GoTo command. On the other hand, the code for an error trap can (and often will) use other Sub or Function procedures.

Since you don't want Visual Basic to inadvertently "fall" into the error-trapping code, it is a good idea to have an Exit (Sub or Function) on the line immediately preceding the label for the error trap.

The On Error GoTo command can occur anywhere in an event, Sub, or Function procedure. Usually, the error-trapping code is inside that procedure. The only exception to this is when one procedure has been called by another. In this case, Visual Basic will look to see if an error trap was enabled in the earlier procedure if one does not exist in the second procedure.

Once you start error trapping with the On Error GoTo command, a run-time error such as a disk not being accessible will no longer bomb the program. The On Error GoTo command should transfer control to a piece of code that identifies the problem and, if possible, fix it.

If the error can be corrected, the Resume statement takes you back to the statement that caused the error in the first place. However, you can't correct an error if you don't know why it happened. Identify the problem by means of the Err object. The Err object has several properties and methods you can use to get information on run-time errors. When a run-time error occurs, the Err object's properties are set with information specific only to the error and you can use the error information to handle the error. You can also Raise errors at run time in your code. The following table summarizes the Err object's main properties and methods.

Property or Method	Description
Number	This is a long integer value specifically identifying an error.
Source	This is a string containing the name of the Visual Basic project.
Description	This is a string containing the error message, if one exists.
LastDLLError	LastDLLError is a long integer that contains the system error code for the last call into a DLL (if the DLL supports returning an error).
Clear	The Clear method resets the Err object.
Raise	The Raise method triggers a run-time error in your code.

When debugging a program, it's helpful to know what the error message for the last error was (for example, to place it in a message box). This would be the string given by:

```
Err.Description
```

Of course, this may be location-dependent so you are better off using the error number. Err.Number is, in fact, the default property for the Err object and the long integer it gives can be used to identify the error. For example, if:

```
ErrorNumber = Err.Number
```

the value of the variable ErrorNumber can help you pick up the type of error. Visual Basic can identify many run-time errors. This table gives some examples of error numbers.

Error Code	Explanation
5	Invalid procedure call or argument
7	Out of memory
13	Type mismatch
57	Device I/O error (for example, trying to print when the printer is off-line)
68	Device unavailable (the device may not exist or is currently unavailable)
71	Disk not ready

 An Out of Memory error does not necessarily mean that your application has run out of memory. It is possible for VBA to return this generic error because it cannot determine a more appropriate error. You still need to find out the cause for the error in your code, but you should not try to figure out why your system is low on memory when there is a very good chance that the error has nothing to do with memory. ⊃

The way you use this information is simple. Suppose an event procedure will be using the printer. Somewhere in the procedure, before the error can occur, place a statement such as this:

```
On Error GoTo PrinterCheck
```

Now, before the End Sub, add code that looks like this:

```
Exit Sub
PrinterCheck:
   ErrorNumber = Err.Number
   Beep
   Select Case ErrorNumber
     Case 25
       MsgBox "Your printer may be off-line."
     Case 27
       MsgBox "Is there a printer available?"
     Case Else
       M$ = "Please tell the operator (= program
         author?) that"
       M$ = M$ & vbCrLf
       M$ = M$ & "error number" & ErrorNumber &_"
         occurred."
       MsgBox M$
       End
   End Select

 M$ = "If the error has been corrected click on OK."
 M$ = M$ &vbCrLf
```

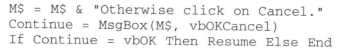

```
M$ = M$ & "Otherwise click on Cancel."
Continue = MsgBox(M$, vbOKCancel)
If Continue = vbOK Then Resume Else End
```

The idea of this error trap is simple, and the Select Case statement is ideal. Each case tries to give some indication of where the problem is and, if possible, how to correct it. If you reach the `Case Else`, the error number has to be reported. In any case, the final block gives you the option of continuing or not by using a message box with two buttons. You might want to get into the habit of writing a general procedure that analyzes the error code. The error trap inside a procedure just sends control to the general procedure. If you do this, you can reuse the general procedure in many different projects.

When developing a program, you may want to test how your error handler works. Visual Basic includes the statement

```
Error(errorcode number)
```

which, when processed, makes Visual Basic behave as if the error described by the given error number had actually occurred. This makes it easier to develop the error trap.

Finally, you can define and then raise your own errors in addition to the ones built into Visual Basic. You can even have your functions directly return an instance of the Err object whenever they return variants. Raising your own errors is especially useful when building a control, as you need to provide feedback to the user. Of course, you do not want to overwrite any of Visual Basic's built-in errors. By convention, the way to number your own errors is to follow this prescription:

1. Use the global constant vbObjectError which defines the range of VB's internal errors.

2. Add 512 to this constant.

3. Start defining your errors with this number.

For example:

```
Const DataNotFound = 1 + vbObjectError + 512

Error.Raise DataNotFound
```

(If your control depends on third-party controls, you have to avoid their error numbers along with VB's intrinsic error codes.)

Resume Revisited

A variant on the Resume command lets you bypass the statement that may have caused the problem. If you use

```
Resume Next
```

or

```
On Error Resume Next
```

to do this automatically.

This kind of code is especially important for a user control since the End statement is forbidden. Roughly speaking, use Resume if the error trap clears the error up and Resume Next otherwise.

Visual Basic begins processing at the statement following the one that caused the error. You can also resume execution at any line of code that has been previously identified with a label. For this, use

```
Resume Label
```

Both the Resume and Resume Next commands behave differently if Visual Basic has to move backward to find the error trap in another procedure. Recall that this happens when one procedure is invoked by a previous procedure and the current procedure doesn't have an error trap. In both cases, the statement executed by Visual Basic will not be in the procedure where the error occurred. For the Resume command, Visual Basic will call the original procedure again. For the Resume Next command, Visual Basic will execute the statement after the call to the original procedure. You will never get back to the original procedure.

Suppose the chain of procedural calls goes back even further: Procedure1 calls Procedure2, which calls Function3. Now an error occurs in Function3, but the only error handler is in Procedure1. If there is a Resume command in the error handler in Procedure1, Visual Basic actually goes to the statement that called Procedure2.

Because this is unwieldy and so prone to problems, it is probably better to rely only on error handlers that occur in a specific procedure. If one procedure calls another, turn off the error handler in the calling routine.

Disabling Error Trapping

If you are confident that you will no longer need an error trap, you can disable error trapping with the statement

```
On Error GoTo 0
```

(although, strictly speaking, the 0 is not needed). Similarly, you can change which error trap is in effect by using another On Error GoTo statement. Be sure to have an Exit command between the error traps. Visual Basic uses the last processed On Error GoTo statement to decide where to go. The On Error GoTo statement will clear the Err object. If you do not use this statement after an error has occurred, it is advisable to use Err.Clear to keep the error from bubbling up to the calling subprogram.

The Line that Caused the Error?

There's one other error-handling function, Erl (Error Line). If you get really desperate and need to find the line that caused the error and Visual Basic isn't stopping the program at that line, you can do the following:

1. Add line numbers before every statement in the procedure.

2. Add the Erl statement to the error trap.

Here's an example of what the code might look like.

```
Sub Partition (AnArray(), Start As Integer, Finish As Integer, _
LocOfSplitter As Integer)
   On Error GoTo PartitionErr
   ' LOCAL variables are: SplitPos,NewStart,I,Splitter
   Dim SplitPos As Integer, NewStart As Integer
   Dim I As Integer, Splitter

10   SplitPos = (start + finish) \ 2
20   Splitter = AnArray(SplitPos)
30   SWAP AnArray(SplitPos), AnArray(start)
40   LeftPos = start
50      For I = start + 1 To finish
60         If AnArray(i) < Splitter Then
70            LeftPos = LeftPos + 1
80            SWAP AnArray(LeftPos), AnArray(i)
```

```
90        End If
100     Next i
110   SWAP AnArray(start), AnArray(LeftPos)
120   LocOfSplitter = LeftPos
  Exit Sub
PartitionErr:
  MsgBox Err.Description & " occurred on line " & Erl
End Sub
```

With information this precise, you can often track down the problem more quickly. We don't recommend this as a common practice, but it may be the only way to debug certain applications or user controls which seem to act differently in various situations.

Chapter 6

Now that you have learned most of the non-object oriented programming techniques needed to build controls with the CCE, it's time to turn to the user interface again. In this chapter, you'll see how to use the Windows common controls including the common dialog boxes, more on the graphics controls, and even how to use VB graphics commands to do graphics from scratch. Finally, since users of your control will expect you to handle mouse operations in a sophisticated manner, we discuss that as well.

More on the
User Interface

More Controls

Although we do not have the space to cover the many custom controls that are available to you, we want to spend a bit of time on the Windows 95 common controls that are part of every Windows 95 or NT installation.

Microsoft does try to keep a rough count of commercial controls available; the last we heard, there were more than 2,000. The Microsoft ActiveX gallery at Microsoft's Web site (www.microsoft.com\activex\gallery) gives you a hint at what's available—we highly recommend this site.

Common Controls

The first common controls are found in the COMCTL32.OCX file. Since these are not part of the standard CCE toolbox, you'll need to add them. Go to Project|Components and choose Microsoft Windows Common Controls 5.0. Here are brief descriptions of the common controls.

TabStrip Control

A TabStrip Control, as shown in Figure 6-1, works like the dividers in a notebook or the labels on a group of file folders.

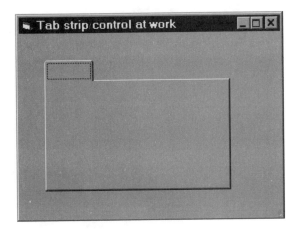

Figure 6-1
Tab Strip Control

Toolbar Control

A Toolbar Control, as shown in Figure 6-2, contains a collection of Button objects used to create a toolbar that is associated with your control or application. The toolbar can either be aligned to the top of its container, as it is usually used, or placed anywhere on the form to provide a set of buttons or a button group.

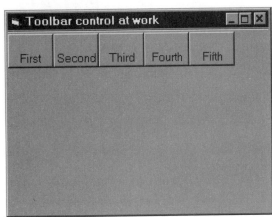

Figure 6-2
Toolbar Control

Getting images on a Toolbar Control requires using an ImageList control to hold the images. ⊃

StatusBar Control

A StatusBar Control, as shown in Figure 6-3, provides a window, usually at the bottom of a parent form, through which an application can display various kinds of status data. The status bar can be divided into a maximum of 16 Panel objects that are contained in a Panels collection. Each panel may have text or a graphic on it that can be added at design time or run time.

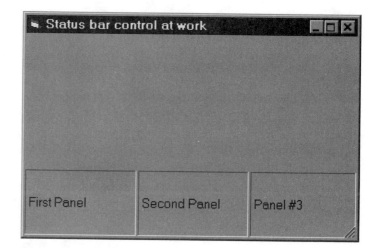

Figure 6-3
StatusBar control

ProgressBar Control

The ProgressBar Control, as shown in Figure 6-4, shows the progress of a lengthy operation by filling a rectangle with one or more chunks at a time, from left to right. The amount of fill is determined by the Value property relative to the progress bar's Min and Max properties.

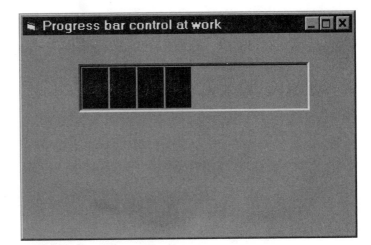

Figure 6-4
ProgressBar
Control

TreeView Control

A TreeView displays a hierarchical list of objects similar to Window Explorer or the Project Explorer in the CCE. Each object is called a *Node*. Each Node consists of a label and an optional bitmap. A TreeView Control is used when you need to display the headings in a document, the entries in an index, the files and directories on a disk, or any other kind of information where seeing it in the form of an outline is helpful. This is the same control used in the Win95 Explorer that displays your system folders including drives, network shares, etc.

ListView Control

The ListView Control displays items using one of four different views: Large Icons, Small Icons, List, or Report. You can arrange items into columns with or without column headings, as well as display accompanying icons and text. This is the control used to display the contents of the folders in the Win95 Explorer.

ImageList Control

An ImageList Control contains a collection of ListImage objects, each of which can be referred to by its index or key. The ImageList Control is not meant to be used alone, but as a way to hold images that other controls such as the ToolBar, TreeView and ListView Controls can use.

Slider Control

A Slider control is a window containing a slider and optional tick marks. You can manipulate the slider by dragging it, clicking the mouse to either side of the slider, or using the keyboard. An example of a Slider control is shown in Figure 6-5.

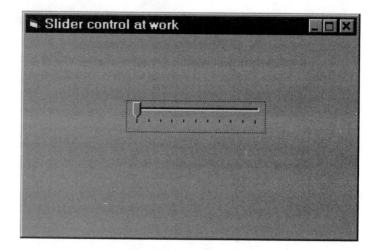

Figure 6-5
Slider Control

An Example Using the Common Controls: DateTime

The CD has the full code for a control that extends the StatusBar control. We call it the DateTime control because it simply uses the built-in functionality of the status bar to display the current date and time. In addition, it exposes a property called ShowKeyboardStatus that, when set to True, widens the DateTime control in order to display the Caps Lock, Scroll Lock and Num Lock status on the keyboard. This demonstrates how to take a complex control and make a simple version of it; one that you may use in its specialized form more often than the basic control. It is easy to imagine doing this with all of the common controls.

Common Dialog Boxes

Working with Windows, you've become accustomed to seeing one of five standard dialog boxes for opening or saving a file, printing, choosing fonts, or setting colors. If your control does any of these operations, users will expect to see the familiar interface at work. This means you will want to build using the common dialog box as your base.

First off, a common dialog control, like a Timer control, has no visible interface. To actually pop up a specific common dialog box requires calling the appropriate method of the common dialog control while the program is running. For example, if you have an Open File item on a File menu and the associated Click procedure is in `OpenFile_Click`, the code to pop up a File Open dialog box using the default name of the control looks like this

```
Sub OpenFile_Click ()

    ...

    CommonDialog1.ShowOpen

    ...
```

The common dialog boxes take no actions; they accept information only. You will always need to write the code that tells Visual Basic what to do with the information entered and then have this code processed when the user closes the common dialog box. ⊃

Working with Common Dialog Boxes

Common dialog boxes are easier to use in principle than in practice. This is because they require a fair amount of initializing to get them to look exactly the way you want. Before you pop up the box, you usually need to initialize the various properties that determine how the common dialog box looks. For example, you might want to set the default in the Print dialog box Print Range to print only page 1. This is done by adjusting the value of the FromPage and ToPage properties of the common dialog control, as shown in the following listing.

```
CommonDialog1.FromPage = 1
CommonDialog1.ToPage = 1
```

All the common dialog boxes allow you to generate an error if the user clicks the Cancel button. Setting up an error trap for this is necessary in most (if not all) cases. To do this, use the following code:

```
[FormName].CommonDialog1.CancelError = True
```

The default is False, so no error is reported when the Cancel button is activated. Set it to True and an error with error number 32755 is generated if the user clicks Cancel or presses Esc. (Again, since nobody would want to use this kind of number in their code—even if they could remember it—use the symbolic constant cdlCancel instead.)

Setting this property to be True and then trapping this error is important because whether the user clicks OK or Cancel, certain values may have changed. Since you only want to use the information when the OK button was clicked, you must have a way to know if the Cancel button was used to close the dialog box.

Here's a general framework for working with a common dialog box that uses an error trap to detect if the Cancel button was pressed.

```
CommonDialog1.CancelError = True
On Error GoTo IsOK
  .
  .
  .
'Make sure the code after the IsOK label
'is always processed
IsOK:
  If Err = 0 Then  'no error so OK clicked
    'code to process data as needed
  ElseIf Err = cdlCancel
    'do nothing cancel invoked
  Else
    'wow you have a real error to handle
  End If
End Sub
```

The File Open and File Save Boxes

The following table gives short descriptions of the most important properties used for these dialog boxes.

Property	Use
DefaultExt	This sets the default extension for files shown in the box.
DialogTitle	This sets the title bar. In particular, you do not need to use Open and Save if you are using these boxes in other contexts.
FileName	This gives the name and path of the file selected.
FileTitle	This gives the name without the path.
Filter	Changes here show up in the Type box. You can have multiple filters by separating them with the pipe symbol (a Chr(124) |). The format is the string for the description, the Chr(124), the filter, another Chr(124), and so on.
FilterIndex	This is used when you set up many filters using the Filter property.
Flags	This property is used to set various possible options on how the box will look. The values needed are stored in constants that begin with `cdlOFN_`.
InitDir	This specifies the initial directory.
MaxFileSize	This sets the maximum size of the filename including all the path info.

The Flags property is very important in determining the final look and feel of the box. For example, a line of code like

```
CommonDialog1.Flags =  cdlOFNAllowMultiselect
```

allows the Filename list box to use multiple selections. You can combine more than one flag with an Or and read back the values using bit-masking techniques with the And operator.

Once the user clicks the OK button, you have to write code to read back the information that was entered and take appropriate actions based on these values. For example, `CommonDialog1.FileName` would contain the name of the file chosen.

The Color Choice Box

Here is a table with descriptions of the important properties used for these dialog boxes.

Property	Use
Color	Shows or gets the color
Flags	As with File Save/File Open, specifies the form of the box.

The symbolic constants for this box begin with `cdlCC`. For example,

```
CommonDialog1.Flags = cdlCCFullOpen
```

would display the whole dialog box (including the one for defining custom colors). When the user clicks the OK button, the value of, for example, `CommonDialog1.Color` is the long integer code for the color selected.

The Font Choice Box

Before we get to the table showing the remaining properties for this box, you'll need to know something about how the Flag property works here. Since you might want to have the font choice box reflect printer fonts only, screen fonts only, or both at once, Visual Basic requires you to set the Flag parameter correctly before it will display the Font box. The symbolic constants used are `cdlCFPrinterFonts`, `cdlCFScreenFonts`, or `cdlCFBoth`. If you don't set the CommonDialog.Flag property to one of these three values and still try to show the Font box, the program generates an error and dies.

There are 14 different Flag property values. As always, you combine them by adding them together.

Here is a table with descriptions of the important remaining properties used for this dialog box.

Property	Use
Color	Only used for color printers.
FontBold, FontItalic, FontStrikeThru, FontUnderline	True/False properties. If the `cdlCFEffects` flag is set, you can allow the user to choose these properties.
FontName	Sets or returns the font name.
FontSize	Sets or returns the size of the font.
Max, Min	These change the point sizes shown in the size box. You need to have the `cdlCFLimitSize` flag set before you can use these properties.

Read back the value of the various font properties to see what the user wants. For example, the value of `CommonDialog1.FontName` is the name of the font the user chose. Then have Visual Basic process the code to have the new value go into effect.

The Printer Dialog Box

As before, the Flags property controls how the box appears. For example, if the Flag parameter is `cdlPDAllPages`, then the All option button in the Print Range frame is set. Specifically, this means you will need bit-masking techniques to check out what the user did with the box. Use code like this:

```
If CommonDialog1.Flags And cdlPDAllPages = _
cdlPDAllPages Then
    'all pages button checked
```

Here is a table with descriptions of the remaining properties used for these dialog boxes.

Property	Use
Copies	Sets or returns the number of copies the user wants.
FromPage, ToPage	What pages are wanted.
HDC	This is the device context number. It is used for API function calls.
Max, Min	Specifies the maximum and minimum pages the user can put in the Print Range frame.
PrinterDefault	Set this to True and the user can click the Setup button to change the WIN.INI file.

The Line and Shape Controls

These two controls let you quickly display simple lines and shapes or print them on a printer. They are different than most other controls because they do not respond to any events: they are for display or printing only. They are also quite sparing of Windows resources.

The Shape control can be used to display rectangles, squares, ovals, or circles. You can also use it to display rounded rectangles and rounded squares. The icon for the Shape control is three overlapping shapes. The Line control can be used to display lines of varying thickness on a form. The icon for the Line control on the toolbox is a diagonal line.

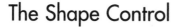

The Shape Control

The Shape control has 20 properties. Usually, you change them dynamically with code while the application is running. The most important properties for the Shape control at design time are described in the following sections.

The Shape Property

This determines the type of shape you get. There are six possible settings.

Setting of Shape Property	Effect
VbShapeRectangle (=0)	Rectangle (default)
VbShapeSquare (=1)	Square
VbShapeOval(=2)	Oval
VbShapeCircle (=3)	Circle
vbShapeRoundedRectangle (=4)	Rounded rectangle
vbShapeRoundedSquare (=5)	Rounded square

For example, if you add a Shape control in the default size and shape to an ordinary EXE form and write the following in the `Form_Click` procedure, you can see the shapes for yourself.

```
Private Sub Form_Click
   Static I As Integer
   Shape1.Shape = I
   I = I + 1
   I = I Mod 6 'to prevent error
End Sub
```

The BackStyle Property

This property determines whether the background of the shape is transparent or not. The default value is 1, which gives you an opaque border; BackColor fills the shape and obscures what is behind it. Set it to 0 (Transparent) and you can see through the shape to what is behind it.

BorderWidth

BorderWidth determines the thickness of the line. It is measured in pixels and can range from 0 to 8,192 (rather too large to display on a form).

BorderStyle

Unlike the case for Image controls, the BorderStyle for Shape controls have seven possible settings, as shown in the following table. Having no border (BorderStyle = 0) prevents the control from being visible unless you modify the FillStyle and FillColor properties.

Value of BorderStyle Property	Effect
VbTransparent (=0)	No border shown
VbBSSolid (=1)	Solid (default)
VbBSDash (=2)	A dashed line
VbBSDot (=3)	A dotted line
VbBSDashDot (=4)	A dash-dot line
VbBSDashDotDot (=5)	A dash-dot-dot line
VbBSInsideSolid (=6)	Outer edge of border is the outer edge of the shape.

 If you set the BorderWidth property to greater than 1, then resetting the BorderStyle property has no effect. ⊃

(To see these in effect, add the line `Shape1.BorderStyle = I` to the previous demonstration program.)

FillColor, FillStyle

The FillColor property determines the color used to fill the shape in the manner set by the FillStyle property. You can set the FillColor property in the same way as setting any color property, either directly via a hexadecimal code or by using the color palette. The FillStyle property has eight possible settings, as shown in the following table.

195

Setting For FillStyle Property	Effect
VbFSSolid (=0)	Solid
VbFSTransparen (=1)	Transparent (default)
VbHorizontalLine (=2)	Horizontal line
VbVerticalLine (=3)	Vertical line
VbUpwardDiagonal (=4)	Upward diagonal
VbDownwardDiagonal (=5)	Downward diagonal
VbCross (=6)	Cross
VbDiagonalCross (=7)	Diagonal cross

The Line Control

The Line control has 15 properties. Usually, you change them dynamically with code while the application is running. The most important properties for the Line control at design time are the BorderWidth property and the BorderStyle property. BorderWidth determines the thickness of the line. It is measured in pixels and can range from 0 to 8,192 (too large to display on most forms). Like the Shape control, the BorderStyle property has six possible settings, but as before, only the last five are really useful.

The most important properties at run time for the Line control are the X1, Y1, X2, Y2 properties. These govern where the edges of the line appear. The X1 property sets (or tells you) the horizontal position of the left end of the line. The Y1 property sets (or tells you) the vertical position of the left-hand corner. The X2 and Y2 properties work similarly for the right end of the line.

These properties use the underlying scale of the container of the Line control. ⊃

Behind the Scenes with Visual Basic's Graphics

To draw on the screen, Visual Basic tells Windows what to display. What this means is that what you can do with Visual Basic's graphics statements depends on the driver programs that Windows uses to control the screen and printer. However, using these driver programs is automatic. You do not have to worry about all the possible hardware combinations a user may have. This is different from what MS-DOS programmers are used to. When graphics are programmed under DOS, part of the program must check to see what kind of graphics board (if any) is installed, and the program must be adjusted accordingly.

However, nothing comes for free. Windows has to do a lot to manage a graphics environment, and this forces trade-offs. For example, unless you set the AutoRedraw property to True so that Visual Basic saves a copy of the object in memory, you will have to manage the redrawing of graphics yourself. (The jargon says that AutoRedraw controls whether graphics are *persistent* or not.)

 Images derived from setting the Picture property of a control or those coming from the Line and Shape controls are always persistent. ⊃

There are slight differences between how the AutoRedraw property being set to True works for forms and picture boxes:

- For a resizable form or user control, Visual Basic saves a copy of the entire screen. Thus, when you enlarge the form, no graphics information is lost. This option requires much more memory, instead of leaving AutoRedraw at False since Visual Basic needs to reserve enough memory for a bit-by-bit description of the whole form. However, if your graphics do not currently fit on a form but will when the form is enlarged, choose this option.

- For a picture box, Visual Basic saves an image only as large as the current size of the box. Nothing new will appear even if the box is enlarged later.

Thus, drawing to picture boxes requires less memory than drawing to the form, even if the picture box fills up the form.

A Feature of the AutoRedraw Property

There is one other interesting feature of AutoRedraw: Suppose you change AutoRedraw to False while a program is running. Then you clear the object by using the Cls method. Whatever you drew before you changed the AutoRedraw property will remain, but everything that was drawn after the switch will disappear. This feature can be very useful. To see how it works, start a new Standard EXE project and try the following demonstration program (recall that text is treated as graphics output on a form). For the `Form_Load` procedure, write

```
Private Sub Form_Load ()
   AutoRedraw = True
   Print "Please click to see a demonstration of
      AutoRedraw."
   Print "These two lines will stay on the screen
      after you double click."
End Sub
```

Now, for the `Click` procedure, add

```
Private Sub Form_Click ()
   AutoRedraw = False        'keeps old stuff
   Cls
   Print: Print: Print       'third line
   Print "But this line will disappear after you
      double click."
End Sub
```

Finally, the `Double_Click` procedure is simply

```
Private Sub Form_DblClick ()
   Cls       'Clears line from Click() procedure
End Sub
```

The ClipControls Property and the Paint Event

Visual Basic activates the Paint event each time a part of the form is newly exposed. What happens within the Paint event, in this case, depends on how the ClipControls property is set at design time. If the ClipControls property is set to True (the default) and the AutoRedraw property is False, then Visual Basic repaints the entire object. If ClipControls is set to False, Visual Basic repaints only the newly exposed areas.

 The ClipControls property has a few other features worth noting. Setting ClipControls to True also creates what Microsoft calls a *clipping region* around non-graphical controls on the object. This means Visual Basic creates an outline of the form and the controls on it in memory. Because the clipping region is created in memory, setting this property to False can reduce the time needed to paint or repaint the object. More time is needed if the object is graphically complex. Clipping regions exclude the Image, Label, Line, or Shape controls. ⊃

If AutoRedraw is set to True, you can speed up your program by setting ClipControls to False. ⊃

More on the Paint Event

In any case, if AutoRedraw is False, you need to write the necessary code in the Paint procedure whenever you want to redraw part or all of a form or picture box. Therefore, the least memory-intensive way to handle the problem of graphics disappearing because a user covered a form or picture box is to redraw the image in the form or picture box in the Paint event procedure. Setting AutoRedraw to True uses up memory (if you have it), potentially speeding up the program, (although the image may take longer to appear at first). You have to choose what's best for the application. At the extremes, the choice is easy: If the amount of drawing to be done is minimal, using the Paint event procedure is better. In any case, Visual Basic calls the Paint procedure for the object only if the AutoRedraw property of the object is set to False.

Be very careful about including in the Paint event procedure any commands that move or resize the object. If you include such commands, Visual Basic will just call the Paint procedure again, and you'll be stuck in an infinite regress. ⊃

The Refresh Method

You will occasionally need to use the Refresh method when working with graphics. This method applies to both forms and controls. It forces an immediate refresh of the form or control, and will let you see an image develop even when AutoRedraw is True. (If AutoRedraw is set to True, Visual Basic waits for the image to be finished or some other idle time before displaying the image.) If you use the Refresh method, Visual Basic will also call any Paint event procedure you have written for the object. This method is commonly used in the ReSize procedure to redisplay any graphics that are calculated in the Paint event procedure. Also, while Visual Basic handles refreshing the screen during idle time, occasionally you will want to control this process yourself. Whenever Visual Basic processes an ObjectName.Refresh statement, it will redraw the object immediately and generate the Paint event, if the object supports this feature.

Saving Pictures

Finally, Visual Basic makes it easy to save the pictures you've drawn to a form or picture box. The SavePicture statement uses the following syntax:

```
SavePicture ObjectName.Image, Filename
```

The operating system uses the Image property to identify the picture in the form or picture box. If you leave off ObjectName, then, as usual, Visual Basic uses the current form. The syntax for this version of the method is

```
SavePicture Image, Filename
```

If you originally loaded the picture from a file by assigning an image to the Picture property of the form or picture box, Visual Basic saves the picture in the same format as the original file. (For example, icon files stay icon files.) Otherwise, Visual Basic saves the picture as a bitmap (.BMP) file.

Fundamentals of Programming Graphics

You can draw on a picture box on a form. Using code, you'll take complete control of each dot on the screen or on the printer. Of course, if all you want to do is draw a few shapes on the screen, there is no need to use any of the graphical methods.

Screen Scales

There are six other possible scales besides the default scale, as well as a totally flexible user-defined scale that you'll see in the next section. These scales are set by changing the ScaleMode property at design or run time, as shown in the following table.

ScaleMode Constants	Units
vbTwips	Twips (the default)
vbPoints	Points (72 per inch)
vbPixels	Pixels (the number of dots, as reported by Windows)
vbCharacters	Characters (units default as 12 points high and 20 points wide)
vbInches	Inches
vbMillimeters	Millimeters
vbCentimeters	Centimeters

Once you set the ScaleMode property, you can read off the size of the *drawing area*, which is the area inside the form or control or the printable area on the paper. This is reported in the current units when you use the ScaleHeight and ScaleWidth properties. Since both ScaleHeight and ScaleWidth report their results using the units selected by ScaleMode, they are very convenient for resetting form-level or global variables in a Resize event procedure. On the other hand, the Height and Width properties of an object are less useful for graphics except for a user control form. This is because these properties give you the area of the object including the borders and title bar, if there are any. In graphics, you usually care more about the dimensions of the drawing area.

 Use form-level or global variables for the Height and Width properties of the Screen object and recalculate these in the Resize event. Then you can use a percentage of these variables in your code in order to make it easier to have your code independent of the particular monitor and card. ⊃

Custom Screen Scales

Regardless of which scale you choose, the drawing area is normally numbered with (0, 0) as the top-left corner. This is obviously inconvenient for drawing tables, charts, graphs, and other mathematical objects. In most of these situations, you want the coordinates to decrease as you move from top to bottom and increase as you move from left to right. For example, mathematics usually uses an X-Y (Cartesian) system, with X measuring distance across from a central point (the origin) and Y measuring distance up or down from the center.

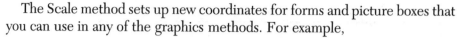

The Scale method sets up new coordinates for forms and picture boxes that you can use in any of the graphics methods. For example,

```
Scale (-100, 100) - (100, -100)
```

sets up a new coordinate system with the coordinates of the top-left corner being (–100, 100) and the bottom-right corner being (100, –100). After this method, the four corners are described in a clockwise order, starting from the top left:

```
(-100, 100)
(100, 100)
(100, -100)
(-100, -100)
```

Now, (0, 0) is roughly the center of the screen. This placement occurs because whenever Visual Basic processes a Scale method that changes to a custom scale, the program automatically finds the pixel that corresponds to your coordinates (by rounding, if necessary).

In general, the Scale method looks like this:

```
Scale (LeftX, TopY) - (RightX, BottomY)
```

where LeftX is a single-precision real number that will represent the smallest X coordinate (left-most), TopY is a single-precision number for the largest Y (top), RightX is the right corner, and BottomY the bottom edge. For example,

```
Scale (-1E38, 1E38) - (1E38, -1E38)
```

gives you the largest possible scale, which means the smallest amount of detail. Large X and Y changes are needed to light up adjacent pixels.

If you use the Scale method with no coordinates, Visual Basic will reset the coordinates back to the default scale of (0, 0) for the top left-hand corner and the units being twips.

 Some programmers prefer using a custom scale rather than percentages of the Screen.Height and Screen.Width objects in their code. ⊃

Another Way to Set Up Custom Scales

Although the Scale method is the simplest way to set up a custom scale, there is one other way that may be useful. You can specify the coordinates of the top left-hand corner and how Visual Basic should measure the vertical and horizontal scales. You do all this by using combinations of the ScaleLeft, ScaleTop, ScaleWidth, and ScaleHeight properties. For example, after Visual Basic processes

```
Object.ScaleLeft = 1000
Object.ScaleTop = 500
```

the coordinates of the top left-hand corner of the object are (1000, 500). After Visual Basic processes a statement like this one, all graphics methods for drawing within the object are calculated based on these new coordinates for the top left-hand corner. For example, if you made these changes to a form, then to place an object at the top left-hand corner now requires setting its Top property to 500 and its Left property to 1000.

Similarly, if you set the ScaleWidth to 100 and the ScaleHeight to 200, the horizontal units are $\frac{1}{100}$ of the graphics area and the vertical units are $\frac{1}{200}$ of the height of the graphics area.

Just as with the Scale method, you can use any single-precision number to reset these four properties. If you use a negative value for ScaleWidth or ScaleHeight, the orientation changes. If ScaleHeight is negative, the coordinates of the top of the object are higher values than those of the bottom. If ScaleWidth is negative, the coordinates of the left side of the object are higher values than those of the right side.

Colors

Visual Basic has quite a few ways to define colors. The easiest, by far, is to use the built-in color constants such as vbBlack or vbRed. Of course, this restricts you to only 8 colors. If you want access to the potentially millions of colors that are available on some graphics adapters, you have two choices.

First you can use the RGB function, whose syntax is:

```
RGB(red, green, blue)
```

The redness, blueness and greenness are set on a scale from 0 to 255. For example:

Color	RGB setting
Black	RGB(0, 0, 0)
Blue	RGB(0, 0, 255)
Cyan	RGB(0, 255, 255)
Yellow	RGB(255, 255, 0)
White	RGB(255, 255, 255)

Next, you can use the hexadecimal code that the RGB function is returning. This is in the form &HBBRRGG, where each two hex digits (00 to FF) give you that color intensity of blue, red, and green on a scale of 0 to 255.

Controls use a data type called OLE_COLOR to pass color codes. This is simply the six hexadecimal digits in the code mentioned above. ⊃

Pixel Control

Now you know how colors are assigned and can change the scale of your screen as you see fit. How do you turn a pixel on? The syntax for this method is

```
PSet(Col, Row) [, ColorCode]
```

Since the color code is optional (as indicated by the square brackets), all you need to do is replace the parameters with the values you want. The value of the first entry determines the column and the second determines the row. After Visual Basic processes this statement, the pixel defined by that point lights up. Obviously, where that point is depends on what scale you've chosen. For example, in the ordinary scale, using the default size for a form, the statement

```
Pset(2400, 1800)
```

would turn on the center pixel in the default size of a user control on our 800 × 600 but after a ScaleMode=3 command, this would likely cause an overflow run-time error. It is possible to use PSet outside the current limits of the form, but if you exceed the limits on the size of the screen, you'll almost certainly get an overflow run-time error. When you use PSet to turn on a point that is outside the form, Visual Basic records this information but doesn't plot any points. This is where the AutoRedraw property's being set to True can help. Suppose you ask Visual Basic to plot a point that is too large to fit the current size of the form, and AutoRedraw is True for the form. Then the information isn't lost; set the WindowState property to 2 (maximized), and the point will show up.

 In a situation like this where you need to know how many twips correspond to a single pixel, turn to Visual Basic's built-in `TwipsPerPixelX/TwipsPerPixelY` functions. (Since Windows API functions usually require pixels, these functions are often needed for using API graphics calls.) ⊃

You can use the Point method to determine the color code of any point on the screen. This returns a long integer using the &HRRGGBB& code. The syntax is:

```
object.Point(x, y)
```

where x, y are single-precision values giving the x (the left/right position) and y (up/down position) and vertical (y-axis) coordinates of the point using the ScaleMode property of the Form or PictureBox.

Lines and Boxes

Obviously, if you had to draw everything by plotting individual points, graphics programming would be too time-consuming to be practical. In addition to line and shape controls, Visual Basic comes with a rich supply of graphics tools, usually called *graphics primitives*, that allow you to plot such geometric figures as lines, boxes, circles, ellipses, and wedges with a single statement. The statement

```
Line (StartColumn, StartRow) - (EndCol, EndRow), ColorCode
```

gives you a line connecting the two points with the given coordinates, using the color specified by ColorCode.

An Example: A Special Effects Control

For example, suppose you wanted to design a Special Effects control that gives you a starburst-like effect that runs continuously when the user clicks in it. To do this, simply set up a user control with a border style property set to Fixed Single. Then add the following code:

```
Private Sub UserControl_Click()
  Dim I As Integer, Col As Single, Row As Single
  ReDim CCode(1 To 3) As Integer
  Randomize
  Scale (-100, 100)-(100, -100)
  Do
    X = DoEvents()
    Cls
    For I = 1 To 150
      CCode(1) = 255 * Rnd
      CCode(2) = 255 * Rnd
      CCode(3) = 255 * Rnd
      Col = 100 * Rnd
      If Rnd < 0.5 Then Col = -Col
      Row = 100 * Rnd
      If Rnd < 0.5 Then Row = -Row
      Line (0, 0)-(Col, Row), RGB(CCode(1), CCode(2), _
      CCode(3))
    Next I
  Loop
End Sub
```

There is one subtle point about the code in this control. Since we want the control to work continuously, it is a good idea to have a DoEvents statement in order to allow other events to be processed.

Last Point Referenced

Visual Basic keeps track of where it stopped plotting. This location is usually called the *last point referenced (LPR)*, and the values of the CurrentX and CurrentY variables store this information. If you are continuing a line from the last point referenced, Visual Basic allows you to omit the LPR in the Line method.

When you start any graphics mode with a ScaleMode method or a custom scale, the last point referenced has the coordinates (0, 0) in that scale. For custom scales, this need not be the top left-hand corner. After a Line method, the last point referenced is the end point of the line (the second coordinate pair).

Relative Coordinates

Up to now, you've been using *absolute coordinates*. Each point is associated with a unique row and column. It's occasionally helpful to use *relative coordinates*, where each point is defined by how far it is from the last point referenced. For example, if you write

```
PSet(12, 100)
```

which makes (12, 100) the last point referenced, then you can write

```
PSet Step(50, 10)
```

to turn on the point in column 62 (50 + 12) and row 110 (10 + 100). In general, when Visual Basic sees the statement

```
Step (X, Y)
```

in a graphics method, it uses the point whose coordinates are X units to the right or left and Y units up or down from the last point referenced (depending on whether X and Y are positive or negative).

DrawWidth, DrawStyle

When you draw on the printer or the screen by using the PSet or Line method (and circles—see the section "Circles and Ellipses" later in this chapter), Visual Basic uses dots that are normally drawn one pixel wide. If you need to change the width of points or lines, use the DrawWidth property. The syntax for this method is

```
Object.DrawWidth = Size%
```

The theoretical maximum size for DrawWidth is 32,767.

If you do not want a solid line, all you need to do is change the DrawStyle property. You can see the effect of DrawStyle only when the DrawWidth is 1. There are seven possible settings when DrawWidth is 1, as shown in the following table.

Value of DrawStyle Property	Description
VbSolid (default = 0)	Solid
VbDash (1)	Dash
VbDot (2)	Dot
VbDashDot (3)	Dash-dot-dash-dot pattern
VbDashDotDot (4)	Dash-dot-dot pattern
VbInvisible (5)	Transparent—nothing shown
VbInsideSolid (6)	Inside solid (see the next section)

Boxes

A modification of the Line method lets you draw a rectangle. The statement

```
Line (FirstCol, FirstRow) - (SecCol, SecRow), CCode, B
```

draws a rectangle in the given color code (CCode) whose opposite corners are given by FirstCol, FirstRow and SecCol, SecRow. For example, another way to get a Special Effects control is with code that looks like this:

```
Dim I As Integer
  Scale (-100, 100)-(100, -100)

  For I = 1 To 90 Step 5
    Line (-100 + I, 100 - I)-(100 - I, -100 + I), , B
  Next I
```

Notice that this program leaves off the color code but still keeps the comma to separate out the B. Without this comma, Visual Basic would think the B was the name of a variable rather than the Box command. Leave out the comma, and Visual Basic would think you're asking for a line connecting

```
(5*I, I)-(639-5*I, 199-I)
```

with color code the current value of B. (Since an uninitialized numeric variable has value 0, you'd probably get a color code of 0.)

The width of the line defining the boundary of the box is determined by the current value of DrawWidth for the object on which you are drawing. When you have a fairly wide line for the boundary, you can see the effect of using the "inside solid" (DrawStyle = 6). Using the InsideSolid line makes a boundary of the box that is half inside, half outside.

Filled Boxes

You can arrange for the variant on the Line method that gives boxes to also fill the box. Use BF rather than B, and you get a filled box. Therefore,

```
Line (FirstCol, FirstRow) - (SecCol, SecRow), CCode, BF
```

will yield a solid rectangle whose opposite corners are given by FirstCol, FirstRow and SecCol, SecRow.

FillStyle, FillColor

Boxes (and circles—see the next section) are usually empty or solid, but Visual Basic allows you seven different patterns to fill boxes as well as using no fill pattern at all. To do this, you need to change the FillStyle property of the form or picture box, using properties from the following table.

Value of FillStyle Property	Description
vbFSSolid = 0	Solid
vbFSTransparent (default =1)	Transparent
vbHorizontalLine (=2)	Horizontal line
vbVerticalLine (=3)	Vertical line
vbUpwardDiagonal (=4)	Upward diagonal
vbDownwardDiagonal (=5)	Downward diagonal
vbCross (=6)	Cross
vbDiagonalCross (=7)	Diagonal cross

Once you have changed the FillStyle property from its transparent default (FillStyle = 1), you can use the FillColor property to set the color used for FillStyle. This property has the syntax

```
Object.FillColor = ColorCode
```

where, as usual, you can set the color code in any of the four ways mentioned previously.

Circles and Ellipses

Normally, to describe a circle in Visual Basic, you give its center and radius. The following fragment draws a circle of radius 0.5 units, starting at the center of the screen:

```
Scale (-1, 1) - (1, -1)
Circle (0, 0), 0.5
```

The last point referenced (CurrentX, CurrentY) after a Circle method is always the center of the circle. You can also add a color code to the Circle method. For example,

```
Circle (0, 0), 0.5 , CCode
```

would draw a circle of radius 0.5 in the color code indicated here by the variable CCode.

To draw a sector or an arc, you have to tell Visual Basic which angle to start at and which angle to finish at. You do this using radian measure, which you may have seen in high school. (It is also used in the trigonometric functions in Visual Basic.) Radian measure isn't very difficult. It measures angles by what percentage the radian measure would give of the circumference of a circle of radius 1. For example, all the way around a circle of radius 1 is 2π units. It is also 360 degrees, so 360 degrees is equal to 2π radians. One-half of a circle of radius 1 is 180 degrees and π units. Therefore, 180 degrees is π radians. Similarly, one-quarter of a circle (90 degrees) is $\frac{\pi}{2}$ radians, and so on. To go from degrees to radians, multiply by $\pi/180$; to go back, multiply by $180/\pi$. (Since π is roughly 3.14159, 360 degrees is roughly 6.28 radians.) In any case, the statement

```
Circle (XRad, YRad), Radius, CCode, StartAngle, EndAngle
```

draws an arc of the circle starting at the angle given in radians by StartAngle and ending with EndAngle. (The Circle method does not, unfortunately, support named arguments.) To get a sector, use negative signs.

There are a few peculiarities of these methods that you should be aware of. The first is that, although mathematics allows negative angles, Visual Basic does not. The negative sign only serves to indicate, "Draw a sector rather than an arc." The second is that if you want your arc to start with a vertical line pointed due east (that is, 0 degrees = 0 radians), you shouldn't use –0 for the StartAngle or EndAngle. Instead, use $-2 * \pi$ (= –6.28 . . .). The final peculiarity is that angles in the Circle method can only have values between -2π (–6.28 . . .) and 2π (6.28 . . .).

210

Ellipses and the Aspect Ratio

You convert the Circle drawing method to an ellipse drawing command by adding one more option. This also lets you override Visual Basic's default settings if you need to adjust the aspect ratio for your monitor. The syntax for this method is

```
Circle [Step] (XCenter, YCenter), radius, , , , aspect
```

The four commas must be there even if you are not using the color code and angle options that you saw earlier. (Step is optional, of course.) This version of the Circle method lets you change the default ratio of columns to rows. (It's really an Ellipse command.) If the aspect parameter is less than 1, the radius is taken in the column direction and the ellipse is stretched in the horizontal direction. If the aspect parameter is greater than 1, the radius is taken in the row direction and the ellipse is stretched in the vertical.

The PaintPicture Method

One problem with earlier versions of Visual Basic is that there was no quick way to paint a picture at a specific place on a form or picture box. (You had to use the BitBlt API call.) Visual Basic has now added a version of this API call directly to its language. This new method is called PaintPicture. It has many uses, for example, it lets you do simple animation quite effectively within Visual Basic. The simplest version of the syntax for PaintPicture looks like this:

```
object.PaintPicture picture, x1, y1, width, height
```

The object can refer to any form, picture box, or the printer. (If you leave it out, Visual Basic assumes you mean the form.) The picture parameter gives the source of the graphic to be drawn. (For example, it could be the Picture property of a Picture Box.) Finally, the x1 and y1 parameters give the coordinates of the upper left-hand corner where you want the picture to appear (using the scale of the object parameter).

To see the PaintPicture method at work, add a Picture box with the default size and width to the form. Assign the Picture property of the Picture box to any bitmap you might have. (Use Paint to make one, for example.) Now try the following code:

```
Private Sub Form_Click()
  Dim I As Integer, J As Integer
  Dim NumberOfCols As Integer, NumberOfRows As
    Integer
  Picture1.Visible = False
  NumberOfRows = Form1.ScaleHeight / Picture1.Height
  NumberOfCols = Form1.ScaleWidth / Picture1.Width
  For I = 1 To NumberOfRows
    For J = 1 To NumberOfCols
        Form1.PaintPicture Picture1.Picture, (J - 1) _
* Picture1.Width, (I - 1)*Picture1.Height, _
Picture1.Width
    Next J
  Next I
End Sub
```

What this code does first is figure out the number of copies of the picture we can place on the form. For example, if the picture box was 400 twips high and the form was 4400 twips high, we can have 11 rows. (A similar calculation is made for the columns.) Next comes the crucial line,

```
Form1.PaintPicture Picture1.Picture, (J - 1)* _
Picture1.Width, (I - 1)* Picture1.Height, _
Picture1.Width
```

which paints multiple copies of the picture on the form.

Finally, the full version of PaintPicture has the following syntax (it doesn't use named parameters, unfortunately):

```
object.PaintPicture picture, x1, y1, width1, _
height1, x2, y2, width2, height2, opcode
```

The first three parameters you have already seen—they are all required. All the remaining parameters are optional. However, if you want to use an optional argument, you must specify all the optional arguments that would appear before it. (No empty commas allowed!)

The optional width1 and height1 parameters are single-precision values that let you set the width and height of the resulting picture. The optional x2 and y2 parameters let you specify single-precision values that give the left/right (x) and up/down (y) coordinates of a clipping region within the original picture. The optional width2 and height2 parameters are single-precision values that give the coordinates of a clipping region within the original picture.

The optional opcode parameter is a Long integer that is used only with bitmaps. This parameter will affect how the picture blends with whatever image was at the location. Its uses are highly specialized, so we don't cover it here.

You can flip a bitmap horizontally or vertically by using negative values for the destination height (height1) or the destination width (width1) arguments. ⊃

Z-Order: How Visual Basic Displays Work

Visual Basic paints the parts of a control or form in three layers. The back (bottom) layer is where you draw information directly on the form using the graphical methods that will be discussed later in this chapter. The middle layer contains the graphical controls (lines, shapes, picture boxes, and the image control). The top layer contains the non-graphical controls like command buttons, list boxes, and check and option buttons. Certain controls, such as labels, have a FontTransparent property that lets information from the layers below shine through.

Within each layer, you can control the order in which controls appear. For example, if you use an MDI form, you can control which one is on top after you use the Arrange method. Or, if you overlap two command buttons, you can specify which one appears on top.

You can do this in two ways. At design time, you can use the Bring To Front and Send To Back options from the Edit menu to specify the initial ordering of what's on top. To change it dynamically while the program is running, you need the ZOrder method. Its syntax is

```
[object.]ZOrder [position]
```

The position parameter can be 0 or 1. If it is 0 or omitted, the object named moves to the front. If it is 1, the object moves to the back. If you omit the object name, the current form moves to the top.

When you start adding many different components to a form, the way they overlap becomes more important. This chapter has a section on the order that Visual Basic uses to display interface elements. This section explains what happens if you draw overlapping components, which ones appear on top and how this can be changed. (It's called *Z-Order*. The Z stands for the Z-axis, the conventional way to describe depth.)

Monitoring Mouse Activity

Windows, and, therefore, Visual Basic, constantly monitors what the user is doing with the mouse. Up to this point, all you have used are the Click and Double Click events. These detect whether the user clicked the mouse once or twice in a form or control. The next few sections show you how to obtain and use more subtle information. Was a mouse button pressed? Which button was it? Is the mouse pointer over a control? Did the user release a button, and if so, which one? Did the user move the mouse out of one form and into another? Exactly where inside the form is the mouse? Visual Basic can detect all these events. Of course, as with all Visual Basic operations, you must write the event procedures that determine how Visual Basic will respond to the event.

Mouse Event Procedures

There are three fundamental mouse event procedures:

Name	Event That Caused It
MouseDown	User clicks one of the mouse buttons.
MouseUp	User releases a mouse button.
MouseMove	User moves the mouse pointer.

In many ways, these procedures are analogous to the KeyUp, KeyDown event procedures. For example, as with those event procedures, you use bit-masking to determine if the user was holding down the SHIFT, ALT, or CTRL key at the same time he or she pressed or released a mouse button.

Only forms and picture boxes return where the mouse pointer is in terms of their internal scales. For the other controls, it's necessary to calculate this information by using the scale of the surrounding container—a method that may or may not be practical.

Controls recognize a mouse event only when the mouse pointer is inside the control; the underlying form recognizes the mouse event in all other cases. However, if a mouse button is pressed and held while the mouse pointer is inside a control or form, that object captures the mouse. This means that no other Visual Basic object can react to mouse events until the user releases the mouse button, regardless of where the user moves the mouse.

All mouse event procedures take the same form and use the same parameters:

```
Object_MouseEvent(Button As Integer, Shift As _
Integer, X As Single, Y As Single)
```

If the object was part of a control array, then, as usual, there is an optional first Index parameter:

```
ObjectInControlArray_MouseEvent(Index As Integer, _
Button As Integer, Shift As Integer, X As Single, _
Y As Single)
```

As the next sections show, bit-masking lets you use the Button argument to determine which mouse button was pressed. Similarly, you can find out if the user was holding down any combination with the SHIFT, ALT, or CTRL keys by bit-masking, using the Shift parameter. Finally, X and Y give you the information you need to determine the position of the mouse pointer, using the internal coordinates of the object, if they exist (forms and picture boxes).

The MouseUp/MouseDown Events

To see this event procedure at work, start up a new project. Double-click to open the Code window and move to the MouseDown event procedure. Now enter the following:

```
Sub Form_MouseDown(Button As Integer, Shift As _
Integer, X As Single, Y As Single)
   Circle (X,Y), 75
End Sub
```

This simple event procedure uses the positioning information passed by X and Y. Each time you click a mouse button, a small circle is centered exactly where you clicked—namely, at CurrentX = X and CurrentY = Y, of size 75 twips. If you add a MouseUp event procedure that looks like

```
Sub Form_MouseUp(Button As Integer, Shift As _
Integer, X As Single, Y As Single)
   Dim CCode As Integer
   Randomize
   CCode = Int(15*Rnd)
   FillStyle = 0
   FillColor = QBColor(CCode)
   Circle (X,Y), 75
End Sub
```

then each time you release the same button, Visual Basic fills the circle with a random color. On the other hand, even though you may have two or even three mouse buttons, Visual Basic will not generate another MouseDown event until you release the original mouse button. This prevents you from filling some circles and leaving others empty when using these two procedures.

Suppose, however, you wanted to make some circles filled and some empty. One way to do this is to use the added information given by the Button argument. For example, suppose the user has a two-button mouse. You can easily write code so that pressing the correct mouse button gives the user a filled circle; pressing the wrong one gives only a colored circular outline. The Button argument uses the lowest three bits of the value of the integer, as shown here:

Button	Value of Button Argument
Left	vbLeftButton
Right	vbRightButton
Middle	vbMiddleButton

Visual Basic will tell you about only one button for the MouseUp/MouseDown combination. You cannot detect if both the left and right buttons are down simultaneously, for example. Thus, you can rewrite the MouseUp event procedure to allow both filled and empty circles using the left/right buttons:

```
Sub Form_MouseUp(Button As Integer, Shift As _
Integer, X As Single, Y As Single)
   Dim CCode As Integer
   Randomize
   CCode = Int(15*Rnd)
   Select Case Button
     Case vbLeftButton, vbMiddleButton
       Circle (X,Y), 75, QBColor(CCode)
       FillColor = &HFFFFFF&
     Case vbRightButton
       FillStyle = 0
       FillColor = QBColor(CCode)
       Circle (X,Y), 75
   End Select
End Sub
```

If you want a pop-up menu in response to a right mouse click, use a line of code like this:

```
If Button = vbRightButton Then PopUpMenu MenuName
```

You can also let the user combine the keyboard with a mouse. For example, you can have the SHIFT-right mouse button combination drop down a special menu. This uses the SHIFT argument in the MouseUp or MouseDown event procedure. Here's a table of the possible values for the lower three bits of the Shift parameter:

Action	Bit Set and Value	Symbolic Constant
SHIFT key down	Bit 0: Value = 1	VbLeftButton
CTRL key down	Bit 1: Value = 2	VbRightButton
ALT key down	Bit 2: Value = 4	VbMiddleButton
SHIFT+CTRL keys down	Bit 0 and 1: Value = 3	VbLeftButton + vbRightButton
SHIFT+ALT keys down	Bit 0 and 2: Value = 5	VbLeftButton + vbMiddleButton
CTRL+ALT keys down	Bit 1 and 2: Value = 6	VbRightButton + vbMiddleButton
SHIFT+CTRL+ALT keys down	Bits 0, 1, and 2: Value = 7	VbLeftButton + vbRightButton + vbMiddleButton

At the present time, most people seem to be writing code for the Shift key by using a Select Case statement, as follows:

```
Select Case Shift
  Case vbShiftMask
    Print "You pressed the Shift key."
  Case vbCtrlMask
    Print "You pressed the Ctrl key."
  Case vbShiftMask + vbCtrlMask
    Print "You pressed the Shift + Ctrl keys."
  Case vbAltMask
    Print "You pressed the Alt key."
```

and so on.

Microsoft suggests not using this kind of code, reserving the possibility of using the higher order bits for something else, and using the And operator to isolate the first three bits before proceeding. You can do this as follows:

```
Shift And 7
Select Case Bits
  Case vbShiftMask
    Print "You pressed the Shift key."
  Case vbCtrlMask
    Print "You pressed the Ctrl key."
  Case vbShiftMask + vbCtrlMask
    Print "You pressed the Shift + Ctrl keys."
  Case vbAltMask
    Print "You pressed the Alt key."
```

The line Shift And 7 (binary pattern of 7 = 111) eliminates any information that may eventually be contained in the higher order bits, letting the program concentrate on the information contained in the lowest three bits. You might also want to apply the same prevention against future problems for the Button argument.

The constants assign the values you'll need for the mouse events to the following global constants:

The MouseUp/MouseDown event procedures work similarly for picture boxes, the only difference being that, as you've seen, you must use the control name of the picture box (and the index if the picture box is part of a control array), as shown here:

```
Sub CntrlName_MouseDown(Button As Integer, Shift As _
Integer, X As Single, Y As Single)
```

The MouseMove Event

Visual Basic calls the MouseMove event procedure whenever the user moves the mouse. This is the most powerful of the mouse event procedures because, unlike the MouseUp/MouseDown event pair, you can use it to analyze completely the state of the mouse buttons. For this event procedure, the Button argument tells you whether some, all, or none of the mouse buttons are down.

You should not get into the habit of thinking that the MouseMove event is generated continuously as the mouse pointer moves across objects. In fact, a combination of the user's software and hardware determines how often the MouseMove event is generated. To see the MouseMove event at work, start a new project and enter the following MouseMove event procedure:

```
Sub Form_MouseMove(Button As Integer, Shift As _
Integer, X As Single, Y As Single)
    DrawWidth = 3
    PSet (X,Y)
End Sub
```

Now run the project and move your mouse around the form at different speeds. As you can see, the dots are more tightly packed when you move the mouse slowly than when you move it rapidly. This happens because Visual Basic relies on the underlying operating system to report mouse events, and such events are generated frequently but not continuously. Because the MouseMove event procedure is not called continuously, the dots are relatively sparse when the mouse is moved rapidly.

Nonetheless, since the MouseMove event procedure will be called relatively frequently, any code inside this event procedure will be executed often. For this reason, you will want to tighten the code inside the MouseMove event procedure as much as possible or provide a flag to prevent repetitive processing. For example, use integer variables for counters and do not recompute the value of variables inside this procedure unless the new value depends on the parameters for the event. Always remember that accessing object properties is much slower than using a variable.

Dragging and Dropping Operations

To move a control as you are designing the interface in your Visual Basic project, hold down a mouse button (the left one) and then move the mouse pointer to where you want the control to end up. A gray outline of the control moves with the mouse pointer. When you are happy with the location, release the mouse button. The Microsoft Windows documentation calls moving an object with the mouse button depressed *dragging* and calls the release of the mouse button *dropping*. Visual Basic makes it easy to program this potential into your projects. You can even drag and drop from one form to another if your project uses multiple forms.

Controls permit two types of dragging. These correspond to two different values of the DragMode property. The default is to not allow you to drag controls around except under special circumstances. (As always, you'll need to write the code for these special circumstances; see the next section.) This is called manual dragging, and the DragMode property will have the value of 0. Changing the value of this property to 1, automatic, means that the user may drag the control around the project. Regardless of the setting for the DragMode property, the control will actually move only if you write the code using the Move method to reposition it, as shown in the next example.

For this example, start up a new project and add a single command button to it. Set the DragMode property of that command button to 1, automatic. The event that recognizes dragging and dropping operations is called the DragDrop event, and it is associated with the control or form where the drop occurs. Thus, if you want to drag a control to a new location on a form, you write code for the form's DragDrop event procedure. For example, to allow dragging and dropping to move the single command button around the form in this example, use the following:

```
Sub UserControl1_DragDrop(Source As Control, X As _
Single, Y As Single)
   Source.Move X, Y
End Sub
```

or if you are using a standard form, the code would look like this:

```
Private Sub Form_DragDrop(Source As Control, X As _
Single, Y As Single)
   Source.Move X, Y
End Sub
```

Since the type of the Source parameter is a control, you can refer to its properties and methods by using the dot notation, as in the preceding example. If you need more information about what type of control is being dragged before applying a method or setting a property, use the If TypeOf Control Is... statement.

If you run this example, you will notice that the object remains visible in its original location while the gray outline moves. You cannot use the DragDrop event to make a control invisible while the dragging/dropping operation takes place, because this event procedure is called only after the user drops the object. In fact, the DragDrop event need not move the control at all. You often use this event to allow the user to just initiate some action. This is especially common when dragging from one form to another. The reason is that the only way a similar control can appear on a new form in Visual Basic is if you created it on another form to place an invisible control of the same type on the new form at design time, to make the control part of a control array, or to use object variables. The top left corner of the control will be placed where the mouse button was released.

To change the gray outline that Visual Basic uses during a drag operation, set the DragIcon property of the control at design time. To do this, select the DragIcon property from the Properties box. Now click the three dots to the left of the Settings box. This opens up the Load Icon dialog box for choosing icons. You can also assign the drag icon of one object to another:

```
FirstControl.DragIcon = SecondControl.DragIcon
```

The final possibility is to use the LoadPicture function. For example:

```
Control.DragIcon=LoadPicture("C\VB\ICONS\MISC\CLOCK01.ICO")
```

If you design a custom icon, a common practice is to reverse the colors for the drag icon. An Icon Editor program makes this easy to do.

The following table summarizes the events, methods, and properties used for dragging and dropping.

Item	Description
DragMode property	Allows automatic dragging (vbAutomatic) or manual dragging (vbManual)
DragIcon property	Changes from the gray rectangle to a custom icon when dragging
DragDrop event	Associated with the target of the operation; generated when the source is dropped on the target control
DragOver event	Associated with any control the source control passes over during dragging
Drag Method	Starts or stops dragging when DragMode is set to manual

Manual Dragging

If you have left the value of the DragMode property at its default value of zero, then you must use the Drag method to allow dragging of the control. The syntax for this method is

```
Control.Drag TypeOfAction
```

The TypeOfAction is an integer value from 0 to 2, as shown here:

```
Control.Drag vbCancel 0          Cancel dragging
Control.Drag vbBeginDrag 1       Begin dragging
Control.Drag vbEndDrag 2         Drop the control
```

If you omit the TypeOfAction argument, the method has the same effect as the statement Control.Drag 1. That is, Visual Basic initiates the dragging operation for the control.

One way to use the flexibility this method gives you is to allow expert users to drag and drop controls, but make the default that users cannot do this. For example, use the CTRL+MouseDown combination to allow dragging to take place. You can do this by beginning the MouseDown event procedure with the following:

```
Sub CntrlName_MouseDown(Button As Integer, Shift As _
Integer, X As Single, Y As Single)
   If (Shift And 7) = vbCtrlMask Then
     CntrlName.DragMode = vbAutomatic
   .
   .
   .
End Sub
```

Another example of where you might want to use this method is in self-running demonstration programs. You can use a value of 1 to start the dragging operation and a value of 2 to drop the control. This lets you show off dragging and dropping operations.

The DragOver Event

All Visual Basic objects, except menus and timers, will detect if a control is passing over them. You can use the DragOver event to allow even greater flexibility for your projects. This event lets you monitor the path a control takes while being dragged. You might consider changing the background color of the control being passed over. The event procedure template for forms is

```
Sub Form_DragOver(Source As Control, X As Single, Y _
As Single, State As Integer)
    .
    .
    .
End Sub
```

For controls, this event procedure template takes the form

```
Sub CtrlName_DragOver([Index As Integer,]Source As _
Control, X As Single, Y As Single, State As Integer)
    .
    .
    .
End Sub
```

As usual, the optional Index parameter is used if the control is part of a control array. The Source is the control being dragged, but the event procedure is associated with the control being passed over. The X and Y parameters give you the CurrentX and CurrentY values in terms of the scale of the object being passed over for forms and picture boxes and the underlying form for all other controls. The State parameter has three possible values:

Value of State Parameter	Description
VbEnter 0	Source is now inside target.
VbLeave 1	Source is outside the target.
VbOver 2	Source moved inside target.

An Example: A Circular Command Button

We want to put everything you have seen so far about pixel graphics and mouse detection to work by showing you how to build a "circular" command button. To make it simple, we'll simply use a solid red circle.

The way this button works is:

1. The user control form contains a red circle.
2. Using the MouseUp event, we determine if the user clicks inside the circular area.
3. Then we raise the Click event for the control.

Actually, the hard part of programming this control is remembering the tiny bit of math that is needed to check that the user clicks inside the circle. To make the math a little easier, we use a custom scale method that puts the center of the user control at coordinates (0, 0). To do this, we use the following Scale statement:

```
Scale (-ScaleWidth / 2, ScaleHeight / 2)-(ScaleWidth _
/ 2, -ScaleHeight / 2)
```

The idea is that the usual scale of a form runs from 0 to ScaleWidth and 0 to ScaleHeight. We make it more symmetrical by moving half the units to their negatives. Next, we need a little geometry (sorry!). Geometry tells us if all the points inside a circle of radius r satisfy the equation:

```
x*x + y*y <= r*r
```

We use the x and y parameters of the MouseUp event to check that this condition is true. This is summarized in Figure 6-6, shown on the next page.

While the whole code is on the CD in the CH6 directory (CircleButton.vbp), here is what you'll need to follow along. First, set the AutoRedraw property of the control to True so the user of the control can see our red circle all the time. Next, we have the module level declarations for one variable and the custom Click event:

```
Private mRadius As Single 'for the radius
Public Event Click()
```

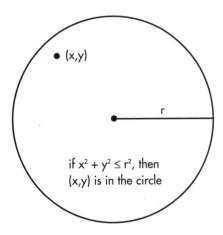

Figure 6-6
Designing a circular button

Here is the code in the MouseUp event that uses the algebraic test described above to test where the button was clicked.

```
Private Sub UserControl_MouseUp(Button As Integer,_
Shift As Integer, X As Single, Y As Single)
   Scale (-ScaleWidth / 2, ScaleHeight / 2)- _
(ScaleWidth / 2, -ScaleHeight / 2)
   If Button = vbLeftButton And (X * X + Y * Y _
<=mRadius * mRadius) Then RaiseEvent Click
End Sub
```

 There is actually a faster way to do this kind of checking for where you are in a graphic, in our case, assuming the color of the circle is different than the color of the rest of the user control. (This is a natural assumption but you can check for this in code, of course.) Simply check the color at the point (X,Y) using the built-in Point method. ⊃

Finally, we need the code to make sure we keep a circle when the user resizes the control at design time. This must be placed in the Resize event of the control. We use a bare Scale command in order to set the scale mode back to the default scale before recalculating the scale of the circle:

```
Private Sub UserControl_Resize()
  Scale 'reset scale back
  Cls
  FillColor = vbRed
  FillStyle = vbSolid
  If ScaleHeight < ScaleWidth Then
    mRadius = ScaleHeight / 2
  Else
    mRadius = ScaleWidth / 2
  End If
  Scale (-ScaleWidth / 2, ScaleHeight / 2)- _
(ScaleWidth / 2, -ScaleHeight / 2)
  Circle (0, 0), mRadius
End Sub
```

 Because of how VB draws circles, you might want to slightly reduce the value of the mRadius variable to, say, 0.98 of its current value. This will help prevent the circle from looking flattened. ⊃

To test the control, you can add a new project and use code like this:

```
Private Sub UserControl1_Click()
  MsgBox "You clicked in the circle"
End Sub
```

If you did everything right, then you'll see the message box only if you click inside the circle.

 The version of this control on the CD adds a shading feature to the perimeter of the circle so the circle looks pressed in when you click it. ⊃

Chapter 7

You are probably comfortable with manipulating most of the Control Creation Edition's built-in objects. The version of the VB5 language that underlies the CCE is far more object oriented than earlier versions of VB. Creating a control is one way of using new, general, techniques built into the VB language for creating and manipulating objects. To go further with the CCE, you need to go beyond the "point and shoot" object manipulation techniques that you have seen so far.

Also, it is worth keeping in mind that Object-Oriented Programming (or OOP) seems to be well on its way to becoming the dominant programming paradigm. OOP is rapidly replacing the structured programming techniques developed in the early '70s. However, if you haven't worked with OOP before, you are probably wondering why so many people are convinced that the change is worthwhile—or even necessary. This chapter will help to answer that question.

Since there is a fair amount of terminology needed to make sense of OOP, you'll start by learning some concepts and definitions. After this, you'll see how the CCE implements its version of OOP. This will let you get started on more sophisticated ways to create your own objects including (at the beginning of the next chapter) adding properties to the simple controls you have seen so far.

Even the most experienced VB programmers might want to think about shifting to a more object-oriented approach to VB. You won't be able to take charge of the control creation process as long as you stick to this older way of thinking.

Objects

Introduction to OOP

Here's a question that seems to have nothing to do with programming: How did companies like Compaq, Dell, Gateway, Micron Technologies, and the other major personal computer manufacturers get so big, so fast? Most people would probably say they made good computers and sold them at rock-bottom prices in an era when computer demand was skyrocketing. But dig a little deeper—how were they able to this? How could they manufacture so many models so fast and respond to the changes that were happening so quickly?

Well, a big part of the answer is that these companies farmed out a lot of the work. They bought components from reputable vendors and then assembled them. They almost never invested time and money in designing and building power supplies, disk drives, motherboards, and other components. In a nutshell, what the personal computer manufacturers were doing was buying "prepackaged functionality." When they bought a power supply, they were buying something with certain properties (size, shape, and so on) and a certain functionality (smooth power output, amount of power available, and so on). Compaq showed the power of this approach; when they moved from engineering all of the parts in their machines to buying many of the parts, they dramatically improved their bottom line. Their stock has gone up more than 10 times since they made the changeover.

OOP springs from the same idea. Your program is made up of objects, with certain properties of the objects and certain operations that the objects can perform. The current state of an object may change over time, but you always depend on the objects in your program to not interact with each other in undocumented ways. Whether you build an object or buy it might depend on your budget or on the time you have available. But, basically, as long as the objects satisfy your specifications as to what they can do and how they respond to outside stimuli, you don't much care how the functionality is implemented. In OOP-speak, you say you only care about what the objects *expose*. So, just as PC manufacturers don't care about the internals of a power supply as long as it does what they want, the users of your control won't care how the control is implemented as long as it does what they want it to.

The key to being most productive in OOP is to make each object responsible for carrying out a small set of related tasks. (To do this successfully also means that the object has to be responsible for maintaining information about its internal data.) If an object needs to do something that isn't its responsibility, it needs to have access to an object which can do that task. The first object then asks the second object to carry out the task using a more generalized version of the function and procedures that you are familiar with from procedural programming. (You have seen a lot of these generalized function calls at work already—they are nothing more than the methods or properties of a control.) In OOP jargon, what people say is that client objects are supposed to send *messages* to server objects.

How the term *messages* is used in OOP is only distantly related to the way the term "messages" is used in Windows programming. For example, the "message" used for API functions such as SendMessage that communicate between the windows in your programs is not an OOP-like message. ⊃

The standard joke to check whether you really understand OOP's way of thinking is the following: Question: How many OOP programmers does it take to change a light bulb? Answer: none, a properly OOP-designed light bulb would accept a ChangeBulb message. ⊃

In particular, an object should never directly manipulate the internal data of another object. All communication between objects should only be done via messages. By designing your objects to handle a certain set of appropriate messages and then leaving them to manipulate their internal data, you maximize reusability and minimize debugging time. In the CCE, this means you create objects that can be manipulated only by changing properties or calling methods. No public variables should be inside the CCE controls you create.

Just as with modules in a procedure-oriented language, you will not want an individual object to do too much. Both design and debugging are simplified when you build small objects that perform a few tasks, rather than overly complicated objects with complex internal data that need hundreds of properties and methods to manipulate them.

The Vocabulary of OOP

The most important OOP term is *class*. A class is usually described as the template or blueprint from which the object will be made. Each object is said to be an *instance* of the class. This idea leads to the standard way of thinking about classes: as cookie cutters. Objects are the cookies. The dough, in the form of memory, will need to be allocated as well. The CCE is pretty good about hiding this "dough preparation" step from you. As you will soon see, you simply use the New keyword to obtain memory. (At some point, the analogy breaks down: you usually have to reclaim the memory for reuse—you'll see how to do this later as well.)

 When you create an object from a class, the terminology used is to say that you have created an *instance* of the class or *instantiated* an object of that class type. ↄ

Encapsulation

Encapsulation is the key concept in working with objects in all versions of OOP—including the one in the CCE. Formally, encapsulation is nothing more than combining data and behavior in one package and hiding how the data is implemented from the user of the object. As mentioned above, the data in an object are usually called its member variables, instance variables, or instance fields. It is the implementation of this internal data that you keep hidden from the user of the object. Note that an object that is an instance of a class will have certain values for its instance fields. These values define its current state. On the other hand:

- The functions and procedures in a CCE class correspond to the object's methods and properties.
- Only by using these methods and properties should the user gain access to the object's current state (i.e, its instance fields).

It cannot be stressed enough that the key to making encapsulation work is to make sure that the other parts of your programs can never access the instance variables (fields) in a class. Programs should interact with this data only through the objects properties and methods. Encapsulation requires this. Keeping data private is the only way to give an object its "black box" behavior (or *data hiding*, as it is sometimes called). Data hiding is critical to reuse and reliability. ⊃

Inheritance

Traditionally, in OOP, when you write your own classes, another tenet of OOP can make this easier: classes in many OOP languages can be built on other classes. OOP terminology says that a class that builds on another class *extends* it. The general concept of extending a base (or *parent*) class is called *inheritance*. The inheritance relationship denotes specialization. In traditional OOP, if a class A extends class B, class A inherits methods from (hence, extends) class B, but has more capabilities. What this means is that the extended class starts out with all the properties of its parent. You then pick and choose which methods of the parent class to override by changing their behavior. In addition to overriding existing methods of the parent to give them new functionality, you can even introduce new methods in your child objects that have no relation to the methods contained in the parent.

The CCE does not support inheritance in the classic OOP sense. (Actually, it is not just the CCE; any language that uses VBA 5.0 will not support classic style OOP inheritance.) However, when you create a control from an existing control, the process gives the *appearance* of using inheritance. One would think that an IntegerTextBox inherits from an ordinary TextBox. But, under the hood in the CCE, there is no parent-child relationship between the two.

The reason that the designers of the VBA language that underlies the CCE did not want to include the more usual OOP version of inheritance is that there is always a tension between inheritance and encapsulation. If Object B inherits all the properties of Object A and you change Object A, you may inadvertently break B's functionality. (This is sometimes called the problem of the fragile base class.) ⊃

231

The CCE gets around the fragile base class problem when using inheritance by using a concept called an *interface.* As you will see below, interfaces give you most, if not all, of the functionality you want out of inheritance without risking the problem of fragile base classes. Of course, nothing is free; as you will see in the next few chapters, using interfaces require more coding than would using classic OOP inheritance. Luckily, the CCE comes with a Control Interface Wizard (see Chapter 9) that does much of the routine coding that the CCE's interfaces require.

Sometimes using inheritance is called *subclassing*. Purists, therefore, do not like it when people use the word subclassing for the process of creating a new control out of an existing one in the CCE because the CCE doesn't support inheritance. We aren't purists. ➲

Polymorphism

Traditionally, polymorphism (from the Greek "many faces") means that inherited objects know what methods they should use depending on where they are in the inheritance chain. For example, when a motorcycle and a car (both inheriting from an abstract "Vehicle" class) get a "right turn" method they would use different methods to accomplish this task.

For a more serious example, suppose you are designing an object-oriented program for dealing with payroll and similar issues in your business. When you have an OOP language that allows inheritance, you would start with an Employee class and specialize this to get Manager, Executive, and so on. Classes like Manager would inherit from an Employee class. (They certainly share many properties such as having a hire date, a social security number, and so on.) The Employee parent class and, therefore, the Manager class both have a method for changing the salary of their instances. But things being the way they are, the RaiseSalary method probably works differently for Manager objects than Employee objects. The way polymorphism would work in this classic situation is that an Employee object would know if it was a plain old employee or really a manager. When it got the word to use the RaiseSalary method,

- If it were a manager, it would call the RaiseSalary method in the Manager class rather than the one in the Employee class.
- Otherwise, it would use the usual RaiseSalary method.

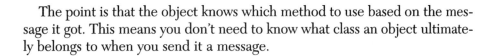

The point is that the object knows which method to use based on the message it got. This means you don't need to know what class an object ultimately belongs to when you send it a message.

How Visual Basic Deals With Polymorphism: Interfaces

Of course, Visual Basic and, hence, the CCE do not have inheritance so polymorphism works a little differently than the classic version just described. However, the last sentence of the previous section remains the key:

You don't need to know what class an object belongs to when you send it a message. All you need to know is the name of the message and its parameters.

(The name and parameters of a method is usually called its *signature*.)

What the CCE does is to use the notion of *interface* to implement this key part of polymorphism. An interface is nothing more than a contract between the class and the user of the class that says: "I have a method with this signature; if you call me and pass me the name and the parameters indicated in the methods signature, I will use my version of the method and you won't have to worry."

One advantage to interfaces is that they make talking to your control possible in an efficient manner. If you call a method to change a property of a control, Visual Basic can find out at compile time (*early bind* is the technical term) what code to call in your control. This works at compile time roughly as follows:

1. Visual Basic looks to see if your object says it supports the method in one of its interfaces. (*Implements* is the term for supporting an interface.)

2. If your object does expose this method in one of its interfaces, then at compile time, Visual Basic looks in the code for the object and generates code that says "Go to this method."

Now, compare this to what happens if you don't give your objects an interface that makes a contract that you will support a method.

1. Since your code hasn't promised it will support the method, at compile time Visual Basic is smart enough to not go looking for what may or may not be there yet.

2. So, at compile time, Visual Basic generates a lot more code. This code politely asks the object if it supports the method with the signature you specified and would it mind running the method if it does?

This kind of code has two features that make it slower to execute:

1. It needs error trapping in case you were wrong, and
2. In any case, since you can't know where to "jump" to the location of the method inside the object, you have to rely on the object to send you the information at run time.

(By the way, this whole process is called *late binding* and is many times slower than early binding.)

Another advantage of the interface approach is that objects that support interfaces can make multiple contracts—support multiple interfaces—without the complexity of managing multiple inheritance chains (one of the real pains in C++!).

Finally, when you use the CCE, the interfaces needed for the users of your control are created for you automatically. The CCE hides the required OCX interface code so you probably don't have to worry about interfaces when you are creating a control.

How to Objectify Your Programs

In the traditional "structured" procedure-oriented programming, you identify what needs to be done and then you either

1. Break the task to be accomplished into subtasks, and these into smaller subtasks, until the subtasks are simple enough to be implemented directly (this is the *top-down approach*); or
2. Write procedures to solve simple tasks and combine them into more sophisticated procedures, until you have the functionality you want (this is the *bottom-up approach*).

Most programmers, of course, use a mixture of the top-down and bottom-up strategies to solve a programming problem. The usual way for discovering procedures turns out to be pretty much the same as the rule for finding methods in OOP: Look for verbs, or actions, in the problem description. There are two important differences between OOP and procedure-oriented programming.

1. In OOP, you first isolate the classes in the project. Only then do you look for the methods of the class.
2. Each method is associated with the class that is responsible for carrying out the operation, and methods do not exist independently of a class.

So, the obvious question is: How do we find the classes?

A good rule of thumb is that classes are the nouns in your analysis of the problem. The methods in your objects correspond to verbs that the noun does. The properties are the adjectives that describe the noun. ⊃

Of course, the "noun-verb-adjective" correspondence to classes, methods and properties is only a first step. Only experience can help you decide which nouns, verbs and adjectives are the important ones when building classes and controls in the CCE.

For example, suppose you want to design a program to manage your checking account using an object-oriented approach. Some nouns are:

- Accounts
- Checks
- Check registers
- Deposit Slips

These nouns may lead to the classes Account, Check, CheckRegister, DepositSlip, and so on. Next, look for verbs. Accounts need to be opened or closed. Checks need to be added to the register. The check register needs to reconciled. Deposit slips need to be totaled. With each verb, such as "add," "reconcile," and "total," you have to identify the one object that has the major responsibility for carrying it out. For example, the deposit slip has the major responsibility for totaling itself up. Thus, Total should be a method of the DepositSlip class.

Summarizing Class Relationships

In traditional OOP, there are three common relationships between classes:

- use
- containment ("has—a")
- inheritance ("is—a")

The *use* relationship is the most obvious and also the most general. For example, the CheckRegister class uses the Account class, since a check register needs to know what account it is working with. But the DepositSlip class does not use the Check class, since deposit slips have nothing to do with checks. Thus, a class uses another class if it manipulates objects of that class. More generally, a class A uses a class B if:

- a method or property of A sends a message to an object of class B,

or

- a method or property of A creates, receives, or returns objects of class B.

Try to minimize the number of classes that use each other. The point is, if a class A is unaware of the existence of a class B, it doesn't care about any changes to B. (And this means that changes to B do not introduce bugs into A!) ⊃

The *containment* relationship is easy to understand; for example, a CheckRegister object could contain Check and DepositSlip objects. Containment simply means that instances of class A contain objects of class B. Of course, containment is a special case of use; if an A object contains a B object, then at least one method of the class A will make use of that object of class B type.

Finally, the third relationship, inheritance, was described above. Since it isn't really used in the CCE, we wont say anything more about it. Instead, you should think of a fourth relationship to add to the classic three; let's call it "supports a." This corresponds to Visual Basic's notion of an interface.

Documenting relationships between classes for doing OOP programming is so important that a whole industry has sprung up to make diagrams to show the relationships. Figure 7-1 shows a diagram for an order-taking system using the Booch-Rumbaugh unified notation. We won't bother with these diagrams here. ⊃

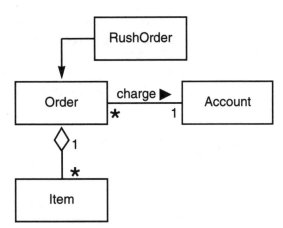

Figure 7-1
A class diagram

What About Individual Objects?

Suppose you have decided on the classes in your project and will soon be working with objects that are specific instances of each class. The key to working with a specific object in OOP is to identify the "three whats" of an object. The three key questions to ask yourself are:

1. What is the object's behavior?
2. What is the object's state?
3. What is the object's identity?

In particular, all objects that are instances of the same class share a family resemblance by behaving the same. (As we said before, in OOP-speak, the behavior of an object is defined by the messages it accepts; in the CCE, this means by the object's methods and properties.)

Next, each object stores information about what it currently looks like and how it got that way. This is what is usually called the object's *state*. An object's state isn't fixed, but any change in the state of an object must be because of messages that were sent to the object.

However, the state of an object does not completely describe it. Each object also has a distinct *identity*. This means that despite two objects appearing to be in the same state and looking, feeling and reacting the same, they are still different objects. In the CCE, the identity of an object is usually visible through the object's Name property unless it is part of a control array (see later in the chapter). For example, each command button on a form is different though they may look and work the same, and even have the same event procedures with identical code.

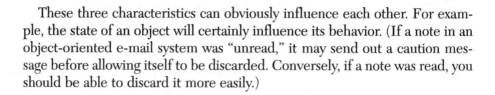

These three characteristics can obviously influence each other. For example, the state of an object will certainly influence its behavior. (If a note in an object-oriented e-mail system was "unread," it may send out a caution message before allowing itself to be discarded. Conversely, if a note was read, you should be able to discard it more easily.)

Advantages To OOP

For small problems, the breakdown into procedures used in structured programming works very well. But for larger problems, the OOP approach that leads to classes and their associated methods and properties has the advantage that classes provide a way to group—convenient clustering mechanism for methods and properties. A simple Web browser may require 2,000 functions for its implementation, or it may require 100 classes with an average of 20 methods and properties per class. A single class that is this simple and its relationship to other classes is much easier to grasp by the programmer. Similarly, the relationships between classes is also easier to handle if the classes themselves are not overly complex. (OOP is also ideal for projects that involve teams of or to handle by teams of programmers since the classes make a natural way to decompose the problem.) In this case, The encapsulation that is built into OOP classes helps you as well. You don't have to worry about data contamination since classes hide their data representations from all code except their own properties and methods.

You may be thinking that encapsulation isn't any different than *modularization*. It really isn't: modules that communicate with each other through procedure calls only, not by sharing data, also hide data implementations from the user of the module. ⊃

There is another advantage that classes have over modules: classes are factories for producing multiple objects with the same behavior. You have seen this at work repeatedly: you can make multiple instances of a control easily once it is on the toolbox. In procedure-oriented programming, you cannot easily get multiple copies of a useful module. You can add a module to your program once, but without some code changes, that's it.

Manipulating Objects Built into Visual Basic

The key to working with objects in Visual Basic is variables of the special object type. For example, when you use the Me keyword to refer to the current object, you are using an object variable. There are also special variables for various system objects. Short descriptions of them follow:

The application object (App is its name) encapsulates lots of information about the currently running application. For example, `App.Path` is the current applications path, `App.HelpFile` is the filename of the help file associated to your application, and so on. The Debug object refers to the Immediate window. You'll see more about this in Chapter 12. The Printer object lets you access the currently selected printer. You can use statements like `Printer.Print` to print, or `Printer.Font.Size = 18` to change the size of the font in the Printer. `Printer.Fonts` returns an array that gives you the names of the fonts supported by your printer.

In general, you declare an object variable with the same Dim, Private, Public, Static, keywords that you've already seen. Thus, you can have local, form level, or public (global) object variables. Microsoft suggests using an appropriate 3-letter prefix for object variables. Here are some examples:

```
Dim frmHelpForm As Form
Dim txtTextInfoBox As TextBox
Public cmdOKButton As CommandButton
```

Generally, the name to use for an object variable of a given control type is the name you see in the top of the Properties window. For user controls, it is the value of the Name property you give the control at design time (which is yet another reason not to leave it at the default value of UserControl1).

There are a few general types of object variables for use in situations where you need to refer to objects of many different types. For example:

```
Dim ctlAnyControl As Control
```

gives you a way to refer to any control. Similarly,

```
Dim objVeryGeneral As Object
```

Finally, objects can also be stored in a variable declared to be of Variant data type.

```
Dim anyThing As Variant
```

239

Set

When you want to make an object variable refer to a specific object of that type in your CCE code, use the Set keyword. For example, if your project had a command button named Command1, your code would look like this:

```
Set cmdAButton = Command1
```

In particular, you cannot use an assignment statement to make an object variable equal to, say, a text box. Code like this:

```
Dim txtNoGood As TextBox
txtNoGood = Text1
```

will simply give you an error message.

The Set command can also be used to simplify lengthy control references. Here's an example:

```
Set fntInner = frmHelp.picInfo.Font
```

Now you can write

```
fntInner.Size = 18
```

instead of

```
frmHelp.picInfo.Font.Size = 18
```

 It is important to note that the Set command does not make a copy of the object, as an ordinary assignment statement would. Instead, the Set command points the object variable to the other object; therefore, you can occasionally cause bugs without being aware of them. If you change a property of an object variable that is Set to another object, the property of the original object changes as well. For example, if you use:

```
Set frmMain.Font = txtLastName.Font
```

then executing

```
txtLastName.Font.Size = 18
```

will also change the font size of frmMain because they both point to (share) the same font object. ⊃

 Always use the most specific object variable you can find when using Set. Your programs will run faster as a result. ⊃

For example, code with this statement

```
Dim txtFoo As TextBox
Set txtFoo = Text1
```

will always run faster than

```
Dim ctlFoo As Control
Set ctlFoo = Text1
```

which, in turn, will always run faster than

```
Dim objFoo As Object
Set objFoo = Text1
```
* p239

In particular, when you use variant variables to hold objects instead of object variables, this slows your program down the most (and probably makes it harder to debug). ꓚ

The Is Keyword

You can use the Is keyword in an If-Then to test if two object variables refer to (have been Set to) the same object. Suppose FirstControl and SecondControl are two control object variables. A line of code like

```
If FirstControl Is SecondControl Then
```

lets you test whether these object variables refer to the same object. (It is a wise programmer who always checks if changing the properties of one object variable will also, perhaps inadvertently, change the properties of another object!)

Manipulating Objects via Code

It is quite common to need a general procedure that manipulates properties of forms or controls or even the forms and controls themselves. First, properties of forms and controls can only be passed by value. For example, consider the following simple Sub procedure:

```
Sub ChangeText (ByVal X As String, Y As String) Y = X
End Sub
```

If you call it using the following code:

```
Call ChangeText(Form1.Caption, Y$)
```

then the current value of Y$ is the new caption for Form1.

If you set the Tag property of the form or control to contain information otherwise not available at run time, you can write a general procedure using this technique to analyze the Tag property. This lets you find out information about the control that would otherwise not be available at run time. ⊃

On the other hand, you will often want to affect the properties of a form or control by using a general procedure. For this, you have to pass the form or control as a parameter by reference. To do this, declare the argument to the procedure to be of one of the object types. (You could use variants, too, of course, but this should be avoided unless absolutely necessary because it is slower and creates harder-to-debug code.)

If you often find yourself writing code to center a form on the screen, why not use the following general procedure?

```
Public Sub CenterForm(AForm As Form)
  AForm.Move (Screen.Width - AForm.Width)/2, _
  (Screen.Height - AForm.Height)/2
End Sub
```

Then, whenever you are in a procedure attached to a specific form, you can simply say

```
CenterForm Me
```

to center the form on the screen. (You could also think about making CenterForm a custom property of a form—see later in the chapter for more on this.)

Similarly, you can have a Sub or Function procedure that affects a property of a control. A first approximation to a general procedure to change the caption on a control might look like this:

```
Sub ChangeCaption (X As Control, Y As String)
  X.Caption = Y
End Sub
```

Notice that this procedure used the general Control type. However, suppose you tried to use this procedure in the form of

```
Call ChangeCaption(Text1, "New text")
```

where Text1 was the name of a text box. Then Visual Basic would give you a run-time error because text boxes do not have a Caption property.

There are two ways around this. The simplest, as far as code goes, is to use the On Error Resume Next statement, as in the following:

```
Sub ChangeCaption (X As Control, Y As String)
  On Error Resume Next
  X.Caption = Y
End Sub
```

However, this kind of code requires being sure that no other error is being inadvertently handled. (In a one-line procedure, this is a good bet—in a more complicated procedure, you might have to be more careful.)

For this reason, it is sometimes preferable to use a variant on the If-Then-Else loop. This allows you to determine what type of control is being manipulated in the code. (This construct has many other uses.) In our situation, the code would take the form:

```
If TypeOf Control Is ControlType Then
  .
  .Else
  .   .
End If
```

where the ControlType parameter is the same as that used in declaring an object variable (Form, Label, TextBox, and so on).

For example, if all you wanted to do was work with Text boxes, and all the other controls you wanted to change did have caption properties, you could use

```
Sub ChangeCaptionOrText (X As Control, Y As String)
  If TypeOf X Is TextBox Then
    X.Text = Y
  Else
    X.Caption = Y
  End If
End Sub
```

You cannot use the keyword Not in this type of control structure, so you will often find yourself using an empty If clause. For example, if you wanted to play it safer:

```
Sub ChangeCaption (X As Control, Y As String)
  If TypeOf X Is TextBox Then
    '  Do Nothing
  Else
    X.Caption = Y
  End If
End Sub
```

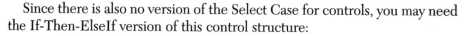
Since there is also no version of the Select Case for controls, you may need the If-Then-ElseIf version of this control structure:

```
If TypeOf X Is...Then
 .  .
ElseIf TypeOf X Is...Then
 .
ElseIf TypeOf X Is...Then
 .
Else
 .. .
End If
```

Creating New Objects at Run Time

You can build classes three ways for object creation in Visual Basic. One is by adding custom properties and events to an existing form. Then, you can use that form as a class (template) for new instances of the form. Each new instance of the form will have the new properties you added.

The second method is by creating a special type of module called a Class module. Class modules are not visual. Class modules have the advantage that, if you have access to a full version of Visual Basic, they can be compiled separately and used by other Windows applications as a convenient library of code. Think of class modules as being something like non-visual controls. Since they have a smaller footprint, you may want to add them to a user control to provide the functionality needed for the control, rather than using a non-visual embedded additional user control.

For example, Visual Basic (and, hence, the CCE) has no convenient way to deal with the individual bits of a value except by writing the masking functions as needed. It makes sense to encapsulate the functionality of a bit-twiddling into a class module. (See this example later in this chapter for how to do this. See the next chapter for how to convert it into a control.)

 If all you have is the CCE, one could make a good argument that you are best off making any class module into a non-visible OCX. We decided to include this material here because the techniques are certain to be of use if you decide to move on to a fuller version of Visual Basic. ⊃

In general, a Class module object contains the code for the custom properties, methods and events that objects created from it will have. Each Class module you create gives you, naturally enough, a single class (template) for building new instances of that class. You can then create new instances of the class via code that belongs to any other code module or form in your project. However, you can have as many Class modules in a project as you like (subject only to operating system constraints, of course), and Class modules can be added both to user control projects and Standard EXE projects.

The third method is to build a user control. In this chapter, we discuss the first two situations and leave user controls to their own chapter. After all, this is a book on the CCE; an in-depth look at user control creation would seem in order. (Besides, creating properties for user controls is a little trickier to code because user controls can exist in so many states. Think of it this way: at the very least, the control has to distinguish between the design time of the test form and the run time of the test form. We will leave these questions and more to the next chapter.)

The Form as a Class

The first case we want to show you of creating a new object at run time is when you want to use the form you designed as a template to create new instances of itself. The form may or may not contain controls on it. Once you create these new instances of your original form, they exist independently. Changing any property of a new instance of your original form has no effect on the original form.

For example, a word processing program might want to be able to create identical windows for use by different documents. More generally, when one has an MDI (multiple document interface application), your "child" windows will often need to be cut from the same cookie cutter (although, over time, their contents will almost surely diverge).

Assume you have a form named Form1 in your project already. Then the statements

```
Dim frmAnotherInstance As Form1
Set frmAnotherInstance = New Form1
```

create a new instance of Form1. You can also combine the two statements into one:

```
Dim frmAnotherInstance As New Form1
```

but most people find the two-statement version clearer and easier to understand.

This new instance starts out with the same properties as the original Form1 at the time the code is executed. In particular, it will have copies of all the controls that were on Form1 in exactly the same places. However, a new form instance isn't yet visible. To make it visible, you have to use the Show method. Then, you have to move it away from its parent form using the Move method or changing a property like Left or Top. For example,

```
Dim frmAForm As New Form1
Dim frmBForm As New Form1
frmFirstForm.Show
frmSecondForm.Show
frmFirstForm.Move Left - 199, Top + 100
frmSecondForm.Move Left - 399, Top + 200
```

shows two copies of the original Form1. The locations are determined by the value of the Left and Top properties of the original Form1. (We needed to use the Move method to prevent the child forms from stacking one on another because instances inherit all the properties of their parent—including their initial location properties.)

 You do not use the New keyword to create new controls. Only Forms in the CCE are classes (templates for new objects). (To see the method for creating new controls at run time in the CCE, see the section on "Control Arrays" later in the chapter.) ⊃

One final point: creating a new instance of a Form at run time via a call to New is completely different than adding another form to a project at design time and then using Load or Show to bring the second form into memory. Every form you add at design time is a new cookie cutter. When you use the New keyword to create a new one, you are stamping out the form cookies. In this case, the new form is an instance of what you made it look like at design time. When you create another instance of a form using New, you have *cloned* an object at run time.

Adding Properties and Events to Forms

You use the same ideas for adding properties to all three ways of creating classes in the CCE, although the terminology is confusing at first. However, if you think about it the right way, the terminology actually makes sense. Let's start off with the obvious question: what are the most basic things you will want to be able to do with a new property?

- Get its current value.
- Assign a new value to it.

For the first situation, you use a special type of procedure called a Property Get procedure. For the second, you use a Property Let procedure (or a Property Set procedure, if the value is itself an object).

 One good way to remember the distinction between Property Gets and Property Lets is that a Let statement will let you make an assignment in Visual Basic and, hence, in the CCE, so it is natural to use it for assigning to properties. ⊃

For example, suppose you want to add a custom property to a form that will tell you whether a form name is centered. Also, you want setting this property to be True to automatically center the form. Here's what you need to do. Set up a Private variable in the declarations section of the form to enforce encapsulation.

```
Private CheckCentered As Boolean
```

Then add the following property procedures to the form:

```
Public Property Let CenterForm(X As Boolean)
    CheckCentered = X 'get the current state of the
                      'property
    If X then
        Me.Move (Screen.Width - Me.Width)/2, _
        Screen.Height - Me.Height)/2
    End If
End Sub
```

The first line of code uses the Private variable to store the current value of the property. Now you can use a line of code like

```
Me.CenterForm = True
```

to center the form (or any instance of it). From another form or code module, you can use a line of code like

```
CustomForm.CenterForm = True
```

to center the form named CustomForm.

Of course, it might be useful to know if a form is centered. For this, we need to use a Property Get procedure that returns a Boolean:

```
Public Property Get CenterForm() As Boolean
    CenterForm = CheckCentered
End Sub
```

The one line of code in this procedure uses the current value of the CheckCentered (Private) Boolean variable that we are using to hold the information about the current value of the property and assigns it as the value of the Property Get procedure. (Property Get procedures are similar to Function procedures in that you assign a value to them inside the body of the property procedure.)

You may be wondering: Why all this bother? Why not query or assign the variable CheckCentered directly? The point is that you are trying to give objects as much "black box" behavior as you can. You would not want another object in your project to query the CheckCentered instance variable directly. Since, in our example, it was declared Private, you couldn't. Making the CheckCentered variable Public to let someone query the instance variable directly to check if a form is centered defeats encapsulation. At the risk of sounding overly-repetitive: never use Public variables for property access. ⊃

General property procedures

Property Let and Property Get procedures work in tandem, as do Property Set and Property Get. The value returned by the Property Get procedure is of the same type as the one used in the assignment for the Property Let or Set. In general, the number of arguments for a Property Get is also one less than that of the corresponding Property Let or Set. The difference between Let and Set is explained later. (The last argument is the one that will be changed.) A Property Get procedure that you write without a corresponding Property Let procedure gives you a read-only property, since you have no way to change it.

The full syntax for a Property Let procedure template looks like this:

```
[Public | Private][Friend] [Static] Property Let
     name [(arglist)]
     [statements]
     [name = expression]
     [Exit Property]   if need be
End Property
```

- Use Public to make the Property Let procedure accessible to every procedure in every module.

- Use Private to make the Property Let procedure accessible only to other procedures in the form, class module or user control where it is declared.

- Use the new Friend keyword to make the property available to any part of the project.

The other Visual Basic keywords work as they would in any procedure. Use the Static keyword if you need all the Property Let procedure's local variables preserved between uses. The Exit Property keywords give you a way to immediately exit from a Property Let procedure, and so on. The name of the Property Let procedure must follow standard procedure naming conventions, except that the name will be the same as the corresponding Property Get or Property Set procedure in the same module.

The full syntax for a Property Get procedure template looks like this:

```
[Public | Private][Friend][Static] Property Get name _
[(arglist)][As type]
    [statements]
    [name = expression]
    [Exit Property]   if need be
End Property
```

The name and type of each argument in a Property Get procedure must be the same as the corresponding arguments in the corresponding Property Let procedure, if it exists. The type of the value returned by a Property Get procedure must be the same data type as the last argument in the corresponding Property Let procedure, if it exists. See the OptionCaption property in the sample code for Chapter 17 for an example of this. ⊃

The last type of Property procedure is the Property Set statement. Its syntax is:

```
[Public | Private][Friend] [Static] Property Set
name [(arglist)]
  [statements]
  [Exit Property]
  [statements]
End Property
```

This is used when the value you are setting is an object itself. For example, if you wanted to add a custom Font property, you would need a Property Set because Font is itself a Visual Basic object.

Adding Events to a Form Instance

Just as you can add custom properties to forms, you can add custom events to a form class and then create a new instance of the form that will expose that event. For example, suppose we want to have a new instance of a form with the added functionality that whenever someone presses any key with the focus in the form, we raise an event. To see this at work, we are going to create three forms.

The original form is automatically added to a Standard EXE. We will add a line of code to this form that says that instances of our form can raise an event. However, it turns out, if you run the application with this form as the startup form, the first form can't actually raise the event. This seems so weird, at first, that it deserves a bit of explanation. The reason is that the first form instance was created before you added the code for raising the event. The first instance of the form was, after all, created in the design environment before you added any code. For this reason, we will use another form as the startup form.

What it turns out we need is a new instance of the first form. This new instance will be created using code that tells the new form instance that it should notify anyone who asks about its custom event. All we need is to create (remember, *instantiate* is the buzzword) a slightly modified version of the original form, which has an "event raising" capability.

Finally, we need a startup form to manage the creation of the form from Step 2. This "manager" form will:

1. Create the second instance of the original form—the one that has the ability to send out events to objects that care to listen for them. (Having the ability to listen to events requires code as well!)

2. Have an event handler that is triggered when the form from Step 2 sends out its custom event to all who ask.

This kind of curious behavior where you have to distinguish the instance of an object at design time from additional instances of it created at run time will be important in the next chapter when we go deeper into the control creation process. ⊃

Let's go through the needed steps one by one.

1. Start up a Standard EXE.

2. For the First form, change its caption to read "No Keys."

3. Set this form's KeyPreview property to True.

4. Add the following code to the Declarations section of the No Keys form:

```
Public Event NoKeyPresses(Key$)
```

This line tells VB that instances of the form will have the potential to raise an event that accepts a single string parameter. Now, make the KeyPress event for the No Keys form read.

```
Private Sub Form_KeyPress(KeyAscii As Integer)
   RaiseEvent NoKeyPresses(Chr(KeyAscii))
End Sub
```

This line says that instances of the form will have the ability to raise the NoKeyPresses event when someone presses a key inside of it. The string equivalent of that key will be sent out along with the event notification.

Now, we want to create the form that will manage everything, so:

5. Choose Project|Add Form.

6. Change the name of the new form to ManagerForm.

7. Add the following Declaration to the General section of this Form:

```
Public WithEvents Foo As Form1
```

This is the key line. It tells VB that the second form will be referring to an instance of the first form that can send out events. Now make the Form_Load of the ManagerForm read as follows:

```
Private Sub Form_Load()
   Set Foo = New Form1 'create an instance of Foo
   Foo.Caption = "Please don't press any keys inside
      of me."
   Foo.Show
End Sub
```

The first line in this code actually creates the instance of Form1 named Foo. However because we declared Foo using the WithEvents keyword in the ManagerForm, this new instance has the needed event signaling ability. The remaining lines of code justify position Foo so it isn't hidden by its parent.

Finally, you may have noticed that once you added the line

```
Public WithEvents Foo As Form1
```

the IDE automatically added a Foo object to the Object list box in the Code window for the Manager form. The Foo object has a NoKeyPresses event. We can now write the code in the Foo_NoKeyPresses event:

```
Private Sub Foo_NoKeyPresses(Key$)
  MsgBox "You pressed an " & Key$ & _
          ". No keypresses allowed in this form!"
End Sub
```

8. Now set the Startup Object in Project|Properties to ManagerForm.

That's it. If you run the application and click in the Foo form (the one with the clever caption) to give it focus, then press a key, VB will pop up the message box, thus proving that the Foo form is sending out an event.

The Nothing Keyword

Once you create a new object, you have used up some memory and resources. When you are done with the object, you must release the memory that was used by the object. This is done by setting the object variable to the keyword Nothing. For example,

```
Dim frmFrm As New Form1
'code to manipulate the new instance of Form1
'would then be used but eventually you need to say:
Set frmForm = Nothing
```

Since object variables merely point to the object, it is possible for several object variables to refer to the same object. When several object variables refer to the same object, then you must set all of them to Nothing in order to release the memory and system resources associated with the object. ⊃

Memory may be released automatically, for example, after the last object variable referring to the object goes out of scope. However, relying on this is sloppy and not guaranteed to work. If you set a local object variable inside a procedure, set it to Nothing before the Sub is exited; don't rely on Visual Basic to clean up after you!

A good place to clean up object references by setting them to nothing is in the QueryUnload event of the startup form. ⊃

Creating a New Class Module

You create a new Class module at design time by choosing Project|Add Class Module. Once you have a Class module, you use the New keyword to create new instances of it in code elsewhere in your project. For example, if MyClass is the name of a Class module in your project,

```
Dim FirstInstance As New MyClass
```

would create an instance of it.

Use Property procedures to define the properties of your class and use Public Sub and Function procedures for its methods. (You can raise events in a Class module, but if you are going to do this, you might as well go all the way and make a control out of it.)

Each Class module can respond to only two events: Initialize and Terminate. As their names suggest, these events are triggered when someone creates an instance of your class or terminates it. Use the Initialize event to give the instance fields in your classes their initial data.

Compared to constructors in languages like Java or C++, the Initialize event in VB is crippled. In particular, it is impossible to pass parameters to the Initialize event and impossible to override it. If you need to send parameters to a Class module in order to set its initial state, add a Create event to the Class module with whatever parameters are necessary. Then call the Create event explicitly immediately after the call to New that creates the class. ⊃

The Terminate event for a Class module is triggered when all references to the class are Set to Nothing or when the object falls out of scope. (This means that local objects declared in procedures would be automatically garbage collected—but, it is not good to rely on this.)

One of the things you will want to do in the Terminate event is set any objects you may have created inside the Class module to Nothing to reclaim the memory they were using.

The Terminate event is not triggered if the application stops because of the End statement. This means that necessary cleanup may not take place if you use End statements promiscuously. ⊃

The only property you can set for a class module in the CCE in both an EXE and a control project is the Name property. Inside a UserControl project, you can also set what is called the Instancing property. There are two possible values. The default is that outside users of your control can create a copy of your class module. You can also set this to Private and only your control will have access to the class module.

Class Modules and User-Defined Types

You can think of a class module as a user-defined type with properties and methods added, but, in fact, user-defined types and class modules have only an uneasy coexistence. One reason is that user-defined types can only be Private inside a Class module. This usually won't cause problems since you shouldn't have any Public data in a Class module anyway. However, in keeping with a more object-oriented approach to VB, we suggest replacing most uses of a user-defined type to hold the Private data used for properties by other VB objects such as classes or collections. There are two reasons for this, other than aesthetics:

1. The user-defined type can't be the value of a property anyway.

2. Even if you could use a user-defined type, using a Visual Basic object (and, therefore, a Property Set) gives you more freedom. This is because the class or collection that holds the property data will now have a much richer structure.

Data Structures and Pointers

Point 2 leads to what appears to be one of the well kept secrets of all versions of Visual Basic since VB4, namely because:

1. The Set statement creates a reference to an object.
2. Class modules can have objects as instance fields.

You can do all the traditional data structures such as linked lists, binary trees, and so on, that usually use pointers with class modules. (Collections described below also play a role.)

For example, here is the declaration you would need for a traditional linked list using Class modules.

```
Class Node
Private NextNode As Node
Private PrevNode As Node
```

Then you can use Property Set to link the various nodes. (For more on data structures in VB using class modules, please see our book, *Core Visual Basic,* due out in late March from Prentice Hall.)

An Example: A Bit/Byte Class

We want to create a class that lets you manipulate the byte equivalent of a zillion bits (actually, we will allow the number of bits to be a long). Then, we want to be able to work with any individual bits in the various bytes. For example, our class should have:

- A read-only property called getBit. This property tells us whether a specific bit is on.
- Write properties called turnBitOn and turnBitOff that can turn an individual bit on. (Notice that a property that merely switched the current state of a bit couldn't do this.)

So, the first question is, how to store the information in the class. For simplicity's sake, we will use an array of Booleans for the bytes. (This is not quite the most space efficient because VB does not implement the Boolean type in a single bit but rather in an integer.)

Anyway, to start building the BitClass Module, add a Class module to a Standard EXE. First you need the Private array to hold the bits:

```
Private BitArray() As Boolean
```

Next, you need the property that resizes the array correctly, depending on the size it is sent.

```
Public Property Let MakeBitSet(N As Long)
   ReDim BitArray(1 To N)
End Property
```

Now, we need the three Property procedures. They are pretty simple: getBit reads off the current value in the array and returns this as the value of the property; TurnOnBit makes a specific bit True; and TurnOffBit makes a specific bit False.

```
Public Property Get getBit(whichBit As Long) As _
Boolean
   getBit = BitArray(whichBit)
End Property

Public Property Let turnOffBit(N As Long)
   BitArray(N) = False
End Property

Public Property Let turnOnBit(N As Long)
   BitArray(N) = True
End Property
```

An Example: The Sieve of Eratosthenes

One of the reasons to implement a bit class is it lets us program one of the standard benchmarks called the Sieve of Eratosthenes. This is a method discovered more than 2,000 years ago for listing all the *primes*. (A prime is a number like 7 that can only be divided by itself and 1.)

The idea behind the Sieve is that you make a list of all the integers:
2 3 4 5 6 7 8 9 10 11 12 13 14 15 16 17 18 19 20 21 22 23 24 25 26

Now you cross out all the multiples of 2 (except 2, of course)
2 3 ~~4~~ 5 ~~6~~ 7 ~~8~~ 9 ~~10~~ 11 ~~12~~ 13 ~~14~~ 15 ~~16~~ 17 ~~18~~ 19 ~~20~~ 21 ~~22~~ 23 ~~24~~ 25 ~~26~~

Now strike through all the remaining multiples of 3.
2 3 ~~4~~ 5 ~~6~~ 7 ~~8~~ ~~9~~ ~~10~~ 11 ~~12~~ 13 ~~14~~ ~~15~~ ~~16~~ 17 ~~18~~ 19 ~~20~~ ~~21~~ ~~22~~ 23 ~~24~~ 25 ~~26~~

and so on. You continue this process until you have gaps that can't be struck through by using the preceding numbers. (For example, 5 is a prime because you can't get to it by striking out multiples of 2 or 3.)

We will imitate this process by flipping a bit instead of striking through the number. To make the Sieve more of a benchmark, we also flip all the bits to True first. The code works as follows. First, we have the routine that makes the bit class the right size and turns on all the bits. The key parts of this code look like this:

```
Dim testArray As New BitArray
testArray.BitSet = Size
For I = 1 To Size
  testArray.turnOnBit = I
Next I
```

Next, we have the code that imitates the crossing-out procedure described above. (We only have to go up to when I*I < =Size because every non-prime number has a factor smaller than its square root.)

```
I = 2
  Do While I * I <= Size
    If testArray.getBit(I) Then
      K = 2 * I
      Do While K <= Size
        testArray.turnOffBit(K)
        K = I + K
      Loop
    End If
    I = I + 1
  Loop
```

Finally, we count the number of bits that are still on.

```
For I = 2 To Size
    If testArray.getBit(I) Then Count = Count + 1
Next I
```

That's it, the Count variable holds the number of primes.

The Full Code for a Sieve Example

The following form adds a Click procedure to a command button and a text box to enter the size to use for the bit array, but is otherwise quite straight-forward.

```
VERSION 5.00
Begin VB.Form frmSieve
    BorderStyle     =   4  'Fixed ToolWindow
    Caption         =   "Sieve Test"
    ClientHeight    =   2565
    ClientLeft      =   3795
    ClientTop       =   2685
    ClientWidth     =   4410
    LinkTopic       =   "Form1"
    MaxButton       =   0    'False
    MinButton       =   0    'False
    PaletteMode     =   1    'UseZOrder
    ScaleHeight     =   2565
    ScaleWidth      =   4410
    ShowInTaskbar   =   0    'False
    Begin VB.TextBox Text1
        Height      =   330
        Left        =   2925
        TabIndex    =   0
        Top         =   1305
        Width       =   1200
    End
    Begin VB.CommandButton Command1
        Caption     =   "Start Sieving"
        Default     =   -1   'True
        Height      =   492
        Left        =   1230
        TabIndex    =   1
```

```
        Top                   =    1875
        Width                 =    1740
    End
    Begin VB.Label Label1
        Alignment             =    2   'Center
        Caption               =    "Enter the ending number:"
        Height                =    330
        Left                  =    135
        TabIndex              =    2
        Top                   =    1335
        Width                 =    2550
    End
End
Attribute VB_Name = "frmSieve"
Attribute VB_GlobalNameSpace = False
Attribute VB_Creatable = False
Attribute VB_PredeclaredId = True
Attribute VB_Exposed = False
Private Sub Command1_Click()
  Dim testArray As BitArray
  Dim Size As Long, Foo As Variant
  Dim I As Long, Count As Long, K As Long

  Foo = Text1.Text
  If Not IsNumeric(Foo) Or Val(Foo) < 0 Then
   MsgBox ("Enter a positive number please")
   Text1.Text = vbNullString
   Text1.SetFocus
   Exit Sub
  End If

  Screen.MousePointer = vbHourglass
  Size = Val(Text1.Text)
  'start the timer
  theTime = Timer

  'set the array size
  Set testArray = New BitArray
  testArray.MakeBitSet = Size
```

```
'turn all bits on
For I = 1 To Size
  testArray.turnOnBit = I
Next I

'set the values in the array
I = 2
Do While I * I <= Size
   If testArray.getBit(I) Then
    K = 2 * I
    Do While K <= Size
       testArray.turnOffBit = K
      K = I + K
    Loop
   End If
   I = I + 1
Loop

'count the set bits
For I = 2 To Size
   If testArray.getBit(I) Then Count = Count + 1
Next I
Screen.MousePointer = vbDefault

'print out the results on the form
Cls
Print "There are " & Count & " primes up to " & Size & "."
Print "Total time taken was " & Timer - theTime & " seconds."

'destroy the class instance
Set testArray = Nothing

End Sub
```

```
VERSION 1.0 CLASS
BEGIN
  MultiUse = -1   'True
END
Attribute VB_Name = "BitArray"
Attribute VB_GlobalNameSpace = False
Attribute VB_Creatable = False
Attribute VB_PredeclaredId = False
Attribute VB_Exposed = False
Private BitArray() As Boolean

Public Property Let MakeBitSet(N As Long)
  ReDim BitArray(1 To N)
End Property

Public Property Get getBit(whichBit As Long) As Boolean
  getBit = BitArray(whichBit)
End Property

Public Property Let turnOffBit(N As Long)
  BitArray(N) = False
End Property

Public Property Let turnOnBit(N As Long)
  BitArray(N) = True
End Property
```

Collections

We want to turn to one of the neatest and most useful Visual Basic objects you can create at run time—a *Collection* object. A Collection object is an object whose parts can be referred to individually as needed, and you still can refer to the object as a whole when necessary. It looks and works like a very smart version of an ordinary array. Here's a hint of what it can do:

- You'll never have to use a construct like Redim Preserve with a collection. The collection automatically resizes itself to accept more elements.

- Even better, a collection automatically shrinks itself when you remove an element. No more manually "compactifying" an array by finding the "empty entries" and copying higher numbered entries into it.

Next, Visual Basic and, therefore, the CCE have built-in collections that give you information about all the forms loaded in a project, the controls on a specific form, or the printers that are installed. These collections are called Forms, Controls, and Printers. The Count property of a collection tells you how many items are in the collection. For example, Forms.Count is the number of forms you have loaded.

You can access individual forms or controls by saying, for example, Forms(0), Forms(1), and so on. Unfortunately, although the count starts at 0, Forms(0) is not necessarily the startup form. The order of the Forms, Controls, or Printers collection is unpredictable. (Since the Count property starts at 0, we go to one less than Forms.Count–1.) The Forms collection is zero-based.

Although using a For-Next loop to iterate through a collection works, it is much slower than using the For Each construct to iterate through a collection. The For Each structure also makes your code a bit clearer when you need to iterate through all the elements in a collection. A framework for this structure takes the following form:

```
For Each Element In TheCollection

Next
```

Here's an example that prints the captions of all the loaded forms in a project in the Debug window.

```
Dim frmForm As Form
For Each frmForm In Forms
   Debug.Print frmForm.Caption
Next
```

Building Your Own Collections

You will often want to build your own collections The items in a collection (usually called its *members,* or *elements)* can be of any type, and you can mix types in a collection if you need to. Since a collection is an object, you must create it as an instance of a built-in class in Visual Basic. The class you need is called, naturally enough, the Collection class. For example,

```
Dim MyCollection As New Collection
```

creates a new collection as an instance of the Collection class.

Just as with the Forms, Controls, or Printers collection, the Count property of each collection you create tells you the number of items in a collection. However, collections you create are one-based. The first element in a user-created collection has index 1. (Collections start out with no elements, so the Count is 0.) Each element in a collection can be referred to by its index, just as you saw in the Forms and Controls collections. This means that the following gives you one way of dealing with all the elements in a collection

```
For I = 1 To NameOfCollection.Count
   work with NameOfCollection(I)
Next I
```

but

```
For Each Foo In NameOfCollection
   work with Foo
Next
```

is preferable since it runs faster and also you don't have to worry about the difference between 0- and 1-based collection.

Collections you create start with an index of 1 and go up to the count of the collection. The built-in Forms, Controls, and Printers collections start at 0 and go up to the Count–1. (To make it more confusing, objects like Toolbars that have a collection as a property are usually 1-based. In the Toolbars case, this is the Buttons collection.) ⊃

The Item Method

The Item method is the default method for a collection; it is how you refer to (or return) a specific element of a collection. Its syntax is:

```
CollectionObject.Item(index)
```

but since it is the default method for a collection, you can just say:

```
CollectionObject(index)
```

(We confess: this is one of the few cases where we use the default method for an object so that we can code with the shorter form.)

The index parameter specifies the position of a member of the collection. It is a long integer (you can have lots of elements in a collection) and goes to the number of items in the collection. For example,

```
MyCollection.Item(1)
MyCollection(1)
```

are both the first item in the collection.

However, you rarely refer to an item using its index. After all, the index may change over time. A better way is to use a key to access the elements in a collection. This key is a string that you set up at the time you add the element to the collection (see the next section). Using a key rather than an index is much more useful; you can easily associate a useful mnemonic to the item for the key and then you always know what you are getting back. The syntax for accessing a collection member using a key is simply:

```
MyCollection.Item(StringKeyGoesHere)
MyCollection(StringKeyGoesHere)
```

The Add Method

Once you create the collection by using the New keyword, use the Add method to add items to it. For example:

```
Dim VBVersions As New Collection
Dim Foo As String
Foo = ("Visual Basic 3.0")
VBVersions.Add Foo
Foo = ("Visual Basic 4.0")
VBVersions.Add Foo
Foo = ("Visual Basic CCE")
VBVersions.Add Foo
```

In general, the Add method has the following syntax (it supports named arguments, by the way):

```
CollectionObject.Add item [, key as string] _
[, before As Long] [, after As Long]
```

In particular, you can (and probably should) use something like the following modified version of the above example:

```
Dim VBVersions As New Collection
Dim Foo As String
Foo = ("Visual Basic 3.0")
VBVersions.Add Foo, Old
Foo = ("Visual Basic 4.0")
VBVersions.Add Foo, Current
Foo = ("Visual Basic CCE")
VBVersions.Add Foo, "The Future"
```

and now you can simply say,

```
Print "The best way to create ActiveX controls is "
& VBVersion ("The Future")
```

Here's another example that uses the With keyword to simplify the object references.

```
Dim Presidents As New Collection
Dim Foo As String
With Presidents
  Foo = "George Washington"
  .Add Foo, "Didn't lie"
  Foo = "Thomas Jefferson"
  .Add item := Foo, key:= "Smartest?"
End With
```

Now you can access Thomas Jefferson by

```
Presidents.Item("Smartest?")
```

or

```
Presidents("Smartest?")
```

The match to the string in the key must be perfect. For example, using
```
Presidents.Item("smartest?")
```
and
```
Presidents("didn't lie")
```
won't work. ➲

Finally, here's an example of combining the built-in Controls collection with a user-defined collection to store information about all the text boxes on a form. We will also use the Name property of the control as the key.

```
Dim AllTextBoxes As New Collection
Dim Foo As Control
For Each Foo in Controls
   If TypeOf Foo = TextBox Then
      AllTextBoxes.Add Foo, Foo.Name
   End If
Next
```

Now you can access the TextBoxes by their name. (Although, as it turns out, this little program has a subtle bug. If you used a control array of text boxes, the key would not be unique since all control array elements have the same name. This leads to a run-time error.) To fix it just add an OnErrorResumeNext statement.

Here are short descriptions of the Add method parts.

Collection Object

This is any Collection object or object variable that refers to a collection except that you cannot use the Add method on the Forms, Controls or Printers collections.

item

This is required. Since the information will be held in a variant variable, it can be an expression of any type. (As mentioned previously, you can mix types in a collection.)

key

The key parameter is optional. It must be a string expression, and within the collection it must be unique or you'll get a run-time error.

before, after

These optional parameters are usually numeric expressions that evaluate to a (long) integer. The new member is placed right before (right after) the member identified by the before (after) argument. If you use a string expression, then it must correspond to one of the keys that was used to add elements to the collection. You can specify before or after positions, but not both. Generally speaking, you will not want to use indices keys as you are better off keying an entry (since the numerical index you set for an entry can change over time without you being aware of the change).

The Remove method

When you need to remove items from a collection, use the Remove method. It, too, supports named arguments, and its syntax is

CollectionObject.Remove *index*

where, as you might expect, the index parameter is used to specify the element you want removed. If the index is a numeric expression, then it must be a number between 1 and the collection's Count property. If it's a string expression, it must exactly match a key to an element in the collection. As with the Add method, you cannot use the Remove method to remove objects from the Printers, Forms or Controls collections.

Control Arrays

It would be logical if you could also use the New keyword to create controls at run time; unfortunately, that isn't the way it works. The CCE still uses the older (and somewhat clumsier) method of control arrays to create new controls of a specific type. (You may have discovered control arrays inadvertently if you gave two controls of the same type the same control name, or tried to copy a control using the Edit menu. If you did, then you saw a dialog box that looks like the one shown in Figure 7-2.

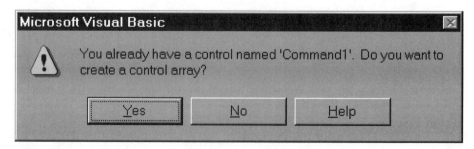

Figure 7-2
Message Box to create control array

Any time you use the same control name more than once while designing a Visual Basic form or a user control form, the CCE asks you whether you really want to create a control array. Click the Yes button (or press ENTER), and you now can add more controls of the same type while the application is running. Each new control in a control array is called an *element* of the control array.

Since both controls now have the same name, Visual Basic needs a way to distinguish them. You do this with the Index property. When you ask Visual Basic to create a control array, Visual Basic gives the first control an Index property of 0 and the second control an Index property of 1. Like any properties of Visual Basic objects, you can change them at design time using the Properties window. In fact, if you assign any number to the Index property of a control at design time, Visual Basic automatically creates a control array. This lets you create a control array without having to use two controls at design time.

Create the control array first before writing any event procedures for its first element. (Although you do not have to create all the elements in the control array before coding them, this is one of the big advantages to the index parameter.) ⊃

Suppose you want to work with the Click event procedure for an element of the command button control array created as in Figure 7-2. Suppose you gave it the control name of cmdInArray. When you move to the Code window by, say, double-clicking one of these the command buttons in the control array, your code event template looks like this:

```
Private Sub cmdInArray(Index As Integer)


End Sub
```

Notice how, instead of having no parameters, as the Click event procedure ordinarily does, this event procedure now uses a new parameter, Index As Integer. This index parameter is the key to the smooth functioning of control arrays. If you want to use the Click procedure for any element of the control array, call it with the appropriate index parameter:

```
cmdInArray_Click(0)  'applies to the original command
                     'button

cmdInArray_Click(1)  'applies to the second one
```

For example, add the following code to the event procedure template shown here:

```
Private Sub cmdInArray_Click (Index As Integer)
   If Index = 0 Then
      MsgBox "You clicked button 0"
   Else
      MsgBox "You clicked button 1"
   End If
End Sub
```

or even more simply:

```
Private Sub cmdInArray_Click (Index As Integer)
   MsgBox "You clicked button " & Index
End Sub
```

When you click one of command buttons, the CCE calls this event procedure and passes the index parameter to the procedure. In this way, the event procedure can use the index to determine what to do.

If you inadvertently added a control to a control array at design time, you can remove it by changing the control name or deleting the control. However, once Visual Basic creates a control array, you must change all the control names or delete all the controls that were in the array in order to eliminate the control array. At that point, you can reuse the name.

Finally, we think it is worth noting the difference between an array of controls and a control array. An array of controls is simply a usual CCE array that happens to contain control objects rather than numbers; a control array is a dynamic object used to create new controls at run time.

Adding and Removing Controls in a Control Array

You must create a control array at design time, but, after that, you can add new elements to the control array while the application is running. Use a variation of the Load command that can also be used to load a new form in an application with multiple forms. For example, suppose you want to add three more command buttons to the example control array created in the previous section. To do this when the startup form loads, you only need to add the following code to the Form_Load event procedure for the startup form:

```
Private Sub Form_Load()
   Dim I As Integer

   For I = 2 To 4
      Load cmdInArray(I)
      cmdInArray(I).Caption = "Command Button #" & I
   Next I
End Sub
```

Whenever the CCE loads a new element of a control array, the object is invisible—the visible property is set to False. All other properties (except the Tab Index and Control Array Index) are copied from the object that has the lowest index in the array. ⊃

This means that newly created controls in a control array default to being stacked one on top of the other. Because of this, you'll often find yourself applying the Move method to controls in a control array after you tell the CCE to load them.

You can use the Unload statement to remove any element of a control array that you added at run time. You cannot use the Unload statement to remove the original elements of the control array that you created at design time. For example, if you add the

```
Private Sub Form_Click()
   Static I As Integer

   If I < 4 Then
     Unload cmdInArray(I + 2)
     I = I + 1
   Else
     Exit Sub
   End If
End Sub
```

each click on an empty place in the form removes the next command button in the control array, but no routine like this can remove the initial element in the control array.

You must be careful, of course; you can only load or unload an element of a control array once. If you try to load or unload a control array element twice in succession, Visual Basic gives a run-time error you can trap (Err = 360).

The Object Browser

In Chapter 2, you saw how to use the Object Browser (shortcut is F2—an example is shown in Figure 7-3) to look at the built-in constants in Visual Basic. The Object Browser can do far more.

1. It makes it easier to navigate among the procedures and functions you added to your project.

2. Even more importantly, the Object Browser gives you complete access to the classes that you can use in your CCE projects.

More precisely, objects that are usable in Visual Basic are usually collected into *type libraries*. These type libraries contain descriptions of the constants, events, properties and methods of the class. A type library can be as sophisticated as the one in Excel or as simple as the one underlying a user-defined control. The Object Browser uses the information from the type library to present its information.

If you are using the MDI interface for the CCE, you can move back to the Object Browser by using CTRL+TAB. ⊃

For example, as shown in Figure 7-3, every control project starts out with the ability to browse itself along with the VB (Visual Basic) type library, the VBA (Visual Basic for Applications) type library, the VBRUN type library (the Visual Basic Virtual machine), the stdole (the OLE library which handles communications between controls and their containers), or all of them at

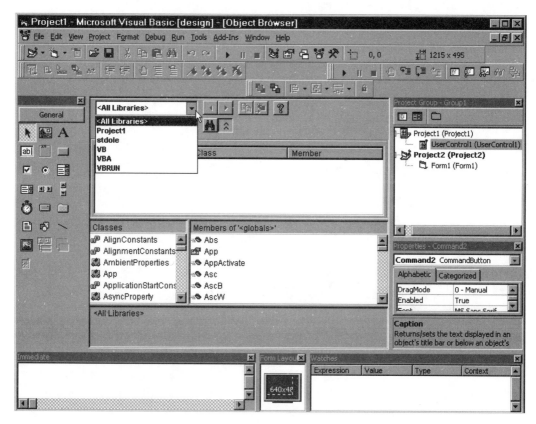

Figure 7-3
The Object Browser with initial libraries showing

270

once. There are also type libraries for Excel, Access—most anything you might imagine. Figure 7-4 shows the Tools|References dialog box on a typical machine. As you can see, there are dozens of type libraries available to the CCE. All you have to do is check off the box for the library you want to browse and then select it from the Libraries drop-down list box at the top of the Object Browser.

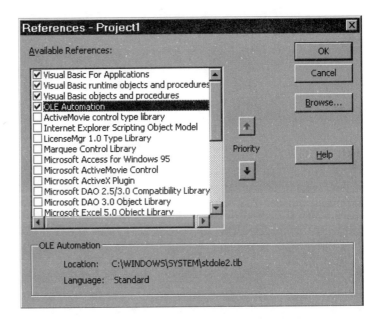

Figure 7-4
The References
dialog box

In general, you use the Libraries/Projects drop-down list box to choose from the available object libraries, including the ones in the current Visual Basic project. Once you choose a library, the left-hand Classes pane gives you access to all the classes in the library and the right-hand pane gives you access to all the *members* of the class highlighted in the left-hand pane. (Members is a fancy name for the constants, properties and methods of the class.) Properties have little letter icons, methods have green icons whose identity escapes us, events have a yellow lightning bolt icon, and constants have gray boxes to their left. The bottom pane gives you the signature of the member if it is a method. It also gives you a more or less useful description of the member.

 If you are browsing the code that you created, simply double-click on any bold-faced item in the Members pane and you will immediately be taken to where the code for that member is located in the Code window. (Boldface is how the Object Browser indicates that here is code for that member.) ⊃

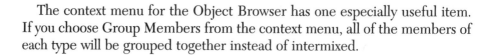

The context menu for the Object Browser has one especially useful item. If you choose Group Members from the context menu, all of the members of each type will be grouped together instead of intermixed.

Navigating in the Object Browser

First off, like many list boxes in Windows, typing a letter highlights the first object whose name begins with that letter in the pane that has the focus. The Object Browser also has a search facility. Simply type anything in the text box below the library box on the left and press ENTER and the Browser will display a list of every item whose name contains those characters.

Next, the descriptions in the bottom pane of the Object Browser often have hyperlinks. These are underlined in green. Simply click on one to go to that item.

Adding Your Own Descriptions for Class Members

For both your class modules and your user controls, it would be courteous if you added the kind of descriptions to your objects that you have seen the Object Browser display for the built-in type libraries. For this:

1. Open the Object Browser and choose the current project.
2. Highlight the name of the class you want to document.
3. Right-click on the member of the class you want to document.

For example, for a Public member you will see a dialog box like the one shown in Figure 7-5. Enter a description of the property in the middle text box.

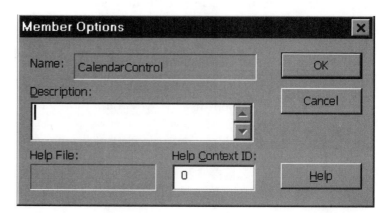

Figure 7-5
Procedure
Attributes
dialog box

Chapter 8

Although you can certainly choose File|Make .ocx and get a reusable OCX from the sample code we have already shown you; the controls you have seen so far really can't do much. Since we're roughly at the halfway point of the book, you're probably itching to start creating some full-blown controls. The purpose of this chapter is to show you what you need to know in order to build full-featured controls. (Just making a full-featured OCX is usually not enough; Chapter 12 shows you what goes into setting up and distributing your controls.)

Here are examples of some of the problems in the sample controls you have seen so far:

- While the sample controls we showed you had custom events, they didn't have any custom properties or methods.
- The user interfaces for the controls you have seen so far were often not very sophisticated.

For example, the controls that we placed on our user controls didn't resize themselves properly when the user control itself was resized in the test form. In this chapter, we will take care of this problem by showing you general code for making your controls resize and reshape themselves properly.

User Controls: Beyond the Basics

We have not yet taken advantage of one really neat feature of the CCE, the ability to make one control using many individual controls. As you will soon see, the CCE makes it easy to combine lots of existing controls into one really powerful control. For example, how often do you need to get someone's address? Usually, what you do is put all the individual text boxes and labels one by one on a form and write the necessary code, tying them together. With the CCE, you won't have to do this anymore. You can build a single control that encompasses the more than a dozen individual controls that a reasonable Address Control would require. We will start the process of building this kind of Address Control in this chapter and finish it off in the next chapter. (The controls you place inside your user control form are often called its *constituent* controls.)

Of course, once you decide to place multiple constituent controls on a single user control form, the way that they interact with each other, with the user control form that contains them, and with the developer using the custom control, becomes much more complex. This means the designer of the custom control needs to do more in the case of multiple constituent control to manage the multiple possible interactions between the constituent controls, the custom control as a whole, and the developer who is using the control. This chapter gets you started on this very important, complex topic. (The next chapter finishes it off.)

The Anatomy of a User Control

As far as the user interface of your control goes, simply use the techniques from Chapter 3 to "paint" the needed constituent controls onto the user control form. These constituent controls can be any controls on your system for which you have the appropriate license. In particular, they can be other custom controls that you have already created. You can do this by explicitly adding the other user control to the Project Group or by registering the control (see Chapter 12) on your system and then choosing Project|Components.

For example, Figure 8-1 is the way your screen would look if you were designing the address control that we will discuss in the next chapter. Notice that this user control has 15 (!) constituent controls (7 text boxes, 7 labels, and a command button).

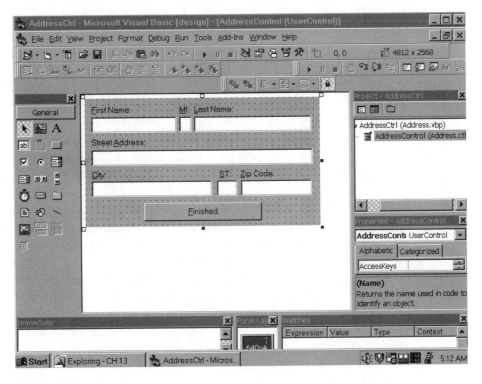

Figure 8-1
The Address Control at design stage

Next, you have to decide on what properties, events, and methods your control should expose to its users. (The methods, events and properties of your user control are often called its *members*. We will often use the "member" shorthand for these elements as well.) The members of your control can be public, private or friend (visible to everything in the same project). The visibility is controlled by your use of the Public, Private or Friend access specifier in the relevant code.

Similarly, the possible events your user control can raise to anyone who uses the control are those declared with the Public keyword (or no keyword, since Public is the default for a user control). For example, placing

```
Public Event BadKey()
```

or

```
Event BadValue(bSetToLimit As Boolean)
```

in the Declarations section of your user control would give you the ability to raise these two events to the user of your control. (You can also have private or friendly custom events in a control but these are rarely useful and, therefore, are uncommon.) In general, the distinction is:

- Public events give the developer using your control (simply referred to as the *user* from now on) the opportunity to react to something.
- Private events give your control the opportunity to react to something.
- Friend events give the other components of your user control project the opportunity to react to something but not the user of your control (relatively rare).

The properties of your control come from the Property Procedures you write. The Public Property Procedures become the properties of your user control that can be used by the user of your control. The Private Property Procedures are for those properties you don't want the user or the other parts of the project to be able to manipulate. The Friendly properties are those you do want other parts of your project to manipulate. More precisely, a Public Property Get/Property Let or Public Property Set/Property Let combination becomes a property that the user of your control can both read and write to. Unless you change the CCE's defaults, the Public Properties are exactly the same properties of your user control that are visible in the Properties window of the IDE when the user of your control adds an instance of that control to their form. (See the next section for how to change this.)

Similarly, when you use a Public Property Get procedure without the corresponding Property Set/Let procedure in the code for your control, you have a user-readable read-only property. (It is also possible, as you will soon see, to create read/write properties that can be set only at design time or only at run time.)

Finally, the methods that a user of your user control can call are exactly the same Public functions and procedures you write. Any Private functions and procedures you write will never be seen by the user of your control. This lets you hide whatever code was needed to carry out the tasks of the control and furthers encapsulation. In particular, if you come up with a better way to carry out an internal task, you probably won't break any existing code. The user of the control never sees internal implementation details.

The Mechanics of Writing the Code in Your User Controls

As with writing any procedures, the Tools|Add Procedure dialog box is probably the most convenient method to get the templates for the members of your control into the Code window, (although you can always simply start typing in the Code window anywhere outside an existing procedure or function).

For example, open up the Add Procedure dialog box and add a Public Property procedure named ExampleProperty. The IDE will automatically generate the following templates:

```
Public Property Get ExampleProperty() As Variant _
End Property
Public Property Let ExampleProperty(ByVal vNewValue _
As Variant)
End Property
```

Notice that the IDE, by default, created both the Property Let and the Property Get. The default parameter for a Property procedure is a variant named vNewValue and this parameter is passed by value and not by reference. Obviously, you will often need to change these defaults for the Property procedures you write.

If you chose to add a public event named TestEvent using this dialog box, you would simply get the following declaration in the General object of your user control:

```
Public Event TestEvent()
```

As with Property procedures, you would have to add any parameters you want to this template by hand.

Finally, since methods are nothing but the Public Subs and Functions of your user control, there's no special box in the Add procedure dialog box for them. Simply write the code and use the appropriate identifier (or none, since Public is the default).

The Procedure Attribute Dialog Box

Once you have created the header for one of the members of your control, you can change its *attributes*. These are things like the description of a property that the user of the control sees in the Properties window—or even if he or she can see the property in the Properties windows at all.

To bring up the Procedure Attributes dialog box, simply position the cursor inside the member you want to work with and choose Tools|Procedure Attributes. Figure 8-2 is an example of what you see for a property named SampleProperty. As you can see, this box has only room for a description of the Property and the Help Context ID (used for associating context-sensitive help).

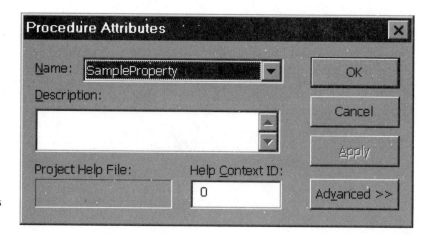

Figure 8-2
Procedure Attributes
dialog box

However, if you click on the Advanced button shown in Figure 8-2, the Procedure Attribute dialog box "grows" to look like Figure 8-3. We want to go over the less obvious features in the full version of this dialog box one by one.

If you aren't used to an Apply button, this simply applies what you have set but doesn't close the dialog box—unlike the OK button, which applies what you have done and closes the dialog box. It is a good idea in your own dialog boxes to add an Apply button with similar functionality for any possible repetitive action. For example, it used to drive one of the authors mad when early versions of Word could only insert one symbol per use of the Insert Symbol dialog box. ⊃

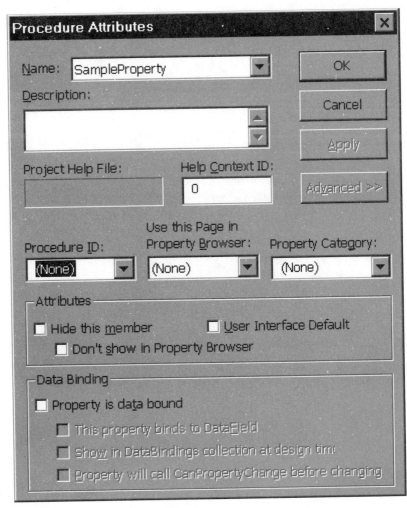

Figure 8-3
The full Procedure
Attributes dialog box

279

Name Drop-Down List Box

Although the CCE defaults to showing the attributes for the member where the cursor is currently located, this drop-down list box gives you quick access to the attributes of all the properties, methods, and events currently defined.

Description TextBox

This text box lets you describe the property, method, or event currently showing in the Name drop-down box. The description shows up in the bottom pane of the Object Browser and also in the bottom of the Properties window.

Project Help File TextBox

You can only see the value here, you cannot set it. You set it in the General tab in the Project|Properties dialog box.

Help Context ID TextBox

This text box specifies the help context ID for the member you are working with. This, in turn, would connect up to the appropriate part of the Help file specified in the General tab in the Project|Properties dialog box (and shown in the Project Help File text box.).

Procedure ID

Many applications that use ActiveX Control have some knowledge of the standard events and properties a control can expose. This combo box lets you choose one of these standards.

 These settings are advisory, not proscriptive. For example, calling something a BackColor property in this combo box doesn't make it behave the way a BackColor property should. You still need to write the code to do this. This box simply tells the user of your control to expect some standard behavior from your member. ⊃

For a property, choosing the Default option in this combo box makes that property the default property for your control. This makes it act like the Text property of a textbox or the Caption of a label control. (Although, as we mentioned before, we rarely use default properties and so, most often, do not provide them for our controls.)

Use this Page in Property Browser

This is important when using Property Pages. Setting it adds an ellipsis button to the property in the Properties window that will load the custom Property Page selected when the user clicks it. See Chapter 10 for more information on this option.

Property Category

As you have seen, the Properties window has the ability to display properties either alphabetically or in categories. Use this combo box to set the category. You can use one of the supplied ones like Behavior or add your own by typing in the name in this combo box.

Attributes

These check boxes allow you to set things like whether the property is a design-time or run-time property. The three check boxes are described in the following table.

Hide This Member	This gives you a property that is not visible to the outside world, although it can still be accessed with code. If you check this box, the CCE will not show the property in the Properties window ever and will only show it in the Object Browser if you choose Show Hidden Members from the Object Browser's context menu. Think of this option as telling the user of your control that this is a secret property and they should use it at their own risk.
Don't Show in Property Browser	This simply determines if the CCE shows the property in the Properties window. The property will still always shows up in the Object Browser and you can continue to write code to work with it.
User Interface Default	This determines which property is highlighted in the Properties window when the user presses F4 with focus in your user control. It also sets the event that the CCE displays in the Code window when you double-click the control. Obviously, there can be only one default property and one default event.

You can make a property settable or readable only at run time but this requires code. See the discussion on the Ambient object in this chapter. ⊃

Data Binding

These check boxes (grayed in Figure 8-3) are used with the VB data control. We will have a short discussion on using these options in Chapter 17 when we make the option group control we build in that chapter data bound.

Being data bound is not enough to make a control able to read and write data from a database, you also need a data control to orchestrate the connection between the data bound control and the database. The CCE does not come with VB's data control because it does not include the data access library needed to make the data control work. You need to have access to this control or some equivalent functionality in order to actually use any data bound controls you create. (But remember that the controls built with the CCE will work in Visual Basic version 4.0, so you can use VB 4's data control.) ⊃

Mapping Properties, Methods, and Events

Consider the address control from Figure 8-1. It should obviously be able to raise a "Finished" event that the user of the control can work with when the end user clicks on the Finished button. This event must, equally obviously, be connected somehow to the Click event of the command button that we put on the user control form.

We need a way to connect these two events. To do this, suppose the Finished command button inside the user control form has the name cmdFinished. Then, here's what you need to have in your code to connect the Finished custom event with the intrinsic Click event for the constituent command button.

1. Put the following declaration for the Public Finished event in the Declarations section of the user control:

```
Public Event Finished()
```

(Again, the keyword Public is optional since it is the default.)

2. Next you need the code that actually connects the two events.
   There's not much to it:

```
Private Sub cmdFinished_Click()
   RaiseEvent Finished
End Sub
```

However, short as this code is, it does have some points worth noting. For example, notice that the cmdFinished_Click event is marked as Private. This means that the user of the Address control will never see it. He or she will have no way to write an event procedure for the Click event of the button. However, Windows doesn't care about the code you write. It still triggers the Click event for the cmdFinished button when the end user of the Address control clicks on it.

So what happens? Well, because of the key RaiseEvent line in this event procedure, a click on this button simply raises the (Public) Finished event of the user control—which is what we want. As you can see, it is natural to call what we just did a *map* between the click event of the command button and the custom Finished event of the user control and to call the whole process *mapping*.

After you design the interface for your control, you should start thinking about how you want to map the methods, events, and properties (members) of your control to the methods, events and properties of the constituent controls. Although we will have more to say about the whole topic of mapping the members of your user control in the next chapter when we discuss the *Control Interface Wizard*, it is still a good idea to get the basics down pat. This is because, while the Control Interface Wizard automatically generates a lot of the code needed for mapping the members of your user control, it may not be able to do it all. Moreover, as a general rule, if you don't understand what the Wizard does, you will be completely at the Wizard's mercy. We don't recommend this for the Control Interface Wizard—good as it is! (By the way, it may seem somewhat ironic in an age of computers, but a piece of paper with two columns marked user control Members and Constituent Control Members is often the best way to keep things straight whether you write the mapping code yourself or use the Control Interface Wizard.)

Mapping Properties

Mapping properties is a little more subtle than mapping events, so let's go through another example for the Address Control in a bit more detail. Notice that all the labels in the Address Control have their own ForeColor property. Suppose we decide that all the labels inside our control should have the same ForeColor property. We want the user of the control to have the ability to set this property, and it should affect all the labels inside the user control. To do this, we need to map a ForeColor property of the user control to all the ForeColor properties of the labels.

First off, we need a Public Property Let procedure to allow the user of the control to set the ForeColor. The code for this procedure must, in turn, set the ForeColor for all the labels in our control. Here's the code:

```
Public Property Let ForeColor(ByVal New_ForeColor As OLE_COLOR)
    Dim i As Integer
    For i = 0 To 6
        lblLabels(i).ForeColor = New_ForeColor
    Next
    UserControl.ForeColor() = New_ForeColor
    PropertyChanged "ForeColor"
End Property
```

Let's go through the above code line by line. First, because of the Public access specifier, the user of this control can see this property. Since it is a Property Let, he or she can assign to this property. This property takes as a parameter an unsigned long integer for the color. (OLE_COLOR is a built-in data type for color codes.)

Next, we have a loop that runs through all the labels on the form. (Notice the advantage of using a control array of labels!). In each case, the loop assigns the current value of the ForeColor property parameter to the ForeColor of the individual labels. This has the effect of changing the colors of all the constituent labels whenever the user of the control sets the ForeColor property of the user control. The next two lines are the key. First we have:

```
UserControl.ForeColor() = New_ForeColor
```

Here we are giving the new value to the ForeColor property of the user control, based on the parameter passed to the Property Let Procedure.

Next, in the line:

```
PropertyChanged "ForeColor"
```

you see a method you haven't seen before, the PropertyChanged method. Think of this as a flag that tells the CCE that the user of the control activated code that made a change in a property value.

If you fail to include the call to the PropertyChanged method using the name of the property that you have changed in code, your user control and the form designer that is using it will get out of sync. For example, leave it out and the Properties window for the form that uses your user control will have no way to update itself. Also, you won't be able to save the current state of the user control to the .frm file for the project. (See below for how to save and restore the state of your user control.) ⊃

Next, let's analyze the associated Property Get procedure. As with any Property Let/Get pair, the associated Property Get has one fewer parameter (i.e., none, in this case) and returns the type of the missing parameter. So its header looks like this:

```
Public Property Get ForeColor() As OLE_COLOR
```

and the one line of code needed is simply:

```
ForeColor = UserControl.ForeColor
```

What this line of code does is check the current setting of the ForeColor property of the user control. Notice because of the line:

```
UserControl.ForeColor() = New_ForeColor
```

in the Property Let procedure, these are in sync whenever the user assigns to the ForeColor property of the control.

Attributes

If you look at the code for your control in a standalone editor, as opposed to the editor in the IDE, you will often see lines containing the keyword Attribute. Attributes are things like the description of the property (what shows up at the bottom of the Properties window). More often than not, attributes are the things that you set via dialog boxes in the IDE, as in the section on Procedure Attributes dialog box that you just saw.) The code for the various attribute settings is hidden from you in the IDE and it is not a good idea to mess with it by loading the .ctl file in a standalone Code Editor (where it will be visible).

For example, here's the code for the above Property Get as you would see it in a standalone editor:

```
Public Property Get ForeColor() As OLE_COLOR
    Attribute ForeColor.VB_Description = _
"Returns/sets the foreground color used
to display text and graphics in an object."
    ForeColor = UserControl.ForeColor
End Property
```

What the Attribute line does, in this case, is tell the CCE to embed the description for the method inside the method. This setting corresponds to what you enter in the Description text box in the Property Attributes dialog box. (One case where you might change these hidden lines with an editor is if you are a terrible typist and decide to run these kind of lines through a spelling checker.)

Managing the State of a User Control

Once you have created the Property procedures that define your custom properties, changes to the properties are done when the CCE processes the code in your Property Lets and Property Sets.

One way to see this at work is to use the debugging techniques described in Chapter 12 to stop execution whenever the CCE is processing code inside a Property Let. Then change that property via the Properties window. You would see that the CCE really does go to the Property Let anytime you change a property. ⊃

There are two ways to change a property via code. The most common is indirectly via a change to one or more of the instance variables in your control. This works because the Property procedures themselves have code that reads off the current state of the instance variables that they are concerned with inside themselves. Thus, whenever the Property procedure code is processed, you would see the change. Notice that there can be a lag between the change in the instance variables and its effect on the property.

Occasionally, you need to make sure that changes are made directly to a property without waiting for the Property Let to be called at some future time. You would want to do this if changing one property affected other properties that were showing in the Properties window. For example, a little later on in this chapter you will see an IntegerTextBox. This control is an extension of the one you saw in Chapter 1 because, among other things, it has MinValue and MaxValue properties that determine how large or small the value that the end user enters can be. Suppose we wanted to add a Range property to this control. The Range property would let you automatically set up a symmetric range. For example, if you set the Range to be 50, the MinValue would automatically be –50 and the MaxValue would automatically be +50. We obviously want any change in the Range propetry to be immediately reflected in what shows in the Properties window for the MinValue and MaxValue properties. The first step in doing this is to directly change the MinValue and MaxValue properties, as in the following code:

```
Public Property Let Range(ByVal vNewValue As Variant)
   If vNewValue <= 0 Or Not (IsNumeric(vNewValue)) Then
      MsgBox "Range must be positive!"
   Else
      'change MinValue and MaxValue properties directly
      MinValue = -vNewValue
      MaxValue = vNewValue
      'update the instance variable
      m_Range = vNewValue
      PropertyChanged "Range" 'always necessary
   End If
End Property
```

The key to this synchronization process is the lines that directly change the MinValue and MaxValue properties:

```
MinValue = -vNewValue
MaxValue = vNewValue
```

Here's another example of this at work (although we refer you to Chapter 17 for more details). In coding the Option Group control in Chapter 17, we decided to have a ZeroBased property that would let you start counting the option buttons in the group from 0 or 1. We also had an OptionValue property that gave the current value of a specific button in the group. If the user changed the ZeroBased property at design time, we have to change the OptionValue property directly to keep these two properties in sync. The required code looks like the following:

```
Public Property Let ZeroBased(bData As Boolean)
  If bData = mbZeroBased Then Exit Property
  mbZeroBased = bData
  'must've changed
  If mbZeroBased Then
    OptionValue = OptionValue - 1
  Else
    OptionValue = OptionValue + 1
  End If
  PropertyChanged "ZeroBased"
End Property
```

Again, the key is the line:

```
OptionValue = OptionValue - 1
```

This line directly changes the value of the property that we called OptionValue.

The Life Cycle of a User Control

When you change a property of a user control on a form, you certainly want this information to be preserved in the .frm file. Similarly, if a user loads a .frm file, you need to have your user control use the information about its properties that were preserved in the .frm file. Or, to take it from another angle, we certainly want the Properties window to reflect any changes we make to the properties in the various Property procedures. The key to all this is putting the right code in the "life cycle" events of your user control. Since the details of the life cycle for a user control are a bit strange, we will concentrate on what you need to get your controls up and running. First, though, here again are the lifestyle events for a user control in the order in which they occur.

```
At birth: Initialize, InitProperties, ReadProperties, Resize
At death: WriteProperties, Terminate
```

You would most likely use the InitProperties event to read off data from the instance variables to set the initial state of your control. Next, recall in the Property procedure code above there was a call to the PropertyChanged method. The general syntax for this method is:

```
PropertyChanged PropertyName
```

where the PropertyName is a string expression for the name of the property (for example, the line PropertyChanged "Range" in the above code). What the PropertyChanged method does is notify whatever object is using the control that a property value has been changed. In Visual Basic, this immediately triggers the WriteProperties event. You must write the code in the WriteProperties event to save the current values of the properties. Here is a typical example (taken from the IntegerTextBox example given below) of what a WriteProperties event procedure looks like.

```
Private Sub UserControl_WriteProperties(PropBag As PropertyBag)
  On Error Resume Next
  Call PropBag.WriteProperty("MinValue", m_MinValue, m_def_MinValue)
  Call PropBag.WriteProperty("MaxValue", m_MaxValue, m_def_MaxValue)
  Call PropBag.WriteProperty("Value", m_Value, m_def_Value)
End Sub
```

Before we go through this code line by line, we want to emphasize: Every control you create must have code that looks like this.

(In general, you will have one PropBag.WriteProperty statement for each Public writable property in your control.)

Having said how important this type of code is, let's go over it line by line to make sure you understand it. First, the parameter for a WriteProperties event is a PropertyBag object. You haven't seen these CCE objects yet, but think of a property bag as simply a container that holds property names, their current values, and, possibly, a default value. Some people like to think of it as a specialized collection but, in fact, how PropertyBags are implemented is completely irrelevant. All you have to know is you can take out and put in the current state of a property into a property bag (just as the OOP theory you saw in the last chapter would want you to do).

Next, we have the On Error Resume Next statement. This is absolutely necessary when writing out property values to a PropertyBag. The reason is that certain environments do not let you write out properties from the design environment. (The CCE does, but remember people may use your user control in many different environments.) You must catch this error; otherwise, any program that uses your control in one of these non-standard environments will crash.

Next, we have the lines that write out the properties. The syntax, in general, is:

```
PropBag.WriteProperty(DataName, Value[, DefaultValue])
```

The DataName parameter is simply a string that gives the name of the property. (Think of this as the key for the specialized property bag collection.) The Value parameter is simply the current value of the property. Finally, the DefaultValue parameter is a default value for the property.

You may be wondering, why bother with a default value? One reason is that, otherwise, the .frm file could grow absurdly big. If you supply a default value for a property, the CCE will write out the value of your property only when the value you want the CCE to save is different from the default.

The mirror image to the WriteProperties event and the WriteProperties method are the ReadProperties Event and the ReadProperties method. The syntaxes are also parallel. For example,

```
Sub UserControl_ReadProperties(PropBag As PropertyBag)
```

and

```
UserControl.ReadProperty(DataName[, DefaultValue])
```

The idea is that you use the appropriate number and kind of ReadProperty methods to restore the previous state of the control, such as the ReadProperty event for the IntegerTextBox. (Notice how this code parallels the code in the WriteProperty event.)

```
Private Sub UserControl_ReadProperties(PropBag As PropertyBag)
  On Error Resume Next
  m_MinValue = PropBag.ReadProperty("MinValue", m_def_MinValue)
  m_MaxValue = PropBag.ReadProperty("MaxValue", m_def_MaxValue)
  Value = PropBag.ReadProperty("Value", m_def_Value)
End Sub
```

Presenting the Best Face to the User of Your Control

There are two aspects to presenting the best face to the user of your control. The first is trivial but should not be neglected. Would our Finance Control have been as professional looking if we hadn't chosen the following icon for it?

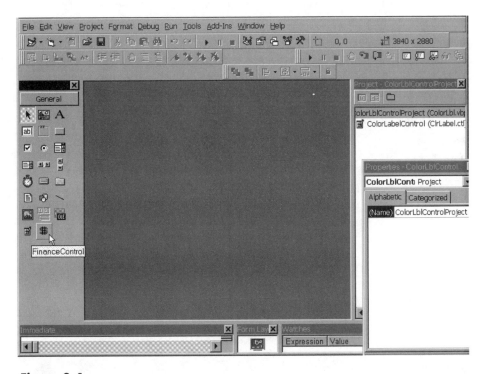

Figure 8-4
The Icon for the Finance Control

The bitmap for the icon the user sees on the toolbox is simply the value of the ToolboxBitmap property. Once you assign this property and compile the control into an OCX, the bitmap is made part of the OCX file so you don't have to supply it separately to the user of your control.

 There are many tools for creating bitmaps. You can even use the Paint program supplied with Windows. We put an excellent shareware one on the CD. (Its only problem that we are aware of is the horrible pun in the title: it's called Microangelo.) ↻

If you use Microangelo (or any other shareware product, for that matter) for longer than the trial period, we hope you will be willing to pay the small license fee required to the creator.

The second and most important issue is to insure the proper sizing of your control and its constituent controls. If you don't make the constituent controls that are inside the form behave properly, your control will look unprofessional. One place to make the code look the way a user would expect it to is in the UserControl_Resize event. For example, suppose you start out with a PictureBox that is supposed to fill up the whole user control form, as shown in Figure 8-5. (We use the Globe.wmf file supplied with Access.)

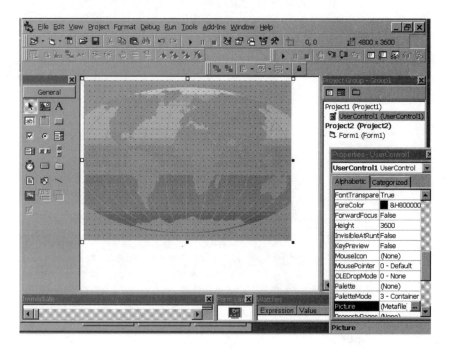

Figure 8-5
A Picture Box at design time

Now, place this control on a test form and start enlarging it. The result, as shown in Figure 8-6, is less than ideal. (To make it more dramatic, we changed the BackColor property of the user control form to Blue, which shows up in Black in Figure 8-6.)

Figure 8-6
Resize problems at design time

The problem is that the constituent PictureBox control that is inside the user control is not resizing itself properly in response to changes in the size of the containing user control form.

The way to fix the bad behavior shown in Figure 8-6 is in the UserControl_Resize event. This event is triggered whenever the user of your control resizes the control (that is, the user control form). For example, to fix up the display shown in Figure 8-6 requires only two lines of code:

```
Private Sub UserControl_Resize()
    'stretch to width and height of the control
    Picture1.Width = Width
    Picture1.Height = Height
End Sub
```

Now, the constituent picture box will always be as wide and as high as its container.

For an ordinary form, you would use ScaleHeight and ScaleWidth in similar code. The reason is that ScaleHeight and ScaleWidth give the internal area of an ordinary form—without the title bar and such. Height and Width give the actual height and width, including the title bar. Since user control forms do not have a title bar, it doesn't matter which you choose. ⊃

Generic Resize Code

The above code works fine when you have a single constituent control, but what happens if you have lots of them inside your user control? In this case, if you need to preserve the proportions of the controls inside the user control form, you will have to work a bit harder.

What we need to do is sometimes described as making a container *elastic.* ⊃

It is possible to buy an elastic container control. For example, VideoSoft has a shareware control called Elastic (supplied on the CD in the \VideoSoft\Vs-OCX directory) that is a quite powerful generic elastic container. (We should point out that we did have some trouble getting it to work in the beta of the CCE. You may want to contact the company for an update.)

Using a third party elastic control does have some definite costs, and we don't only mean the cost of the control. For example, using an elastic control inside your own user control might enlarge the footprint of your control too much. ⊃

If you choose to write the code yourself, the trick is to get out of the habit of thinking of controls as having a fixed size. Instead, think of them as having certain proportions relative to the user control form.

To see what we mean, let's start with a simple example: you want to write the code that will guarantee that the command button will always show up centered at the bottom of the user control form with the same proportions it had when you started out.

Here are the relative dimensions on a 640 × 480 video display of a user control form and a default size command button. (Use the ScaleHeight and ScaleWidth properties to get at the dimensions of the interior of the user control form for other resolutions.)

Object	Height	Width
Command button	495	1215
Form	4140	6690

Thus, the ratio of the heights is 495/4140, and that of the widths, 1215/6690. Given this information, you can use the Move method in the UserControl_Resize event to make sure the command is always centered on the bottom of the form and has the correct proportions.

```
Sub UserControl_Resize()
    Dim TheHeight As Single, TheWidth As Single
    TheHeight = (495/4140)*ScaleHeight
    TheWidth = (1215/6690)*ScaleWidth
    Command1.Move ScaleWidth/2 -(TheWidth/2), _
ScaleHeight -_ TheHeight, TheWidth, TheHeight
End Sub
```

The key line

```
Command1.Move ScaleWidth/2 -(TheWidth/2), _
ScaleHeight -_ TheHeight, TheWidth, TheHeight
```

moves the command button exactly where you want it.

If you haven't set AutoRedraw to True, you will want to have the Paint event procedure call the Resize event procedure. ⊃

Of course, this is rather cumbersome to do by hand if you have many controls on a form. However, it is not hard to see how to automate this process.

1. Set up a type called ProportionsForAControl in the Declaration section of a code module:

```
Type ProportionsForAControl
    WidthProportions As Single
    HeightProportions as Single
    TopProportions As Single
    LeftProportions as Single
End Type
```

2. Set up a form-level array of these records:

```
Dim ControlProportionsArray() As ProportionsForAControl
```

3. In the UserControl_Initialize event, use the Controls.Count property to redimension the ControlProportionsArray array we are using to hold the proportion information. (Every time you add a control by using a control array, update the information.)

4. Fill the array with the correct values by iterating through the Controls collection to get the proportions of all the controls on the form.

5. Use the information now contained in the ControlProportionsArray in the UserControl_Resize procedure to resize all the controls on the form whenever the form is resized.

 The only thing to be aware of in writing the code is that you want to avoid checking the size of invisible controls such as Timers or CommonDialog controls. We do this using On Error Resume Next; you could also directly check the type of the control. ⊃

Here's the complete code for one version of a generic resize routine for your user controls that follows the above outline.

```
Private Type ControlProportions
    WidthProportions As Single
    HeightProportions As Single
    TopProportions As Single
    LeftProportions As Single
End Type
Dim ArrayOfProportions() As ControlProportions

Sub InitResizeArray()
    On Error Resume Next
    Dim I As Integer
    ReDim ArrayOfProportions(0 To Controls.Count - 1)
    For I = 0 To Controls.Count - 1
        With ArrayOfProportions(I)
            .WidthProportions = Controls(I).Width / ScaleWidth
            .HeightProportions = Controls(I).Height / _
                ScaleHeight
            .LeftProportions = Controls(I).Left / ScaleWidth
            .TopProportions = Controls(I).Top / ScaleHeight
        End With
    Next I
End Sub

Sub ResizeControls()
    On Error Resume Next
    Dim I As Integer
    For I = 0 To Controls.Count - 1
        With ArrayOfProportions(I)
            'we will move the controls to where they should be
            'resizing them proportionally
            Controls(I).Move .LeftProportions * ScaleWidth, _
                           .TopProportions * ScaleHeight, _
```

```
                                  .WidthProportions * ScaleWidth, _
                                  .HeightProportions * ScaleHeight
            End With
         Next I
      End Sub

      Private Sub UserControl_Initialize()
         InitResizeArray
      End Sub

      Sub UserControl_Resize()
         ResizeControls
      End Sub
```

A Full-Blown Example: An Integer Text Box

Although we have a few more points to cover about user controls, we have covered enough so that you can understand the code for an IntegerTextBox that:

- Accepts only integers
- Has a minimum and maximum possible acceptable value as custom properties
- Resizes itself properly

Let's go through the main point of the control. The full code of the control will be found in the CH 8 directory on the CD. Note that you have already seen the ReadProperties and WriteProperties event codes, so we won't repeat them in this section.

First, we have the general declarations. They look like this:

```
Option Explicit

Public Event BadValue(bSetToLimit As Boolean)
Public Event BadKey()
'Default Property Values:
Const m_def_Value = 0
```

```
Const m_def_MinValue = 0
Const m_def_MaxValue = 1000
'Property Variables:
Dim m_Value As Integer
Dim m_MinValue As Integer
Dim m_MaxValue As Integer
```

Besides the Option Explicit to enforce good programming habits, we have the declaration for the two Public events, one for a bad keystroke and the other if the value the end user enters (or pastes) is too large. The Constants give us some reasonable defaults for the MinValue and MaxValue properties.

The first code you write for a control will almost always be in the Initialize event. Ours simply looks at the form level constants to set up the Initial values. (These values, in turn, could be changed by the ReadProperties event code that you already saw.) The code for the Initialize event looks like this:

```
'Initialize Properties for User Control
Private Sub UserControl_InitProperties()
  m_Value = m_def_Value
  m_MinValue = m_def_MinValue
  m_MaxValue = m_def_MaxValue
End Sub
```

Next, here's the simple code we chose to use for the Resize event:

```
Private Sub UserControl_Resize()
  'stretch to width of control
  txtValue.Width = Width
  'set to fixed height
  Height = 330
End Sub
```

Notice that we decided to have the text box that is the only constituent of the user control to have a fixed height but its width will always be as large as the user control container.

Next, here's the code for the Change event. At this point, it should be pretty straightforward. The idea is simply to check whether what has been entered is bigger than the current settings of the m_MinValue and m_MaxValue instance variables:

```
Private Sub txtValue_Change()
  Dim bSetToLimit As Boolean
  'check the value for proper range
  If Val(txtValue.Text) < m_MinValue Then
    'raise the event

    RaiseEvent BadValue(bSetToLimit)
    If bSetToLimit Then
      'reset to the min value
      txtValue.Text = m_MinValue
    Else
      'reset to previous value
      txtValue.Text = m_Value
    End If
  ElseIf Val(txtValue.Text) > m_MaxValue Then
    'raise the event
    RaiseEvent BadValue(bSetToLimit)
    If bSetToLimit Then
      'reset to the max value
      txtValue.Text = m_MaxValue
    Else
      'reset to previous value
      txtValue.Text = m_Value
    End If
  End If
  'set the value var
  m_Value = Val(txtValue.Text)
End Sub
```

The KeyPress event needs to be a little more sophisticated than the one you saw in Chapter 1. We want to allow the end user of the control to use the Backspace key as well as a negative sign if it is in the first position in the text box. (This occurs when the value of txtValue.SelStart is 0. You could allow trailing spaces if you want by first using the LTrim function before checking for the minus sign.)

```
Private Sub txtValue_KeyPress(KeyAscii As Integer)
    'minus sign only at first character
    Dim GoodEntry As Boolean
    'backspace allowed
    If KeyAscii = Asc(vbBack) Then Exit Sub
    ' need to check for minus  sign only at beginning
```

```
Select Case txtValue.SelStart
   Case 0
      If KeyAscii = Asc("-") Or (KeyAscii >= _
      Asc("0") And KeyAscii <= Asc("9")) Then
         GoodEntry = True
      End If
   Case Else
      If (KeyAscii >= Asc("0") And KeyAscii _
<= Asc("9")) Then
         GoodEntry = True
      End If
   End Select
   If Not GoodEntry Then
      KeyAscii = 0
      RaiseEvent BadKey
   End If
End Sub
```

Then we have the code for the three custom properties. Here's the code for the Value property. It simply reads off the current state of the m_Value instance variable.

```
Public Property Get Value() As Integer
   Value = m_Value
End Property
```

The associated Property Let procedure updates the value of the m_Value instance variable after checking that the bounds haven't been breached. (We pop up a message box if it has.) The code looks like this:

```
Public Property Let Value(ByVal New_Value As Integer)
   If New_Value < m_MinValue Then
      MsgBox "Minimum Limit Exceeded!"
      m_Value = m_MinValue
   ElseIf New_Value > m_MaxValue Then
      MsgBox "Maximum Limit Exceeded!"
      m_Value = m_MaxValue
   Else
      m_Value = New_Value
   End If
   txtValue.Text = m_Value
   PropertyChanged "Value"
End Property
```

The Property Procedures for the MinValue and MaxValue propeties are similar:

```
Public Property Get MinValue() As Integer
   MinValue = m_MinValue
End Property


Public Property Let MinValue(ByVal New_MinValue As _
Integer)
   If New_MinValue > m_MaxValue Then
     MsgBox "Minimum cannot exceed Maximum!"
   Else
      m_MinValue = New_MinValue
      PropertyChanged "MinValue"
   End If
End Property

Public Property Get MaxValue() As Integer
   MaxValue = m_MaxValue
End Property

Public Property Let MaxValue(ByVal New_MaxValue As _
Integer)
   If New_MaxValue < m_MinValue Then
     MsgBox "Maximum cannot be less than Minimum!"
   Else
      m_MaxValue = New_MaxValue
      PropertyChanged "MaxValue"
   End If
End Property
```

Interacting with the User of Your Control

One of the things the code in your user control has to know is whether the control is being used at design time or run time. After all, you may want to only allow setting certain properties at design time or run time. This is done by checking the current state of the UserMode of the Ambient object in your code. For example, in Chapter 11 we have a label that changes color depending on Timer events from a Timer control. We don't want the label to change color when it is in design mode. So our Timer event looks like this:

```
Private Sub Timer1_Timer()
  On Error Resume Next
  Static nColor As Integer
  If Not Ambient.UserMode Then Exit Sub 'don't
                          ' execute in design mode
  If nColor = 15 Then
    nColor = 0                         'start over again
  Else
    nColor = nColor + 1                'increment it
  End If
  lblLabel.ForeColor = QBColor(nColor)  'set the forecolor
End Sub
```

The point is that we don't want the Timer event to do anything when the user of our control is designing a form with our custom control. (The Ambient.UserMode value is True if we are in design time and False otherwise.)

Use similar code in Property Procedures to give design-time or run-time properties. Simply check for the state of Ambient.UserMode before executing the code in the Property procedure. ⊃

What is going on under the hood is actually kind of interesting; we want to spend a little more time on the Ambient keyword. First off, what the Ambient property is really doing is returning an AmbientProperties Object. This object, in turn, has properties like the UserMode property that you can query to find interesting information about the container in which your control is sitting.

In addition, the AmbientProperties object lets you check for suggested values for some of the more common properties. For example, you can use the value of Ambient.BackColor or Ambient.ForeColor to find out what the container is suggesting for the back color and forecolor of your control. You can use the Ambient.DisplayName value to see if the container has a suggested name for the control. The value of the Ambient.LocaleID property is a long integer that follows Windows conventions in telling you the language and country of the user. (We suggest looking at the on-line help for more information on this useful object.)

Extender Object

The Extender object is often more useful than the AmbientProperties object. This object gives you access to certain properties, methods, and events that come from the container control. For example, if you have a label or text like object, perhaps you want the default caption or text to be the same as the name the user gives to the current instance of your user control. Notice that this is a value given in the Properties window of the form designer and it is not immediately clear how to access this information. Through the wonder of the Extender object, all you have to do is query the current value of the Extender.Name property!

The following table lists the most useful Extender properties.

You cannot be sure all the environments that are using your control will provide the Extender properties, methods, and events described in the following tables. For example, browsers would not normally provide a property like the Extender.Left property to tell you how far from the left edge of the container you are. ⊃

Extender Property	Description
Name	Gives the name the user of your control gave the current instance.
Visible	Tells if the instance of your user control is currently visible.
Parent	Gives the name of the container for your control on the user's form (usually the name of the form, but could be a picture box or a frame, for example).
Cancel	Used for button-like objects. Tells you whether your control is the default Cancel button for the container.
Default	As with Cancel, this property tells you if the user control is the default button for the container.
Container	Returns a read-only object that represents the visual container of the control.
DragIcon	A read/write property that specifies the icon to use when your user control is dragged someplace.
DragMode	This read/write property tells you whether you are in manual or automatic mode for dragging.
Enabled	This read-only property tells you if the instance of your control is currently enabled.
Height	A read/write property that returns an integer that gives the height of the control in the container's scale units.

Extender Property	Description
HelpContextID	A read/write property that specifies the context ID in the associated Help file that should be used when the user of the object presses the F1 key when the instance of your control has the focus.
Index	A read-only property that specifies the position in a control array this instance of the control occupies.
Left	A read/write property that specifies the position of the left edge of the control relative to the left edge of the container. (Uses the scale of the container of your control.)
TabIndex	A read/write property that gives the tab order for your control.
TabStop property	This read/write property specifies whether your control can be tabbed to.
Tag	Gives the value of the Tag property that the user gave the instance of your control.
ToolTipText	A read/write property that gives exactly what the name implies.
Top	This read/write property specifies the position of the top edge of the instance of your control relative to the top edge of the container. (As with the other size properties, uses the scale of the container.)
Width	This read/write property gives the width of the instance of your user control in the container's scale units.

The Extender object also has some methods your control can use. The most useful are described in the following table.

Method	Description
Drag	Use this method to begin, end, or cancel someone trying to drag your control.
Move	Lets you move the instance of your control around.
SetFocus	Sets the focus to your control.
Zorder	Lets you change the Z-order for your control (see Chapter 6).

Next, we have the Extender events that you can work with.

Event	Description
DragDrop	This event is raised when another control on the form is dropped on your control.
DragOver	This event is raised when another control on the form is dragged over your control.
GotFocus	This event is triggered when your control gets the focus.
LostFocus	This event is raised when your control loses the focus.

An Example: The Guaranteed-to-Drive-Your-User-Crazy Command Button

We want to show off the powers of the Extender object with a custom command button that you will probably not want to use in your projects. Why? Well, anytime the mouse gets near it, it runs away.

The full code is on the CD, the code that make it behave the way it does needs to be in the MouseMove event. Although the code is a little complicated, the idea is actually simple: any time the mouse gets inside our control, we move it to a new location. (If need be, we make it appear on the opposite edge of the containing form.) There are two ways to do this. The first is to do what we did and directly reset the UserControl.Extender.Left and the UserControl.Extender.Top properties. The second is to call the UserControl.Extender.Move method.

Here's the mouse move procedure that makes our control so cruel.

```
Private Sub Command1_MouseMove(Button As Integer,_
Shift As Integer, X As Single, Y As Single)
    Dim l As Single
    Dim t As Single
    l = UserControl.Extender.Left
    t = UserControl.Extender.Top

    Const Unit = 100

    'see what direction they moved in from
    If X < (BTN_WIDTH / 2) Then
        'they are on the left half of the button
        l = l + Unit
```

```
      If Y < (BTN_HEIGHT / 2) Then
        'they are on the top half of the button
        t = t + Unit
      Else
        t = t - Unit
      End If
    Else
      l = l - Unit
      If Y < (BTN_HEIGHT / 2) Then
        'they are on the top half of the button
        t = t + Unit
      Else
        t = t - Unit
      End If
    End If

    'check the left setting
    If (l + BTN_WIDTH) < (Unit * 4) Then
      'went off the left side of the screen
      l = UserControl.Extender.Container.ScaleWidth - _
      BTN_WIDTH
    ElseIf (l + Unit) >
UserControl.Extender.Container.ScaleWidth Then
      'went off the right side of the screen
      l = 0 'ScaleWidth + Unit
    End If

    'check the top setting
    If (t + BTN_HEIGHT) < (Unit * 4) Then
      'went off the top of the screen
      t = UserControl.Extender.Container.ScaleHeight - _
      BTN_HEIGHT
    ElseIf (t + Unit) >
UserControl.Extender.Container.ScaleHeight Then
      'went off the bottom of the screen
      t = 0 'ScaleHeight + Unit
    End If

    'now set the new left and top
    UserControl.Extender.Left = l
    UserControl.Extender.Top = t
End Sub
```

Under the Hood of a Control: COM/OLE

We want to end this chapter with a very brief introduction to the technology that underlies ActiveX controls. (The standard reference, Adam Denning's *OLE Controls Inside Out* (Microsoft Press, 1996) is 559 pages and, like all complete treatments of COM, requires some knowledge of C++.) Nonetheless, we would like to give you a short overview.

First, ActiveX controls are Microsoft's attempt to realize one of the rallying cries of OOP: "Objects Everywhere." This has a nice ring to it, but what does it really mean? Well, one problem with OOP is that it was traditionally a technique for working with source code. You built your program up from objects that were supplied as source code. When you distribute an ActiveX control, you will almost certainly not want to distribute your source code for recompiling by the developer who is using your control. (That would be giving away too much.)

Instead, what you want to distribute to developers is something that is ultimately just a bunch of bytes. But, ask yourself, how can a stream of bytes sent over the Internet or pulled off a floppy be translated into an object that you can use in your browser or on a form? The only way this can happen is if there is some translation scheme available that takes the bytes and makes sense out of it.

Microsoft calls its version of the technology needed for doing a translation between byte streams and useful objects COM (which stands for the common object model). There's also a version called DCOM (for the distributed common object model—the one that could be used over a network) but, except for some technicalities, the basic ideas are the same in both cases.

There are competing technologies. The most popular is CORBA (which stands for common object request broker). You might want to visit www.omg.com to learn more about the CORBA specification. ⊃

The way this magic can happen is that every ActiveX control (or, for that matter, every COM compliant object) that comes across the Net, or is pulled off a disk, comes with an identifier that describes the *interfaces* it supports. (Recall from the last chapter that interfaces are contracts between the object and the user of the object that specify the signatures of the messages the object can accept.) There is only one required interface for a COM object, called IUnknown. This interface has three member functions in it called

QueryInterface, AddRef and Release. (The last two are for dealing with the lifetime of COM objects, so we won't cover them here.)

The QueryInterface function is the one that gives you information about the other interfaces the COM object supports. (COM objects can support multiple interfaces.) Once the user of your control knows the interfaces your control can support, it has a fighting chance to gain access to the functionality embedded in your object. It simply has to send a call that uses the right signature via the STDOLE libraries that are part of the support for COM to the object. Although not completely true, think of the STDOLE's libraries as being responsible for the communication link between your code and the COM object.

Technically, what a call to QueryInterface does is return a pointer to the information about the other interfaces that the COM object supports. The user of the control never gets the address of the functions in these other interfaces; instead, what it gets back is a pointer to a pointer in the vtable. If you don't know what these terms mean, don't worry. ⊃

For example, when you use Visual Basic code that looks like this:

```
Dim AnObject As Object
Set AnObject = CreateObject("WordBasic")
```

then under the hood you have made a call to QueryInterface to find out about the IDispatch interface of the WordBasic class. (IDispatch is the interface responsible for OLE automation for those coming from a VB background.)

So, how can a COM object tell the world what interfaces it supports? Roughly speaking, here's what happens: when you compile one of your controls into an OCX, you will have automatically created an enormous (128-bit) number called a GUID (globally unique identifier). This GUID describes the interfaces that your object can expose in the sense that the user of your object (via the COM libraries like STDOLE) knows how to translate the GUID into descriptions of the interfaces that the object supports. You can have multiple GUIDs associated to an object if your object supports multiple interfaces. (Each GUID that represents an interface is sometimes called an IID.)

GUIDs are stored in the registry under Windows 95 and Windows NT in HKEY_CLASSES_ROOT. If you look at the registry with RegEdit, you can see the GUIDs for the components installed on your machine. Since 128-bit numbers are so large and the method used to create the 128-bit GUID is designed to give you a unique one, there is no chance that two objects will share the same GUID. (The number in the registry is actually a 32-hex digit equivalent of the GUID.) ⊃

Finally, the uniqueness of the GUID for each compiled version of your control can lead to problems when you create multiple OCXs from essentially the same source file. For one thing, your registry can get cluttered and the Project|Components dialog box will, too. (See Chapter 12 for some ways around this problem.)

Chapter 9

The last chapter painted a picture of what goes into making a user control, using pretty wide brush strokes. This chapter goes into the nitty gritty of how best to expose the control methods, properties and events (that is, how to expose the members of your control).

 In this chapter, as in the previous one, we are using the term *members* to refer, collectively, to the methods, properties and events of a user control. ⊃

To give the user of your control the ability to fine tune the control for specific use may require exposing dozens of members. Of course, as you saw in the last chapter, exposing the members of the constituent controls that make up your user control is not conceptually difficult; it just requires writing lots of routine code.

For example, every member you want to make public needs to be distinguished from every member you want to keep private, and, regardless of the scope, both may require writing two routine Property procedures. Also, once you have a lot of constituent controls in your user control, it becomes more complicated to *map* the members correctly. (As you saw in the last chapter, mapping simply refers to how members of the user control pair up with members of the constituent controls.) For example, if you have 5 labels and a caption property for your control, do you want to map the caption property of your user control to the caption property of the first label, the second? Perhaps you don't want to map it to the caption property of a label at all!

Using the Control Interface Wizard

Of course, you could write all the needed code by hand following the models from the last chapter, but the process is tedious, at best. Even the most experienced VB developer would not willingly do what is required if there was an easier way. And, there is. The *Control Interface Wizard* that comes with the CCE (on the Add-Ins menu) writes a lot of the necessary code automatically. Even the most experienced control developers (including those at Microsoft!) use the Control Interface Wizard to build the functionality into their controls. Then, they tweak the resulting code by hand to finish off their control.

This chapter walks you through using the Control Interface Wizard and the necessary hand tweaking in two realistic situations. The first is a simple banner control. The second control is a fairly sophisticated address control. It uses multiple controls inside the user control form in order to provide more functionality and a richer user interface. (This makes how you map the members more difficult, but also more important.)

In both cases, we take you through the steps needed to use the Wizard. After each step, we explain what is going on behind the scenes given the choices we made. After all, all of the Wizards that come with the CCE are there to simplify generating the needed code. If you don't understand the code generated by a Wizard, you will never be able to take full advantage of the CCE.

A Simple Banner Control

This control is simple in the sense that it has no visible controls on it. It consists of a timer control that is invisible at run time and the user control itself used to display the text. We will create this control from scratch. Follow these steps:

1. Load the Control Creation Edition and start up a new ActiveX Control project.
2. Set the AutoRedraw property of the user control form to True. This way, the text will persist if the control is covered or moved.
3. Double-click the Timer control in the Toolbox. Using a Timer control lets us set the rate at which the banner moves.
4. Set the Interval property of the timer to 100 (milliseconds). This gives our control a default value other than the usual 0 (meaning inactive) that timers start out with.

Using the Wizard

Once you have created the user control form, you are ready to run the Control Interface Wizard. Load the Control Interface Wizard from the Add-Ins menu. Figure 9-1 shows the opening screen of the Wizard.

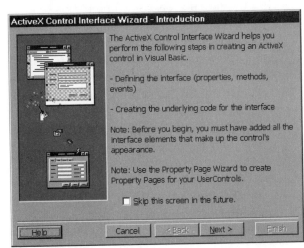

Figure 9-1
Opening screen of the Wizard

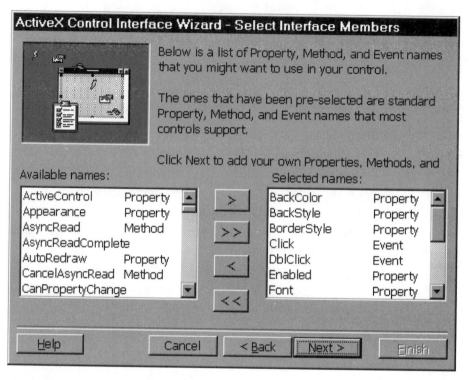

Figure 9-2
Select Interface Members screen of the Wizard

Click Next to go to the "Select Interface Members" step, as shown in Figure 9-2. As you can see, this screen is divided into two list boxes. The left one, called Available names, lists all the methods, properties and events of all the constituent controls on your user control. For example, if you scroll down you can see methods like the Cls method of the form or the Timer event of the Timer control. The right list box, called Selected names, lists the members of the constituent controls that the Wizard will make public (or *expose*, as it is usually called). For example, you probably want the user to be able to set the BackColor property of the form.

On the other hand, we do not want the user able to change the BackStyle property of our user control. (Recall the possible values are Opaque and Transparent. Why would you want a Transparent banner?) Do this by double-clicking on the BackStyle property. Double-clicking in the Wizard moves any item to the other list.

Any member you remove from the Selected names list becomes Private to your control. Removing these items tells the Wizard to not add the code needed to expose them. ⊃

Now, remove the keyboard events from the Selected names list by double-clicking them: KeyDown, KeyPress, KeyUp. These events are not needed because this control doesn't use the keyboard.

In addition to double-clicking, which moves the item to the other pane immediately, you can use the ordinary click, SHIFT + click or CTRL + click methods to select, respectively, one name, a continuous list of names, or a discontinuous group of names from a pane. Then press either the ← or → buttons to move the selected items to the other pane. ⊃

Move the Interval property from the Available names list to the Selected names list by double-clicking it. Once it is in the Selected names list, we know it will be exposed (made Public). This property needs to be exposed so the user can set the interval for the control to scroll the text.

Click Next to go to the Create Custom Interface Members screen, as shown in Figure 9-3. (A *custom interface member* is Wizard-speak for any property, event, or method that is special to your control.)

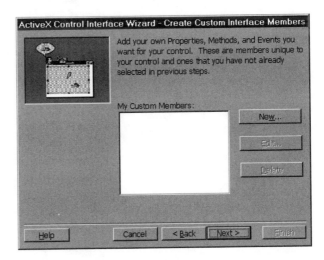

Figure 9-3
Create Custom Interface Members

We want to add our own member called Caption. This will be a string property that the user can set for the text that the banner displays. (We could have called it BannerText or some such name but it is easier for your users if you use the obvious VB equivalent of the property.) Notice that we need to add a custom property for this because the user control itself does not have a caption property. (User controls are essentially forms without title bars—no title bar, no caption!)

To do this, click New. The Add Custom Member dialog box, shown in Figure 9-4, pops up.

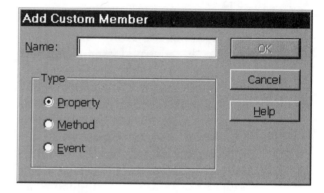

Figure 9-4
Add Custom Member
dialog box

Add a Property called Caption and click on OK.

Click Next to go to the Set Mapping step, as shown in Figure 9-5. The Set Mapping page of the Wizard is where you tell the Wizard which properties, methods and events of the user control are to be tied to properties of its constituent controls. For example, the Timer event of the user control has to be associated to the Timer event of the Timer control.

The contents of the Public Name list box in this screen are exactly the names you had in the Selected names box in the step shown in Figure 9-2. This is why you won't, for example, see a BackStyle property listed here. ⊃

Make sure the focus is at the top of the list of Public Names and press SHIFT+END to select the entire list. Now hold down the CTRL key and click on the Interval and Caption items in order to deselect them. The point is that

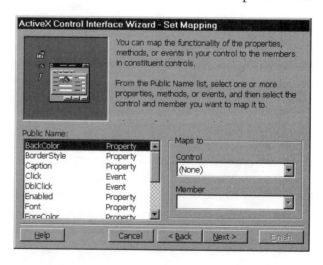

Figure 9-5
Set Mapping dialog box

these two properties need to be mapped differently than all the rest of the Public Names.

Now, in the Maps to frame, select UserControl in the Control drop-down. This will map all of the selected items to the equivalent member of the user control itself. For example, the BackColor of the banner control will come from the BackColor of the user control form.

We now need to tell the Wizard what to do with the Caption and Interval properties which do not yet have a home. Let's take up the Caption property first. For this:

1. Make sure only the Caption property is selected in the Public Name box.

2. Select None in the Control drop-down list. This is because the Caption property is not going to correspond to any property of the constituent controls.

3. Click Next to go to the Set Attributes step, as shown in Figure 9-6. This is where we set up the custom caption property. This screen tells us that this is where we can clean up the loose ends of "unmapped members."

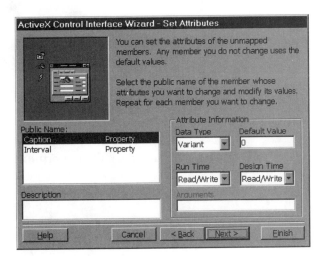

Figure 9-6
Set Attributes screen

4. Select String in the Data Type drop-down.

5. Type in This is a Banner! in the Default Value field. Leave the other drop-down boxes alone. We want our Caption property to be both readable and writable at run time and design time.

Next, we need to map the Interval property. For this:

6. Click Back to go back to the Set Mapping screen.

7. Click on Interval to set its mapping.

8. Choose Timer1 from the Control drop-down box.

9. The Interval Property pops up in the Member drop-down list box. (In general, the Member box contains a list of all the members of any constituent control you are mapping your Public names to. For a timer, this is only the Enabled and Timer members. However, since the Wizard automatically puts the default property of the control you are mapping to, the Interval property is listed here.)

Figure 9-7
Finished screen for the
Wizard

That's it. Click on Finish to go to the Finish Screen, shown in Figure 9-7, where you are given the opportunity to see the summary report, shown in Figure 9-8. (The summary report contains nothing you don't already know.)

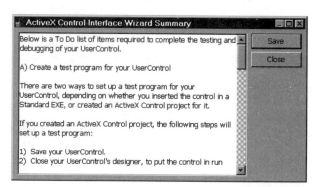

Figure 9-8
Summary screen for the
Wizard

What the Wizard Did

After you click on Finish and close the Wizard, the Wizard goes off and performs its wizardry. It creates all of the code needed to expose the properties, events and methods to the user of our user control. It also adds code to set the default values when the control is initialized. Take a look at what the Wizard created. We apologize for the length of the code, but we hope this will convince you that you would never want to write all this code yourself. The elements that go into this kind of code were explained in earlier chapters, so we won't do it again here. Note that the Wizard uses m_ to indicate its module level variables rather than a simple m as we usually do. It also leaves off the Public modifier for events, since this is the default.

```
'Default Property Values:
Const m_def_Caption = "This is a Banner!"
'Property Variables:
Dim m_Caption As String
'Event Declarations:
Event Click() 'MappingInfo=UserControl,UserControl,-1,Click
Event DblClick() 'MappingInfo=UserControl,UserControl, _
-1,DblClick
Event MouseDown(Button As Integer, Shift As Integer, _
X As Single, Y As Single)
   'MappingInfo=UserControl,UserControl,
   -1,MouseDown
Event MouseMove(Button As Integer, Shift As Integer, _
X As Single, Y As Single)
   'MappingInfo=UserControl,UserControl,-1,MouseMove
Event MouseUp(Button As Integer, Shift As Integer, X As _
Single, Y As Single) 'MappingInfo=UserControl,UserControl,
                    '-1,MouseUp

'WARNING! DO NOT REMOVE OR MODIFY THE FOLLOWING COMMENTED LINES!
'MappingInfo=UserControl,UserControl,-1,BackColor
Public Property Get BackColor() As OLE_COLOR
   BackColor = UserControl.BackColor
End Property

Public Property Let BackColor(ByVal New_BackColor As OLE_COLOR)
   UserControl.BackColor() = New_BackColor
   PropertyChanged "BackColor"
End Property
```

```
'WARNING! DO NOT REMOVE OR MODIFY THE FOLLOWING COMMENTED LINES!
'MappingInfo=UserControl,UserControl,-1,ForeColor
Public Property Get ForeColor() As OLE_COLOR
   ForeColor = UserControl.ForeColor
End Property

Public Property Let ForeColor(ByVal New_ForeColor As OLE_COLOR)
   UserControl.ForeColor() = New_ForeColor
   PropertyChanged "ForeColor"
End Property

'WARNING! DO NOT REMOVE OR MODIFY THE FOLLOWING COMMENTED LINES!
'MappingInfo=UserControl,UserControl,-1,Enabled
Public Property Get Enabled() As Boolean
   Enabled = UserControl.Enabled
End Property

Public Property Let Enabled(ByVal New_Enabled As Boolean)
   UserControl.Enabled() = New_Enabled
   PropertyChanged "Enabled"
End Property

'WARNING! DO NOT REMOVE OR MODIFY THE FOLLOWING COMMENTED LINES!
'MappingInfo=UserControl,UserControl,-1,Font
Public Property Get Font() As Font
   Set Font = UserControl.Font
End Property

Public Property Set Font(ByVal New_Font As Font)
   Set UserControl.Font = New_Font
   PropertyChanged "Font"
End Property

'WARNING! DO NOT REMOVE OR MODIFY THE FOLLOWING COMMENTED LINES!
'MappingInfo=UserControl,UserControl,-1,BackStyle
Public Property Get BackStyle() As Integer
   BackStyle = UserControl.BackStyle
End Property

Public Property Let BackStyle(ByVal New_BackStyle As Integer)
   UserControl.BackStyle() = New_BackStyle
   PropertyChanged "BackStyle"
End Property
```

```
'WARNING! DO NOT REMOVE OR MODIFY THE FOLLOWING COMMENTED LINES!
'MappingInfo=UserControl,UserControl,-1,BorderStyle
Public Property Get BorderStyle() As Integer
   BorderStyle = UserControl.BorderStyle
End Property

Public Property Let BorderStyle(ByVal New_BorderStyle As
   Integer)
   UserControl.BorderStyle() = New_BorderStyle
   PropertyChanged "BorderStyle"
End Property

'WARNING! DO NOT REMOVE OR MODIFY THE FOLLOWING COMMENTED LINES!
'MappingInfo=UserControl,UserControl,-1,Refresh
Public Sub Refresh()
   UserControl.Refresh
End Sub

Private Sub UserControl_Click()
   RaiseEvent Click
End Sub

Private Sub UserControl_DblClick()
   RaiseEvent DblClick
End Sub

Private Sub UserControl_MouseDown(Button As Integer,
   Shift As Integer, X As Single, Y As Single)
   RaiseEvent MouseDown(Button, Shift, X, Y)
End Sub

Private Sub UserControl_MouseMove(Button As Integer,
   Shift As Integer, X As Single, Y As Single)
   RaiseEvent MouseMove(Button, Shift, X, Y)
End Sub

Private Sub UserControl_MouseUp(Button As Integer,
   Shift As Integer, X As Single, Y As Single)
   RaiseEvent MouseUp(Button, Shift, X, Y)
End Sub
```

```
'WARNING! DO NOT REMOVE OR MODIFY THE FOLLOWING COMMENTED LINES!
'MappingInfo=Timer1,Timer1,-1,Interval
Public Property Get Interval() As Long
   Interval = Timer1.Interval
End Property

Public Property Let Interval(ByVal New_Interval As Long)
   Timer1.Interval() = New_Interval
   PropertyChanged "Interval"
End Property

Public Property Get Caption() As String
   Caption = m_Caption
End Property

Public Property Let Caption(ByVal New_Caption As String)
   m_Caption = New_Caption
   PropertyChanged "Caption"
End Property

'Initialize Properties for User Control
Private Sub UserControl_InitProperties()
   Set Font = Ambient.Font
   m_Caption = m_def_Caption
End Sub

'Load property values from storage
Private Sub UserControl_ReadProperties(PropBag As PropertyBag)

   UserControl.BackColor = PropBag.ReadProperty("BackColor",
     &H8000000F)
   UserControl.ForeColor = PropBag.ReadProperty("ForeColor",
     &H80000012)
   UserControl.Enabled = PropBag.ReadProperty("Enabled", True)
   Set Font = PropBag.ReadProperty("Font", Ambient.Font)
   UserControl.BackStyle = PropBag.ReadProperty("BackStyle", 1)
   UserControl.BorderStyle =
     PropBag.ReadProperty("BorderStyle", 0)
   Timer1.Interval = PropBag.ReadProperty("Interval", 0)
   m_Caption = PropBag.ReadProperty("Caption", m_def_Caption)
End Sub
```

```
'Write property values to storage
Private Sub UserControl_WriteProperties(PropBag As PropertyBag)

  Call PropBag.WriteProperty("BackColor",
    UserControl.BackColor, &H8000000F)
  Call PropBag.WriteProperty("ForeColor",
    UserControl.ForeColor, &H80000012)
  Call PropBag.WriteProperty("Enabled", UserControl.Enabled,
    True)
  Call PropBag.WriteProperty("Font", Font, Ambient.Font)
  Call PropBag.WriteProperty("BackStyle",
    UserControl.BackStyle, 1)
  Call PropBag.WriteProperty("BorderStyle",
    UserControl.BorderStyle, 0)
  Call PropBag.WriteProperty("Interval", Timer1.Interval, 0)
  Call PropBag.WriteProperty("Caption", m_Caption,
    m_def_Caption)
End Sub
```

Activating the Banner

We still need to add some code to make the control actually act as a banner.
The following code lets the text scroll from right to left at the desired interval.

```
Private Sub Timer1_Timer()
  Static nPos As Integer
  Static msBanner As String

  If Not Ambient.UserMode Then Exit Sub  'design mode
                          'so no scroll in design mode
  If Len(msBanner) = 0 Then
    msBanner = Caption & Space(Len(Caption))
    While TextWidth(msBanner) < (Width * 2)
      'pad with spaces to fill the whole control twice
      msBanner = msBanner & " "
    Wend
    nPos = 1
  End If
```

```
'move left the corrected number of positions based on
'the character width of the current left most character
nPos = nPos + ((TextWidth("W") \ TextWidth(Mid$(msBanner,_
nPos, 1))))
'check for being past the end of the string and reset if so
If nPos > Len(msBanner) Then nPos = 1
'shift it to the right
m_Caption = Mid$(msBanner, nPos) & Left$(msBanner, nPos)
RefreshCaption
End Sub
```

Since the caption is drawn directly on the user control itself, we need to write code to do this. We need to do this from a lot of places, so it is best to encapsulate it in a subroutine.

```
Sub RefreshCaption()
   'print the caption
   UserControl.Cls: UserControl.Print m_Caption
End Sub
```

Now, we need to add the RefreshCaption call to some spots in the code the Wizard generated. Basically, any Property Let routine that changes the user control needs to also reset the caption, such as the Property Let associated to the BackColor, ForeColor, Font and Caption properties. Add a call to the sub, above the PropertyChanged call, as in the following example.

```
Public Property Let BackColor(ByVal New_BackColor As OLE_COLOR)
   UserControl.BackColor() = New_BackColor
   RefreshCaption
   PropertyChanged "BackColor"
End Property
```

Just a few more code changes and we'll be done. In order to make the control look a little nicer in its default state, let's add some defaults of our own to the UserControl_InitProperties event. We need to replace the subroutine that the Wizard created with the one given next. This code will make the control start off with a border, a red background, blue text and a bold Courier font.

```
'Initialize Properties for User Control
Private Sub UserControl_InitProperties()
  'set the defaults
  BackColor = &HFFFF00
  ForeColor = &HFF&
  BorderStyle = 1
  UserControl.FontName = "Courier New"
  UserControl.FontBold = True
  m_Caption = m_def_Caption
End Sub
```

Now, in order to make the control properly display the caption when we place one on a form, we need to add the RefreshCaption call to the resize event of the user control, as in:

```
Private Sub UserControl_Resize()
  RefreshCaption
End Sub
```

Finally, to make it even neater, let's add code to resize the font when the user of the control resizes it.

```
Private Sub UserControl_Resize()
  Static sglLastHeight As Single
  Dim sglCurrHeight As Single
  Dim nFont As Single

  If sglLastHeight = 0 Then
    'initialize it
    sglLastHeight = Height
  End If

  nFont = UserControl.FontSize
  sglCurrHeight = Height

  'resize the font to match the control size
  If (sglLastHeight <= sglCurrHeight) And (TextHeight("A") _
< sglCurrHeight) Then
    'they enlarged it
    While TextHeight("A") <= sglCurrHeight
      nFont = nFont + 0.25
      UserControl.FontSize = nFont
    Wend
  Else
```

```
     'they reduced it
     While (TextHeight("A") >= sglCurrHeight) And (nFont > 1.25)
        nFont = nFont - 0.25
        UserControl.FontSize = nFont
     Wend
  End If
'save the current height to compare against next time
  sglLastHeight = Height
  RefreshCaption
End Sub
```

Testing the Banner Control

Now, we have a pretty cool banner control that we created in about an hour using the power of the Control Interface Wizard and a little code of our own. To test it, follow these steps:

1. Close the user control.
2. Add a Standard EXE project using File|Add Project.
3. Place an instance of the newly created BannerControl on Form1.
4. Press F5.

It should display "This is a Banner!" in a scrolling fashion from right to left.

An Address Control

Now, we are going to move on to a more complex control that requires more programming and a greater use of the Control Interface Wizard in order to add and map its own custom properties, events and methods. This control has a much more substantial user interface, as shown in Figure 9-9. Notice that this control has fifteen constituent controls. The idea, of course, is that anytime you need to allow a user to enter an address in a VB project or on a Web page, you can use this ActiveX control rather than recoding it from scratch.

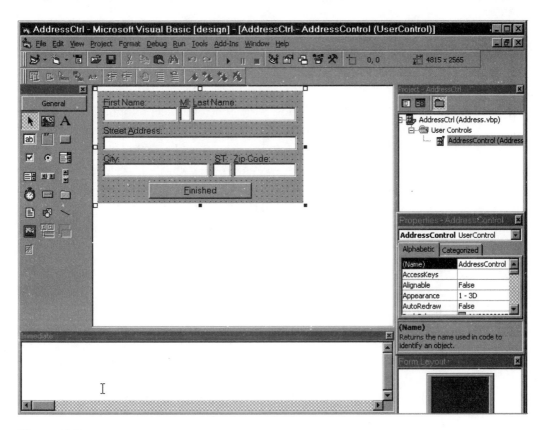

Figure 9-9
The designer for the Address Control

This control uses two control arrays: one for the various text boxes and the other for the labels. As you will see, using control arrays considerably simplifies the code for the control.

Given the complexity of the user interface, you might want to load the form for the user control from the CD. The control in its raw state is named `AddressFirstStage.vbp` and may be found in the CH9 directory of the CD. Of course, the `AddressFirstStage.vbp` is currently unusable because it does not expose any members. The user of this control in its current state couldn't do anything useful with it. Therefore, it's time to use the Control Interface Wizard to make our job easier.

The Control Interface Wizard and the Address Control

Load the `AddressFirstStage.vbp` control project into the CCE and start up the ActiveX Control Interface Wizard from the Add-Ins menu. Click Next to go to the Select Interface Members step. At this step:

1. Click the DOUBLE LEFT ARROW button to move all of the default selections to the Available names list. If we stopped at this point, we would be exposing nothing to the user of the control.

2. Double-click the following member items from the Available names list in order to move them to the Selected names list:

`BackColor, BorderStyle, Change, Enabled, Font and ForeColor`

These are the properties, events and methods we want to expose to the user. We now want to add a few custom members to our Address Control. The tricky thing here is that since our Address Control has so many constituent controls of the same type, we need to be careful about what member of our control gets mapped to what member of one of the eight constituent controls. So, click Next to go to the Create Custom Interface Members step. Now:

1. Click New and add a property called DataFont.
2. Click New and add a property called DataBackColor.
3. Click New and add a property called DataForeColor.
4. Click New and add a property called FirstName.
5. Click New and add a property called LastName.
6. Click New and add a property called MI.
7. Click New and add a property called Address.
8. Click New and add a property called City.
9. Click New and add a property called State.
10. Click New and add a property called Zip.
11. Click New and add a method called ClearAll.
12. Click New and add an event called Finished.

The result is shown in Figure 9-10.

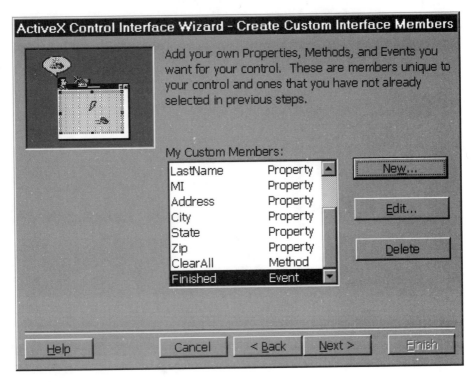

Figure 9-10
Custom Interface Members for the Address Control

The idea is to present the user of the control with a property like FirstName but map that to the Text property of the appropriate text box. This is the role of the Set Mapping screen in the Control Interface Wizard. So click on Next to take you to the Set Mapping screen, as shown in Figure 9-11 on the next page. Notice that the Public Name box lists all the names we had in the Select names box in the second screen of the Wizard, plus all the custom members we just created.

Mapping the Members

This is where we tell the Wizard how to map the various members we have selected so it will know what code to generate in order to do the mapping. The following table shows how to map the members.

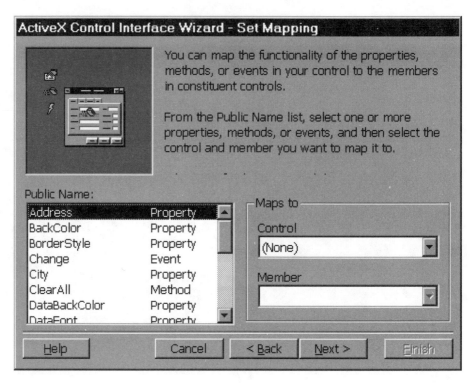

Figure 9-11
The Set Mapping screen for the Address Control

Member Name	Maps to Control	Maps to Member
Address	Control = "txtData(3)"	Member = "Text"
BackColor	Control = "UserControl"	Member = "BackColor"
BorderStyle	Control = "UserControl "	Member = "BorderStyle"
Change	Control = "txtData(0)"	Member = "Change"
City	Control = "txtData(4)"	Member = "Text"

The ClearAll method does not really map to any member of the constituent controls or the user control form, so we need to leave it unmapped. Any unmapped members like this one will need hand-tweaked code to make it work correctly. For this, simply map the ClearAll property to the user control but leave the Member box blank.

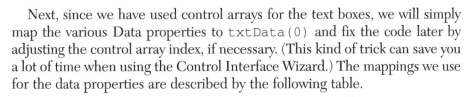

Next, since we have used control arrays for the text boxes, we will simply map the various Data properties to `txtData(0)` and fix the code later by adjusting the control array index, if necessary. (This kind of trick can save you a lot of time when using the Control Interface Wizard.) The mappings we use for the data properties are described by the following table.

Member Name	Maps to Control	Maps to Member
DataBackColor	Control = "txtData(0)"	Member = "BackColor"
DataFont	Control = "txtData(0)"	Member = "Font"
DataForeColor	Control = "txtData(0)"	Member = "ForeColor"

Next, make the mapping described in the following table.

Member Name	Maps to Control	Maps to Member
Enabled	Control = "UserControl "	Member = "Enabled"
Finished	Control = "cmdFinshed"	Member = "Click"
FirstName	Control = "txtData(0)"	Member = "Text"
Font	Control = "UserControl "	Member = "Font"
ForeColor	Control = "UserControl "	Member = "ForeColor"
LastName	Control = "txtData(2)"	Member = "Text"
MI	Control = "txtData(1)"	Member = "Text"
State	Control = "txtData(5)"	Member = "Text"
Zip	Control = "txtData(6)"	Member = "Text"

That's it. Click Next to go the "Finished" step and click Finish.

Tweaking the Code

The Wizard creates a lot of the code needed for our address control. However, because of the many constituent controls and the fairly complex mapping, we need to go in and modify the code slightly to get it working correctly.

We will start at the top of the code module and work our way down, making additions and corrections as we go. You can see that the Wizard did a tremendous amount of work for us. Even where we need to add code of our own, the Wizard often provided a template for adding what we need.

The Wizard adds lots of comments beginning with `"WARNING!"`. These comments are used by the Wizard to know what it did previously when you run it another time in order to add or change something. If you change or remove any of these comments, you risk confusing the Wizard so that it may not perform as expected the next time you run it. ↝

In order to set the individual sub control property values, we need to add a loop that walks through all of the labels in the `lblLabels` control array. For example, for the Font objects, the Wizard generated this code:

```
Public Property Set Font(ByVal New_Font As Font)
   Set UserControl.Font = New_Font
   PropertyChanged "Font"
End Property
```

We need to replace this with:

```
Public Property Set Font(ByVal New_Font As Font)
   Dim i As Integer
   For i = 0 To 6: Set lblLabels(i).Font = _
   New_Font: Next
   Set UserControl.Font = New_Font
   PropertyChanged "Font"
End Property
```

in order to be sure that the fonts are changed for all the elements in our control array. (The ease of adding this kind of code is one of the main reasons why control arrays are so useful when making a user control.)

Do the same thing for the ForeColor property. Replace:

```
Public Property Let ForeColor(ByVal New_ForeColor _
As OLE_COLOR)
   UserControl.ForeColor() = New_ForeColor
   PropertyChanged "ForeColor"
End Property
```

with

```
Public Property Let ForeColor(ByVal New_ForeColor _
As OLE_COLOR)
   Dim i As Integer
   For i = 0 To 6: lblLabels(i).ForeColor = _
   New_ForeColor: Next
   UserControl.ForeColor() = New_ForeColor
   PropertyChanged "ForeColor"
End Property
```

Next, you'll need to modify the DataBackColor, DataForeColor and DataFont properties. For this, replace:

```
Public Property Let DataBackColor(ByVal
New_DataBackColor As OLE_COLOR)
   txtData(0).BackColor() = New_DataBackColor
   PropertyChanged "DataBackColor"
End Property
```

with

```
Public Property Let DataBackColor
   (ByVal New_DataBackColor As OLE_COLOR)
   Dim i As Integer
   For i = 0 To 6: txtData(i).BackColor() = _
   New_DataBackColor: Next
   PropertyChanged "DataBackColor"
End Property
```

and replace:

```
Public Property Let DataForeColor
   (ByVal New_DataForeColor As OLE_COLOR)
   txtData(0).ForeColor() = New_DataForeColor
   PropertyChanged "DataForeColor"
End Property
```

with

```
Public Property Let DataForeColor
   (ByVal New_DataForeColor As OLE_COLOR)
   Dim i As Integer
   For i = 0 To 6: txtData(i).ForeColor() = _
   New_DataForeColor: Next
   PropertyChanged "DataForeColor"
End Property
```

Finally, replace:

```
Public Property Set DataFont(ByVal New_DataFont _
As Font)
   Set txtData(0).Font = New_DataFont
   PropertyChanged "DataFont"
End Property
```

with

333

```
Public Property Set DataFont(ByVal New_DataFont _
As Font)
  Dim i As Integer
  For i = 0 To 6: Set txtData(i).Font = _
  New_DataFont: Next
  PropertyChanged "DataFont"
End Property
```

Creating a Member from Scratch— The ClearAll Method

The Wizard did not know how to handle the ClearAll method because we did not map it to anything, so we need to replace the function it created. For this, replace:

```
Public Function ClearAll() As Variant
  ClearAll = UserControl.()
End Function
```

with

```
Public Sub ClearAll()
  Dim i As Integer
  For i = 0 To 6: txtData(i).Text = _
  vbNullString: Next
End Sub
```

Mapping Common Properties

Properties like ForeColor should be set once for all the constituent controls when the user of the control works with the property. For all of the constituent controls to reflect the single value entered by the user for the ForeColor, DataBackColor and DataForeColor properties of the user control, replace the following lines in the UserControl_ReadProperties sub:

```
UserControl.ForeColor = _
PropBag.ReadProperty("ForeColor", &H80000012)
txtData(0).BackColor = _
PropBag.ReadProperty("DataBackColor", &H80000005)
txtData(0).ForeColor = _
PropBag.ReadProperty("DataForeColor", &H80000008)
```

with

```
ForeColor = PropBag.ReadProperty( _
  "ForeColor", &H80000012)
DataBackColor = _
PropBag.ReadProperty("DataBackColor", &H80000005)
DataForeColor = _
PropBag.ReadProperty("DataForeColor", &H80000008)
```

This works directly with the property rather than with the private variable and, thus, makes the change we want.

Summing Up

The control is now ready to use. It is a full-featured control that allows the user to set all of the text box values. It also allows the user to set color and font in one step. The Wizard can save a lot of time but, unfortunately, it does not do everything you need in every circumstance. The purpose of this chapter was to show what the Wizard actually did and how to use it to get you as close as possible to the code for the finished control you are trying to create. The trick is to learn what to expect from the Wizard and what you have to do yourself.

Whenever you tweak code by hand that the Wizard creates, you will probably not be able to use the Wizard again.

This is because if you ran the Wizard again, it would change a lot of the code you modified. In particular, we suggest not trying to run it again once you have your control working the way you like. You are better off continuing to put the final touches on it by hand. ⊃

If you do want to run the Wizard again, make sure you have saved and backed up your control to a different location. This way, you can go back to where you were before running the Wizard the second time. ⊃

Chapter 10

If you played around with the Windows 95 custom controls briefly described in Chapter 6, you saw they all have a property called Custom. If you clicked on this, you saw a screen that let you set the properties of the control more easily. For example, Figure 10-1 shows you the Property Pages for the Tab Strip Control.

In general, a property page makes it easier for the user of your control to use it, so you should seriously consider adding one for any control that has complex properties to set. The purpose of this chapter is to show how to build custom property pages using the CCE.

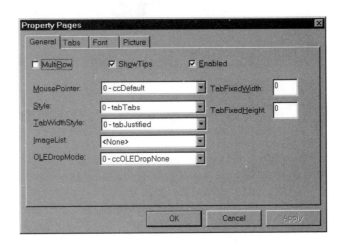

Figure 10-1
Property Pages for
the Tab Strip Control

Property Pages

Getting Started

A property page is attached to a user control as the value of its PropertyPages property. The CCE comes with three standard property pages called StandardFont, StandardColor and StandardPicture. For example, start up a user control and go to the PropertyPages property and click on the three dots. This will open up a screen like Figure 10-2.

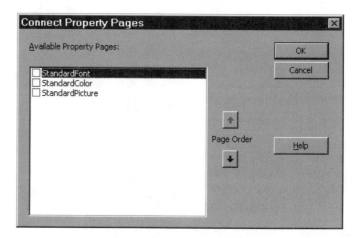

Figure 10-2
The Connect Property Pages dialog box

Choose the StandardPicture page and click on OK. At this point, your control designer doesn't look very interesting. However, if you add a Standard EXE to give a form to test the user control on and close the control designer, you will notice a new (custom) property listed for the user control, as shown in Figure 10-3.

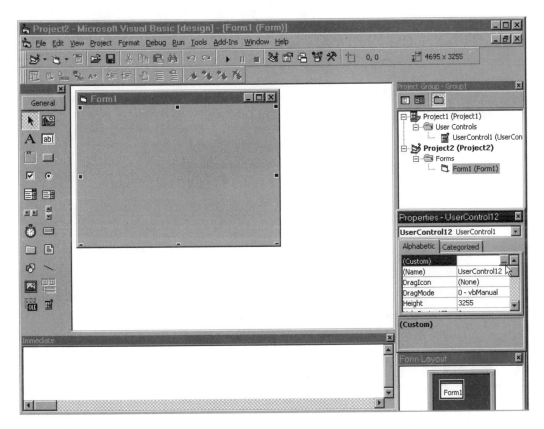

Figure 10-3
A (Custom) property

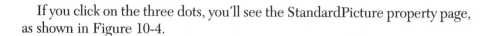

If you click on the three dots, you'll see the StandardPicture property page, as shown in Figure 10-4.

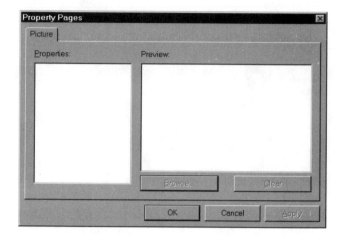

Figure 10-4
The StandardPicture
property page

Of course, this property page can't do anything because there is no code behind it. We'll show you the code needed to activate a property page shortly.

 If a control has a property page, then right-clicking on the control and clicking on Properties brings up the property page. ⊃

Finally, you can have multiple property pages by clicking off the appropriate check boxes in the Connect Property Pages dialog box. The arrow keys on this dialog box let you order them.

A Simple Property Page

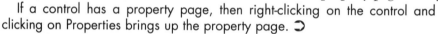

Let's start with a fairly simple example of creating a property page. To show you how to do this, let's create a control that has a property whose value is potentially a list of items. Rather than require the user to type in a long list of items separated by commas in the Properties window, we will create a property page that contains a list box with those values in it. All the user of the control has to do is select from this box using the ordinary Windows techniques for list box selection.

First, we need to create the control. This control is going to be a list box that only displays a subset of a group of possible values. For example, lets say you want to make a control that lists the days of the week for users to select from. Sometimes, you want all the days available; other times, you want just weekdays or weekend days. The property page will show a list of all the days and allow the user to select which days to display. Start up a new ActiveX project in the Control Creation Edition using the CtrlGroup so that you also have the test form. Now,

1. Add a standard list box control to the user control.
2. Set the following properties to the user control.

Constituent control	Property	Value
User Control	Name	DayListControl
List1	IntegralHeight	False
List1	Left	0
List1	MultiSelect	1 – Simple
List1	Top	0

The user control form looks like Figure 10-5.

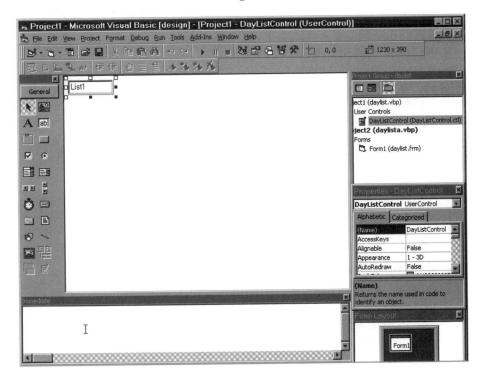

Figure 10-5
DayListControl in design time

Writing the Code for the DayList Control

Double-click the user control and add the usual code to the Resize event in order to keep the list box the same size as the surrounding user control form.

```
Private Sub UserControl_Resize()
   List1.Width = Width
   List1.Height = Height
End Sub
```

Save the control project and call it DayList.

Now, we are ready to add the ListValues property that will tell the list box which values to display when it is loaded in an application or HTML page. Internally, this will be a semicolon delimited string. To add this read/write property, we need to add the appropriate Property Get/Let procedures along with a private variable for data transfer. To do all this, add the following code to the General section of the code for the user control.

```
Dim msDays As String

Public Property Get Days() As String
   Days = msDays    'a semi-colon delimited list
End Property

Public Property Let Days(sData As String)
   Dim nEnd As Integer
   Dim nStart As Integer

   msDays = sData

   'clear out any previous items
   List1.Clear

   'add the current items to the list box by walking through the
   'delimited string and pulling out each item. This loop
   'assumes
   'that each item is followed by a ";" including the final one
   nStart = 1
   nEnd = InStr(msDays, ";")
```

```
While nEnd > 0
   List1.AddItem Mid$(msDays, nStart, nEnd - nStart)
   nStart = nEnd + 1
   nEnd = InStr(nStart, msDays, ";")
Wend

End Property
```

Next, we want to add the controls to read and write the properties back from the PropertyBag.

```
Private Sub UserControl_ReadProperties(PropBag As PropertyBag)
   'Load property values from storage
   Days = PropBag.ReadProperty("Days", msDays)
End Sub

Private Sub UserControl_WriteProperties(PropBag As PropertyBag)
   On Error Resume Next
   'Write property values to storage
   Call PropBag.WriteProperty("Days", msDays)
End Sub
```

Finally we need some code to initialize the control:

```
Private Sub UserControl_Initialize()
   msDays = Days
End Sub
```

Testing the DayList Control

Close the user control designer so the control will be available for use in the test project. Now the DayList user control is ready to test. If you don't already have a test project, select File|Add Project and add a Standard EXE project to the CCE. Add the new DayListControl and place one on the test form of the project, as shown in Figure 10-6 on the next page.

Notice that the Property window contains the Days property. Try setting it to something like Monday;Wednesday;Thursday;. If you have done everything correctly up to this point, the list should display "Monday", "Wednesday" and "Thursday". The problem is that users will have to type out the words, spell them correctly, use the right delimiter, etc., so this is not very user friendly.

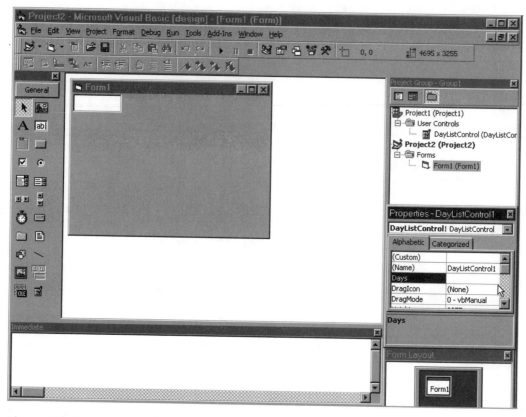

Figure 10-6
The Test form for the DayList Control

Adding the Property Page

Now, we are ready to create a Property page that allows users to set this property simply by picking days from a list. To do this, we will add a Property page that allows the user to set the Days property from it. For this:

1. Make sure that the current project is the user control.
2. Select Project|Add Property Page on the main menu bar. The Add Property Page screen shown in Figure 10-7 will show up.

Choose PropertyPage and click on Open. You should have a Property page displayed on your screen, as shown in Figure 10-8. Notice your Project window should include a Property Pages item on the same level as the user control item.

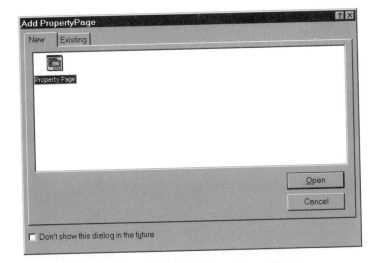

Figure 10-7
Add Property Page
dialog box

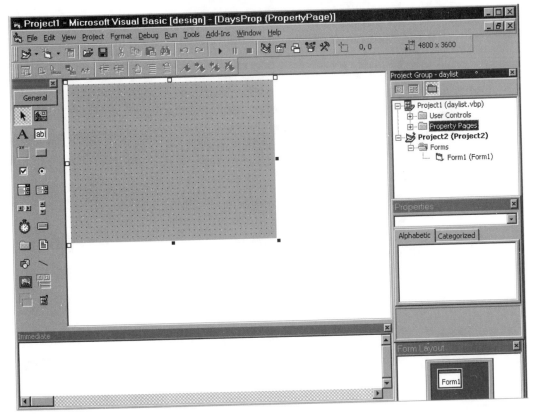

Figure 10-8
Property Page in design mode

The Property page designer looks like an ordinary form designer. The only clue is in the title bar. This is because a Property page is really just an ordinary form. In particular, that means you need to design it the way you want it to look using the techniques from Chapter 3. Add any custom controls to the tool bar of the Property page designer by choosing Project|Components.

To make our Property page:

1. Set the Name property of the Property page to DaysProp.

2. Set the Caption property of the Property page to Day List.

3. Add a List Box Control and call it 1stDays. Enlarge it to show the days of the week.

Add the days of the week to the List property of 1stDays.

Use CTRL + ENTER to separate the lines in the List box. ⊃

Your Property page designer should look like Figure 10-9.

4. Set the MultiSelect property of 1stDays to 1 – Simple.

That finishes the design stage for the Property page.

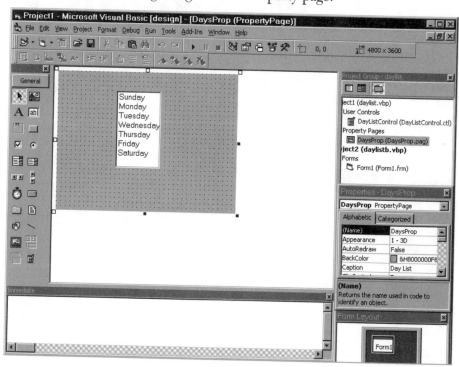

Figure 10-9
Property Page designer in progress

Activating the Property Page

We need to add the code to activate the Property page. Before we do that, however, we need to tell the user control it now has a Property page. For this:

1. Open up the Connect Property Pages dialog box by double-clicking in the PropertyPages property of the user control.
2. DaysProp should show up, in addition to the standard three Property pages that the CCE comes with. Choose it.

We need to know whether the user clicks inside the list box on the Property page. The way to do this in the CCE is by working with the value of the Changed property. For this, open a Code window for the Property page and add the three procedures that we discuss next to the Property page code.

```
Private Sub lstDays_Click()
   Changed = True
End Sub
```

This tells us that when the user clicks in the list box, the Property page has changed. (Changed is a built-in property of a Property page that returns or sets a value to tell you whether a property on a Property page has changed.)

Next, we need a procedure to apply the changes after the user makes them. This is done with the ApplyChanges event procedure that, like Changed, is one of the standard procedures that a Property page has. The code will build up the delimited string from what the user selected in the Property page and then assign it to the Days:

```
Private Sub PropertyPage_ApplyChanges()
   Dim i As Integer
   Dim sTmp As String

   'build the delimited string from the selected items
   For i = 0 To lstDays.ListCount - 1
     If lstDays.Selected(i) Then
       sTmp = sTmp & lstDays.List(i) & ";"
     End If
   Next
   SelectedControls(0).Days = sTmp
End Sub
```

`SelectedControl(0)` is the currently selected control on the form. If the user selects more than one control, `SelectedControl(0)` is the primary control in the group. None of our Property page code deals with the controls in a multiselected group. ⊃

Finally, we need the standard SelectionChanged() procedure of a Property page. This event gets triggered when the user changes anything in the Property page. This code tells us which items were selected by assigning the value of the appropriate entry in the Selected array that is associated with any list or combo box. Here is the code needed for this event.

```
Private Sub PropertyPage_SelectionChanged()
   Dim i As Integer

   'select the items that are in the string
   For i = 0 To lstDays.ListCount - 1
     If InStr(SelectedControls(0).Days,
          lstDays.List(i) & ";") > 0 Then
        lstDays.Selected(i) = True
     End If
   Next
End Sub
```

Testing the Completed Property Page

Now the property page is ready to test. Reload Form1 of the EXE project we added earlier. It should still have Monday, Wednesday and Thursday in it. Right-click the user control and select properties. The property page you just created with the 3 days selected is as shown in Figure 10-10.

Now we need to check that our property page really works. For this:

1. Make sure the DayList property page and Form1 are visible on your screen, as in Figure 10-10.

2. Click on some other day or days.

3. Then click Apply and OK.

You should see the list on Form1 change to the newly selected items and the Days property list in the Properties window will be updated as well. This is clearly much easier for the user than typing in a delimited string of entries to use our control!

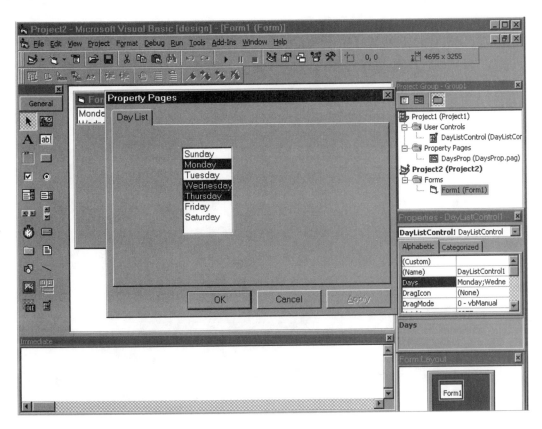

Figure 10-10
The DayList property page at work

Polishing Up Our Property Page

There are many more ways to embellish our Property page. This section will describe a few of them. First, you may have noticed that even though we created a custom Property page for the Days property, the results are still displayed in the Properties window as a delimited string that users might try to edit directly. If you want to prohibit the user of your control from doing this, you need to set an attribute of the property. To do this:

1. Load the user control code window.

2. Open the Tools menu and select Procedure Attributes.

3. Click Advanced. This brings up a screen like Figure 10-11, shown on the next page.

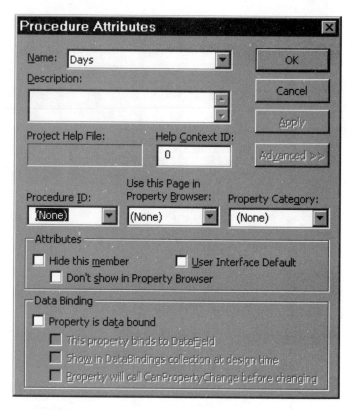

Figure 10-11
Advanced Procedure
Attributes screen

4. Check the check box titled "Don't show in property browser."

5. Click on OK to close the dialog box.

Another possibility is to leave the Days property listed in the Properties window but allow users to load the custom property page from this line of the Properties window. This is also done by setting another attribute on the Procedure Attributes dialog box. In this case:

1. Select the user control code window.

2. Click the Tools menu and select Procedure Attributes.

3. Click Advanced.

4. Uncheck the check box titled "Don't show in property browser" if it is still checked.

5. Select DaysProp from the "Use this Page in Property Browser" list.

6. Click on OK to close the dialog box.

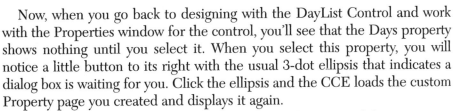

Now, when you go back to designing with the DayList Control and work with the Properties window for the control, you'll see that the Days property shows nothing until you select it. When you select this property, you will notice a little button to its right with the usual 3-dot ellipsis that indicates a dialog box is waiting for you. Click the ellipsis and the CCE loads the custom Property page you created and displays it again.

What we just did does not prohibit the user of the control from typing directly into the Properties window, but at least the Property page is there if needed. ⊃

If you want to, you can also add usability features to the Property page, such as buttons for None and All, so the user does not have to click every entry to select them all. The DayList sample project in the CH10 directory on the CD has these buttons.

The Property Page Wizard

If you create a custom control with a lot of exposed properties, CCE comes with a Property Page Wizard that makes the job of creating property pages a bit easier. However, the current version can only create text boxes and check boxes. Thus, you will need to add things like list boxes and combo boxes by hand if your property page design calls for them. Still, it is often easier to use the Wizard to reduce the amount of busy work that you would otherwise need to do. To show how the Wizard works, let's go through a typical session using it.

First, we need to create a simple control and add some properties to it in order to have something to work with. To do this, start with a simple text box and run the Control Interface Wizard to expose some properties. We will then place those properties on the Property pages we create. So, start up a new ActiveX Control project.

1. Add a text box to the user control.
2. Load the Control Interface Wizard from the Add-Ins menu.
3. Click Next to go to the Select Interface Members step.
4. Move the Locked and MaxLength properties from the Available names list to the Selected names list.
5. Move the BackStyle property from the Selected names list to the Available names list, because it does not apply to a text box.
6. Click Next to go to the Create Custom Interface Members step.

7. Click New… to create a custom member.

8. Enter P1 in the Name field.

9. Click New… again. Enter P2 in the Name field, make sure the Property button is clicked, and then click OK and click OK.

10. Click Next to go to the Set Mapping step.

11. Select the entire list of Public Names by going to the top of the Public Names and using SHIFT/END.

12. In the Control drop-down, select Text1.

13. Click Next to go to the Set Attributes step. As shown in Figure 10-12, we have only two custom properties to set attributes for.

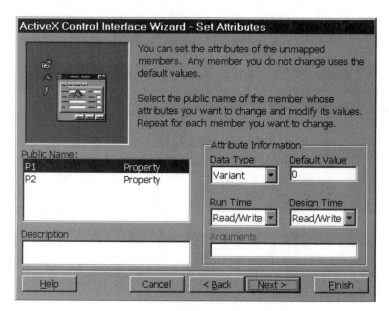

Figure 10-12
Set Attributes dialog box

14. With P1 selected in the Public Names list, select String in the Data Type drop-down list.

15. Enter abcd in the Default Value field.

16. Select P2 in the Public Names list.

17. Select Boolean in the Data Type drop-down list.

18. Click Next, then Finish to make the Wizard do its job.

The result is a simple control with lots of properties of various types. Now we are ready to create a set of Property pages for this control using the Wizard. Save your control before we go on.

Using the Property Wizard

We now have a control to show off the Property Wizard. Start up by choosing Add-Ins|Property Page Wizard. You'll probably see an introductory screen like Figure 10-13. (If not, you will see a screen like Figure 10-14.)

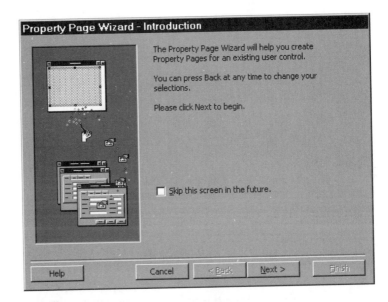

Figure 10-13
Introductory screen for the Property Wizard

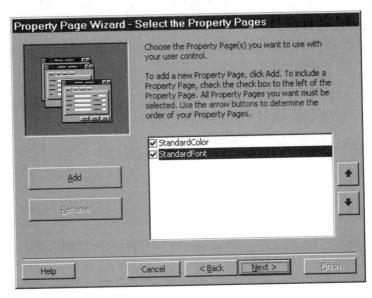

Figure 10-14
Select the Property Pages screen in the Property Wizard

Click Next to go to the first functional screen in the Wizard, as shown in Figure 10-14. Notice in Figure 10-14 that the Wizard detects that you have some properties of type Color and Font and, therefore, selects the Standard pages for these types of properties. Properties of type Font, Picture and OLE_COLOR are automatically placed on the standard pages for you. To use them, select the pages in the PropertyPages property of the user control. The Wizard will do this for you if you leave these boxes checked on this screen.

We now want to add a Property page. For this, click the Add button. A dialog box like Figure 10-15 pops up to give the name of the property page.

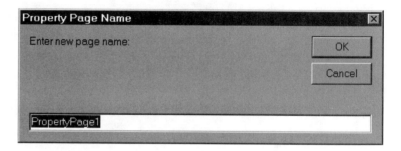

Figure 10-15
Property Page Name
dialog box

Let's call our property page General. So enter General for the new name of the Property Page and click OK to confirm the new name. Notice that the Select Property Pages screen adds the General page with a checkmark. Next, follow the procedure to add a property page named Other.

To rearrange the order the user will see the Property pages, select the page that you want to move by clicking the Up and Down arrows keys. See if you can get them in this order: General, Other, StandardColor, StandardFont.

We now want to add the appropriate properties to the Property pages we created. For this, click Next to go to the Add Properties step, as shown in Figure 10-17. This screen is where you place the properties you want on each particular page. You cannot place properties on any of the three *Standard* pages. They are simply here for reference to give you a somewhat clearer view of your final Property page collection.

There are numerous ways to get a property onto a page at this step. The most obvious is to:

1. Select a page.

2. Select a property.

3. Then click the single right arrow button to move the property to the current page.

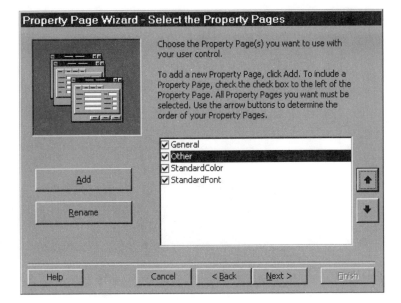

Figure 10-16
Select the Property Pages
screen completed

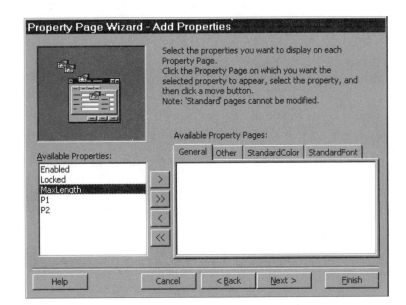

Figure 10-17
Add Properties page in
the Property Wizard

However, since this Wizard supports "drag and drop," an easier way is to simply drag the desired property from the Available Properties list to either the current page or the tab of the desired page and drop it. (There's a neat hand icon when you drag and drop, as shown in Figure 10-18.)

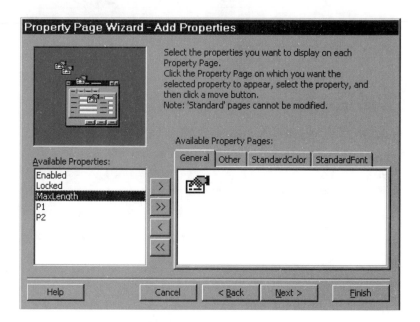

Figure 10-18
Drag and Drop in the Add Properties page

It is a good idea to add the properties in the order you want them to be displayed on the final Property pages, otherwise the Wizard will lay them out in the order you added them. ⊃

Using either technique, place the P1 and P2 properties on the Other page and the other 3 properties on the General page. Click Next, then click Finish to have the Wizard create the Property pages you have set up.

Now that the Wizard has created the Property pages, it is time to see what they look like. To do this, add a form to the control project and place a user control on it. Then you can either right-click and choose Properties, or select the Custom property in the Property Browser and click the little "…" button. The result will look like Figure 10-19.

Polishing Up the Wizard's results

The Property Page Wizard is a simple utility intended to help you get started with building Property pages. It will remove a lot of the tedium of writing the code needed to hook up the properties. It will not, however, produce sophis-

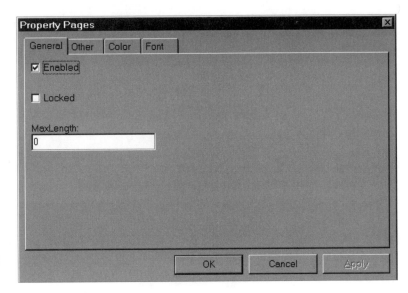

Figure 10-19
Property Pages that the
Wizard created

ticated Property pages with controls such as list boxes, option buttons or frames without you massaging the output by hand.

There is a lot you can do to enhance Property pages and make them easier to use. As you have seen with our simple DayList example, lots of properties have values that come from a set list of possibilities. If you use the Property Page Wizard, these properties will be displayed simply as multiple text boxes because it is impossible for the Wizard to determine what the predefined list of possible values is. It is fairly easy to convert a text box property to a drop-down combo. To do this with the P properties from the previous example, simply follow these steps:

1. Load the Other property page.
2. Delete the text box under the P1 caption and add a combo box in its place.
3. Set the Name property to cboP1.
4. Add some items to the List property, such as A, B, C.
5. Open the code module for the property page.
6. Replace all occurrences of txtP1 with cboP1.
7. Add the following code:

```
Private Sub cboP1_Click()
    Changed = True
End Sub
```

Now load Form1 again and right-click the user control and choose Properties to display the Properties pages. Select the Other page and notice that, instead of a text box, the user now has a drop-down combo box from which to choose a value.

Chapter 11

When you bring up the New Project dialog box in the standard install of the CCE, one of the items you see is a *Control Group Project*. This is nothing more than a User Control Project and a Standard EXE Project combined into one *project group*. This project group combines the two pieces you need to start building a control into one easy-to-use package. The Control Group Project is an example of a powerful feature called *templates* in the CCE that enables you to easily reuse objects. These objects can be controls, classes, forms, or combinations of them in a group. More precisely, a template is any Visual Basic object such as a form, class, user control, project group, etc., that can serve as a starting point for a new object of that type.

The CD supplied with this book contains a set of five user control templates based on the PictureBox, Label, TextBox, Command Button and ListBox Controls. We also added five control group projects that add the necessary EXE project for testing a control you develop from one of the five user control templates. Using our control templates, you can easily extend and test (or *subclass,* as it is usually called—although, as mentioned in Chapter 7, this isn't quite what traditional OOP uses the term for) one of these five standard controls. These templates let you enhance the most common controls without needing to do any of the preliminaries outlined in previous chapters. You won't have to run the Control Interface Wizard because we did it for you. Our templates also include the extra code needed to allow the use of design time properties such as MultiLine for a TextBox at run time.

Templates

Using Our Templates

To use the templates on the CD, you will need to copy the directories in the Template directory in the CodeFromBook directory over to the Template directory of the CCE. (This is usually called `VB5cce\Template`.) When you do this, you will have a subdirectory of the Template directory for Property Pages (PropPage), for User Controls (UserCtls), for Forms (Forms), and Control Groups (Ctlgroup).

Once you have copied our Template directory over the Template directory of the CCE, load the CCE to use one of our group templates. As shown in Figure 11-1, the New Project dialog box now automatically shows you control groups for all our user controls. Figure 11-2 shows you what the Add User Control dialog box looks like once you have copied the UserCtls directory. (You would see the dialog box in Figure 11-2 whenever you choose Project|Add User Control.)

 Any project or project groups you save to one of the subdirectories of the Template become templates themselves. They will be available when you choose to add a component of that type to your project. ⊃

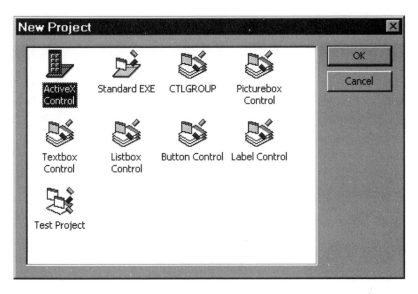

Figure 11-1
New Project dialog box with templates

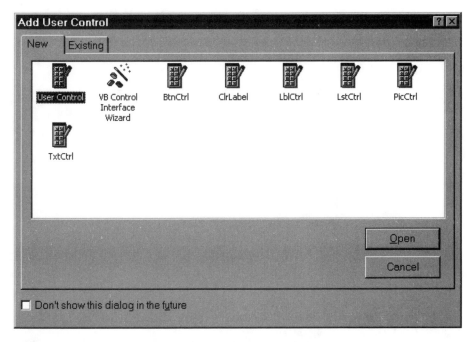

Figure 11-2
Add User Control dialog box with templates

Using One of Our Templates

Suppose you want to further customize a label and test it as well. Choose Label Control from the New Project dialog box shown in Figure 11-1. (To further customize our label control, choose LblCtrl from the Add User Control dialog box shown in Figure 11-2.)

Never use Add File from a template directory unless you want to risk changing the template. Once you save the template, it will no longer be in its original state and may not be as useful anymore. If you want to modify a template, it is best to simply load it into the CCE and then save it with your changes. ⊃

A Step-By-Step Session

In this section, we want to run through a step-by-step session with one of our templates. Load the CCE if it isn't already loaded.

1. Select the Label Control from the New Project dialog box.

2. Open the LabelControl User Control (for example, by double-clicking in the Project Explorer). You should see a screen like Figure 11-3.

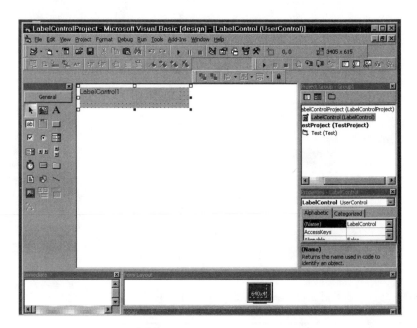

Figure 11-3
Our Label Control template in design mode

We are now going to add some code to the base control to make it cycle through colors on a timed interval. For this, we need a timer control, so add one from the toolbox by double-clicking it. (Recall the timer control is invisible at run time so you don't need to move it.) Set the Interval property of the Timer to 100 (1/10 of a second).

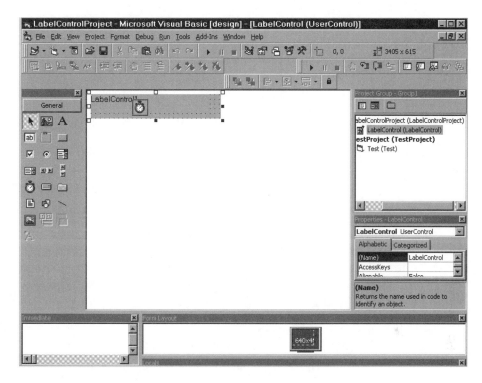

Figure 11-4
Timed Label in design stage

Next, we need to run the Control Interface Wizard to:

1. Expose the Timer Interval property.
2. Create a custom property called TimerEnabled.
3. Map the Interval property for the user control to the Timer1 control's Interval property.
4. Map the custom TimerEnabled property to the Timer1 control's Enabled property.
   (If you need help with this, refer to Chapter 10.)

Add the following code to the user control.

```
Private Sub Timer1_Timer()
  On Error Resume Next
  Static nColor As Integer
  If Not Ambient.UserMode Then Exit Sub 'don't execute in
                                        'design mode
  If nColor = 15 Then
    nColor = 0                          'start over again
  Else
    nColor = nColor + 1                 'increment it
  End If
  lblLabel.ForeColor = QBColor(nColor)  'set the forecolor
End Sub
```

(One could also use nColor = (nColor + 1) Mod 15 instead of the If-Then-Else.)

Now, you are ready to test your new control but first you should save it to a new directory. This prevents you from changing the base template. Save it to any directory and name it something like ColorLbl. That way it will have no link to the original template. Notice we got this new control by simply adding a timer, a couple of properties, and some code. Since we used our Label Control group, we already have the form ready to test the control. To do this,

1. Close the designer for your user control.

2. Open up the Test form and add an instance of the user control to the form.

3. The exposed Interval property needs to be set (try 100 or $\frac{1}{10}$ second). The TimerEnabled property has a default value of True, so all you have to do to test this label is press F5. The CCE will run the project and you should see a label with the color of the caption changing rapidly.

Next, notice that our label has a Custom property so there is a property page available, as shown in Figure 11-5. This makes it easy to experiment with other settings such as different font sizes and background colors.

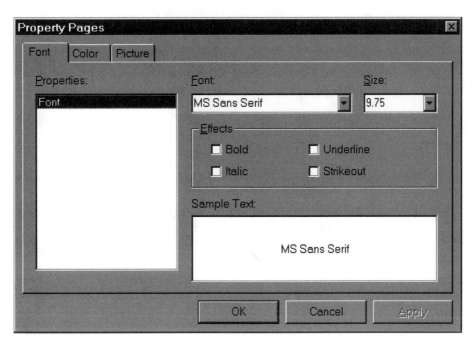

Figure 11-5
The Property Pages for our Label Control

Creating a Template

If you often need a control based on a different type of control than one of the five given in our templates, this section shows you how to create your own templates. Creating a user control template involves saving the control file (i.e., the `.ctl` file) to the correct directory. As mentioned earlier, the templates the CCE knows about need to lie in subdirectories of its Template directory. By default, the CCE only creates a Projects directory and a Ctlgroup directory when it is set up. In order to create other types of templates, follow our model and create the following directories.

Template	Name of directory
for Forms	Template\Forms
for Classes	Template\Classes
for Code Modules	Template\Modules
for MDIForms	Template\MDIForms
for Property Pages	Template\PropPage
for User Controls	Template\UserCtls

If you have already copied our Template tree from the CD, in addition to the default you should have the Forms, PropPage and UserCtls directories. If you want to create templates of the other types, you need to create those directories manually.

Your Own Templates

Once you have the directory structure in place, you are ready to create your own template. First, decide what type of template you need. For example, suppose that you always like to have a certain type of About Box and you want to include it with all of your controls. Of course, you would probably want to tweak it just a little for each control. Creating a form template is the perfect way to do this. Just follow these steps to create your own About Box template.

1. Load Visual Basic Control Creation Edition.
2. Load a Standard EXE project.
3. Rename Form1 to frmAbout.
4. Make it the size you want it to be.

Now set the following properties:

Property	Value
BorderStyle	4 - Fixed ToolWindow
Caption	"About MyControl"
MaxButton	False
MinButton	False
StartUpPosition	2 - CenterScreen

Next, add the controls you want to add to the About Box, such as an OK button, some labels for the name of the object, its version, etc. Then add an image control with the Stretch property set to True to display the control's icon. (If you need help doing this, refer to Chapter 3 for instructions on how to place controls on a form.) The only code you will need to add is the code in the OK Button Click event, as follows:

```
Private Sub cmdOK_Click()
   Unload Me
End Sub
```

Now you are ready to save the form in the correct subdirectory of the Template directory. Press CTRL+S and you should get a save dialog for the form. You need to save it in the Template\Forms directory. Call it simply MyAbout.frm. That's it, you have just created an About Box template that can be added to any project.

Chapter 12

Most of the controls you build will be enhanced versions of either the standard controls that come with the CCE, or of other commercial controls. However, any extension of a control, no matter how simple, can cause major problems if it is not written carefully and tested thoroughly. The first part of this chapter shows you how to test and debug the controls that you build with the Control Creation Edition. In particular, we cover fully the various (and quite powerful) debugging tools built into the CCE.

Testing requires both organized and extensive execution of the code you have written. Make sure that all code paths in your control are tested by having them all processed by the host application. This has to be done by running an exhaustive set of scenarios on the code. Realistically, though, testing is one aspect of a project that is never really finished, so you also must know when good enough is good enough and just ship it.

Next, after you have debugged and tested the control, you will most likely want to give it to others to use. Sharing your controls with others in your company, selling it, or just giving it to friends means you need a way to set it up on other machines. This can be as simple as using the Browse feature in Visual Basic or as complex as a Web-based setup using compression in the form of CAB files. (See later in the chapter for more on this.) The last part of this chapter discusses deployment of your control. (Usually, distributing a control requires dealing with various setup and registration issues, which we also cover here.

Testing, Debugging, and Deployment

 Of course, for completely testing and debugging a control, mastering the mechanics of the debugging tools is not enough. The more testing and debugging methods you know, the better off you will be. This chapter can only cover the most common methods. More techniques may be found in our book, *Core Visual Basic* (also from Prentice Hall), which will be available at the end of the first quarter of 1997. However, even that book is not exhaustive; a full treatment of testing and debugging would require a substantial book of its own. And, unfortunately, to the best of our knowledge, no book devoted solely to Visual Basic testing and debugging exists. ⊃

Introduction

As you have seen, controls cannot be run in the traditional way you run a Visual Basic application. They must work "in the process" of another application. This usually means that you add the control to a form or forms that are part of a Standard EXE project. The most common way to test your control is:

1. Add a Standard EXE project to your current session. This gives you a form on which to place the control you are testing.

2. Close the designer for the user control. This puts the control in what is usually called *run* mode. (You can always tell you are in run mode by looking for the enabled icon of your user control on the toolbox.)

3. Completing Step 2 allows you to place an instance of your user control on the test form (or forms) from Step 1 and then start the test project.

On to Debugging

Visual Basic is certainly one of the best development environments available when it comes to debugging. One important reason is an extraordinarily useful feature usually called *edit and continue*. After you stop a program in midstream, putting the IDE in what is usually called *break* mode, the edit and continue feature lets you examine and even modify your code and then continue execution from the stopping point or some other point.

You can put a program in break mode either by hitting a breakpoint (see later in the chapter for more on this feature), using a Stop statement in code, or by pressing CTRL+BREAK. ⊃

Of course, only breakpoints and the Stop statement give you precise control of what line was being executed when the program stopped.

When you are in break mode, you can often find the value of a variable by holding the mouse cursor over the variable for a moment. This depends on the variable being *in context* (VB-speak for the variable being in the scope of the code that was executing when you broke execution). As shown in Figure 12-1, if the variable is in context, a little box will pop up showing the current value of the variable. ⊃

CTRL+BREAK

Pressing CTRL+BREAK (usually) stops the execution of your application and puts the CCE into break mode. The IDE will also highlight the current line of executable code if a line of code is executing. However, if the application is not currently executing any code, it will simply go into break mode and no line will be highlighted.

Figure 12-1
Variable Info
in Break mode

An obvious but important question is, how can your application be running but no code is executing? The most common cause of this is that the application is waiting for input perhaps from the user or another application or module (such as a DLL). If you stop a program in this state, the IDE regards the active form as being in the current scope. So, if you were in this state and entered:

```
Print Caption
```

in the Immediate window, it would display the current form's caption.

 Almost everybody we know uses the ? shortcut for the Print keyword when working in the Immediate window. Just type ? caption and press RETURN and its value will be printed out. ⊃

Run/Restart

As you know, pressing F5 is used to run an application from the beginning. However, if you are in break mode, pressing F5 actually makes the application continue from the current line. The way to restart a program from the beginning when you are in break mode is to use SHIFT+F5. (You can also use the equivalent tools on the Standard or Debugging toolbars.)

End

There is no shortcut key for this. It is available on the Run menu and the Debug toolbar. Using the End tool immediately stops the program.

More on the Immediate Window (Debug Window)

If the Immediate window isn't visible, choose View|Immediate window or press CTRL+G. (Although Immediate window is its official name, most people, including us, call it the Debug window or the I-Pane.)

In the CCE, you can do more with the Debug window than ever before. For example, in Visual Basic 4.0, you could not execute one of your own procedures unless you were in break mode. With the Control Creation Edition, you can execute any available procedure in your code or VBA simply by typing the proper call statement.

Another thing you can do now is load a form, although the designer for that form must be closed for this to be possible. Of course, the form may not act entirely correctly if it is dependent upon the application to be in a particular state when it is loaded. The really weird thing in this case is that the form is running but the rest of the application is still in an uncompiled, non-running state.

The Debug window is primarily used to evaluate variables and expressions. We use it extensively in break mode after a run-time error has occurred in order to fix the problem code. For example, a common problem is trying to access a character in a string by using a function like Mid with an invalid index such as a negative number, zero or something larger than the length of the string. For example, consider the following code:

```
Function GetMiddleInitial(sName As String) As String
  GetMiddleInitial = Mid$(sName, InStr(sName, ".") - 1, 1)
End Function
```

The problem is that this code assumes the name passed to it will have a period after the middle initial. If it doesn't, a run-time error of "Invalid Procedure Call" will occur and the line of code will be highlighted. At this point, you can evaluate the parts of your code line. For example, if you had passed in John Doe, you would see that InStr(sName, ".") is 0 and thus, subtracting 1 yields –1. This, however, is an invalid index for accessing the characters of a string variable. At this point, you would simply add the following code to the procedure and run it again:

```
If InStr(sName, ".") Then
  GetMiddleInitial = Mid$(sName, InStr(sName, ".") - 1, 1)
End If
```

The ability to do this in break mode makes debugging very efficient.

A word of caution is needed here. If you make many changes that you want to keep, we suggest you stop the application and save the code before continuing. It is not possible to save your changes while in break mode, so if you happen to crash your application or system, you will lose everything you did while in break mode. ⊃

Breakpoints

A breakpoint is a line where you want execution to stop right before the Control Creation Edition is going to process it. To set a breakpoint, go to an executable line of code and press F9 or left-click in the left margin. A (red) dot, as shown in Figure 12-2, will appear in the margin of the line. This dot indicates that the breakpoint has successfully been set.

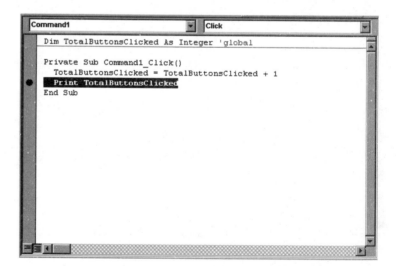

Figure 12-2
A Line with a
Breakpoint set

Setting a breakpoint is probably the most common and useful method of stopping code execution. One disadvantage to it, though, is that breakpoints do not persist across programming sessions; you will need to set them up each time you reload the project. (See the section on the Assert method for another way to handle breakpoints that avoids this problem.) ⊃

Advanced Breakpoints

There are other ways to tell Visual Basic to break at a certain time that are quite powerful in certain situations. The most common is to use the *watch feature* of the IDE. This, in turn, depends on a concept called a *Watch Point*. As the name suggests, a Watch Point lets you tell the IDE to watch what is going on and stop when something you specify happens. To create a Watch Point, select Debug|Add Watch and the dialog box shown in Figure 12-3 will appear.

In Figure 12-3, there are three watch types which are described as follows.

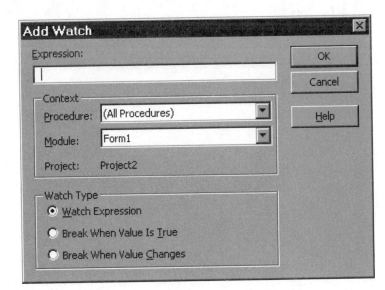

Figure 12-3
Add Watch
dialog box

Watch Expression

Choosing this simply displays the value of whatever expression you have in the Expression field in the Add Watch dialog box of the Watch window. An example of this was shown in Figure 12-3. Note that the CCE defaults to placing what you have highlighted in the Expression box. You can combine this feature with the single step mode to watch the state of an expression continuously.

You can only watch expressions that are in the current scope. For example, if Total was a form level variable, you could watch it while any code attached to the form was evaluating. If Counter was local to a procedure, you could only see its value when you were executing code in that procedure. Try this: start up a simple form with a command button and put a Static integer counter in the command button Click event and then add the code `Counter = Counter + 1` to this event procedure. Add Counter as a watch expression. Start the form running. At this point, the Counter variable is out of scope so you simply see an <<Out Of Context>> in the Watches window, as shown in Figure 12-4.

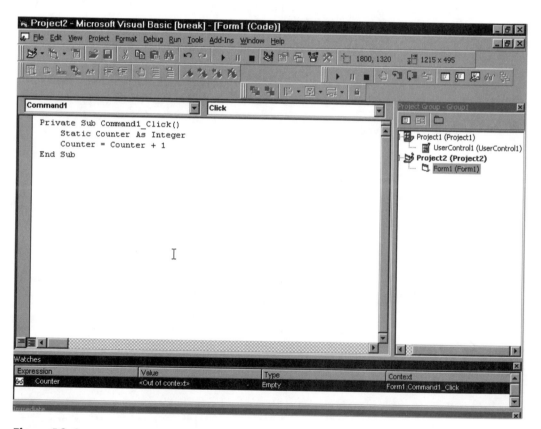

Figure 12-4
Watches window out of context variable

Notice, as in Figure 12-4, that even if a variable is out of context, the Watches window shows you the context of the variable. If you put a breakpoint at the `Counter = Counter + 1` line and start the program again, you can see that the Watches window shows you that the counter is, indeed, initialized to zero. Figure 12-5 illustrates this.

Break When True

This method lets you stop the program and go into break mode when an expression becomes True. This is quite useful when you want to break inside a loop. For example, you can enter a variable or an expression like Text1.Enabled or I = 3, and when the expression becomes True (non-zero), the CCE will stop the program at the line *following* the one that made the expression True.

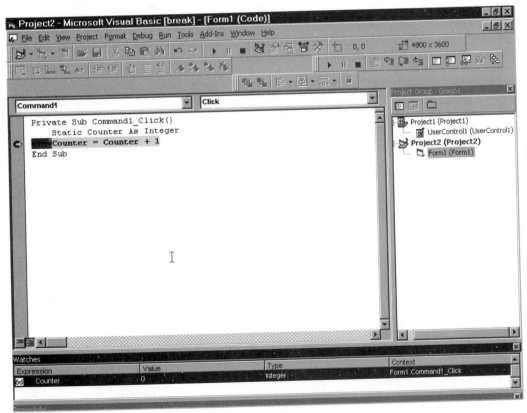

Figure 12-5
Watches window in context

Break When Expression Changes

The third method lets you make the CCE stop executing a program when a value changes. For example, suppose you are having trouble with a particular flag being reset at a time when you do not want it to be. This is probably caused by an event firing when you didn't expect it. The Break When Expression Changes statement is the watch type that will let you stop the program when a property value changes. You can use it to see where, and probably why, the expression changed so you can ensure that it changes only as you intend.

Stepping Through Code

Pressing F8 allows you to step through the code, that is, execute it on a line-by-line basis. If you use F8 instead of F5 to start a program, you can start stepping through your code from the beginning line (usually in the `Form_Initialize`, `Form_Load` events or the Sub Main procedure). You can also use F8 to step through the code one line at a time, starting from the current breakpoint. Stepping through code is extremely useful for checking your logic on a line-by-line basis.

Since you often want to consider a call to another procedure as one step, the IDE has the SHIFT+F8 combination as well as the F8 key. SHIFT+F8 will step over subprocedures. For example, suppose you make Sub Main the start-up code instead of the `Form_Initialize`, then in the following code, you might even add numbering in the code to illustrate the order of the execution.

```
Sub Main()
   Dim i As Integer
   For i = 0 to 10
      Debug.Print MySub(i)
   Next
End Sub
Function MySub(i As Integer) As String
   Debug.Print I am in Mysub
   MySub = "Item Number " & i
End Function
```

Pressing F8 would step into MySub every time through the loop and, therefore, would require two more uses of F8 to get out of the loop. Using

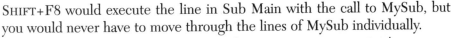

SHIFT+F8 would execute the line in Sub Main with the call to MySub, but you would never have to move through the lines of MySub individually.

If you inadvertently step into a sub routine, you can simply press SHIFT+CTRL+F8 to step "out" and return to the line after the call. ⊃

The final way to use the IDE's stepping features is to choose "Run To Cursor" off the Debug menu or use the shortcut CTRL+F8. As the name suggests, you use this by moving the cursor to a place in your code, then pressing CTRL+F8. The IDE will execute all the code up to that line. One example of where this feature is useful is when you want to run to the end of a loop. Simply click on the line after the Next statement (in our example code) and press CTRL+F8. All of the code in the loop will be executed and you will stop at the line immediately after the loop.

Statements such as GoTo, Exit Sub, or Exit For may cause execution to bypass your cursor location, so you want to make sure this type of code is not present when you use this feature. ⊃

Set Next Statement

Pressing CTRL+F9 on an executable line in the current procedure will make it the next statement to execute. This is extremely useful after you have modified a line of code and want to execute it again. Make sure that all variables have the value you expect them to at this point so the code executes as expected.

Call Stack

The Call Stack dialog box (an example of which is shown in Figure 12-6) is very useful when you need to figure out how you got to where you are. It will show you every function call in the current path of code execution. One common example of where this is helpful is when you are debugging a recursive program where it is not readily apparent that it was recursive in the first place. The call stack will be full of the same calls over and over again, which is a very good indication of a recursion in place.

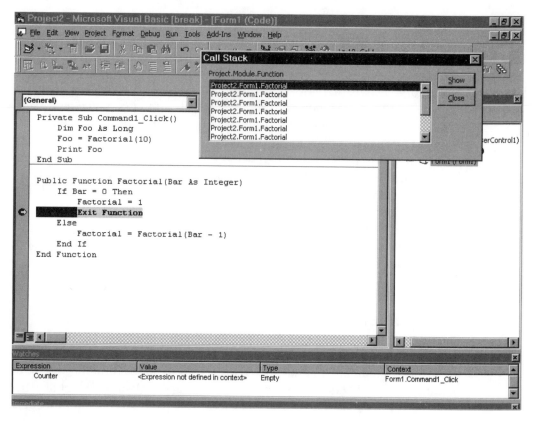

Figure 12-6
The Call Stack window for a recursion

Debugging in Code

In addition to the built-in debugging features in the IDE, it is possible to add code to your application to aid in debugging. The following are the statements used specifically for debugging.

Stop Statement

This is a line of code that stops execution when it is hit, which is very useful when you need a breakpoint to persist across debugging sessions. Make sure not to leave any of these in the finished code as they will produce a run-time error. Also consider using the newer Assert statement described later.

MsgBox Statement

Placing MsgBox statements in your code is probably the oldest method of debugging because they produce visual notification of what the application is doing. Make sure to remove them as well.

One thing to be aware of when using message boxes to debug is that they sometimes don't interact well with other Windows events. For example, if you add a MsgBox call to a control's MouseDown event, you may not get the MouseUp and Click events. (Professionals say that message boxes "consume" extra Windows messages. The result is that you may not get events that would normally be fired.) ⊃

Debug.Print

This is not as visual as a MsgBox but also not as intrusive. The output simply goes to the Debug window in the IDE. You can see all the things you printed to the Debug window simply by scrolling through the window. These statements are ignored by the compiler and, therefore, have no impact on the execution of the final control.

Assert

The idea of the new Assert method of the Debug object is borrowed from the C language. This method can be an extremely useful debugging tool once you get used to the idea of using it routinely. It is simply a statement to the IDE that "I claim this statement is True. If it is not, stop the program at that point and tell me." This means you can use a line of code like:

```
Debug.Assert TestExpression
```

and you will have an automatic breakpoint when TestExpression first becomes False. In particular, you can use:

```
Debug.Assert False
```

for the equivalent of a Stop statement. (The advantage to using the Assert method instead of a Stop statement is that since it belongs to the Debug object, it has no effect on the final OCX.)

Conditional Compilation

The CCE has the ability to compile different branches of your code depending on the state of various flags. This is usually called *conditional compilation*. The advantage to conditional compilation is that code that is excluded by using conditional compilation is not in the final executable file. In particular, it has no size or performance effect. For example, to include "debug code," as it is usually called, your code needs to include a block like the following.

```
#If InDebug Then
    'Place statements that will be used only under
    'debugging here.
    '
#Else
    'Place non-debug statements here
#End If
```

(Notice the similarity to an ordinary If-Then-Else. There is even an #ElseIf if you need it.)

The Option Compare statement doesn't affect the tests in an #If. Visual Basic always uses case-insensitive comparisons in an #If. ⊃

You can define your own compiler constants at any point by defining an ordinary constant. Heres an example:

```
#Const InDebug = True
```

Notice that you use the # to define a conditional compiler constant. Conditional compiler constants defined in code belong to the form control or module in which they appear—they cannot be global (public) in scope.

If you need to define conditional compiler constants that affect the whole project, choose Project | Project Properties and fill in the appropriate line of the Make tab. (Separate multiple compiler constants by colons.) ⊃

Debugging and Error Handlers

Having an active error handler (see Chapter 5) can make debugging confusing and more difficult. After all, getting in a situation where you are dividing by zero is probably a bug and you shouldn't use an error handler to replace weeding out the bad code. The problem is that the active error handler will prevent you from even knowing that such a bug was in your code. The cure for this is to do some of your testing and debugging with all error handlers inactive. To do this:

1. Go to the Tools|Option dialog box.
2. Click on the General tab.
3. Check the "Break on all errors" check box.

Once this option is checked, the IDE will disable all error handlers and go into break mode when any error is encountered. This is certainly more convenient than commenting out all the error handling code!

If this is too drastic, check the "Break on unhandled errors," which will only take you to break mode when you don't explicitly handle the error.

 The remaining option on this tab "Break in class module" is especially useful when you are debugging a control. (Or, for that matter any code that refers to objects—even if those objects come from outside Visual Basic.) The problem is that when you use an object, it may generate an error. You may not want this error silently handled by the object. It is often more useful, if the object you are referring to generates an error, to know about it at the place in your VB code that called the object. When this option is checked, Visual Basic breaks at the code that referenced the object that gave the error. (However, usually all Visual Basic can do is report a generic error. This is because it doesn't know enough about the internal makeup of the object it calls to do much else. Visual Basic will most often use Err.Number = 440 for any error in an object outside itself.) ⊃

Testing Your Control

Obviously, testing a control requires knowledge of what it is supposed to do in various situations. If you developed the control, you should have this information in hand. If not, you must get it from the author or designer of the control—you may even have to go so far as to read the documentation for the control.

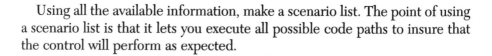
Using all the available information, make a scenario list. The point of using a scenario list is that it lets you execute all possible code paths to insure that the control will perform as expected.

Basic Testing

First, the control must do the basic tasks for which it was designed. For example, does an extension of a text box still accept text? Does it still allow cut and paste using the standard Windows conventions? If a control is designed to be a numeric-only TextBox, you need to verify that it does not accept any non-numeric characters from the keyboard or by pasting from the clipboard. Verifying this is simply a matter of knowing those tasks and trying each one. For example, our original version of the TextBox in Chapter 1 had a bug because it allowed the user to paste in negative numbers. This was found simply by trying to paste a negative number into it and discovering that it worked without error.

Secondly, you must test the so-called *negative cases*. These are cases where you expect the control to fail but you want to verify that, even in failure, it produces an expected result such as a meaningful error message. For example, with a numeric TextBox, suppose we have a maximum value property. You would certainly want to enter a value outside the range and have the control issue an appropriate error, as opposed to simply beeping or failing silently.

Next, you will want to test at the *boundary cases*. For the numeric text box, you will want to test it with exactly the minimum and the maximum values to make sure that they are accepted. Boundary case problems are related to off-by-one errors. When dealing with loops, these are so common that testing for them is usually second nature. (Probably the original off-by-one error is the answer to the question: how many shelves does it take to make a usual five-shelf bookcase? Answer: 6, not 5; you have to take into account the extra shelf for the top. Off-by-one errors are often called Fence Post errors for this reason.)

 Your control should not produce any untrapped run-time errors that could cause the host application to fail. The samples and templates shipped with this book could have significantly more error handling code—they are really designed to serve as starting points for you, i.e. proofs of concept. ⊃

Unless the control was coded with some of the debugging techniques listed above, it will be nearly impossible to determine if you are executing every code path. This is where tools such as a code profiler would come in handy to produce a report of code coverage to show which code was executed or not.

Unfortunately, the CCE does not ship with a profiler. In the absence of such a tool, you could use either a MsgBox or a Debug.Print statement at the top of each procedure to verify that it is getting tested.

Platform Testing

The next phase of testing involves using the control in all of the host applications in which it is intended to be used. Controls can be used in Visual Basic itself, other applications such as Microsoft Access or Excel, and the most important host of late, Internet Explorer. Testing here requires that you first build an OCX using the File|Make *ProjectName*.OCX command. This command pops up the dialog box shown in Figure 12-7. (You can then click on the Options button to go to a dialog box for setting versioning information, as shown in Figure 12-8.)

When you go to make an OCX out of your control, the CCE creates a binary executable file with the extension .ocx but it also registers the control for use on your system. For example, if you have Visual Basic 4.0 on your system, the new control should appear in the list of available controls when you choose Tools|Custom Controls.

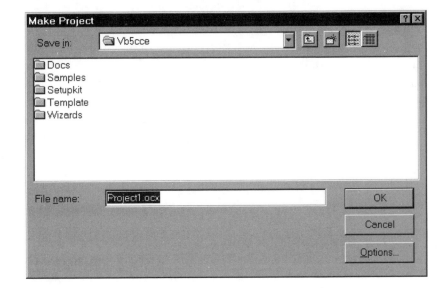

Figure 12-7
Make Project
dialog box

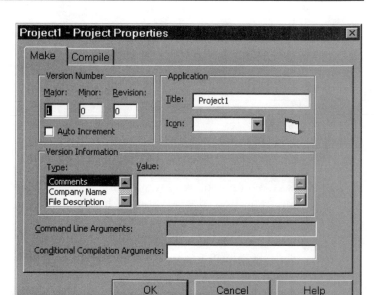

Figure 12-8
Project Properties
dialog box

On the other hand, if you copy the OCX file to another system that has an OCX hosting application, you will have to register the control on that system. If you don't, the user of Visual Basic 4 would not see your control when he or she chooses Tools|Custom Controls.

Here's what you need to do to register a control:

1. Copy the file MSVBVM50.DLL to the other system. (With a default installation, this file will be found in your system directory—probably either the c:\Windows\System or c:\Winnt\System32 directory.) Put this file in the target computer's system directory. (It can be placed in the working directory, but that is not advised as you will most likely end up with multiple copies and version problems if you put it any place other than the system directory).

2. Next, choose the Browse feature in the application's equivalent of the Custom Controls dialog and find the OCX file for your control that you have previously copied to the system.

For example, in testing the control with Visual Basic 4.0, once you have your control in the list of available custom controls, simply check its box like any other .ocx and the control shows up in your toolbox. Now, you can test your control in a Visual Basic 4.0 application to make sure it works there as well.

Testing in Internet Explorer

Testing your user control in Internet Explorer 3.01 or later involves a few more steps. We are going to run through a session with the ActiveX Control Pad utility to show you how to get your control onto a Web page where you can test it in the Internet Explorer. We assume you have already made your OCX file and installed the ActiveX Control Pad on your system. Now follow these steps:

1. Load the Control Pad.

2. Place your edit cursor at the beginning of a line in the Body of the new HTML page. (Failure to do this may cause the Control Pad to insert the control data in an undesirable location that will most likely lead to errors.)

3. Select Edit|Insert ActiveX Control and select the control you want to test from the list. An example of what you will see is shown in Figure 12-9.

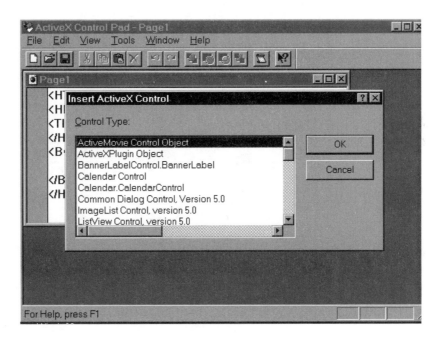

Figure 12-9
The ActiveX Control Pad at work

All of the controls supplied with this book have a sample HTML page in the code directory on the CD so that they can be tested in the Internet Explorer. ⊃

The control may have a strange name if you did not properly name it when you created it in the first place (see the tip that follows). The name that you will see in the ActiveX Control Pad will be the description of the class for the control itself. If you did not put this in the Project Properties dialog box, as you can see in Figure 12-9 by looking for our Banner Control from Chapter 9, the name will be the project name followed by a ".", followed by the name of the user control.

 To give a control a user-friendly name, load the control project, press F2 for the Object Browser, choose the name of the control project in the main drop-down and the control in the "Classes" list. Then, right-click the control name and choose Properties. This will display a Members Options dialog box, as shown in Figure 12-10 (for the Banner Control), that allows you to enter a description that ends up being the friendly name of the control. Now isn't that intuitive? ⊃

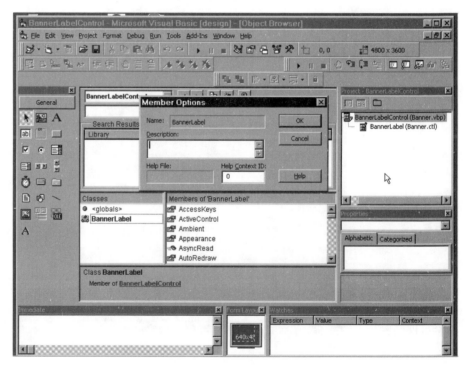

Fig12-10
The Member Options dialog box inside the IDE

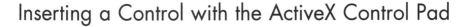

Inserting a Control with the ActiveX Control Pad

After you have selected the desired control, choose OK and your screen should look like Figure 12-11, with a couple of overlapping windows. The currently active window is the property sheet for the control.

Set properties in the ActiveX Control Pads Properties window by highlighting a property and typing in the box next to the Apply button. Then click on Apply. If this control has a custom property page, you can get to it by right-clicking in the control and choosing the last Properties item. ⊃

Partially obscured in Figure 12-11 are windows (see Figure 12-12) for the visual representation of the control (analogous to the user control form) and one for the HTML code.

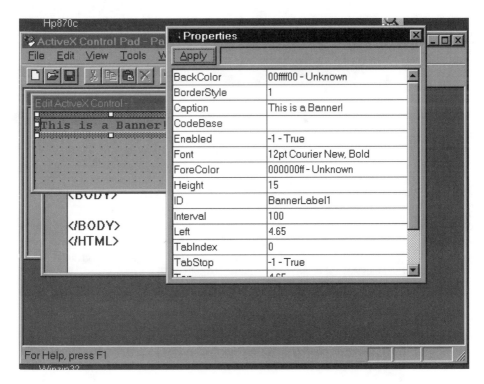

Figure 12-11
The ActiveX Control Pad at design time

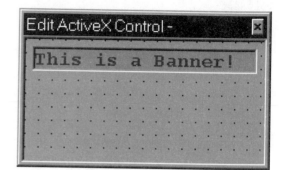

Figure 12-12
The user control form in the
ActiveX Control Pad

Once you have set the properties as you like, close the "Edit ActiveX Control" dialog and the needed information to use the ActiveX control will be added to the HTML page you are creating, as shown in Figure 12-13. (This information consists of the totally inscrutable ClassID property plus the lines needed to set the properties of the controls.)

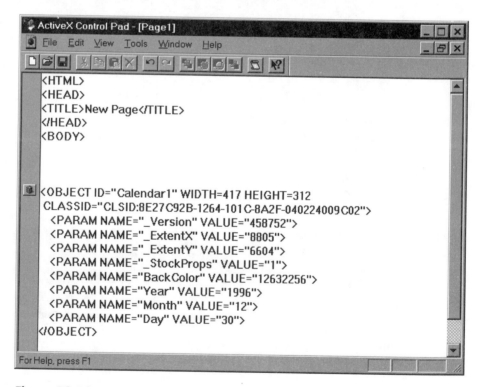

Figure 12-13
The ActiveX Control Pad with needed HTML Object tag

Now:

1. Save the HTML page.

2. Load Internet Explorer 3.01 or greater. (You don't need an active Internet connection, so do not log on to your service provider as you usually do. We're just going to connect to the page on our local machine instead of connecting to one on a remote machine.)

3. Choose File|Open and enter the path name where you saved the HTML page from Step 1. This will probably display a dialog box, as shown in Figure 12-14, informing you of a potential safety violation because the page you are loading contains an ActiveX Control. (See the note in the "Control Deployment" section that follows for information on signing your controls.) Select OK and then Yes and the page should load, displaying the control.

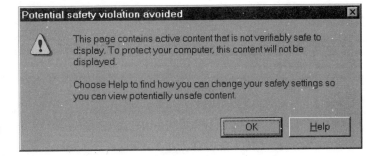

Figure 12-14
Security Warning
dialog box

Scripting Your ActiveX Ccontrol

Of course, if you followed the previous steps, the page doesn't do much except what it is programmed to do in its initial state—because you don't have any code hooked up to it. (For example, the Banner Control would work fine but all it would say is "This is a banner!") To test your control, you have to know how to add some simple VBScript code to interact with the control.

 VBScript is a simple subset of the VB language. It should take someone who has gotten this far only a few hours to master it completely. The Microsoft Web site (www.microsoft.com/vbscript) has sufficient documentation on it for an experienced programmer. ⊃

Go back to the ActiveX Control Pad and select Tools|Script Wizard. This will load a dialog box like the one shown in Figure 12-15. Notice that this dialog box has two treeview lists and a code or list window.

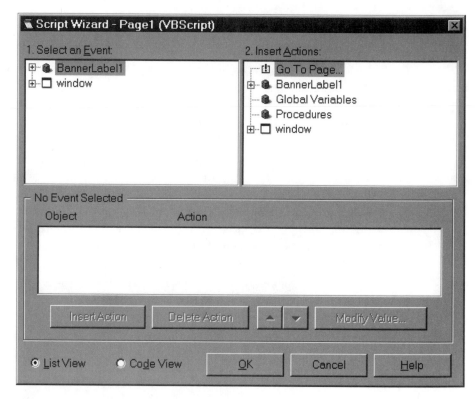

Figure 12-15
The Script Wizard in the ActiveX Control Pad

Suppose you have registered the Address Control from Chapter 9 and want to test it with some simple script code. Follow the steps given previously, only this time add an instance of our Address Control to an HTML page in the ActiveX Control pad. Now start up the Script Wizard again:

1. Select "Code View."

2. Expand the Address Control in the left-hand pane by clicking the "+" to the left of its name.

3. Click on one of the events shown below the control. For example, our Address Control has Change and Finished events. If your control has not exposed any events, there will not be any for you to test so you will not be able to continue with this process on that particular control.

When you clicked on an event name, you should have noticed that the Code window now looks like Figure 12-16 and has code something like:

```
Sub AddressControl1_Finished()
```

in it.

Below this line, simply enter:

```
If AddressControl1.FirstName = "William" Then
    MsgBox "Everybody calls him Bill though!"
End If
```

 Don't put in an End Sub. An annoying peculiarity of the control pad's Scripting Wizard is that it adds the End Sub automatically but doesn't display it! ⊃

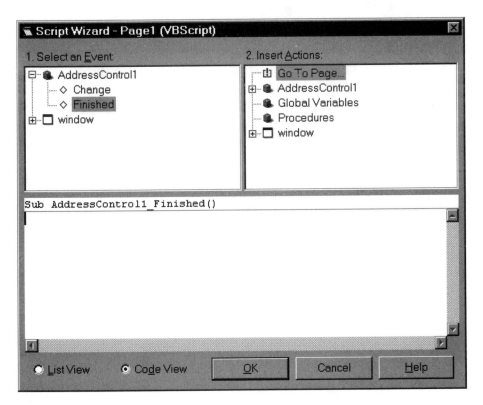

Figure 12-16
Address Control in ScriptWizard

Now click the OK button and the code will automatically be inserted into the HTML page. Save the HTML page and go back to Internet Explorer. If you still have the page loaded, click the Refresh button on the toolbar and the page will reload. If not, simply reload the page using its location as described above.

Click on the Finished button (or do whatever is needed to fire the particular event you chose to test). In our case, enter "William" into the First Name field so the message box will pop up. If you followed all these steps, substituting your control and its events for our event and it worked, you should pat yourself on the back because this is a pretty big accomplishment.

But you aren't done. Next, you need to repeat the steps described above for all of the events your control has exposed.

Control Deployment

Once you have created a control, you may wish to give it to others or maybe even try to sell it. In order to use the control on another system, you must first install it. Depending on the controls and the libraries used on your user control, you will need to distribute the needed OCXs and DLLs along with your control. Make sure that you have the proper license to do this before distributing a custom control or a library purchased from someone else. If you are not sure, contact the company for this information.

If you only used the VBA language and the standard controls as we have in this book, then all you need to distribute is the .ocx itself and the MSVBVM50.DLL library. This file contains the Microsoft Visual Basic Virtual Machine 5.0 library functions. If you used any of the other OCX controls that came with the Visual Basic Control Creation Edition, you are free to distribute them as well.

 For a commercial distribution of a control, you will probably want to sign your controls using a digital certificate available (for a small fee) from Verisign (www.verisign.com). Their Web site has full details on the process of obtaining a certificate for your controls. ⊃

Simple Installation

The simplest installation involves copying the files to the target system and registering the user control and any subcontrols and libraries that it uses. You can register an OCX or DLL using the Regsvr32.EXE utility that Microsoft makes available. To use the registration utility, first copy `Regsvr32.EXE` to your system in a directory in your path such as your `\Windows` directory. Then open up a DOS window and from the command line type:

```
Regsvr32 mycontrol.ocx
```

This will register the control and make it available to any host application that uses this OCX.

Full Setup

The Control Creation Edition comes with a Setup Wizard that does virtually all of the work needed to create a fully functional setup for your control. To see this at work, we will walk through a session with the Wizard to set up one of the controls that we have created in this book. For this, we will use the Banner created in Chapter 9. (If you did not build it by hand, you can always copy it from the CD in the CH9 directory to your system now.) Here's what you need to do to use the Setup Wizard:

1. Launch the Control Creation Edition's Application Setup Wizard from the Start menu. (It is not available from within the CCE.) You'll see an introductory screen like Figure 12-17 (or possibly the screen in Figure 12-18).

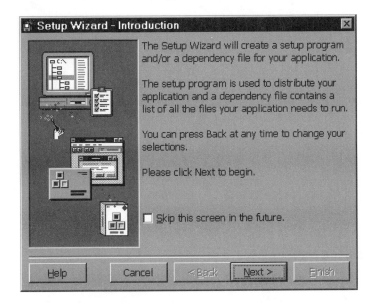

Figure 12-17
Startup screen for the Setup Wizard

2. Click the Browse button, shown in Figure 12-18, and find the Banner.VBP file from wherever you placed it.

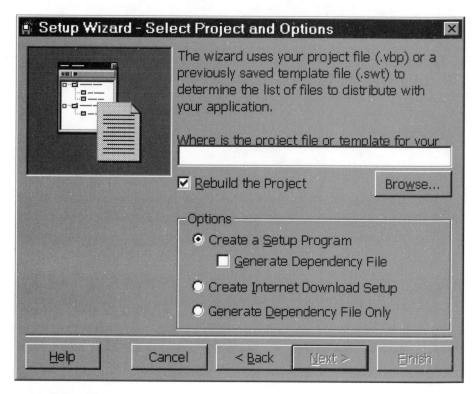

Figure 12-18
Select Project screen in the Setup Wizard

3. In the Options frame shown in Figure 12-18, select "Create a Setup Program" because we want to set up the control for use on other systems.

4. Click Next, then while the Wizard creates a new version of your OCX, you will be taken to the "Distribution Method" step shown in Figure 12-19.

5. Choose "Floppy disk."

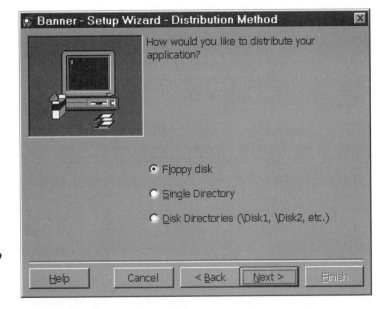

Figure 12-19
Distribution
Method screen

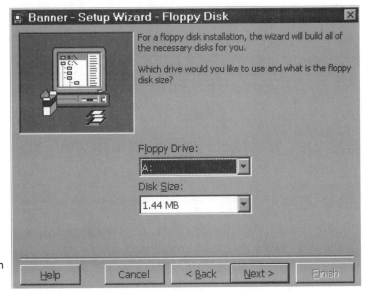

Figure 12-20
Floppy Disk screen
in Setup Wizard

6. Click Next to go to the "Floppy Disk" step shown in Figure 12-20.
   If the defaults are not correct, choose the appropriate settings from
   the drop-down lists.

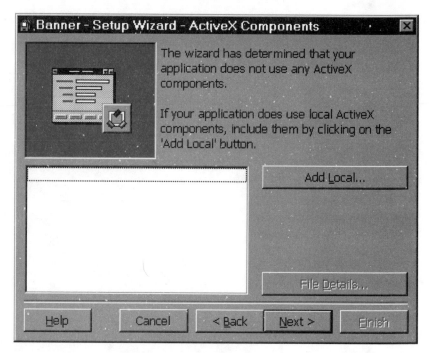

Figure 12-21
The Add Components screen in the Setup Wizard

7. Click Next to go to the "ActiveX Components" step shown in Figure 12-21. This step is where you would tell the Wizard to add in any other necessary components such as specialized libraries and other OCXs if you used them in your user control. Since we do not have any such dependencies for our Banner Control, we will just move on. (Notice that the Wizard is sophisticated enough to tell us that we are not using any other ActiveX Controls that are not already part of the VBVM.)

8. Click Next to go to the "Confirm Dependencies" step shown in Figure 12-22. In this step, you should see the STDOLE.TLB file listed because it is needed by the control. (This is the library needed for OLE; most controls will need it.) Leave this box checked.

9. Click Next, and the Wizard will start performing its magic. You should see a message box as shown in Figure 12-23. This message box asks you whether you want to add the PropertyPage.DLL with the message "if you wish to use this control in a design environment other than Visual Basic." Answer Yes to this prompt so that any font, color, or picture properties your control has will be able to be set with the property pages and will be available to the user of the control.

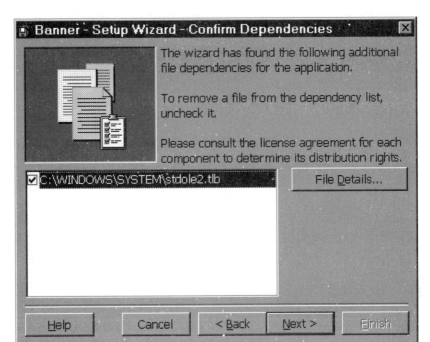

Figure 12-22
Confirm
Dependencies box

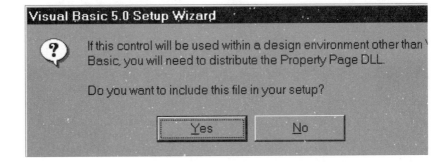

Figure 12-23
Property Page
message box

10. After a short delay, you should be looking at the "File Summary" step shown in Figure 12-24 on the next page. This displays a list of all of the files needed to distribute this control. Click Next to go to the Finish step.

11. Finally, click Finish. The Wizard will start compressing all of the files it needs and prompt you to put disk 1 of 2 in drive A:. Now it will copy the files to the floppy disks.

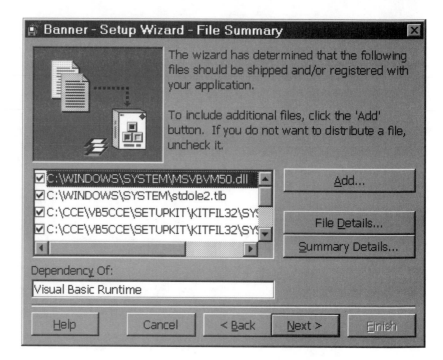

Figure 12-24
File Summary
dialog box

That's it, you're finished. You now have 2 disks that make it possible to set up this control on another system. If the system you work on is available to others across a network, you could have chosen "Single Directory" on Step 5 and the files would have been copied to a directory on your hard drive instead of the floppy disks.

Two disks with 1.5 megs may seem like a lot considering the OCX file is only about 20k. Most of the needed files are probably already on the user's system. If you are in a controlled environment like a corporation, you can be sure that say the STDOLE.TLB library and the VBVM is already on the user system. This cuts the installation files down to a few 100k. ∽

Finally, if you need to deploy the control across the Internet, run the Wizard again and choose "Create Internet Download Setup" on the first step. This will create a CAB file and an HTM file that can be loaded into Internet Explorer. The Internet Explorer will handle the setup for you since it knows exactly what to do with CAB files.

A CAB file (which stands for Cabinet) is Microsoft's archive format. It usually gives about a 2:1 compression ratio in most non-graphical situations. (For graphics, the possible compression ratios are much higher.) ∽

Chapter 13

All of the standard controls have features left out that make them more time consuming to use. Making a control that does everything that a standard control does and saves time when using it enhances the use of Visual Basic and is one of the main selling points of the CCE (especially since it's free).

How many times have you put a label control on a form and wanted the font to be as big as possible for the size of the label? The only way to do this with a standard label is by a trial and error font setting. The control we are about to show you takes a standard Label control and gives it the ability to enlarge or shrink the font automatically based upon the size you set the control. To achieve this, this control should:

1. Change the font size appropriately when you place a control on the form.
2. Resize the font to the best size when you make the control smaller or larger.

The interface for this control is trivial, the code needed is minimal and the Control Interface Wizard is going to do all of the work of exposing the standard properties and events that we need. The resulting OCX is only about 21k.

The Stretch Label

The Idea of the Control

The control we show you here was designed to satisfy the following goals:

1. All the usual things you do with a Label Control should be available.
2. The user should be able to use this control just like a standard Label Control.
3. The control needs to add the font size automatically so as to save time for the user of the control.

Creating the Interface

To accomplish these goals, we need an extremely simple UI. Here's a picture of the control at design time.

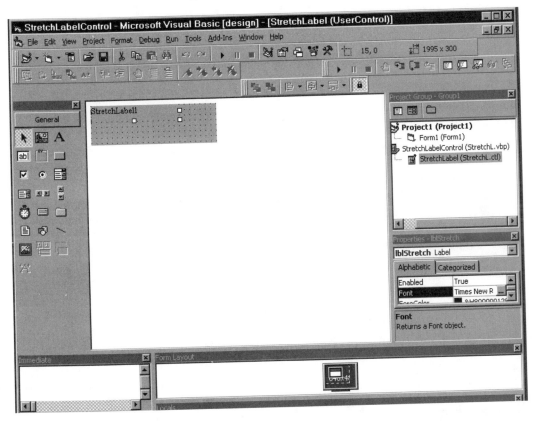

Figure 13-1
The StretchLabel Control at design time

Not much to it—it's just a label control on the surface. As you can imagine, building the interface for this control took about 10 seconds. The label control can keep all its default properties. This way, our user control looks just like a standard Label Control. The following table describes the user control components and their most important properties.

Table 13-1

User Control Components and Properties

Form	
LockControls	-1 'True
Label	
Caption	StretchLabel1
Name	lblStretch
Left	0
Top	0
Font	Times New Roman

(It is best to use a TrueType font like Times New Roman in order to see the font size changes more clearly.)

 The format given in Table 13-1 will be the format we use to describe all the sample controls in the remaining chapters. At the end of this and the following chapters, we will always give the full code for the control including all the properties that we reset from their defaults. The CD contains the code and all the files needed to see the control at work. ⊃

Without code, our user control is quite useless because

1. It won't do anything except display the caption that it starts with. The user of the control has no way to reset the caption.

2. Other controls cannot communicate with it in any way.

Exposing the Properties

First, we want to run the Control Interface Wizard to expose the properties and events so that our control will include all the standard Label properties and events. For example, a user of our control should be able to set the caption, size, and width from the Properties window.

To do this, load the Wizard from the Add-Ins menu and follow these steps:

1. Remove the KeyDown, KeyPress, and KeyUp events from the Selected names list.

2. Add the AutoSize, Caption, MouseIcon, MousePointer, ToolTipText, UseMnemonic, WhatsThisHelpID, and WordWrap properties from the Available names list.

3. Click Next until you get to the "Set Mapping" step.

4. Select all the items in the Public Name list.

5. Choose lblStretch in the Control drop-down list since we want to map all the members of our control to the identically named members of the label that is on the user control form.

6. Click Next to get to the Finish step and click <Finish>.

The Wizard adds all the code we need to expose the properties and events. The one thing that we need to add is an error-handling statement to each of the ReadProperties and WriteProperties events, as follows:

To the existing

```
Private Sub UserControl_ReadProperties(PropBag As _
PropertyBag)
```

add this line before all other lines:

```
On Error Resume Next
```

To the existing

```
Private Sub UserControl_WriteProperties(PropBag As _
PropertyBag)
```

add this line before all other lines:

```
On Error Resume Next
```

This is necessary because certain host applications will produce errors that should be ignored when reading or writing property values. The On Error Resume Next statement will do this.

Now, to see that we hooked up the property correctly,

1. Add a test form (Standard EXE) project to the CCE.

2. Close the designer for the StretchLabel Control.

3. Add the stretch label to the test form.

4. Click the StretchLabel Control and press F4 to view its properties in the Properties window. Notice they are the same as a standard Label Control.

We now have a control that can communicate with code outside of itself.

Resize Logic

Now, we want to add the code that changes the font size when the user resizes the user control. We will add the standard code that prevents the user of the control from seeing any white space between the label inside the StretchLabel Control and its container. Figure 13-2 shows the new Stretch label.

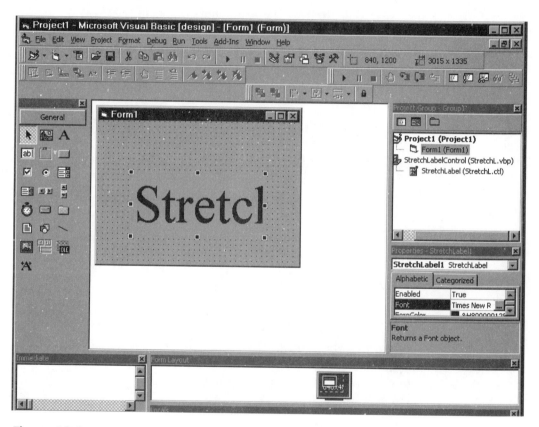

Figure 13-2
Stretch label

Here's the code. We hope it is self-explanatory, given the comments that we added. (There may be other ways of writing this code and there are more than a few ways to further optimize it. The method we chose seems to work fine for our purposes.)

```
Private Sub UserControl_Resize()
  Static sglLastHeight As Single
  Dim sglCurrHeight As Single
  Dim nFont As Single
  If sglLastHeight = 0 Then
     'initialize it
     sglLastHeight = lblStretch.Height
  End If
  'set the label control to the size of the control
  lblStretch.Height = Height
  lblStretch.Width = Width
  'get the current font size
  nFont = FontSize
  'get the current label height
  sglCurrHeight = lblStretch.Height
  'resize the font to match the control size
  If (sglLastHeight < sglCurrHeight) And (TextHeight("A") < _
  sglCurrHeight) Then
     'they enlarged it
     While TextHeight("A") <= sglCurrHeight
       nFont = nFont + 0.25
       FontSize = nFont
     Wend
  Else
     'they reduced it
     While (TextHeight("A") >= sglCurrHeight) And (nFont > _
     1.25)
       nFont = nFont - 0.25
       FontSize = nFont
     Wend
  End If
  'now set the label's font size
  lblStretch.FontSize = FontSize
  'save the current height to compare against next time
  sglLastHeight = lblStretch.Height
End Sub
```

Possible Additions and Potential Problems

This control serves as a great template for other controls that are based on the label where you want this base functionality. The only potential problem isn't really a problem at all but rather something built into the CCE. Every time you change the caption of an ordinary label in the Properties window, it immediately shows up in the label. When you change the caption on our custom control via the Properties window, you won't see the changes go into effect until you press ENTER.

The Full Code for This Control

```
VERSION 5.00
Begin VB.UserControl StretchLabel
   ClientHeight    =    885
   ClientLeft      =    0
   ClientTop       =    0
   ClientWidth     =    2895
   LockControls    =    -1   'True
   PropertyPages   =    "StretchL.ctx":0000
   ScaleHeight     =    885
   ScaleWidth      =    2895
   ToolboxBitmap   =    "StretchL.ctx":0004
   Begin VB.Label lblStretch
      AutoSize         =    -1   'True
      Caption          =    "StretchLabel1"
      BeginProperty Font
         Name             =    "Times New Roman"
         Size             =    8.25
         Charset          =    0
         Weight           =    400
         Underline        =    0    'False
         Italic           =    0    'False
         Strikethrough    =    0    'False
      EndProperty
      Height           =    210
      Left             =    15
      TabIndex         =    0
```

```
      Top                    =    0
      Width                  =    960
   End
End
Attribute VB_Name = "StretchLabel"
Attribute VB_GlobalNameSpace = False
Attribute VB_Creatable = True
Attribute VB_PredeclaredId = False
Attribute VB_Exposed = True
Attribute VB_Description = "Gary and Dave's Stretch Label
  Control"
Option Explicit
'Event Declarations:
Event Click() 'MappingInfo=lblStretch,lblStretch,-1,Click
Event DblClick() 'MappingInfo=lblStretch,lblStretch,
  -1,DblClick
Event MouseDown(Button As Integer, Shift As Integer,
  X As Single, Y As Single)
  'MappingInfo=lblStretch,lblStretch,-1,MouseDown
Event MouseMove(Button As Integer, Shift As Integer,
  X As Single, Y As Single)
  'MappingInfo=lblStretch,lblStretch,-1,MouseMove
Event MouseUp(Button As Integer, Shift As Integer,
  X As Single, Y As Single)
  'MappingInfo=lblStretch,lblStretch,-1,MouseUp


'WARNING! DO NOT REMOVE OR MODIFY THE FOLLOWING COMMENTED LINES!
'MappingInfo=lblStretch,lblStretch,-1,BackColor
Public Property Get BackColor() As OLE_COLOR
Attribute BackColor.VB_Description = "Returns/sets the
     background color used to display text and graphics in an
     object."
   BackColor = lblStretch.BackColor
End Property

Public Property Let BackColor(ByVal New_BackColor As OLE_COLOR)
   lblStretch.BackColor() = New_BackColor
   PropertyChanged "BackColor"
End Property
```

```
'WARNING! DO NOT REMOVE OR MODIFY THE FOLLOWING COMMENTED LINES!
'MappingInfo=lblStretch,lblStretch,-1,ForeColor
Public Property Get ForeColor() As OLE_COLOR
Attribute ForeColor.VB_Description = "Returns/sets the
    foreground color used to display text and graphics in an
    object."
  ForeColor = lblStretch.ForeColor
End Property

Public Property Let ForeColor(ByVal New_ForeColor As OLE_COLOR)
   lblStretch.ForeColor() = New_ForeColor
   PropertyChanged "ForeColor"
End Property

'WARNING! DO NOT REMOVE OR MODIFY THE FOLLOWING COMMENTED LINES!
'MappingInfo=lblStretch,lblStretch,-1,Enabled
Public Property Get Enabled() As Boolean
Attribute Enabled.VB_Description = "Returns/sets a value that
    determines whether an object can respond to user-generated
    events."
  Enabled = lblStretch.Enabled
End Property

Public Property Let Enabled(ByVal New_Enabled As Boolean)
   lblStretch.Enabled() = New_Enabled
   PropertyChanged "Enabled"
End Property

'WARNING! DO NOT REMOVE OR MODIFY THE FOLLOWING COMMENTED LINES!
'MappingInfo=lblStretch,lblStretch,-1,Font
Public Property Get Font() As Font
Attribute Font.VB_Description = "Returns a Font object."
Attribute Font.VB_UserMemId = -512
  Set Font = lblStretch.Font
End Property

Public Property Set Font(ByVal New_Font As Font)
   Set lblStretch.Font = New_Font
   PropertyChanged "Font"
End Property
```

```
'WARNING! DO NOT REMOVE OR MODIFY THE FOLLOWING COMMENTED LINES!
'MappingInfo=lblStretch,lblStretch,-1,BackStyle
Public Property Get BackStyle() As Integer
Attribute BackStyle.VB_Description = "Indicates whether a
    Label or the background of a Shape is transparent or
    opaque."
  BackStyle = lblStretch.BackStyle
End Property

Public Property Let BackStyle(ByVal New_BackStyle As Integer)
  lblStretch.BackStyle() = New_BackStyle
  PropertyChanged "BackStyle"
End Property
'WARNING! DO NOT REMOVE OR MODIFY THE FOLLOWING COMMENTED LINES!
'MappingInfo=lblStretch,lblStretch,-1,BorderStyle
Public Property Get BorderStyle() As Integer
Attribute BorderStyle.VB_Description = "Returns/sets the
    border style for an object."
  BorderStyle = lblStretch.BorderStyle
End Property

Public Property Let BorderStyle(ByVal New_BorderStyle As
    Integer)
  lblStretch.BorderStyle() = New_BorderStyle
  PropertyChanged "BorderStyle"
End Property

'WARNING! DO NOT REMOVE OR MODIFY THE FOLLOWING COMMENTED LINES!
'MappingInfo=lblStretch,lblStretch,-1,Refresh
Public Sub Refresh()
Attribute Refresh.VB_Description = "Forces a complete repaint
    of a object."
  lblStretch.Refresh
End Sub

Private Sub lblStretch_Click()
  RaiseEvent Click
End Sub

Private Sub lblStretch_DblClick()
  RaiseEvent DblClick
End Sub
```

411

```
Private Sub lblStretch_MouseDown(Button As Integer, Shift As
    Integer, X As Single, Y As Single)
  RaiseEvent MouseDown(Button, Shift, X, Y)
End Sub

Private Sub lblStretch_MouseMove(Button As Integer, Shift As
    Integer, X As Single, Y As Single)
  RaiseEvent MouseMove(Button, Shift, X, Y)
End Sub

Private Sub lblStretch_MouseUp(Button As Integer, Shift As
    Integer, X As Single, Y As Single)
  RaiseEvent MouseUp(Button, Shift, X, Y)
End Sub

'WARNING! DO NOT REMOVE OR MODIFY THE FOLLOWING COMMENTED LINES!
'MappingInfo=lblStretch,lblStretch,-1,AutoSize
Public Property Get AutoSize() As Boolean
Attribute AutoSize.VB_Description = "Determines whether a
    control is automatically resized to display its entire
    contents."
  AutoSize = lblStretch.AutoSize
End Property

Public Property Let AutoSize(ByVal New_AutoSize As Boolean)
  lblStretch.AutoSize() = New_AutoSize
  PropertyChanged "AutoSize"
End Property

'WARNING! DO NOT REMOVE OR MODIFY THE FOLLOWING COMMENTED LINES!
'MappingInfo=lblStretch,lblStretch,-1,Caption
Public Property Get Caption() As String
Attribute Caption.VB_Description = "Returns/sets the text
    displayed in an object's title bar or below an object's
    icon."
  Caption = lblStretch.Caption
End Property

Public Property Let Caption(ByVal New_Caption As String)
  lblStretch.Caption() = New_Caption
  PropertyChanged "Caption"
End Property
```

```
'WARNING! DO NOT REMOVE OR MODIFY THE FOLLOWING COMMENTED LINES!
'MappingInfo=lblStretch,lblStretch,-1,MouseIcon
Public Property Get MouseIcon() As Picture
Attribute MouseIcon.VB_Description = "Sets a custom mouse icon."
  Set MouseIcon = lblStretch.MouseIcon
End Property

Public Property Set MouseIcon(ByVal New_MouseIcon As Picture)
  Set lblStretch.MouseIcon = New_MouseIcon
  PropertyChanged "MouseIcon"
End Property

'WARNING! DO NOT REMOVE OR MODIFY THE FOLLOWING COMMENTED LINES!
'MappingInfo=lblStretch,lblStretch,-1,MousePointer
Public Property Get MousePointer() As Integer
Attribute MousePointer.VB_Description = "Returns/sets the type
    of mouse pointer displayed when over part of an object."
  MousePointer = lblStretch.MousePointer
End Property

Public Property Let MousePointer(ByVal New_MousePointer As _
Integer)
  lblStretch.MousePointer() = New_MousePointer
  PropertyChanged "MousePointer"
End Property

'WARNING! DO NOT REMOVE OR MODIFY THE FOLLOWING COMMENTED LINES!
'MappingInfo=lblStretch,lblStretch,-1,ToolTipText
Public Property Get ToolTipText() As String
Attribute ToolTipText.VB_Description = "Returns/sets the text
    displayed when the mouse is paused over the control."
  ToolTipText = lblStretch.ToolTipText
End Property

Public Property Let ToolTipText(ByVal New_ToolTipText As String)
  lblStretch.ToolTipText() = New_ToolTipText
  PropertyChanged "ToolTipText"
End Property
```

```
'WARNING! DO NOT REMOVE OR MODIFY THE FOLLOWING COMMENTED LINES!
'MappingInfo=lblStretch,lblStretch,-1,WhatsThisHelpID
Public Property Get WhatsThisHelpID() As Long
Attribute WhatsThisHelpID.VB_Description = "Returns/sets an
    associated context number for an object."
  WhatsThisHelpID = lblStretch.WhatsThisHelpID
End Property

Public Property Let WhatsThisHelpID(ByVal New_WhatsThisHelpID
    As Long)
  lblStretch.WhatsThisHelpID() = New_WhatsThisHelpID
  PropertyChanged "WhatsThisHelpID"
End Property

'WARNING! DO NOT REMOVE OR MODIFY THE FOLLOWING COMMENTED LINES!
'MappingInfo=lblStretch,lblStretch,-1,WordWrap
Public Property Get WordWrap() As Boolean
Attribute WordWrap.VB_Description = "Returns/sets a value that
    determines whether a control expands to fit the text in
    its Caption."
  WordWrap = lblStretch.WordWrap
End Property

Public Property Let WordWrap(ByVal New_WordWrap As Boolean)
  lblStretch.WordWrap() = New_WordWrap
  PropertyChanged "WordWrap"
End Property

'Load property values from storage
Private Sub UserControl_ReadProperties(PropBag As PropertyBag)
  On Error Resume Next

  lblStretch.BackColor = PropBag.ReadProperty("BackColor",
    &H8000000F)
  lblStretch.ForeColor = PropBag.ReadProperty("ForeColor",
    &H80000012)
  lblStretch.Enabled = PropBag.ReadProperty("Enabled", True)
  Set Font = PropBag.ReadProperty("Font", Ambient.Font)
  lblStretch.BackStyle = PropBag.ReadProperty("BackStyle", 1)
  lblStretch.BorderStyle = PropBag.ReadProperty("BorderStyle", 0)
  lblStretch.AutoSize = PropBag.ReadProperty("AutoSize", False)
```

414

```
    lblStretch.Caption = PropBag.ReadProperty("Caption",
      "StretchLabel1")
    Set MouseIcon = PropBag.ReadProperty("MouseIcon", Nothing)
    lblStretch.MousePointer =
      PropBag.ReadProperty("MousePointer", 0)
    lblStretch.ToolTipText = PropBag.ReadProperty("ToolTipText",
      "")
    lblStretch.WhatsThisHelpID =
      PropBag.ReadProperty("WhatsThisHelpID", 0)
    lblStretch.WordWrap = PropBag.ReadProperty("WordWrap", False)
End Sub


'Write property values to storage
Private Sub UserControl_WriteProperties(PropBag As PropertyBag)
    On Error Resume Next

    Call PropBag.WriteProperty("BackColor",
      lblStretch.BackColor, &H8000000F)
    Call PropBag.WriteProperty("ForeColor",
      lblStretch.ForeColor, &H80000012)
    Call PropBag.WriteProperty("Enabled", lblStretch.Enabled,
      True)
    Call PropBag.WriteProperty("Font", Font, Ambient.Font)
    Call PropBag.WriteProperty("BackStyle",
      lblStretch.BackStyle, 1)
    Call PropBag.WriteProperty("BorderStyle",
      lblStretch.BorderStyle, 0)
    Call PropBag.WriteProperty("AutoSize", lblStretch.AutoSize,
      False)
    Call PropBag.WriteProperty("Caption", lblStretch.Caption,
      "StretchLabel1")
    Call PropBag.WriteProperty("MouseIcon", MouseIcon, Nothing)
    Call PropBag.WriteProperty("MousePointer",
      lblStretch.MousePointer, 0)
    Call PropBag.WriteProperty("ToolTipText",
      lblStretch.ToolTipText, "")
    Call PropBag.WriteProperty("WhatsThisHelpID",
      lblStretch.WhatsThisHelpID, 0)
    Call PropBag.WriteProperty("WordWrap", lblStretch.WordWrap,
      False)
End Sub
```

```
Private Sub UserControl_Resize()
  Static sglLastHeight As Single
  Dim sglCurrHeight As Single
  Dim nFont As Single

  If sglLastHeight = 0 Then
    'initialize it
    sglLastHeight = lblStretch.Height
  End If

  'set the label control to the size of the control
  lblStretch.Height = Height
  lblStretch.Width = Width

  'get the current font size
  nFont = FontSize
  'get the current label height
  sglCurrHeight = lblStretch.Height

  'resize the font to match the control size
  If (sglLastHeight < sglCurrHeight) And (TextHeight("A") <
    sglCurrHeight) Then
    'they enlarged it
    While TextHeight("A") <= sglCurrHeight
      nFont = nFont + 0.25
      FontSize = nFont
    Wend
  Else
    'they reduced it
    While (TextHeight("A") >= sglCurrHeight) And (nFont > 1.25)
      nFont = nFont - 0.25
      FontSize = nFont
    Wend
  End If

  'now set the label's font size
  lblStretch.FontSize = FontSize
  'save the current height to compare against next time
  sglLastHeight = lblStretch.Height
End Sub
```

When you activate a Web site you often need more power than is built into your scripting language. On the other hand, nobody wants to "reinvent the wheel." If your favorite language already has debugged libraries that do what you need, it makes sense to encapsulate that functionality into a control. Then, all you have to do is:

- Place the control on your Web page, and
- Access that control via a scripting language like VBScript.

For example, Visual Basic for Applications (or VBA, as it is usually called) has a powerful library of financial functions for doing everything from mortgage calculation to net present value. Visual Basic for Applications is built into the CCE. These functions are not part of VBScript, however. We, therefore, think it makes sense to encapsulate the financial functions in an ActiveX Control. You can then use VBA's financial functions on any Web page that can handle ActiveX Controls.

 Although we concentrate on the financial functions from VBA in this chapter, the techniques given here would work with any library that you can call from Visual Basic. For example, you could encapsulate your favorite Win32 API functions into an ActiveX Control. ⊃

The Finance Control

The Idea of the Control

We want to build an ActiveX Control that gives easy access to Visual Basic's powerful financial functions (see Chapter 5 if you aren't familiar with them). To do this efficiently, the Finance Control we will build in this chapter must:

1. Be invisible at run time.
2. Expose all of the financial functions built into Visual Basic as (easy-to-use) methods of the control.

The first point means we won't have to build a user interface because the control is going to be invisible at run time. The code we add is simply what is needed to make all the financial functions found in VBA available as methods of the user control. The resulting OCX is only about 16k!

In summary, our design goals were:

1. Expose the financial function of VBA to VBScript.
2. Be as easy to use as the functions themselves.
3. Perform enough error handling so that the control cannot inadvertently cause the application using it to fail.

Creating the Interface

To accomplish the design goals, the only UI necessary is a bitmap to identify the control on a form at design time. This is because, just like using the Timer Control, you will need a way of knowing you have placed an instance of the control on a form. We chose the obvious bitmap, as Figure 14-1 indicates.

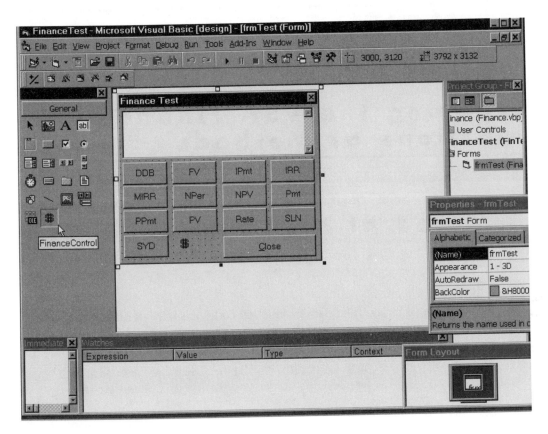

Figure 14-1
The Finance Control

The bitmap used can be found on the CD in the Ch 14 directory.

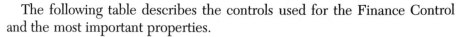

The following table describes the controls used for the Finance Control and the most important properties.

Form

InvisibleAtRuntime	−1 'True
Picture	"Finance.ctx":0000
ToolboxBitmap	"Finance.ctx":0546

As usual, the end of the chapter gives the full code for the control including all the properties that we reset from their defaults. The CD contains the code and all the files needed to see the control at work.

Exposing the VBA Financial Functions as Methods

First, we need to add a generic error routine to handle the possible errors that occur as a result of improper use of one of the functions. Here is a simple routine that displays the error in a somewhat user-friendly formatted fashion.

```
Private Sub ShowError()
  MsgBox "Runtime Error " & Err & " has occurred." & _
  vbCrLf & Err.Description, vbInformation, "Finance Control"
End Sub
```

We need to add the financial function codes as methods of the user control. Here is an example of one of the functions. The entire set of functions appears at the end of the chapter, along with the full code from the user control.

```
Public Function DDB(Cost As Double, Salvage As Double, _
Life As Double, Period As Double, Optional Factor As _
Single) As Double
  On Error GoTo DDBErr
  If Factor = 0 Then
    DDB = VBA.DDB(Cost, Salvage, Life, Period)  Else
    DDB = VBA.DDB(Cost, Salvage, Life, Period, Factor)
  End If
  Exit Function
DDBErr:
  ShowError
End Function
```

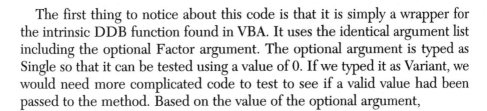

The first thing to notice about this code is that it is simply a wrapper for the intrinsic DDB function found in VBA. It uses the identical argument list including the optional Factor argument. The optional argument is typed as Single so that it can be tested using a value of 0. If we typed it as Variant, we would need more complicated code to test to see if a valid value had been passed to the method. Based on the value of the optional argument,

- we pass the arguments on to the VBA version of DDB
- the method returns the value given by the underlying VBA function.

There is one important point to notice in our code: we must prefix the call to the VBA function with the explicit "VBA.DDB" syntax. This is necessary because of a name conflict between our methods and the VBA functions. If we didn't give the CCE edition a way of distinguishing the name of our method from the name of the VBA function, then it would, by default, call our own method recursively—accomplishing nothing but an eventual "stack overflow" error.

 As an alternative, we could have named our methods something other than the usual VBA names, choosing something like "finDDB" for the method name given in the example. We prefer using the same names for our methods as the VBA functions because it is easier for us to remember when we use the control. ➲

It is also very important to have enough error handling in this type of code. You do not want to have the calling application fail due to your lack of error trapping. To do this, we added an error handler that calls our generic error display routine, and then returns without giving a return value for the function. This way, the calling application can always test for a return value of 0.

To use the control, simply place it on a form and call one of its methods as shown below:

```
Depr = FinanceControl1.DDB(InitCost, SalvageVal, LifeTime, DepYear)
```

We provide you with a sample test application on the CD to see how easy and useful this simple control is. We hope it will convince you that the ability to encapsulate VBA (or any other library language) in a user control is extremely useful.

 By the way—the VB script code on the CD is worth looking over. It shows how to pass arrays to an OCX, which is not well-documented. It does require VBSCRIPT 2.0, though. ➲

Resize Logic

Since we do not want this control to be any bigger than is sufficient to show the bitmap (why obscure any other controls on the form?), we need to add the following code in the Resize event:

```
Private Sub UserControl_Resize()
    Height = 240
    Width = 240
End Sub
```

Possible Additions and Potential Problems

This control is now fairly complete. You could add the ability to:

1. Return the value in some special format by having, for example, a format or locale property.
2. Add a UI that displays the output of the current calculation.
3. Add other functions such as the Date intrinsics (DatePart, DateDiff and DateAdd)

(However, we feel that it would make more sense to leave (2) to the calling routine and put the functionality of (3) into another control.)

A potential problem is insufficient error handling. (One general rule is that you can *always* provide more error information to the user!)

Code for This Control

```
VERSION 5.00
Begin VB.UserControl FinanceControl
    ClientHeight    =    240
    ClientLeft      =    0
    ClientTop       =    0
```

```
      ClientWidth       =      240
      InvisibleAtRuntime=    -1    'True
      Picture           =     "Finance.ctx":0000
      PropertyPages     =     "Finance.ctx":0542
      ScaleHeight       =      240
      ScaleWidth        =      240
      ToolboxBitmap     =     "Finance.ctx":0546
End
Attribute VB_Name = "FinanceControl"
Attribute VB_GlobalNameSpace = False
Attribute VB_Creatable = True
Attribute VB_PredeclaredId = False
Attribute VB_Exposed = True
Attribute VB_Description = "Gary and Dave's Finance Control"
Option Explicit

'each of the financial intrinsic function are encapsulated
'in a method of the control. The optional parameters are
'all types so they can be tested for a non-zero state
'and the defaults can be used if no value is passed in.

Public Function DDB(Cost As Double, Salvage As Double, _
Life As Double, Period As Double, _
Optional Factor As Single) As Double
  On Error GoTo DDBErr
  If Factor = 0 Then
    DDB = VBA.DDB(Cost, Salvage, Life, Period)
  Else
    DDB = VBA.DDB(Cost, Salvage, Life, Period, Factor)
  End If
  Exit Function
DDBErr:
  ShowError
End Function

Public Function FV(Rate As Double, Nper As Integer, Pmt As _
Double, Optional PV As Double, Optional Due As Integer) As _
Double
  On Error GoTo FVErr
  If PV = 0 Then
    FV = VBA.FV(Rate, Nper, Pmt)
  ElseIf Due = 0 Then
```

```
    FV = VBA.FV(Rate, Nper, Pmt, PV)
  Else
    FV = VBA.FV(Rate, Nper, Pmt, PV, Due)
  End If
  Exit Function
FVErr:
  ShowError
End Function

Public Function IPmt(Rate As Double, Per As Double, _
Nper As Integer, PV As Double, Optional FV As Double, _
Optional Due As Integer) As Double
  On Error GoTo IPmtErr
  If FV = 0 Then
    IPmt = VBA.IPmt(Rate, Per, Nper, PV)
  ElseIf Due = 0 Then
    IPmt = VBA.IPmt(Rate, Per, Nper, PV, FV)
  Else
    IPmt = VBA.IPmt(Rate, Per, Nper, PV, FV, Due)
  End If
  Exit Function
IPmtErr:
  ShowError
End Function

Public Function IRR(ByVal Values As Variant, _
    Optional Guess As Double) As Double
  On Error GoTo IRRErr
  Dim dblValues() As Double
  Dim i As Integer
  Dim s As Integer
  Dim f As Integer
  ReDim dblValues(LBound(Values) To UBound(Values))
  For i = LBound(Values) To UBound(Values)
    dblValues(i) = CDbl(Values(i))
  Next
  If Guess = 0 Then
    IRR = VBA.IRR(dblValues())
  Else
    IRR = VBA.IRR(dblValues(), Guess)
  End If
  Exit Function
```

```
IRRErr:
  ShowError
  Resume 0
End Function

Public Function MIRR(ByVal Values As Variant, _
FinanceRate As Double, ReinvestRate As Double) As Double
  On Error GoTo MIRRErr
  Dim dblValues() As Double
  Dim i As Integer
  ReDim dblValues(LBound(Values) To UBound(Values))
  For i = LBound(Values) To UBound(Values)
    dblValues(i) = CDbl(Values(i))
  Next
  MIRR = VBA.MIRR(dblValues(), FinanceRate, ReinvestRate)
  Exit Function
MIRRErr:
  ShowError
End Function

Public Function Nper(Rate As Double, Pmt As Double, PV As _
Double, Optional FV As Double, Optional Due As Integer) As _
Double
  On Error GoTo NperErr
  If FV = 0 Then
    Nper = VBA.Nper(Rate, Pmt, PV)
  ElseIf Due = 0 Then
    Nper = VBA.Nper(Rate, Pmt, PV, FV)
  Else
    Nper = VBA.Nper(Rate, Pmt, PV, FV, Due)
  End If
  Exit Function
NperErr:
  ShowError
End Function

Public Function NPV(Rate As Double, ByVal Values As Variant) _
  As Double
  On Error GoTo NPVErr
  Dim dblValues() As Double
  Dim i As Integer
  ReDim dblValues(LBound(Values) To UBound(Values))
```

```
   For i = LBound(Values) To UBound(Values)
     dblValues(i) = CDbl(Values(i))
   Next
   NPV = VBA.NPV(Rate, dblValues())
   Exit Function
NPVErr:
   ShowError
End Function

Public Function Pmt(Rate As Double, Nper As Integer, PV As _
Double, Optional FV As Double, Optional Due As Integer) As _
Double
   On Error GoTo PmtErr
   If FV = 0 Then
     Pmt = VBA.Pmt(Rate, Nper, PV)
   ElseIf Due = 0 Then
     Pmt = VBA.Pmt(Rate, Nper, PV, FV)
   Else
     Pmt = VBA.Pmt(Rate, Nper, PV, FV, Due)
   End If
   Exit Function
PmtErr:
   ShowError
End Function

Public Function PPmt(Rate As Double, Per As Double, Nper As _
Integer, PV As Double, Optional FV As Double, Optional Due _
As Integer) As Double
   On Error GoTo PPmtErr
   If FV = 0 Then
     PPmt = VBA.PPmt(Rate, Per, Nper, PV)
   ElseIf Due = 0 Then
     PPmt = VBA.PPmt(Rate, Per, Nper, PV, FV)
   Else
     PPmt = VBA.PPmt(Rate, Per, Nper, PV, FV, Due)
   End If
   Exit Function
PPmtErr:
   ShowError
End Function
```

```
Public Function PV(Rate As Double, Nper As Integer, Pmt As _
Double, Optional FV As Double, Optional Due As Integer) As _
Double
   On Error GoTo PVErr
   If FV = 0 Then
      PV = VBA.PV(Rate, Nper, Pmt)
   ElseIf Due = 0 Then
      PV = VBA.PV(Rate, Nper, Pmt, FV)
   Else
      PV = VBA.PV(Rate, Nper, Pmt, FV, Due)
   End If
   Exit Function
PVErr:
   ShowError
End Function

Public Function Rate(Nper As Integer, Pmt As Double, PV As _
Double, Optional FV As Double, Optional Due As Integer, _
Optional Guess As Double) As Double
   On Error GoTo RateErr
   If FV = 0 Then
      Rate = VBA.Rate(Nper, Pmt, PV)
   ElseIf Due = 0 Then
      Rate = VBA.Rate(Nper, Pmt, PV, FV)
   ElseIf Guess = 0 Then
      Rate = VBA.Rate(Nper, Pmt, PV, FV, Due)
   Else
      Rate = VBA.Rate(Nper, Pmt, PV, FV, Due, Guess)
   End If
   Exit Function
RateErr:
   ShowError
End Function

Public Function SLN(Cost As Double, Salvage As Double, _
Life As Double) As Double
   On Error GoTo SLNErr
   SLN = VBA.SLN(Cost, Salvage, Life)
   Exit Function
SLNErr:
   ShowError
End Function
```

```
Public Function SYD(Cost As Double, Salvage As Double, _
Life As Double, Period As Double) As Double
  On Error GoTo SYDErr
  SYD = VBA.SYD(Cost, Salvage, Life, Period)
  Exit Function
SYDErr:
  ShowError
End Function

Private Sub UserControl_Resize()
  Height = 240
  Width = 240
End Sub

Private Sub ShowError()
  MsgBox "Runtime Error " & Err & " has occurred." & _
  vbCrLf & Err.Description, vbInformation, "Finance Control"
End Sub
```

Chapter 15

Entering dates is a common task, but writing the code to allow this can be tiresome. As with any tedious but common programming task, it makes sense to encapsulate this functionality into an ActiveX Control. This way, if your program or script needs to allow the user to enter a date, you can farm the work out to a control. This control should only allow valid dates and make it easy for the user to enter a date quickly.

The Calendar Control we are going to show you accomplishes both of these tasks. The user interface is somewhat complex, but little code is needed. The resulting OCX is only about 25k.

The Calendar Control

The Idea of the Control

Allowing only correct dates is an easy design goal; making a Calendar Control easy to use is another question with many answers. The control we show you here was designed to satisfy the following goals:

1. The date should always be displayed.
2. The user should be able to change day, month or year via (different) button clicks.
3. The user should be able to toggle to easily display the calendar for the current month.

Creating the Interface

Accomplishing all the goals mentioned required us to combine a number of simpler controls in our user control. Figure 15-1 shows the control without the monthly calendar dropped down.

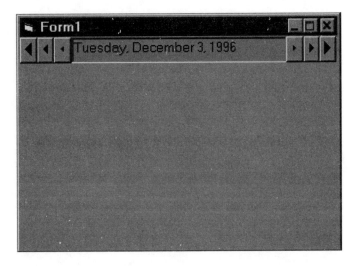

Figure 15-1
The Calendar Control
basic display

We used four types of controls on this user control. The first is a control array of six graphical command buttons. The icons are the various arrows and the control array itself is named cmdChange. The icons represent moving one day, month or year at a time in the indicated direction. As with any user-friendly control, all the controls will have tooltips to tell the user what they do. The second control is a Label Control that we will use to show the currently selected date. The label has the border style property set to 1 (Fixed Single) and the 3D property set as well (Appearance property = 1 = 3D). This way, the label looks just like a text box. However, since it is still a label, the user can't type in it. This prevents users from entering invalid dates. The next control is a PictureBox Control for the monthly calendar. We take advantage of the fact that a PictureBox Control is a container control by adding two control arrays of labels to it. The first control array has seven labels for the days of the week and the second array has 42 labels (6 rows of 7 labels each) that are needed to show any month. (If a month starts on a Friday or Saturday it may need six rows.) Figure 15-2 shows the control at work with the monthly calendar dropped down and a tooltip showing.

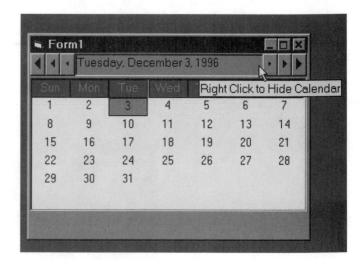

Figure 15-2
The Monthly display in the Calendar Control

The following table describes the controls and their most important properties using the format you have already seen.

Form

AutoRedraw	-1 'True
LockControls	-1 'True

PictureBox

Name	picCalendar

Label (control array)

Name	lblNumbers
Alignment	2 'Center
Appearance	0 'Flat
Index	0

Label (control array)

Name	lblDays
Alignment	2 'Center
Appearance	0 'Flat
Index	0

CommandButton (control array)

Name	cmdChange
Index	5
Style	1 'Graphical
TabStop	0 'False
ToolTipText	"Next Year (Ctrl+PageDown)"

CommandButton

Name	cmdChange
Index	4
ToolTipText	"Next Month (PageDown)"

CommandButton

Name	cmdChange
ToolTipText	"Next Day (Right Arrow Key)"

CommandButton

Name	cmdChange
Index	2
ToolTipText	"Previous Day (Left Arrow Key)"

CommandButton

Name	cmdChange
ToolTipText	"Previous Month (PageUp)"

CommandButton

Name	cmdChange
ToolTipText	"Previous Year (Ctrl+PageUp)"

Label

Name	lblDate
BorderStyle	1 'Fixed Single
Caption	"Wednesday, November 20, 1996"
ToolTipText	"Right Click to View Calendar"

As usual, the end of the chapter gives the full code for the control including all the properties that we reset from their defaults. The CD contains the code and all the files needed to see the control at work.

Building the interface for this control, as shown in Figure 15-3, took only about 1 hour. This was possible because we took full advantage of Visual Basic's handy control array feature. Here's what the control looks like at design time.

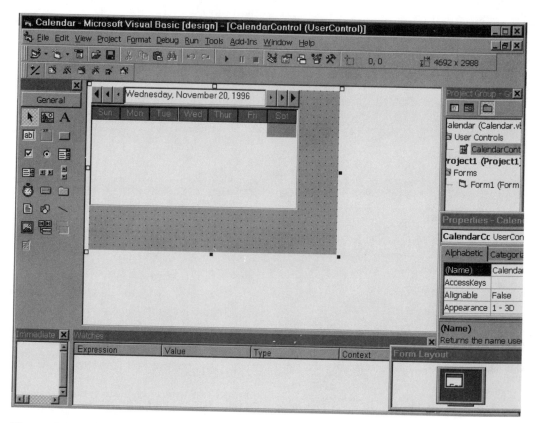

Figure 15-3
The Calendar Control at design time

Although we think the control is designed quite nicely, in its current state it is also quite useless. This is because:

1. It won't do anything except display the date that you see right now.

2. Other controls cannot communicate with it in any way.

We will need to add the necessary code to cure this problem.

Exposing the Properties

First, we want to add the code that will let us expose the current date to any code running in an application that uses our code. To do this, go to the Code window by choosing View|Code (or right-clicking the user control and selecting "View Code").

Now, we need a module level variable to hold the current date. It needs to use the Date data type because we want the date to be a formatted string, not a date value. For this, use the following line of code:

```
Dim m_CurrentDate As Date
```

We also need a module level variable to hold the information about which cell is currently selected.

```
Dim mnCurrentCell As Integer
```

Next, we need a Property Get procedure to allow other controls or code to access the date value. For this, we use

```
Public Property Get CurrentDate() As Date
   CurrentDate = m_CurrentDate
End Property
```

In order to set the property at both design and run time, we need a Property Let function. This Property Let procedure should have a single parameter that takes a date value. It needs to do four things with this value:

1. Display the date in the caption of the label.
2. Store the value passed as a parameter in the module level variable `m_CurrentDate` that we just created.
3. Call a support routine to fill the calendar.
4. Finally, execute the PropertyChanged routine that tells Visual Basic that the current property value has changed. (Recall this is the way a property can persist when the user of the control goes from design to run mode, or saves a form with the user control on it.)

To do all this only requires four lines of code!

```
Public Property Let CurrentDate(ByVal _
New_CurrentDate As Date)
   lblDate.Caption = Format(New_CurrentDate, "dddd,
mmmm d, yyyy")
   m_CurrentDate = New_CurrentDate
   FillCalendar
   PropertyChanged "CurrentDate"
End Property
```

Next, we need a way to initialize the date so that the control starts with today's date. As always, place this kind of code in the InitProperties procedure.

```
Private Sub UserControl_InitProperties()
   CurrentDate = Date
End Sub
```

Finally, we need the two routines that read and write the properties so that they can persist when the user switches modes between design and run time.

```
Private Sub UserControl_ReadProperties(PropBag As _
PropertyBag)
   On Error Resume Next
   CurrentDate = PropBag.ReadProperty("CurrentDate", _
   Date)
End Sub
```

```
Private Sub UserControl_WriteProperties(PropBag As _
PropertyBag)
   On Error Resume Next
   Call PropBag.WriteProperty("CurrentDate",
m_CurrentDate, Date)
End Sub
```

To test the code we have written so far, follow the usual steps of closing the user control designer and adding a Standard EXE project. Now double-click the new icon in the toolbox (the last one) to place a Calendar Control on Form1, as shown in Figure 15-4.

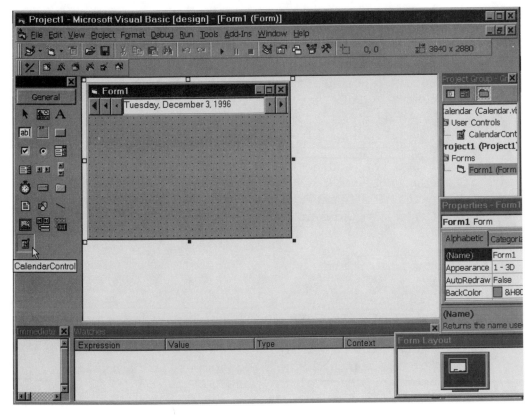

Figure 15-4
The Calendar Control at design time

Now, we need to add the sub routine that fills the calendar grid contained in the PictureBox with the current month and highlights the current day. The code is pretty much self-explanatory, given the comments that we added. (There are a lot of ways of writing this code and there are more than a few ways to further optimize it. The method we chose seems to work fine for our purposes.)

```
Sub FillCalendar()
    Dim i As Integer
    Dim nStart As Integer
    Dim nCurr As Integer
    Dim nLast As Integer
    Dim nLastMonthEnd As Integer
```

```
'figure out the starting cell
nStart = DatePart("w", m_CurrentDate - DatePart("d", _
m_CurrentDate) + 1) - 1
'figure out the ending cell
nLast = nStart + DatePart("d", DateAdd("m", 1, _
m_CurrentDate) - DatePart("d", DateAdd("m", 1, _
m_CurrentDate))) - 1

If nStart > 0 Then
   'figure out the ending value of last month
   'if there are some previous month days visible
   nLastMonthEnd = DatePart("d", m_CurrentDate - _
   DatePart("d", m_CurrentDate)) - nStart + 1
End If

'initialize the current day
nCurr = 1

'now walk through the days and setup the cells
For i = 0 To 41
   If i < nStart Or i > nLast Then
      'out of the range so we need to set it to italic
      lblNumbers(i).BackColor = &HFFFFFF
      lblNumbers(i).BorderStyle = 0
      lblNumbers(i).ForeColor = &HC0C0C0
      If i < nStart Then
        lblNumbers(i).Caption = nLastMonthEnd + i
      Else
        If i = nLast + 1 Then nCurr = _
        1 'reset on the first day of next month
        lblNumbers(i).Caption = nCurr
        nCurr = nCurr + 1
      End If
   Else
      lblNumbers(i).ForeColor = &H0&
      If nCurr = DatePart("d", m_CurrentDate) Then
         'this is the current date so we need to
         'set it's backcolor and borderstyle
         lblNumbers(i).BackColor = &HFFFF00
         lblNumbers(i).BorderStyle = 1
         'save the current cell number
         mnCurrentCell = i
```

```
      Else
        lblNumbers(i).BackColor = &HFFFFFF
        lblNumbers(i).BorderStyle = 0
      End If
      'set the caption
      lblNumbers(i).Caption = nCurr
      'increment our counter
      nCurr = nCurr + 1
    End If
  Next
End Sub
```

To see if we hooked up the property correctly:

1. Press F5 to run the project and see that the form loads and the control displays the date correctly.

2. Stop the application.

3. Click the Calendar Control and press F4 to view its properties in the Properties window.

4. Change the date and press ENTER. Notice that the displayed date changes. This is possible because of the Property Let procedure that we added.

5. Press F5 and notice that the newly entered date is correctly displayed.

We now have a control that can communicate with code outside of itself. We now want to add the code that allows the user to set the date at run time.

Run-Time Logic

We will tackle this in a few steps. First, we need to write the code to accept user input from the arrow buttons and the keyboard. Since we made the buttons a control array, we only need a single sub routine to handle the Click event for all 6 of the buttons. When a user clicks a button, the code simply changes the value of the current date property appropriately. When it is finished doing this, the code sets the focus back to the picCalendar control so that this control is ready to accept keyboard input as needed.

```
'date setting functions
'========================================================
Private Sub cmdChange_Click(Index As Integer)
   Select Case Index
     Case 0   'previous year
       CurrentDate = DateAdd("yyyy", -1, CurrentDate)
     Case 1   'previous month
       CurrentDate = DateAdd("m", -1, CurrentDate)
     Case 2   'previous day
       CurrentDate = CurrentDate - 1
     Case 3   'next day
       CurrentDate = CurrentDate + 1
     Case 4   'next month
       CurrentDate = DateAdd("m", 1, CurrentDate)
     Case 5   'next year
       CurrentDate = DateAdd("yyyy", 1, CurrentDate)
   End Select
   picCalendar.SetFocus
End Sub
```

Now, let's add the code to accept keyboard input. Since the picCalendar control is the only control on our user control that has its TabStop property set to True, we know that it will have focus when the control becomes active. The setFocus line in the code above insures that, after the user clicks a button, our control will get the focus right back. Therefore, all we have to do is trap the right keystroke combinations and process them as if the user had clicked on the equivalent arrow buttons. Pressing the HOME key takes you directly to today's date with a single keystroke. The functions of the ARROW, PAGEUP/DOWN and CTRL+PAGEUP/DOWN keys are given in the tooltips for the buttons but the function of the HOME key is not mentioned anywhere. This makes it undocumented unless the user is told of its existence in some other way—via a help file, for example. (You could remedy this by changing the tooltip property of the lblDate control.)

```
Private Sub picCalendar_KeyDown(KeyCode As Integer, Shift As _
Integer)
   'get the keystrokes from the picture control
   'because that is the only control on our UserControl
   'that can have focus
```

```
    If KeyCode = vbKeyRight Or KeyCode = vbKeyDown Then
        cmdChange_Click 3
    ElseIf KeyCode = vbKeyLeft Or KeyCode = vbKeyUp Then
        cmdChange_Click 2
    ElseIf KeyCode = vbKeyPageDown And Shift = 0 Then
        cmdChange_Click 4
    ElseIf KeyCode = vbKeyPageUp And Shift = 0 Then
        cmdChange_Click 1
    ElseIf KeyCode = vbKeyPageDown And Shift <> 0 Then
        cmdChange_Click 5
    ElseIf KeyCode = vbKeyPageUp And Shift <> 0 Then
        cmdChange_Click 0
    ElseIf KeyCode = vbKeyHome Then
        CurrentDate = Date
    End If
End Sub
```

Now, we need a way to allow the user to click on a cell in the calendar to make it the currently displayed date. To do this, the code below simply uses the module level variable called mnCurrentCell in order to determine how to set the new date. It does this by subtracting the index of the cell clicked from the index of the current cell, and subtracting that amount from the current date.

```
    Private Sub lblNumbers_Click(Index As Integer)
        CurrentDate = CurrentDate - (mnCurrentCell - Index)
    End Sub
```

Now, let's test the control again. You should still have the control on Form1, so all we need to do is press F5 to run the application and see if it works. You should be able to click any of the buttons, press the ARROW, PAGEUP/DOWN and CTRL+PAGEUP/DOWN or click one of the cells in the grid to change the date. In addition, don't forget to test the HOME key to reset to today's date.

Pretty cool, isn't it? This control is almost done. We just need a few finishing touches and some optional display code.

Control Size and Display

The calendar grid is only needed when the user is entering a date and wants to find it using the Calendar view. In order to preserve form space, we are going to add code that will make the control display the calendar grid only when the user needs it. We will also add some code to indicate what the focus is, and then some generic resizing code.

First, we need another module level variable added to the top of the module as follows:

```
Dim mbShowCalendar As Boolean
```

To show the user that the control has the focus, we will add the following code to the GotFocus and LostFocus event. We make them Private because we don't want this event available publicly.

```
Private Sub picCalendar_GotFocus()
   'change it to blue
   lblDate.BackColor = &HFFFF00
End Sub

Private Sub picCalendar_LostFocus()
   'change it back to white
   lblDate.BackColor = &HFFFFFF
   'remove the calendar
   mbShowCalendar = True
   lblDate_MouseUp vbRightButton, 0, 0, 0
End Sub
```

(The GotFocus event occurs when the user tabs to the user control. This is because the picCalendar Control is the only control with the TabStop property set to True on the user control.)

It is easy to waste a lot of space with a user control. To control the size of the control so the user does not make it too small to use, or too big and waste form space, we added the following code. (It is possible to use much more sophisticated control that checks for screen resolution and font sizes, of course.)

```
Private Sub UserControl_Resize()
  'force the size to the only allowable values
  If mbShowCalendar Then
    Height = 2190
  Else
    Height = 330
  End If
  Width = 3945
End Sub
```

Next, we need to add the event that toggles the view of the calendar grid when the user clicks the right mouse button.

```
Private Sub lblDate_MouseUp(Button As Integer, _
Shift As Integer, X As Single, Y As Single)
  If Button = vbRightButton Then
    'right click to toggle the calendar state
    If mbShowCalendar Then
      mbShowCalendar = False
      Height = 330
      lblDate.ToolTipText = "Right Click to View
        Calendar"
    Else
      mbShowCalendar = True
      Height = 2190
      lblDate.ToolTipText = "Right Click to Hide
        Calendar"
      picCalendar.SetFocus
    End If
  End If
End Sub
```

That's it, we're done! Let's test the whole control again. For this,

1. Add a command button to Form1 so we have another control to switch focus to.

2. Press F5.

You should notice right away that the calendar isn't displayed until you right-click the date. Also notice that the current displayed date changes to blue when the control gets focus. Tab back and forth from the command button to the Calendar Control and it should switch from blue to white.

Possible Additions and Potential Problems

The first potential problem is that the control may not display well in all fonts or in all screen resolutions. Two of the many possible ways to fix this are:

1. Exposing a Font property to the user of the control. The user could then set the Font property so that it displays nicely on his or her target machine.

2. Write the code (and there will be a lot of it) to make all the parts of the control resize themselves to the current size and display resolution.

The next problem should become obvious if you play around with our control a lot. Notice that the calendar grid comes up behind other controls on the form. To see this, place a command button on Form1 directly below the Calendar Control and run the application again. When you right-click the date, you will notice that the calendar shows up behind the command button. This is a Zorder problem. It can be fixed by setting the Zorder property of our Calendar Control to be above the command button. To do this,

1. Go back to design mode.
2. Right-click the command button.
3. Choose "Send to Back."

Now run the application again and right-click the date. This time, it should display on top of the command button, as intended.

As for additions, you could:

- Add the Font property we mentioned.
- Add a property that determines if the monthly calendar grid is always visible or not. Remember that the reason we made it invisible by default was to save form space. If you do not need to worry about that for some applications, make it possible to always have the grid visible.
- Add a property that allows weekends to be grayed out.
- Add an enumerated Holiday property that could be set.

(Obviously, the list of possible additions could go on and on!)

The Full Code for This Control

```
VERSION 5.00
Begin VB.UserControl CalendarControl
    AutoRedraw      =    -1   'True
    ClientHeight    =    2985
    ClientLeft      =    0
    ClientTop       =    0
    ClientWidth     =    4695
    LockControls    =    -1   'True
    PropertyPages   =    "Calendar.ctx":0000
    ScaleHeight     =    2985
    ScaleWidth      =    4695
    Begin VB.PictureBox picCalendar
        BackColor       =    &H00FFFFFF&
        Height          =    1845
        Left            =    0
        ScaleHeight     =    1785
        ScaleWidth      =    3870
        TabIndex        =    0
        Top             =    330
        Width           =    3930
        Begin VB.Label lblNumbers
            Alignment       =    2    'Center
            Appearance      =    0    'Flat
            BackColor       =    &H00FFFFFF&
            ForeColor       =    &H00000000&
            Height          =    255
            Index           =    41
            Left            =    3315
            TabIndex        =    55
            Top             =    1530
            Width           =    555
        End
        Begin VB.Label lblNumbers
            Alignment       =    2    'Center
            Appearance      =    0    'Flat
            BackColor       =    &H00FFFFFF&
            ForeColor       =    &H00000000&
            Height          =    255
```

445

```
        Index             =     40
        Left              =     2760
        TabIndex          =     54
        Top               =     1530
        Width             =     555
End
Begin VB.Label lblNumbers
        Alignment         =     2      'Center
        Appearance        =     0      'Flat
        BackColor         =     &H00FFFFFF&
        ForeColor         =     &H00000000&
        Height            =     255
        Index             =     39
        Left              =     2205
        TabIndex          =     53
        Top               =     1530
        Width             =     555
End
Begin VB.Label lblNumbers
        Alignment         =     2      'Center
        Appearance        =     0      'Flat
        BackColor         =     &H00FFFFFF&
        ForeColor         =     &H00000000&
        Height            =     255
        Index             =     38
        Left              =     1650
        TabIndex          =     52
        Top               =     1530
        Width             =     555
End
Begin VB.Label lblNumbers
        Alignment         =     2      'Center
        Appearance        =     0      'Flat
        BackColor         =     &H00FFFFFF&
        ForeColor         =     &H00000000&
        Height            =     255
        Index             =     37
        Left              =     1095
        TabIndex          =     51
        Top               =     1530
        Width             =     555
End
```

```
Begin VB.Label lblNumbers
    Alignment           =    2    'Center
    Appearance          =    0    'Flat
    BackColor           =    &H00FFFFFF&
    ForeColor           =    &H00000000&
    Height              =    255
    Index               =    36
    Left                =    540
    TabIndex            =    50
    Top                 =    1530
    Width               =    555
End
Begin VB.Label lblNumbers
    Alignment           =    2    'Center
    Appearance          =    0    'Flat
    BackColor           =    &H00FFFFFF&
    ForeColor           =    &H00000000&
    Height              =    255
    Index               =    35
    Left                =    -15
    TabIndex            =    49
    Top                 =    1530
    Width               =    555
End
Begin VB.Label lblNumbers
    Alignment           =    2    'Center
    Appearance          =    0    'Flat
    BackColor           =    &H00FFFFFF&
    ForeColor           =    &H00000000&
    Height              =    255
    Index               =    34
    Left                =    3315
    TabIndex            =    48
    Top                 =    1275
    Width               =    555
End
Begin VB.Label lblNumbers
    Alignment           =    2    'Center
    Appearance          =    0    'Flat
    BackColor           =    &H00FFFFFF&
    ForeColor           =    &H00000000&
    Height              =    255
```

```
      Index          =      33
      Left           =      2760
      TabIndex       =      47
      Top            =      1275
      Width          =      555
   End
   Begin VB.Label lblNumbers
      Alignment      =      2      'Center
      Appearance     =      0      'Flat
      BackColor      =      &H00FFFFFF&
      ForeColor      =      &H00000000&
      Height         =      255
      Index          =      32
      Left           =      2205
      TabIndex       =      46
      Top            =      1275
      Width          =      555
   End
   Begin VB.Label lblNumbers
      Alignment      =      2      'Center
      Appearance     =      0      'Flat
      BackColor      =      &H00FFFFFF&
      ForeColor      =      &H00000000&
      Height         =      255
      Index          =      31
      Left           =      1650
      TabIndex       =      45
      Top            =      1275
      Width          =      555
   End
   Begin VB.Label lblNumbers
      Alignment      =      2      'Center
      Appearance     =      0      'Flat
      BackColor      =      &H00FFFFFF&
      ForeColor      =      &H00000000&
      Height         =      255
      Index          =      30
      Left           =      1095
      TabIndex       =      44
      Top            =      1275
      Width          =      555
   End
```

```
Begin VB.Label lblNumbers
    Alignment        =    2    'Center
    Appearance       =    0    'Flat
    BackColor        =    &H00FFFFFF&
    ForeColor        =    &H00000000&
    Height           =    255
    Index            =    29
    Left             =    540
    TabIndex         =    43
    Top              =    1275
    Width            =    555
End
Begin VB.Label lblNumbers
    Alignment        =    2    'Center
    Appearance       =    0    'Flat
    BackColor        =    &H00FFFFFF&
    ForeColor        =    &H00000000&
    Height           =    255
    Index            =    28
    Left             =    -15
    TabIndex         =    42
    Top              =    1275
    Width            =    555
End
Begin VB.Label lblNumbers
    Alignment        =    2    'Center
    Appearance       =    0    'Flat
    BackColor        =    &H00FFFFFF&
    ForeColor        =    &H00000000&
    Height           =    255
    Index            =    27
    Left             =    3315
    TabIndex         =    41
    Top              =    1020
    Width            =    555
End
Begin VB.Label lblNumbers
    Alignment        =    2    'Center
    Appearance       =    0    'Flat
    BackColor        =    &H00FFFFFF&
    ForeColor        =    &H00000000&
    Height           =    255
```

```
        Index              =    26
        Left               =    2760
        TabIndex           =    40
        Top                =    1020
        Width              =    555
End
Begin VB.Label lblNumbers
        Alignment          =    2    'Center
        Appearance         =    0    'Flat
        BackColor          =    &H00FFFFFF&
        ForeColor          =    &H00000000&
        Height             =    255
        Index              =    25
        Left               =    2205
        TabIndex           =    39
        Top                =    1020
        Width              =    555
End
Begin VB.Label lblNumbers
        Alignment          =    2    'Center
        Appearance         =    0    'Flat
        BackColor          =    &H00FFFFFF&
        ForeColor          =    &H00000000&
        Height             =    255
        Index              =    24
        Left               =    1650
        TabIndex           =    38
        Top                =    1020
        Width              =    555
End
Begin VB.Label lblNumbers
        Alignment          =    2    'Center
        Appearance         =    0    'Flat
        BackColor          =    &H00FFFFFF&
        ForeColor          =    &H00000000&
        Height             =    255
        Index              =    23
        Left               =    1095
        TabIndex           =    37
        Top                =    1020
        Width              =    555
End
```

```
Begin VB.Label lblNumbers
    Alignment       =   2   'Center
    Appearance      =   0   'Flat
    BackColor       =   &H00FFFFFF&
    ForeColor       =   &H00000000&
    Height          =   255
    Index           =   22
    Left            =   540
    TabIndex        =   36
    Top             =   1020
    Width           =   555
End
Begin VB.Label lblNumbers
    Alignment       =   2   'Center
    Appearance      =   0   'Flat
    BackColor       =   &H00FFFFFF&
    ForeColor       =   &H00000000&
    Height          =   255
    Index           =   21
    Left            =   -15
    TabIndex        =   35
    Top             =   1020
    Width           =   555
End
Begin VB.Label lblNumbers
    Alignment       =   2   'Center
    Appearance      =   0   'Flat
    BackColor       =   &H00FFFFFF&
    ForeColor       =   &H00000000&
    Height          =   255
    Index           =   20
    Left            =   3315
    TabIndex        =   34
    Top             =   765
    Width           =   555
End
Begin VB.Label lblNumbers
    Alignment       =   2   'Center
    Appearance      =   0   'Flat
    BackColor       =   &H00FFFFFF&
    ForeColor       =   &H00000000&
    Height          =   255
```

```
        Index        =    19
        Left         =    2760
        TabIndex     =    33
        Top          =    765
        Width        =    555
End
Begin VB.Label lblNumbers
        Alignment    =    2    'Center
        Appearance   =    0    'Flat
        BackColor    =    &H00FFFFFF&
        ForeColor    =    &H00000000&
        Height       =    255
        Index        =    18
        Left         =    2205
        TabIndex     =    32
        Top          =    765
        Width        =    555
End
Begin VB.Label lblNumbers
        Alignment    =    2    'Center
        Appearance   =    0    'Flat
        BackColor    =    &H00FFFFFF&
        ForeColor    =    &H00000000&
        Height       =    255
        Index        =    17
        Left         =    1650
        TabIndex     =    31
        Top          =    765
        Width        =    555
End
Begin VB.Label lblNumbers
        Alignment    =    2    'Center
        Appearance   =    0    'Flat
        BackColor    =    &H00FFFFFF&
        ForeColor    =    &H00000000&
        Height       =    255
        Index        =    16
        Left         =    1095
        TabIndex     =    30
        Top          =    765
        Width        =    555
End
```

```
Begin VB.Label lblNumbers
    Alignment       =    2    'Center
    Appearance      =    0    'Flat
    BackColor       =    &H00FFFFFF&
    ForeColor       =    &H00000000&
    Height          =    255
    Index           =    15
    Left            =    540
    TabIndex        =    29
    Top             =    765
    Width           =    555
End
Begin VB.Label lblNumbers
    Alignment       =    2    'Center
    Appearance      =    0    'Flat
    BackColor       =    &H00FFFFFF&
    ForeColor       =    &H00000000&
    Height          =    255
    Index           =    14
    Left            =    -15
    TabIndex        =    28
    Top             =    765
    Width           =    555
End
Begin VB.Label lblNumbers
    Alignment       =    2    'Center
    Appearance      =    0    'Flat
    BackColor       =    &H00FFFFFF&
    ForeColor       =    &H00000000&
    Height          =    255
    Index           =    13
    Left            =    3315
    TabIndex        =    27
    Top             =    510
    Width           =    555
End
Begin VB.Label lblNumbers
    Alignment       =    2    'Center
    Appearance      =    0    'Flat
    BackColor       =    &H00FFFFFF&
    ForeColor       =    &H00000000&
    Height          =    255
```

```
          Index         =    12
          Left          =    2760
          TabIndex      =    26
          Top           =    510
          Width         =    555
       End
       Begin VB.Label lblNumbers
          Alignment     =    2    'Center
          Appearance    =    0    'Flat
          BackColor     =    &H00FFFFFF&
          ForeColor     =    &H00000000&
          Height        =    255
          Index         =    11
          Left          =    2205
          TabIndex      =    25
          Top           =    510
          Width         =    555
       End
       Begin VB.Label lblNumbers
          Alignment     =    2    'Center
          Appearance    =    0    'Flat
          BackColor     =    &H00FFFFFF&
          ForeColor     =    &H00000000&
          Height        =    255
          Index         =    10
          Left          =    1650
          TabIndex      =    24
          Top           =    510
          Width         =    555
       End
       Begin VB.Label lblNumbers
          Alignment     =    2    'Center
          Appearance    =    0    'Flat
          BackColor     =    &H00FFFFFF&
          ForeColor     =    &H00000000&
          Height        =    255
          Index         =    9
          Left          =    1095
          TabIndex      =    23
          Top           =    510
          Width         =    555
       End
```

```
Begin VB.Label lblNumbers
    Alignment        =    2    'Center
    Appearance       =    0    'Flat
    BackColor        =    &H00FFFFFF&
    ForeColor        =    &H00000000&
    Height           =    255
    Index            =    8
    Left             =    540
    TabIndex         =    22
    Top              =    510
    Width            =    555
End
Begin VB.Label lblNumbers
    Alignment        =    2    'Center
    Appearance       =    0    'Flat
    BackColor        =    &H00FFFFFF&
    ForeColor        =    &H00000000&
    Height           =    255
    Index            =    7
    Left             =    -15
    TabIndex         =    21
    Top              =    510
    Width            =    555
End
Begin VB.Label lblNumbers
    Alignment        =    2    'Center
    Appearance       =    0    'Flat
    BackColor        =    &H00FFFF00&
    ForeColor        =    &H00000000&
    Height           =    255
    Index            =    6
    Left             =    3315
    TabIndex         =    20
    Top              =    255
    Width            =    555
End
Begin VB.Label lblNumbers
    Alignment        =    2    'Center
    Appearance       =    0    'Flat
    BackColor        =    &H00FFFFFF&
    ForeColor        =    &H00000000&
    Height           =    255
```

```
      Index        =    5
      Left         =    2760
      TabIndex     =    19
      Top          =    255
      Width        =    555
   End
   Begin VB.Label lblNumbers
      Alignment    =    2    'Center
      Appearance   =    0    'Flat
      BackColor    =    &H00FFFFFF&
      ForeColor    =    &H00000000&
      Height       =    255
      Index        =    4
      Left         =    2205
      TabIndex     =    18
      Top          =    255
      Width        =    555
   End
   Begin VB.Label lblNumbers
      Alignment    =    2    'Center
      Appearance   =    0    'Flat
      BackColor    =    &H00FFFFFF&
      ForeColor    =    &H00000000&
      Height       =    255
      Index        =    3
      Left         =    1650
      TabIndex     =    17
      Top          =    255
      Width        =    555
   End
   Begin VB.Label lblNumbers
      Alignment    =    2    'Center
      Appearance   =    0    'Flat
      BackColor    =    &H00FFFFFF&
      ForeColor    =    &H00000000&
      Height       =    255
      Index        =    2
      Left         =    1095
      TabIndex     =    16
      Top          =    255
      Width        =    555
   End
```

```
Begin VB.Label lblNumbers
    Alignment        =   2   'Center
    Appearance       =   0   'Flat
    BackColor        =   &H00FFFFFF&
    ForeColor        =   &H00000000&
    Height           =   255
    Index            =   1
    Left             =   540
    TabIndex         =   15
    Top              =   255
    Width            =   555
End
Begin VB.Label lblNumbers
    Alignment        =   2   'Center
    Appearance       =   0   'Flat
    BackColor        =   &H00FFFFFF&
    ForeColor        =   &H00000000&
    Height           =   255
    Index            =   0
    Left             =   -15
    TabIndex         =   14
    Top              =   255
    Width            =   555
End
Begin VB.Label lblDays
    Alignment        =   2   'Center
    Appearance       =   0   'Flat
    BackColor        =   &H80000010&
    BorderStyle      =   1   'Fixed Single
    Caption          =   "Sat"
    ForeColor        =   &H00C0C0C0&
    Height           =   255
    Index            =   6
    Left             =   3315
    TabIndex         =   13
    Top              =   0
    Width            =   555
End
Begin VB.Label lblDays
    Alignment        =   2   'Center
    Appearance       =   0   'Flat
    BackColor        =   &H80000010&
```

```
            BorderStyle       =       1    'Fixed Single
            Caption           =       "Fri"
            ForeColor         =       &H00C0C0C0&
            Height            =       255
            Index             =       5
            Left              =       2760
            TabIndex          =       12
            Top               =       0
            Width             =       555
         End
         Begin VB.Label lblDays
            Alignment         =       2    'Center
            Appearance        =       0    'Flat
            BackColor         =       &H80000010&
            BorderStyle       =       1    'Fixed Single
            Caption           =       "Thur"
            ForeColor         =       &H00C0C0C0&
            Height            =       255
            Index             =       4
            Left              =       2205
            TabIndex          =       11
            Top               =       0
            Width             =       555
         End
         Begin VB.Label lblDays
            Alignment         =       2    'Center
            Appearance        =       0    'Flat
            BackColor         =       &H80000010&
            BorderStyle       =       1    'Fixed Single
            Caption           =       "Wed"
            ForeColor         =       &H00C0C0C0&
            Height            =       255
            Index             =       3
            Left              =       1650
            TabIndex          =       10
            Top               =       0
            Width             =       555
         End
         Begin VB.Label lblDays
            Alignment         =       2    'Center
            Appearance        =       0    'Flat
            BackColor         =       &H80000010&
```

```
      BorderStyle       =     1    'Fixed Single
      Caption           =     "Tue"
      ForeColor         =     &H00C0C0C0&
      Height            =     255
      Index             =     2
      Left              =     1095
      TabIndex          =     9
      Top               =     0
      Width             =     555
   End
   Begin VB.Label lblDays
      Alignment         =     2    'Center
      Appearance        =     0    'Flat
      BackColor         =     &H80000010&
      BorderStyle       =     1    'Fixed Single
      Caption           =     "Mon"
      ForeColor         =     &H00C0C0C0&
      Height            =     255
      Index             =     1
      Left              =     540
      TabIndex          =     8
      Top               =     0
      Width             =     555
   End
   Begin VB.Label lblDays
      Alignment         =     2    'Center
      Appearance        =     0    'Flat
      BackColor         =     &H80000010&
      BorderStyle       =     1    'Fixed Single
      Caption           =     "Sun"
      ForeColor         =     &H00C0C0C0&
      Height            =     255
      Index             =     0
      Left              =     -15
      TabIndex          =     7
      Top               =     0
      Width             =     555
   End
End
Begin VB.CommandButton cmdChange
   Height               =     315
   Index                =     5
```

```
      Left            =     3720
      Picture         =     "Calendar.ctx":0004
      Style           =     1    'Graphical
      TabIndex        =     6
      TabStop         =     0     'False
      ToolTipText     =     "Next Year    (Ctrl+PageDown)"
      Top             =     0
      UseMaskColor    =     -1   'True
      Width           =     210
   End
   Begin VB.CommandButton cmdChange
      Height          =     315
      Index           =     4
      Left            =     3510
      Picture         =     "Calendar.ctx":0546
      Style           =     1    'Graphical
      TabIndex        =     5
      TabStop         =     0     'False
      ToolTipText     =     "Next Month   (PageDown)"
      Top             =     0
      UseMaskColor    =     -1   'True
      Width           =     210
   End
   Begin VB.CommandButton cmdChange
      Height          =     315
      Index           =     3
      Left            =     3300
      Picture         =     "Calendar.ctx":0A88
      Style           =     1    'Graphical
      TabIndex        =     4
      TabStop         =     0     'False
      ToolTipText     =     "Next Day   (Right Arrow Key)"
      Top             =     0
      UseMaskColor    =     -1   'True
      Width           =     210
   End
   Begin VB.CommandButton cmdChange
      Height          =     315
      Index           =     2
      Left            =     420
      Picture         =     "Calendar.ctx":0FCA
      Style           =     1    'Graphical
```

```
        TabIndex        =    3
        TabStop         =    0    'False
        ToolTipText     =    "Previous Day   (Left Arrow Key)"
        Top             =    0
        UseMaskColor    =    -1   'True
        Width           =    210
     End
     Begin VB.CommandButton cmdChange
        Height          =    315
        Index           =    1
        Left            =    210
        Picture         =    "Calendar.ctx":150C
        Style           =    1    'Graphical
        TabIndex        =    2
        TabStop         =    0    'False
        ToolTipText     =    "Previous Month   (PageUp)"
        Top             =    0
        UseMaskColor    =    -1   'True
        Width           =    210
     End
     Begin VB.CommandButton cmdChange
        Height          =    315
        Index           =    0
        Left            =    0
        Picture         =    "Calendar.ctx":1A4E
        Style           =    1    'Graphical
        TabIndex        =    1
        TabStop         =    0    'False
        ToolTipText     =    "Previous Year   (Ctrl+PageUp)"
        Top             =    0
        UseMaskColor    =    -1   'True
        Width           =    210
     End
     Begin VB.Label lblDate
        BackColor       =    &H00FFFFFF&
        BorderStyle     =    1    'Fixed Single
        Caption         =    "Wednesday, November 20, 1996"
        Height          =    315
        Left            =    630
        TabIndex        =    56
        ToolTipText     =    "Right Click to View Calendar"
        Top             =    0
```

```
      Width              =    2670
   End
End
Attribute VB_Name = "CalendarControl"
Attribute VB_GlobalNameSpace = False
Attribute VB_Creatable = True
Attribute VB_PredeclaredId = False
Attribute VB_Exposed = True
Attribute VB_Description = "Gary and Dave's Calendar Control"
Option Explicit

Private mbShowCalendar As Boolean
Private mnCurrentCell As Integer

'Property Variables:
Private m_CurrentDate As Date

Public Property Get CurrentDate() As Date
   CurrentDate = m_CurrentDate
End Property

Public Property Let CurrentDate(ByVal New_CurrentDate As Date)
   lblDate.Caption = Format(New_CurrentDate, "dddd, mmmm d, _
yyyy")
   m_CurrentDate = New_CurrentDate
   FillCalendar
   PropertyChanged "CurrentDate"
End Property

'Initialize Properties for User Control
Private Sub UserControl_InitProperties()
   CurrentDate = Date
End Sub

'Load property values from storage
Private Sub UserControl_ReadProperties(PropBag As PropertyBag)
   On Error Resume Next
   CurrentDate = PropBag.ReadProperty("CurrentDate", Date)
End Sub

'Write property values to storage
Private Sub UserControl_WriteProperties(PropBag As PropertyBag)
```

```
  On Error Resume Next
  Call PropBag.WriteProperty("CurrentDate", m_CurrentDate, Date)
End Sub

Sub FillCalendar()
  Dim i As Integer
  Dim nStart As Integer
  Dim nCurr As Integer
  Dim nLast As Integer
  Dim nLastMonthEnd As Integer

  'figure out the starting cell
  nStart = DatePart("w", m_CurrentDate - _
    DatePart("d", m_CurrentDate) + 1) - 1
  'figure out the ending cell
  nLast = nStart + DatePart("d", DateAdd("m", 1, _
  m_CurrentDate) - DatePart("d", DateAdd("m", 1, _
  m_CurrentDate))) - 1

  If nStart > 0 Then
    'figure out the ending value of last month
    'if there are some previous month days visible
    nLastMonthEnd = DatePart("d", m_CurrentDate - _
    DatePart("d", m_CurrentDate)) - nStart + 1
  End If

  'initialize the current day
  nCurr = 1

  'now walk through the days and setup the cells
  For i = 0 To 41
    If i < nStart Or i > nLast Then
      'out of the range so we need to set it to italic
      lblNumbers(i).BackColor = &HFFFFFF
      lblNumbers(i).BorderStyle = 0
      lblNumbers(i).ForeColor = &HC0C0C0
      If i < nStart Then
        lblNumbers(i).Caption = nLastMonthEnd + i
      Else
        If i = nLast + 1 Then nCurr = _
          1 'reset on the first day of next month
        lblNumbers(i).Caption = nCurr
```

```
            nCurr = nCurr + 1
        End If
    Else
        lblNumbers(i).ForeColor = &H0&
        If nCurr = DatePart("d", m_CurrentDate) Then
            'this is the current date so we need to
            'set it's backcolor and borderstyle
            lblNumbers(i).BackColor = &HFFFF00
            lblNumbers(i).BorderStyle = 1
            'save the current cell number
            mnCurrentCell = i
        Else
            lblNumbers(i).BackColor = &HFFFFFF
            lblNumbers(i).BorderStyle = 0
        End If
        'set the caption
        lblNumbers(i).Caption = nCurr
        'increment our counter
        nCurr = nCurr + 1
    End If
  Next
End Sub


'date setting functions
'=========================================================
Private Sub cmdChange_Click(Index As Integer)
  Select Case Index
    Case 0   'previous year
      CurrentDate = DateAdd("yyyy", -1, CurrentDate)
    Case 1   'previous month
      CurrentDate = DateAdd("m", -1, CurrentDate)
    Case 2   'previous day
      CurrentDate = CurrentDate - 1
    Case 3   'next day
      CurrentDate = CurrentDate + 1
    Case 4   'next month
      CurrentDate = DateAdd("m", 1, CurrentDate)
    Case 5   'next year
      CurrentDate = DateAdd("yyyy", 1, CurrentDate)
  End Select
  picCalendar.SetFocus
End Sub
```

```vb
Private Sub picCalendar_KeyDown(KeyCode As Integer, Shift As _
Integer)
   'get the keystokes from the picture control
   'because that is the only control on our UserControl
   'that can have focus
   If KeyCode = vbKeyRight Or KeyCode = vbKeyDown Then
     cmdChange_Click 3
   ElseIf KeyCode = vbKeyLeft Or KeyCode = vbKeyUp Then
     cmdChange_Click 2
   ElseIf KeyCode = vbKeyPageDown And Shift = 0 Then
     cmdChange_Click 4
   ElseIf KeyCode = vbKeyPageUp And Shift = 0 Then
     cmdChange_Click 1
   ElseIf KeyCode = vbKeyPageDown And Shift <> 0 Then
     cmdChange_Click 5
   ElseIf KeyCode = vbKeyPageUp And Shift <> 0 Then
     cmdChange_Click 0
   ElseIf KeyCode = vbKeyHome Then
     CurrentDate = Date
   End If
End Sub

Private Sub lblNumbers_Click(Index As Integer)
   CurrentDate = CurrentDate - (mnCurrentCell - Index)
End Sub

'calendar display functions
'=======================================================
Private Sub picCalendar_GotFocus()
   'change it to blue
   lblDate.BackColor = &HFFFF00
End Sub

Private Sub picCalendar_LostFocus()
   'change it back to white
   lblDate.BackColor = &HFFFFFF
   'remove the calendar
   mbShowCalendar = True
   lblDate_MouseUp vbRightButton, 0, 0, 0
End Sub
```

```
Private Sub UserControl_Resize()
   'force the size to the only allowable values
   If mbShowCalendar Then
     Height = 2190
   Else
     Height = 330
   End If
   Width = 3945
End Sub

Private Sub lblDate_MouseUp(Button As Integer,
     Shift As Integer, X As Single, Y As Single)
   If Button = vbRightButton Then
     'right click to toggle the calendar state
     If mbShowCalendar Then
       mbShowCalendar = False
       Height = 330
       lblDate.ToolTipText = "Right Click to View Calendar"
     Else
       mbShowCalendar = True
       Height = 2190
       lblDate.ToolTipText = "Right Click to Hide Calendar"
       picCalendar.SetFocus
     End If
   End If
End Sub
```

Chapter 16

All standard controls lack features that would make them more useful in certain circumstances. Making a control that does everything that a standard control does and adds the features you want makes Visual Basic more powerful and easy to use.

For example, how many times have you wanted to be able to overwrite what is in an ordinary text box? Of course you can't: the standard text box is always in insert mode. The control we will show you how to build in this chapter takes a standard text box control and gives it the ability to toggle from insert to overwrite mode at run time. If we want to do this in the most user-friendly fashion, our control should work just like a standard text box except that it must make switching from overwrite to insert mode obvious and intuitive.

We also decided to add one other nifty feature that regular text boxes dont have: the ability to switch between multiline and a single line at run time. We do this by keeping a hidden mirror text box that we can switch to when changing modes. This was done using a control array of two text boxes.

In the end, the user interface is extremely simple, the code needed is minimal and the Control Interface Wizard is going to do most of the work of exposing the properties and events that we need. The resulting OCX is only about 17k!

The Overwritable Text Box

The Idea of the Control

The control we show here was designed to satisfy the following goals:

1. All the things you usually do with a text box control should be possible.

2. The user should be able to use this control just like a standard text box control.

3. The control needs to add the multiline and overwrite switching features in a way that is transparent to the user of the control.

Creating the Interface

To accomplish all these goals, we need an extremely simple UI. Figure 16-1 shows the control at work.

Not much to it, is there? Looks just like an ordinary text box.

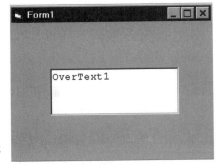

Actually, under the hood things are a bit more subtle than they appear. There is a second invisible text box whose contents mirror the first. One of the text boxes uses mostly default property values; it's the second one that uses some different property settings as shown in

Figure 16-1
An extended text box

Figure 16-2. When the user wants to switch to multiline mode, we simply make the mirror version that is a multiline text box visible at exactly the same location as its sibling.

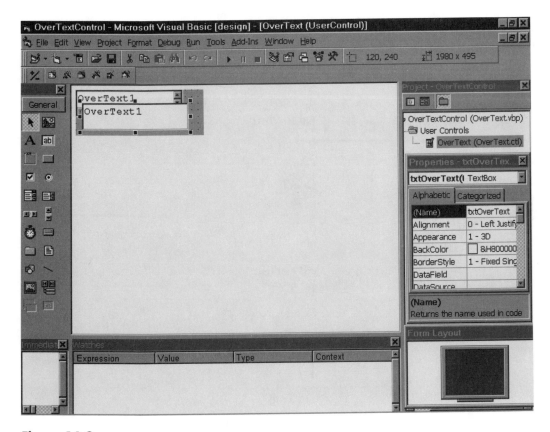

Figure 16-2
The Overwriting text box control at design time

The reason we need two text boxes is that there is no way to set the MultiLine property at run time, so we need one text box to have this property set to False (default) and the other to have it set to True. This lets us have a control that can handle both a single line as well as multiline at design time and run time. ⊃

We also added scroll bars to the multiline version.

Here's what the control looks like at design time.

Not much to this either, is there? On the surface, it is simply two text boxes with identical captions. However, we actually used a control array so both these text boxes are elements of the same control array. Building the interface for this control, as shown in Figure 16-2, took less than 2 minutes.

The following table describes the controls along with their most important properties using the format you have already seen.

Table 16-1
Controls and Their Most Important Properties

Form	
LockControls	−1 'True
TextBox	
Name	txtOverText
Index	0
Font	Courier New
Text	OverText1
Left	0
Top	0
TextBox	
Name	txtOverText
Index	1
Font	Courier New
Text	OverText1
Left	0
Top	0
MultiLine	−1 'True
ScrollBars	3 'Both
Visible	0 'False

We used Courier New as the default font. This is because, in overwrite mode, the control looks best with a non-proportionally spaced font. Feel free to experiment with other fonts. ⊃

As usual, the end of the chapter gives the full code for the control including all the properties that we reset from their defaults. The CD contains the code and all the files needed to see the control at work.

In this state the design is quite useless. This is because:

1. It won't do anything except act like a standard text box. It has no writable properties.

2. Other controls cannot communicate with it in any way.

We will need to add the necessary code to take care of both problems.

Exposing the Properties

First, we want to run the ActiveX Control Interface Wizard in order to expose the properties and events that we need to make our control act just like a standard text box. To do this, load the Wizard from the Add-Ins menu and follow these steps:

1. Remove the BackStyle and BorderStyle properties and the KeyDown, KeyPress and KeyUp events from the Selected names list because we do not wish to expose these properties.

2. Move the Change, Locked, MaxLength, MouseIcon, MousePointer, SelLength, SelStart, SelText, Text, ToolTipText and WhatsThisHelpID property items from the Available names list to the Selected names list since we do want the user of the control to be able to change them.

3. Click Next to go to the Create Custom Interface Members step. Here we are going to add a couple of our own custom properties.

4. Click New, and add a property called MultiLine. (This will be our version of the ordinary MultiLine property that can be switched at run time.)

5. Click New, and add a property called OverwriteColor for the color to be used in overwrite mode. (See below for suggestions on how to improve this.)

6. Click Next to go to the Set Mapping step.

7. Select the entire list of Public Name. (An easy way to do this is to select the first item in the list and then press SHIFT+END).

8. Deselect the MultiLine and OverwriteColor items (Hold down the CTRL key and click the MultiLine and OverwriteColor items). This is necessary to customize these properties.

9. Select txtOverText(0) in the Control drop-down list box.

10. Click Next to go to the Set Attributes step.

11. With MultiLine selected in the Public Name list, select Boolean from the Data Type list. Leave the default value at 0 (False).

12. Select OverwriteColor in the Public Name list and select OLE_COLOR from the Data Type list.

13. Click Next to go to the Finish step.

14. Click Finish.

The Wizard now adds all the code we need to expose the properties and events of our control, roughly seven pages.

We need to add error handling to each of the existing ReadProperties and WriteProperties events, as follows:

```
Private Sub UserControl_ReadProperties(PropBag As PropertyBag)
On Error Resume Next
...


Private Sub UserControl_WriteProperties(PropBag As PropertyBag)
On Error Resume Next
...
```

This is always necessary because certain host applications will cause errors that should be ignored when reading or writing property values. The On Error Resume Next statement lets us do this.

Now, we need to add some code to handle setting the properties on the other text box in the control array. To do this, we need to add a line of code to some of the existing Property Let and Property Set procedures to keep the properties in sync for both text boxes. Here is what the BackColor Property Let should look like.

```
Public Property Let BackColor(ByVal New_BackColor As OLE_COLOR)
   txtOverText(0).BackColor() = New_BackColor
   txtOverText(1).BackColor() = New_BackColor
   PropertyChanged "BackColor"
End Property
```

The second line in the routine sets the txtOverText(1).BackColor property to the same value as its sibling currently has. We need to do the same mirroring process for the ForeColor, Enabled, Font, Locked, MaxLength, MouseIcon, MousePointer, SelLength, SelStart, SelText, Text, ToolTipText and WhatsThisHelp. (Consult the code listing at the end of the chapter to see what this looks like.)

Run-Time Logic

Now, we need to add the code that will allow a user to go into overwrite mode by pressing the INSERT key. To do this, we need to add a couple of module level variables to the general declarations, as follows:

```
Dim mbOverwrite As Boolean
```

This variable is used to tell any routine what overwrite state we are in at present. Next add:

```
Dim mnCtlIndex As Integer
```

This variable will be either 0 or 1, depending on which text box is currently active. (We could save a byte by making it a byte.)

Next, we need to add the code to handle the keystrokes sent to the active text box. We need to check if the INSERT key was pressed; if so, switch modes and text boxes. Otherwise, let the keystroke be processed by the currently visible text box. All this needs to be done in the txtOverText_KeyDown and txtOverText_KeyPress events, as shown here.

```
Private Sub txtOverText_KeyDown(Index As Integer, _
KeyCode As Integer, Shift As Integer)
   If KeyCode = vbKeyInsert And Shift = 0 Then
      'toggle the mode
      mbOverwrite = Not mbOverwrite
      If mbOverwrite Then
         txtOverText(mnCtlIndex).ForeColor = _
         m_OverwriteColor
      Else
         txtOverText(mnCtlIndex).ForeColor = vbBlack
      End If
      Exit Sub
   End If
End Sub
```

```
Private Sub txtOverText_KeyPress(Index As Integer,_
KeyAscii As Integer)
 process ordinary keystrokes
   If mbOverwrite Then
        'set the sellength to 1 and the new keystroke
        'will overwrite at the current cursor position
        txtOverText(mnCtlIndex).SelLength = 1
   End If
End Sub
```

This KeyDown event handles the toggling of the overwrite state since the KeyPress event only handles printable keys. (The KeyPress event is generated between the KeyDown and KeyUp events.) Using the KeyPress event makes the code more robust since KeyDown can get confused by the state of caps lock key. (Of course, the overwrite code could be broken in certain scenarios. We couldn't test it using non-English keyboards, for example.) Also the cursor movement keys such as HOME, DOWN, END, etc., are not processed in the KeyPress event so they continue to operate normally without any special handling.

The next event is optional. We think it is best to have the control go back to regular INSERT mode when it loses focus. This is taken care of in the LostFocus event, which follows. If you want it to retain its state throughout its life, simply leave this code out.

```
Private Sub txtOverText_LostFocus(Index As Integer)
   'the control has lost focus
   'so go back to insert mode
   txtOverText(mnCtlIndex).ForeColor = vbBlack
   mbOverwrite = False
End Sub
```

If you tested the control at this point, you would notice that it does indeed go into overwrite mode when you press the INSERT key, but there is no visual clue to the user that we are in overwrite mode. Also, the MultiLine property has no effect on the control yet. To let the user know that we have switched modes, we will set the default OverwriteColor property to something other than the default color of black. To do this, replace the line near the top of the code module that says

```
Const m_def_OverwriteColor = 0
```

to:

```
Const m_def_OverwriteColor = vbBlue
```

Now, test it again to see how it works. You will need to remove the user control from the form and add it back in order to get the new default value to take effect.

Next, to hook up the MultiLine property, we need to add some code to the MultiLine Property Let procedure, so replace

```
Public Property Let MultiLine(ByVal New_MultiLine _
As Boolean)
   m_MultiLine = New_MultiLine
   PropertyChanged "MultiLine"
End Property
```

with:

```
Public Property Let MultiLine(ByVal New_MultiLine _
As Boolean)
   m_MultiLine = New_MultiLine
   If m_MultiLine Then
     mnCtlIndex = 1
     txtOverText(0).Visible = False
     txtOverText(1).Visible = True
   Else
     mnCtlIndex = 0
     txtOverText(1).Visible = False
     txtOverText(0).Visible = True
   End If
   PropertyChanged "MultiLine"
End Property
```

Now, if you test it, you will see that changing the MultiLine property at design time changes the control from a single line text box to a multiline one with scrollbars.

However, there is still one more problem. You may notice that when we go back to run mode, our control switches back to single line. This is a standard problem of having the state of a control persist during the switch to run time. This is cured by code in the ReadProperties event that uses the correct Property Get procedure. In our case, change

```
m_MultiLine = PropBag.ReadProperty("MultiLine", m_def_MultiLine)
```

to:

```
MultiLine = PropBag.ReadProperty("MultiLine", m_MultiLine)
```

We do this because we have code in our Property Let procedure that needs

475

to execute when the control comes to life and reads the current state of its properties. The Control Interface Wizard adds code to set the module level variable it created (m_MultiLine), but this does not write the code that would make the Property Let procedure fire up. The small change takes care of this by setting the property itself instead of the local variable used to hold the current state of the property. This trick is something you will need to use constantly. Also, because the local variable gets set in the Property Let procedure, we accomplish both tasks with this single line of code.

Now, if you test the control, you will see that the MultiLine property works as expected. In fact, the control logic is finished. All we need to add is the resize logic described below.

Resize Logic

In order to resize the text box controls properly when the user resizes the control, we need to add the following code:

```
Private Sub UserControl_Resize()
   txtOverText(0).Width = Width
   txtOverText(0).Height = Height
   txtOverText(1).Width = Width
   txtOverText(1).Height = Height
End Sub
```

Since controls in a control array automatically have the same position properties as the first control created in the array, we don't need any extra code to properly position the second text box. ⊃

Possible Additions and Potential Problems

This control is essentially complete as is. It can serve as a useful template for other controls that are based on adding functionality to an ordinary text box. A few possible additions would be:

- A better method of indicating the current mode. This would require either using the Windows API or a lot more VB code. But it would be nice to have the cursor change to a block instead of simply changing the color of the text.

- Add more elements to the control array. This would let you handle different values for the Scrollbars property of the control. This would require three more controls in the array to handle the multi-line state with no scrollbars, horizontal scrollbars, or vertical scroll-bars only.

- A potential problem is that the text properties could get out of sync at run time; thus, changing from single line to multiline may cause the text to change. There are numerous ways to fix this. The first is to set the inactive text box in the change event so that they stay in sync. Another is to disallow the multiline property to be changed at run time. This is done by adding code before all other code in the Property Let procedure:

```
If Ambient.UserMode And (Not mbReadingProperties) Then
    MsgBox Error(382)
    Exit Property
End If
```

Adding this code requires that you add the following declaration to your module:

```
Dim mbReadingProperties As Boolean
```

and these lines at the start and end, respectively, of the UserControl_ReadProperties event:

```
mbReadingProperties = True
mbReadingProperties = False
```

This kind of code is very useful for properties that require Property Let procedure code to run at startup but where you do not wish the property to be settable at run time. Of course, allowing this makes the control somewhat less useful but it does remove the requirement that you maintain the text value in all controls in the array at run time. After all, this may end up being a waste of resources if you have more than two controls in the array. ⊃

Finally, you could decide to expose other events such as KeyPress to the user of the control. In any case, the control is quite functional and ready to use in its current state.

The Full Code for This Control

```
VERSION 5.00
Begin VB.UserControl OverText
   ClientHeight    =    825
   ClientLeft      =    0
   ClientTop       =    0
   ClientWidth     =    2385
   PropertyPages   =    "OverText.ctx":0000
   ScaleHeight     =    825
   ScaleWidth      =    2385
   ToolboxBitmap   =    "OverText.ctx":0004
   Begin VB.TextBox txtOverText
      BeginProperty Font
         Name             =    "Courier New"
         Size             =    9.75
         Charset          =    0
         Weight           =    400
         Underline        =    0    'False
         Italic           =    0    'False
         Strikethrough    =    0    'False
      EndProperty
      Height          =    495
      Index           =    0
      Left            =    0
      TabIndex        =    0
      Text            =    "OverText1"
      Top             =    0
      Width           =    1980
   End
   Begin VB.TextBox txtOverText
      BeginProperty Font
         Name             =    "Courier New"
         Size             =    9.75
         Charset          =    0
         Weight           =    400
         Underline        =    0    'False
         Italic           =    0    'False
         Strikethrough    =    0    'False
```

```
        EndProperty
        Height          =     495
        Index           =     1
        Left            =     0
        MultiLine       =     -1    'True
        ScrollBars      =     3     'Both
        TabIndex        =     1
        Text            =     "OverText.ctx":0186
        Top             =     0
        Visible         =     0     'False
        Width           =     2000
    End
End
Attribute VB_Name = "OverText"
Attribute VB_GlobalNameSpace = False
Attribute VB_Creatable = True
Attribute VB_PredeclaredId = False
Attribute VB_Exposed = True
Attribute VB_Description = "Gary and Dave's Overwritable
  Textbox"
Option Explicit
Dim mbReadingProperties As Boolean
Dim mbOverwrite As Boolean
Dim mnCtlIndex As Integer


'Default Property Values:
Const m_def_MultiLine = 0
Const m_def_OverwriteColor = vbBlue
'Property Variables:
Dim m_MultiLine As Boolean
Dim m_OverwriteColor As OLE_COLOR
'Event Declarations:
Event Click() 'MappingInfo=txtOverText(0),txtOverText,0,Click
Event DblClick() 'MappingInfo=txtOverText(0), _
txtOverText,0,DblClick
Event MouseDown(Button As Integer, Shift As Integer, _
X As Single, Y As Single)
'MappingInfo=txtOverText(0),txtOverText,0,MouseDown
Event MouseMove(Button As Integer, Shift As Integer, _
X As Single, Y As Single)
'MappingInfo=txtOverText(0),txtOverText,0,MouseMove
```

```
Event MouseUp(Button As Integer, Shift As Integer, _
X As Single, Y As Single)
'MappingInfo=txtOverText(0),txtOverText,0,MouseUp
Event Change() 'MappingInfo=txtOverText(0),_
txtOverText,0,Change


Private Sub txtOverText_KeyDown(Index As Integer, _
KeyCode As Integer, Shift As Integer)
   If KeyCode = vbKeyInsert And Shift = 0 Then
      'toggle the mode
      mbOverwrite = Not mbOverwrite
      If mbOverwrite Then
         txtOverText(mnCtlIndex).ForeColor = m_OverwriteColor
      Else
         txtOverText(mnCtlIndex).ForeColor = vbBlack
      End If
      Exit Sub
   End If
End Sub


Private Sub txtOverText_KeyPress(Index As Integer, KeyAscii _
As Integer)
   If mbOverwrite Then
      'it is a key that we need to process so
      'set the sellength to 1 and the new keystroke
      'will overwrite at the current cursor position
      txtOverText(mnCtlIndex).SelLength = 1
   End If
End Sub


Private Sub txtOverText_LostFocus(Index As Integer)
   'the control has lost focus
   'so go back to insert mode
   txtOverText(mnCtlIndex).ForeColor = vbBlack
   mbOverwrite = False
End Sub
```

```
'WARNING! DO NOT REMOVE OR MODIFY THE FOLLOWING COMMENTED LINES!
'MappingInfo=txtOverText(0),txtOverText,0,BackColor
Public Property Get BackColor() As OLE_COLOR
Attribute BackColor.VB_Description = "Returns/sets the
    background color used to display text and graphics in an
    object."
  BackColor = txtOverText(0).BackColor
End Property

Public Property Let BackColor(ByVal New_BackColor As OLE_COLOR)
  txtOverText(0).BackColor() = New_BackColor
  txtOverText(1).BackColor() = New_BackColor
  PropertyChanged "BackColor"
End Property

'WARNING! DO NOT REMOVE OR MODIFY THE FOLLOWING COMMENTED LINES!
'MappingInfo=txtOverText(0),txtOverText,0,ForeColor
Public Property Get ForeColor() As OLE_COLOR
Attribute ForeColor.VB_Description = "Returns/sets the
    foreground color used to display text and graphics in an
    object."
  ForeColor = txtOverText(0).ForeColor
End Property

Public Property Let ForeColor(ByVal New_ForeColor As OLE_COLOR)
  txtOverText(0).ForeColor() = New_ForeColor
  txtOverText(1).ForeColor() = New_ForeColor
  PropertyChanged "ForeColor"
End Property

'WARNING! DO NOT REMOVE OR MODIFY THE FOLLOWING COMMENTED LINES!
'MappingInfo=txtOverText(0),txtOverText,0,Enabled
Public Property Get Enabled() As Boolean
Attribute Enabled.VB_Description = "Returns/sets a value that
    determines whether an object can respond to user-generated
    events."
  Enabled = txtOverText(0).Enabled
End Property

Public Property Let Enabled(ByVal New_Enabled As Boolean)
  txtOverText(0).Enabled() = New_Enabled
  txtOverText(1).Enabled() = New_Enabled
  PropertyChanged "Enabled"
End Property
```

```
'WARNING! DO NOT REMOVE OR MODIFY THE FOLLOWING COMMENTED LINES!
'MappingInfo=txtOverText(0),txtOverText,0,Font
Public Property Get Font() As Font
Attribute Font.VB_Description = "Returns a Font object."
Attribute Font.VB_UserMemId = -512
   Set Font = txtOverText(0).Font
End Property

Public Property Set Font(ByVal New_Font As Font)
   Set txtOverText(0).Font = New_Font
   Set txtOverText(1).Font = New_Font
   PropertyChanged "Font"
End Property

'WARNING! DO NOT REMOVE OR MODIFY THE FOLLOWING COMMENTED LINES!
'MappingInfo=txtOverText(0),txtOverText,0,Refresh
Public Sub Refresh()
Attribute Refresh.VB_Description = "Forces a complete repaint
    of an object."
   txtOverText(0).Refresh
End Sub

Private Sub txtOverText_Click(Index As Integer)
   RaiseEvent Click
End Sub

Private Sub txtOverText_DblClick(Index As Integer)
   RaiseEvent DblClick
End Sub

Private Sub txtOverText_MouseDown(Index As Integer, Button _
As Integer, Shift As Integer, X As Single, Y As Single)
   RaiseEvent MouseDown(Button, Shift, X, Y)
End Sub

Private Sub txtOverText_MouseMove(Index As Integer, Button _
As Integer, Shift As Integer, X As Single, Y As Single)
   RaiseEvent MouseMove(Button, Shift, X, Y)
End Sub
```

```
Private Sub txtOverText_MouseUp(Index As Integer, Button As _
Integer, Shift As Integer, X As Single, Y As Single)
  RaiseEvent MouseUp(Button, Shift, X, Y)
End Sub

Private Sub txtOverText_Change(Index As Integer)
  'synchronize the textboxes
  If mnCtlIndex = 0 Then
    txtOverText(1).Text = txtOverText(0).Text
  Else
    txtOverText(0).Text = txtOverText(1).Text
  End If
  RaiseEvent Change
End Sub

'WARNING! DO NOT REMOVE OR MODIFY THE FOLLOWING COMMENTED LINES!
'MappingInfo=txtOverText(0),txtOverText,0,Locked
Public Property Get Locked() As Boolean
Attribute Locked.VB_Description = "Determines whether a
    control can be edited."
  Locked = txtOverText(0).Locked
End Property

Public Property Let Locked(ByVal New_Locked As Boolean)
  txtOverText(0).Locked() = New_Locked
  txtOverText(1).Locked() = New_Locked
  PropertyChanged "Locked"
End Property

'WARNING! DO NOT REMOVE OR MODIFY THE FOLLOWING COMMENTED LINES!
'MappingInfo=txtOverText(0),txtOverText,0,MaxLength
Public Property Get MaxLength() As Long
Attribute MaxLength.VB_Description = "Returns/sets the maximum
    number of characters that can be entered in a control."
  MaxLength = txtOverText(0).MaxLength
End Property

Public Property Let MaxLength(ByVal New_MaxLength As Long)
  txtOverText(0).MaxLength() = New_MaxLength
  txtOverText(1).MaxLength() = New_MaxLength
  PropertyChanged "MaxLength"
End Property
```

```
'WARNING! DO NOT REMOVE OR MODIFY THE FOLLOWING COMMENTED LINES!
'MappingInfo=txtOverText(0),txtOverText,0,MouseIcon
Public Property Get MouseIcon() As Picture
Attribute MouseIcon.VB_Description = "Sets a custom mouse icon."
   Set MouseIcon = txtOverText(0).MouseIcon
End Property


Public Property Set MouseIcon(ByVal New_MouseIcon As Picture)
   Set txtOverText(0).MouseIcon = New_MouseIcon
   Set txtOverText(1).MouseIcon = New_MouseIcon
   PropertyChanged "MouseIcon"
End Property


'WARNING! DO NOT REMOVE OR MODIFY THE FOLLOWING COMMENTED LINES!
'MappingInfo=txtOverText(0),txtOverText,0,MousePointer
Public Property Get MousePointer() As Integer
Attribute MousePointer.VB_Description = "Returns/sets the type
    of mouse pointer displayed when over part of an object."
   MousePointer = txtOverText(0).MousePointer
End Property


Public Property Let MousePointer(ByVal New_MousePointer As _
Integer)
   txtOverText(0).MousePointer() = New_MousePointer
   txtOverText(1).MousePointer() = New_MousePointer
   PropertyChanged "MousePointer"
End Property


'WARNING! DO NOT REMOVE OR MODIFY THE FOLLOWING COMMENTED LINES!
'MappingInfo=txtOverText(0),txtOverText,0,SelLength
Public Property Get SelLength() As Long
Attribute SelLength.VB_Description = "Returns/sets the number
    of characters selected."
   SelLength = txtOverText(0).SelLength
End Property

Public Property Let SelLength(ByVal New_SelLength As Long)
   txtOverText(0).SelLength() = New_SelLength
   txtOverText(1).SelLength() = New_SelLength
   PropertyChanged "SelLength"
End Property
```

```
'WARNING! DO NOT REMOVE OR MODIFY THE FOLLOWING COMMENTED LINES!
'MappingInfo=txtOverText(0),txtOverText,0,SelStart
Public Property Get SelStart() As Long
Attribute SelStart.VB_Description = "Returns/sets the starting
    point of text selected."
  SelStart = txtOverText(0).SelStart
End Property

Public Property Let SelStart(ByVal New_SelStart As Long)
  txtOverText(0).SelStart() = New_SelStart
  txtOverText(1).SelStart() = New_SelStart
  PropertyChanged "SelStart"
End Property

'WARNING! DO NOT REMOVE OR MODIFY THE FOLLOWING COMMENTED LINES!
'MappingInfo=txtOverText(0),txtOverText,0,SelText
Public Property Get SelText() As String
Attribute SelText.VB_Description = "Returns/sets the string
    containing the currently selected text."
  SelText = txtOverText(0).SelText
End Property

Public Property Let SelText(ByVal New_SelText As String)
  txtOverText(0).SelText() = New_SelText
  txtOverText(1).SelText() = New_SelText
  PropertyChanged "SelText"
End Property

'WARNING! DO NOT REMOVE OR MODIFY THE FOLLOWING COMMENTED LINES!
'MappingInfo=txtOverText(0),txtOverText,0,Text
Public Property Get Text() As String
Attribute Text.VB_Description = "Returns/sets the text
    contained in the control."
  Text = txtOverText(0).Text
End Property

Public Property Let Text(ByVal New_Text As String)
  txtOverText(0).Text() = New_Text
  txtOverText(1).Text() = New_Text
  PropertyChanged "Text"
End Property
```

```
'WARNING! DO NOT REMOVE OR MODIFY THE FOLLOWING COMMENTED LINES!
'MappingInfo=txtOverText(0),txtOverText,0,ToolTipText
Public Property Get ToolTipText() As String
Attribute ToolTipText.VB_Description = "Returns/sets the text
    displayed when the mouse is paused over the control."
  ToolTipText = txtOverText(0).ToolTipText
End Property

Public Property Let ToolTipText(ByVal New_ToolTipText As String)
  txtOverText(0).ToolTipText() = New_ToolTipText
  txtOverText(1).ToolTipText() = New_ToolTipText
  PropertyChanged "ToolTipText"
End Property

'WARNING! DO NOT REMOVE OR MODIFY THE FOLLOWING COMMENTED LINES!
'MappingInfo=txtOverText(0),txtOverText,0,WhatsThisHelpID
Public Property Get WhatsThisHelpID() As Long
Attribute WhatsThisHelpID.VB_Description = "Returns/sets an
    associated context number for an object."
  WhatsThisHelpID = txtOverText(0).WhatsThisHelpID
End Property

Public Property Let WhatsThisHelpID(ByVal New_WhatsThisHelpID _
As Long)
  txtOverText(0).WhatsThisHelpID() = New_WhatsThisHelpID
  txtOverText(1).WhatsThisHelpID() = New_WhatsThisHelpID
  PropertyChanged "WhatsThisHelpID"
End Property

Public Property Get MultiLine() As Boolean
  MultiLine = m_MultiLine
End Property

Public Property Let MultiLine(ByVal New_MultiLine As Boolean)
  'un-comment these lines to disallow setting at run time
' If Ambient.UserMode And (Not mbReadingProperties) Then
'   MsgBox Error(382)
'   Exit Property
' End If
  m_MultiLine = New_MultiLine
  If m_MultiLine Then
    mnCtlIndex = 1
```

```
    txtOverText(0).Visible = False
    txtOverText(1).Visible = True
  Else
    mnCtlIndex = 0
    txtOverText(1).Visible = False
    txtOverText(0).Visible = True
  End If
  PropertyChanged "MultiLine"
End Property


Public Property Get OverwriteColor() As OLE_COLOR
  OverwriteColor = m_OverwriteColor
End Property


Public Property Let OverwriteColor(ByVal New_OverwriteColor _
As OLE_COLOR)
  m_OverwriteColor = New_OverwriteColor
  PropertyChanged "OverwriteColor"
End Property


'Initialize Properties for User Control
Private Sub UserControl_InitProperties()
  m_MultiLine = m_def_MultiLine
  m_OverwriteColor = m_def_OverwriteColor
End Sub


'Load property values from storage
Private Sub UserControl_ReadProperties(PropBag As PropertyBag)
  On Error Resume Next

  mbReadingProperties = True
  txtOverText(0).BackColor = PropBag.ReadProperty("BackColor", _
  &H80000005)
  txtOverText(0).ForeColor = PropBag.ReadProperty("ForeColor", _
  &H80000008)
  txtOverText(0).Enabled = PropBag.ReadProperty("Enabled", True)
  Set Font = PropBag.ReadProperty("Font", Ambient.Font)
  txtOverText(0).Locked = PropBag.ReadProperty("Locked", False)
  txtOverText(0).MaxLength = _
  PropBag.ReadProperty("MaxLength", 0)
  Set MouseIcon = PropBag.ReadProperty("MouseIcon", Nothing)
```

```
   txtOverText(0).MousePointer = _
   PropBag.ReadProperty("MousePointer", 0)
   txtOverText(0).SelLength = PropBag.ReadProperty("SelLength", 0)
   txtOverText(0).SelStart = PropBag.ReadProperty("SelStart", 0)
   txtOverText(0).SelText = PropBag.ReadProperty("SelText", "")
   txtOverText(0).Text = PropBag.ReadProperty("Text", _
   "OverText1")
   txtOverText(0).ToolTipText = _
   PropBag.ReadProperty("ToolTipText", "")
   txtOverText(0).WhatsThisHelpID = _
   PropBag.ReadProperty("WhatsThisHelpID", 0)
   MultiLine = PropBag.ReadProperty("MultiLine", _
   m_def_MultiLine)
   m_OverwriteColor = PropBag.ReadProperty("OverwriteColor", _
   m_def_OverwriteColor)
   mbReadingProperties = False
End Sub

'Write property values to storage
Private Sub UserControl_WriteProperties(PropBag As PropertyBag)
   On Error Resume Next

   Call PropBag.WriteProperty("BackColor", _
   txtOverText(0).BackColor, &H80000005)
   Call PropBag.WriteProperty("ForeColor", _
   txtOverText(0).ForeColor, &H80000008)
   Call PropBag.WriteProperty("Enabled", _
   txtOverText(0).Enabled, True)
   Call PropBag.WriteProperty("Font", Font, Ambient.Font)
   Call PropBag.WriteProperty("Locked", _
   txtOverText(0).Locked, False)
   Call PropBag.WriteProperty("MaxLength", _
   txtOverText(0).MaxLength, 0)
   Call PropBag.WriteProperty("MouseIcon", MouseIcon, Nothing)
   Call PropBag.WriteProperty("MousePointer", _
   txtOverText(0).MousePointer, 0)
   Call PropBag.WriteProperty("SelLength", _
   txtOverText(0).SelLength, 0)
   Call PropBag.WriteProperty("SelStart", _
   txtOverText(0).SelStart, 0)
   Call PropBag.WriteProperty("SelText", _
   txtOverText(0).SelText, "")
```

```
Call PropBag.WriteProperty("Text", txtOverText(0).Text, _
"OverText1")
Call PropBag.WriteProperty("ToolTipText", _
txtOverText(0).ToolTipText, "")
Call PropBag.WriteProperty("WhatsThisHelpID", _
txtOverText(0).WhatsThisHelpID, 0)
Call PropBag.WriteProperty("MultiLine", m_MultiLine, _
m_def_MultiLine)
Call PropBag.WriteProperty("OverwriteColor", _
m_OverwriteColor, m_def_OverwriteColor)
End Sub

Private Sub UserControl_Resize()
   txtOverText(0).Width = Width
   txtOverText(0).Height = Height
   txtOverText(1).Width = Width
   txtOverText(1).Height = Height
End Sub
```

Now, to see that we hooked up the properties of our control correctly:

1. Press F5 to run the project and see that the form loads and the control displays the starting text.
2. Stop the application.
3. Click the user control and press F4 to view its properties in the Properties window.
4. Change the Text property and press ENTER. Notice that the displayed text changes. This is possible because of the Property Let procedure that we added.

We now have a control that can communicate with code outside of itself. We want to add the code that allows the user to set the date at run time.

Chapter 17

Whenever your application has more than two option buttons in a single group, it can be frustrating to always have to write the If-Then-Else code that determines which option the user has selected. Unfortunately, with standard option buttons, there is no other way of proceeding. Standard option buttons do not have a way of exposing which button is currently selected within the group except through testing each button individually.

The control we want to show you here extends the idea of an option button group by making it possible to check, with a single statement, which option button was clicked. It does this by adding a property that gives the currently selected button as its value. In a nutshell, what we want is an option group button control that:

1. Is as easy to use as standard option buttons.
2. Will expose a read/write property to the user of the control that sets or returns the currently selected option button.

Finally, the user interface for this control is fairly simple but the code is somewhat complex. So you might want to load the control found on the CD in the CH 17 dir in order to get started. Moreover, since we are not exposing any standard properties, we will not be using the Control Interface Wizard. We will explain the code as we go. In the end, the OCX is only about 28k.

The Option Group Control

The Idea of the Control

The control we will show you in this chapter actually does a bit more than the one described in the introduction. It was designed to satisfy the following goals:

1. Expose enough properties and events of our Option Button Group Control so that it is similar to use as an ordinary option button.
2. Perform the necessary sizing and spacing of the option buttons so the user does not need to.
3. Make the control able to read and write data to a database.
4. Have a Property page that makes adding, ordering, modifying and deleting the option buttons easy and efficient.

This control really requires a property page in order to make it easy to use. This is because the buttons in the group are dynamic. Any time you have a property like this (usually called a *property array*), it will not be exposed in the Properties window. Figure 17-1 shows the finished Property page.

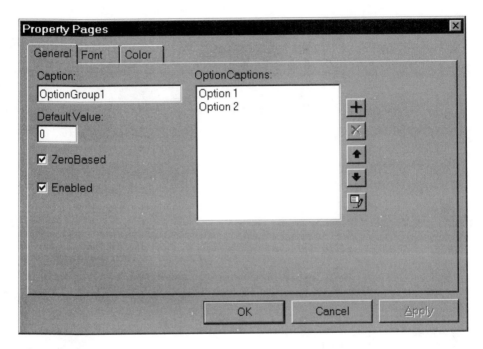

Figure 17-1
The Property Page for the Option Button Control

(See Chapter 10, Property Pages, for more details on how to build this.)

Creating the Interface

To accomplish all these goals, we need a fairly simple UI. Figure 17-2 shows the control at design time.

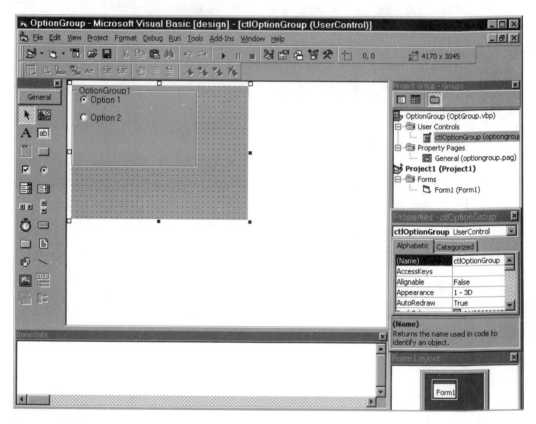

Figure 17-2
The Option Group Control

To build this, we used a Frame Control and an array of two option buttons. Since the minimum number of options buttons in a group is two, we will start with that number. Obviously, the individual buttons we place inside a frame will be part of a control array. Then, based on how the user of the control sets a property, we will change the number of controls in the array dynamically.

The following table describes the controls and their most important properties using the format you have already seen.

Table 17-1: Controls and Their Most Important Properties

Form	
AutoRedraw	–1 'True
LockControls	–1 'True
Frame	
Name	fraOptions
Caption	OptionGroup1
Left	0
Top	0
TabIndex	0
OptionButton	
Name	optOptions
Index	0
Caption	Option 1
Left	180
Top	210
Height	270
OptionButton	
Name	optOptions
Index	1
Caption	Option 2
Left	180
Top	615
Height	270

As usual, the end of the chapter gives the full code for the control including all the properties that we reset from their defaults. The CD contains the code and all the files needed to see the control at work.

Building the interface for this control, as shown in Figure 17-2, took about 10 minutes.

The Code

We will now explain the code in stages. The first stage is the module level variables needed to communicate across the various procedures in the user control.

```
Const CTL_HEIGHT = 270
'Module vars
Private mbReadingProperties As Boolean
Private mbSettingValue As Boolean
```

These module variables are flags used to determine the state of the control. This lets us make sure that certain code will not execute at undesirable times. The reason for this should be clearer as you work through the rest of the code.

Next we need the local variables used to hold property information:

```
'Local Vars for Properties
Private mbZeroBased As Boolean
Private mnValue As Integer
Private mnNumOptions As Integer
```

As you have seen, variables like this are used to store the current value of the properties they represent. Without these variables, there would be no way to pass the value back to other code that calls the Property Get procedure.

Now we need one event declaration. The event we want our control to raise allows the user control to pass on its version of the Click event when the user clicks in our control. This way, the user of our control can write code that will execute when the user clicks the option group, just as they can when a standard option button is clicked.

```
'Event Declarations
Public Event Click()
```

Later in the code, you will see where we call RaiseEvent to actually fire up this event.

Next we will add the design-time/run-time Property procedures for the caption.

```
'Design Time/Runtime Public Properties
Public Property Get Caption() As String
   Caption = fraOptions.Caption
End Property
```

```
Public Property Let Caption(ByVal sVal As String)
  fraOptions.Caption = sVal
  PropertyChanged "Caption"
End Property
Public Property Get CaptionFont() As Font
  Set CaptionFont = fraOptions.Font
End Property
Public Property Set CaptionFont(ByVal vNewValue As _
Font)
  Set fraOptions.Font = vNewValue
  PropertyChanged "CaptionFont"
End Property
```

The Property procedures simply read or write to a property of the frame control. The CaptionFont property allows the user to set a different font for the title of the option group than for the captions in the various buttons.

Next, we need procedures to set the BackColor, ForeColor and Enabled properties for every control on the user control. We do this by iterating the collection of controls using the For/Each/Next control structure.

```
Public Property Get BackColor() As OLE_COLOR
  BackColor = fraOptions.BackColor
End Property

Public Property Let BackColor(ByVal vNewValue As _
OLE_COLOR)
  Dim ctl As Control
  For Each ctl In UserControl.Controls
    ctl.BackColor = vNewValue
  Next ctl
  PropertyChanged "BackColor"
End Property

Public Property Get ForeColor() As OLE_COLOR
  ForeColor = fraOptions.ForeColor
End Property

Public Property Let ForeColor(ByVal vNewValue As _
OLE_COLOR)
  Dim ctl As Control
  For Each ctl In UserControl.Controls
    ctl.ForeColor = vNewValue
  Next ctl
  PropertyChanged "ForeColor"
End Property
```

The next procedures get and set the font of the captions for all of the option buttons in the array.

```
Public Property Get Enabled() As Boolean
   Enabled = UserControl.Enabled
End Property

Public Property Let Enabled(ByVal vNewValue As _
Boolean)
   Dim ctl As Control
   For Each ctl In UserControl.Controls
     ctl.Enabled = vNewValue
   Next ctl
   UserControl.Enabled = vNewValue
   PropertyChanged "Enabled"
End Property

Public Property Get OptionsFont() As Font
   Set OptionsFont = optOptions(0).Font
End Property

Public Property Set OptionsFont(ByVal vNewValue As _
Font)
   Dim i As Integer
   For i = 0 To mnNumOptions - 1
     Set optOptions(i).Font = vNewValue
   Next i
   PropertyChanged "OptionsFont"
End Property
```

The next procedures get and set the caption of an individual option button in the array by accepting an Index argument from the calling routine.

```
Public Property Get OptionCaption(nIndex As _
Integer) As String
   On Error GoTo OptionCaptionGetErr
   If mbZeroBased Then
     OptionCaption = optOptions(nIndex).Caption
   Else
     OptionCaption = optOptions(nIndex - 1).Caption
   End If
   Exit Property
OptionCaptionGetErr:
```

```
    MsgBox Error
End Property
Public Property Let OptionCaption(nIndex As Integer, _
    sCaption As String)
  On Error GoTo OptionCaptionLetErr
  If mbZeroBased Then
    optOptions(nIndex).Caption = sCaption
  Else
    optOptions(nIndex - 1).Caption = sCaption
  End If
  Exit Property
OptionCaptionLetErr:
  MsgBox Error
End Property
```

We next want to have a ZeroBased property to allow the user to start with a count of 0 or a count of 1 (like VBs Option Base statement). Setting the ZeroBased property requires some additional code in the Property Let procedure in order to shift the current OptionValue property based on the new setting.

Eliminating this property would simplify the entire control, but we think that it makes the control more user friendly for some programmers to be able to think in their desired base of 0 or 1. Although many lists of items in Visual Basic are 0-based, more are becoming 1-based, such as collections. This property enables the user to determine what they want the control to use as its base. ⊃

```
Public Property Get ZeroBased() As Boolean
  ZeroBased = mbZeroBased
End Property

Public Property Let ZeroBased(bData As Boolean)
  If bData = mbZeroBased Then Exit Property

  mbZeroBased = bData
  'must've changed
  If mbZeroBased Then
    OptionValue = OptionValue - 1
  Else
    OptionValue = OptionValue + 1
  End If
```

```
   PropertyChanged "ZeroBased"
End Property

Public Property Get OptionValue() As Integer
   OptionValue = mnValue
End Property

Public Property Let OptionValue(nData As Integer)
   On Error GoTo OptionValueErr

   mbSettingValue = True

BadData:

   'check for none set (-1)
   If nData = -1 Then
     'turn the current one off
     If mnValue > -1 Then
       optOptions(mnValue).Value = False
     End If
   ElseIf mbZeroBased Then
     If nData < 0 Or nData > mnNumOptions - 1 Then
       If Not Ambient.UserMode Then
         MsgBox Error(380)
       Else
         'must've been a datacontrol set that caused the error
         'so just turn off all values
         nData = -1
         GoTo BadData
       End If
     End If
     'attempt to set the control
     optOptions(nData).Value = True
   Else
     If nData < 1 Or nData > mnNumOptions Then
       If Not Ambient.UserMode Then
         MsgBox Error(380)
       Else
         'must've been a datacontrol set that caused the error
         'so just turn off all values
         nData = -1
         GoTo BadData
```

```
      End If
    End If
    'they passed in a 1 based number so we need to convert it
    optOptions(nData - 1).Value = True
  End If

  'must've passed so we can set the local var
  mnValue = nData

  PropertyChanged "OptionValue"
  mbSettingValue = False

  Exit Property
OptionValueErr:
  MsgBox Err.Description
  mbSettingValue = False
End Property
```

As you can see, the Property Let procedure for the OptionValue property is fairly complicated. It must test for special cases including –1 for none, out of range values, and whether the control is 0– or 1– based. The mbSettingValue flag is needed to keep the procedure from being called over and over again, because this procedure will trigger the optOptions_ Click event which can, in turn, attempt to set the value again. There is also some error handling specifically written to handle bad data from a database when the control is used in a data-bound application.

The following Property Let procedure is going to correspond to a design time property only. It should give an appropriate error message if the user tries to execute it at run time. The Property Get that lets you read the current value of the property should be available anytime.

The way we make the property unavailable at run time is by testing the value of the Ambient.UserMode property. As you have seen, if this value is True we know we are in run time mode for the control. However, we want to allow the control to read back any stored property values without an error. We do this by adding our own flag called mbReadingProperties. This lets us insure that the procedure does not execute while we are simply reading stored property values. Without this flag, we would get an error every time we went from design time to run time.

```
'Design Time Only Public Properties
Public Property Get NumOptions() As Integer
  NumOptions = mnNumOptions
End Property

Public Property Let NumOptions(nData As Integer)
  Dim i As Integer

  'disallow at run time
  If Ambient.UserMode And (Not mbReadingProperties) Then
    MsgBox Error(382)
    Exit Property
  End If

  'load or unload the option buttons
  If nData < mnNumOptions Then
    'need to get rid of some
    For i = mnNumOptions - 1 To nData Step -1
      Unload optOptions(i)
    Next i
  Else
    'need to add some
    For i = mnNumOptions To nData - 1
      Load optOptions(i)
      optOptions(i).Visible = True
      optOptions(i).Enabled = True
      optOptions(i).Caption = "Option " & i + 1
    Next i
  End If

  mnNumOptions = nData
  UserControl_Resize
  OptionValue = mnValue

  PropertyChanged "NumOptions"
End Property
```

The next two procedures are similar to ones you have seen used repeatedly before. Procedures like this are necessary so that properties of a user control can persist across state changes.

```
'Property Bag Functions
Private Sub UserControl_ReadProperties(PropBag As PropertyBag)
  On Error Resume Next
  Dim i As Integer
  'Load property values from storage
  mbReadingProperties = True
  Caption = PropBag.ReadProperty("Caption")
  ZeroBased = PropBag.ReadProperty("ZeroBased", True)
  OptionValue = PropBag.ReadProperty("OptionValue", 0)
  NumOptions = PropBag.ReadProperty("NumOptions", 2)
  BackColor = PropBag.ReadProperty("BackColor", &H8000000F)
  ForeColor = PropBag.ReadProperty("ForeColor", &H0)
  Set CaptionFont = PropBag.ReadProperty("CaptionFont")
  Set OptionsFont = PropBag.ReadProperty("OptionsFont")
  Enabled = PropBag.ReadProperty("Enabled", True)
  For i = 0 To NumOptions - 1
    If mbZeroBased Then
      OptionCaption(i) = PropBag.ReadProperty(i & _
                                    "OptionCaption")
    Else
      OptionCaption(i + 1) = PropBag.ReadProperty(i & _
                                    "OptionCaption")
    End If
  Next
  mbReadingProperties = False
End Sub

Private Sub UserControl_WriteProperties(PropBag As PropertyBag)
  On Error Resume Next
  Dim i As Integer
  'Write property values to storage
  Call PropBag.WriteProperty("Caption", Caption, "")
  Call PropBag.WriteProperty("ZeroBased", ZeroBased, True)
  Call PropBag.WriteProperty("OptionValue", OptionValue, 0)
  Call PropBag.WriteProperty("NumOptions", NumOptions, 2)
  Call PropBag.WriteProperty("BackColor", BackColor, &H8000000F)
  Call PropBag.WriteProperty("ForeColor", ForeColor, &H0)
  Call PropBag.WriteProperty("CaptionFont", CaptionFont)
  Call PropBag.WriteProperty("OptionsFont", OptionsFont)
  Call PropBag.WriteProperty("Enabled", Enabled, True)
  For i = 0 To NumOptions - 1
```

```
   If mbZeroBased Then
     Call PropBag.WriteProperty(i & "OptionCaption", _
                                 OptionCaption(i))
   Else
     Call PropBag.WriteProperty(i & "OptionCaption", _
                                 OptionCaption(i + 1))
   End If
 Next
End Sub
```

The only code that needs explaining in the above is the For/Next loop that is used to read or write the option captions. They are all stored as separate strings with a numeric prefix attached to them. This is a very useful way of storing lists of items where the number of items is dynamic.

The final two procedures are for the Private events that we must handle internally.

```
'Private events
Private Sub optOptions_Click(Index As Integer)
   If mbSettingValue Then Exit Sub
   If mbZeroBased Then
     OptionValue = Index
   Else
     OptionValue = Index + 1
   End If
   RaiseEvent Click
End Sub
```

We trap the Click event for a constituent button and pass it on to the application that is hosting the control. This way, the host control can process the event itself. The host control is also responsible for setting the OptionValue property based on the current ZeroBased state of the control.

Finally, we need the code to initialize the module level variables to the desired default values. Otherwise, by default, they would both be 0 and this would confuse the control logic that we so laboriously built into the control.

```
Private Sub UserControl_Initialize()
   mnNumOptions = 2
   mbZeroBased = True
End Sub
```

Resize Logic

We want to resize the containing frame control and then properly space and
size the option buttons whenever the user resizes the control. To do this, we
needed to add code that sets the frame control to the current size of the user
control. Then it spaces the controls by calculating how large a button can be,
based on the number of buttons on the control and their current heights (the
value of the CTL_HEIGHT constant).

```
Private Sub UserControl_Resize()
  On Error GoTo UserControl_ResizeErr

  Dim i As Integer
  Dim h As Integer
  Dim t As Integer

  fraOptions.Height = Height - 30
  fraOptions.Width = Width - 45

  'position the option buttons
  h = fraOptions.Height - (CTL_HEIGHT * (mnNumOptions + 1))
  h = h \ (mnNumOptions + 1) 'individual control height

  t = t + (h + 200)

  For i = 0 To mnNumOptions - 1
    optOptions(i).Move 120, t, fraOptions.Width - CTL_HEIGHT
    optOptions(i).TabIndex = i
    t = t + (h + CTL_HEIGHT)
  Next i

  UserControl.Refresh

  Exit Sub
UserControl_ResizeErr:
  MsgBox Error
End Sub
```

Data Binding

Since we would like to be able to make this control have the ability to be data-bound, we must do the following:

1. Load the Tools|Procedure Attributes dialog.
2. Click the <Advanced> button.
3. Select the OptionValue property in the Name drop-down list.
4. Check the Property is data bound check box in the Data Binding frame.
5. Check the This property binds to DataField check box.
6. Click <OK>.

That's it. If you test the control, you will see that it now has a DataSource and DataField property available. This makes it possible to place this user control on a Visual Basic 4.0 form (or any other host that provides a data control) and have the control read the value from the database, then write back the new value.

For example, you might have a field for Mr., Mrs. or Miss in your database. This easily translates to 0, 1 and 2 or, if you prefer, 1, 2 and 3. So all you need to do is use our user control and bind it to that field. Then, when the form becomes active, the control will select the correct option, based on the what is in the database, and write out the selected option when the user changes the record.

Property Page

The Captions for the Options in this control cannot be set at design time without a property page. They are not exposed because they are stored as a collection. Property Pages were discussed in Chapter 11, so we will not discuss them again here other than to show you how to connect the one we have supplied on the CD.

Follow these steps to add the Property Page to the control you have just created.

1. Copy the OptionGroup.pag and .pgx files to your project directory.

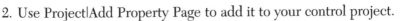

2. Use Project|Add Property Page to add it to your control project.

3. Load your control in design mode and double-click the PropertyPages property on the Properties window.

4. Select General, Standard Font and Standard Color.

5. Close the dialog and you now have a custom Property Page connected to your control.

Possible Additions and Potential Problems

This control is quite complete as is. A few possible additions that come to mind are:

- Make it possible to list the options from left to right instead of just top to bottom.
- Provide a way to do multi-column option groups.

A problem you might run into is that the control doesn't handle too many options buttons in a group. If a user of the control puts too large a number of options in the group, they simply overwrite each other and you cannot see the group correctly. This could be remedied by having the control only accept a limited number of buttons. (A reasonable number might be 10; after all, a UI with more than 10 buttons in a single group isn't likely to be too user friendly.)

The Full Code for This Control

```
VERSION 5.00
Begin VB.UserControl ctlOptionGroup
    AutoRedraw      =    -1   'True
    ClientHeight    =    3045
    ClientLeft      =    0
    ClientTop       =    0
    ClientWidth     =    4170
```

```
ClipControls      =    0     'False
LockControls      =    -1    'True
PropertyPages     =    "optiongroup.ctx":0000
ScaleHeight       =    3045
ScaleWidth        =    4170
ToolboxBitmap     =    "optiongroup.ctx":002D
Begin VB.Frame fraOptions
    Caption           =    "OptionGroup1"
    Height            =    1860
    Left              =    0
    TabIndex          =    0
    Top               =    0
    Width             =    2985
    Begin VB.OptionButton optOptions
       Caption           =    "Option 2"
       Height            =    270
       Index             =    1
       Left              =    180
       TabIndex          =    2
       Top               =    615
       Width             =    2715
    End
    Begin VB.OptionButton optOptions
       Caption           =    "Option 1"
       Height            =    270
       Index             =    0
       Left              =    180
       TabIndex          =    1
       Top               =    210
       Value             =    -1    'True
       Width             =    2715
    End
    End
   End
End
Attribute VB_Name = "ctlOptionGroup"
Attribute VB_GlobalNameSpace = False
Attribute VB_Creatable = True
Attribute VB_PredeclaredId = False
Attribute VB_Exposed = True
Attribute VB_Description = "Gary and Dave's Option Group
   Control"
Option Explicit
```

```
Const CTL_HEIGHT = 270
'Module vars
Private mbReadingProperties As Boolean
Private mbSettingValue As Boolean

'Local Vars for Properties
Private mbZeroBased As Boolean
Private mnValue As Integer
Private mnNumOptions As Integer

'Event Declarations
Event Click()

'Design Time/Runtime Public Properties
Public Property Get Caption() As String
  Caption = fraOptions.Caption
End Property

Public Property Let Caption(ByVal sVal As String)
  fraOptions.Caption = sVal
  PropertyChanged "Caption"
End Property

Public Property Get CaptionFont() As Font
  Set CaptionFont = fraOptions.Font
End Property

Public Property Set CaptionFont(ByVal vNewValue As Font)
  Set fraOptions.Font = vNewValue
  PropertyChanged "CaptionFont"
End Property

Public Property Get BackColor() As OLE_COLOR
  BackColor = fraOptions.BackColor
End Property

Public Property Let BackColor(ByVal vNewValue As OLE_COLOR)
  Dim ctl As Control
  For Each ctl In UserControl.Controls
    ctl.BackColor = vNewValue
  Next ctl
  PropertyChanged "BackColor"
End Property
```

```
Public Property Get ForeColor() As OLE_COLOR
   ForeColor = fraOptions.ForeColor
End Property

Public Property Let ForeColor(ByVal vNewValue As OLE_COLOR)
   Dim ctl As Control
   For Each ctl In UserControl.Controls
     ctl.ForeColor = vNewValue
   Next ctl
   PropertyChanged "ForeColor"
End Property

Public Property Get Enabled() As Boolean
   Enabled = UserControl.Enabled
End Property

Public Property Let Enabled(ByVal vNewValue As Boolean)
   Dim ctl As Control
   For Each ctl In UserControl.Controls
     ctl.Enabled = vNewValue
   Next ctl
   UserControl.Enabled = vNewValue
   PropertyChanged "Enabled"
End Property

Public Property Get OptionsFont() As Font
   Set OptionsFont = optOptions(0).Font
End Property

Public Property Set OptionsFont(ByVal vNewValue As Font)
   Dim i As Integer
   For i = 0 To mnNumOptions - 1
     Set optOptions(i).Font = vNewValue
   Next i
   PropertyChanged "OptionsFont"
End Property

Public Property Get OptionCaption(nIndex As Integer) As String
   On Error GoTo OptionCaptionGetErr

   If mbZeroBased Then
     OptionCaption = optOptions(nIndex).Caption
```

```
   Else
     OptionCaption = optOptions(nIndex - 1).Caption
   End If

   Exit Property
OptionCaptionGetErr:
   MsgBox Error
End Property

Public Property Let OptionCaption(nIndex As Integer, _
sCaption As String)
   On Error GoTo OptionCaptionLetErr

   If mbZeroBased Then
     optOptions(nIndex).Caption = sCaption
   Else
     optOptions(nIndex - 1).Caption = sCaption
   End If

   Exit Property
OptionCaptionLetErr:
   MsgBox Error
End Property

Public Property Get ZeroBased() As Boolean
   ZeroBased = mbZeroBased
End Property

Public Property Let ZeroBased(bData As Boolean)
   If bData = mbZeroBased Then Exit Property

   mbZeroBased = bData
   'must've changed
   If mbZeroBased Then
     OptionValue = OptionValue - 1
   Else
     OptionValue = OptionValue + 1
   End If

   PropertyChanged "ZeroBased"
End Property
```

```
Public Property Get OptionValue() As Integer
Attribute OptionValue.VB_MemberFlags = "24"
  OptionValue = mnValue
End Property

Public Property Let OptionValue(nData As Integer)
  On Error GoTo OptionValueErr

  mbSettingValue = True

BadData:

  'check for none set (-1)
  If nData = -1 Then
    'turn the current one off
    If mnValue > -1 Then
      optOptions(mnValue).Value = False
    End If
  ElseIf mbZeroBased Then
    If nData < 0 Or nData > mnNumOptions - 1 Then
      If Not Ambient.UserMode Then
        MsgBox Error(380)
      Else
        'must've been a datacontrol set that caused the error
        'so just turn off all values
        nData = -1
        GoTo BadData
      End If
    End If
    'attempt to set the control
    optOptions(nData).Value = True
  Else
    If nData < 1 Or nData > mnNumOptions Then
      If Not Ambient.UserMode Then
        MsgBox Error(380)
      Else
        'must've been a datacontrol set that caused the error
        'so just turn off all values
        nData = -1
        GoTo BadData
      End If
    End If
    'they passed in a 1 based number so we need to convert it
    optOptions(nData - 1).Value = True
  End If
```

```
    'must've passed so we can set the local var
    mnValue = nData

    PropertyChanged "OptionValue"
    mbSettingValue = False

    Exit Property
OptionValueErr:
    MsgBox Err.Description
    mbSettingValue = False
End Property

'Design Time Only Public Properties
Public Property Get NumOptions() As Integer
    NumOptions = mnNumOptions
End Property

Public Property Let NumOptions(nData As Integer)
    Dim i As Integer

    'disallow at run time
    If Ambient.UserMode And (Not mbReadingProperties) Then
        MsgBox Error(382)
        Exit Property
    End If

    'load or unload the option buttons
    If nData < mnNumOptions Then
        'need to get rid of some
        For i = mnNumOptions - 1 To nData Step -1
            Unload optOptions(i)
        Next i
    Else
        'need to add some
        For i = mnNumOptions To nData - 1
            Load optOptions(i)
            optOptions(i).Visible = True
            optOptions(i).Enabled = True
            optOptions(i).Caption = "Option " & i + 1
        Next i
    End If
```

```
    mnNumOptions = nData
    UserControl_Resize
    OptionValue = mnValue

    PropertyChanged "NumOptions"
End Property


'Property Bag Functions
Private Sub UserControl_ReadProperties(PropBag As PropertyBag)
    On Error Resume Next
    Dim i As Integer
    'Load property values from storage
    mbReadingProperties = True
    Caption = PropBag.ReadProperty("Caption")
    ZeroBased = PropBag.ReadProperty("ZeroBased", True)
    OptionValue = PropBag.ReadProperty("OptionValue", 0)
    NumOptions = PropBag.ReadProperty("NumOptions", 2)
    BackColor = PropBag.ReadProperty("BackColor", &H8000000F)
    ForeColor = PropBag.ReadProperty("ForeColor", &H0)
    Set CaptionFont = PropBag.ReadProperty("CaptionFont")
    Set OptionsFont = PropBag.ReadProperty("OptionsFont")
    Enabled = PropBag.ReadProperty("Enabled", True)
    For i = 0 To NumOptions - 1
      If mbZeroBased Then
        OptionCaption(i) = PropBag.ReadProperty(i & _
                                        "OptionCaption")
      Else
        OptionCaption(i + 1) = PropBag.ReadProperty(i & _
                                        "OptionCaption")
      End If
    Next
    mbReadingProperties = False
End Sub


Private Sub UserControl_WriteProperties(PropBag As
PropertyBag)
    On Error Resume Next
    Dim i As Integer
    'Write property values to storage
    Call PropBag.WriteProperty("Caption", Caption, "")
    Call PropBag.WriteProperty("ZeroBased", ZeroBased, True)
    Call PropBag.WriteProperty("OptionValue", OptionValue, 0)
```

```
   Call PropBag.WriteProperty("NumOptions", NumOptions, 2)
   Call PropBag.WriteProperty("BackColor", BackColor, _
   &H8000000F)
   Call PropBag.WriteProperty("ForeColor", ForeColor, &H0)
   Call PropBag.WriteProperty("CaptionFont", CaptionFont)
   Call PropBag.WriteProperty("OptionsFont", OptionsFont)
   Call PropBag.WriteProperty("Enabled", Enabled, True)
   For i = 0 To NumOptions - 1
      If mbZeroBased Then
         Call PropBag.WriteProperty(i & "OptionCaption", _
                                    OptionCaption(i))
      Else
         Call PropBag.WriteProperty(i & "OptionCaption", _
                                    OptionCaption(i + 1))
      End If
   Next
End Sub


'Private events
Private Sub optOptions_Click(Index As Integer)
   If mbSettingValue Then Exit Sub
   If mbZeroBased Then
      OptionValue = Index
   Else
      OptionValue = Index + 1
   End If
   RaiseEvent Click
End Sub


Private Sub UserControl_Initialize()
   mnNumOptions = 2
   mbZeroBased = True
End Sub


Private Sub UserControl_Resize()
   On Error GoTo UserControl_ResizeErr

   Dim i As Integer
   Dim h As Integer
   Dim t As Integer

   fraOptions.Height = Height - 30
```

```
fraOptions.Width = Width - 45

'position the option buttons
h = fraOptions.Height - (CTL_HEIGHT * (mnNumOptions + 1))
h = h \ (mnNumOptions + 1)

t = t + (h + 200)

For i = 0 To mnNumOptions - 1
  optOptions(i).Move 120, t, fraOptions.Width - CTL_HEIGHT
  optOptions(i).TabIndex = i
  t = t + (h + CTL_HEIGHT)
Next i

UserControl.Refresh

Exit Sub
UserControl_ResizeErr:
  MsgBox Error
End Sub
```

Index

Center Form procedure p 242

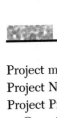

LICENSE AGREEMENT AND LIMITED WARRANTY

READ THE FOLLOWING TERMS AND CONDITIONS CAREFULLY BEFORE OPENING THIS SOFTWARE PACKAGE. THIS LEGAL DOCUMENT IS AN AGREEMENT BETWEEN YOU AND PRENTICE-HALL, INC. (THE "COMPANY"). BY OPENING THIS SEALED SOFTWARE PACKAGE, YOU ARE AGREEING TO BE BOUND BY THESE TERMS AND CONDITIONS. IF YOU DO NOT AGREE WITH THESE TERMS AND CONDITIONS, DO NOT OPEN THE SOFTWARE PACKAGE. PROMPTLY RETURN THE UNOPENED SOFTWARE PACKAGE AND ALL ACCOMPANYING ITEMS TO THE PLACE YOU OBTAINED THEM FOR A FULL REFUND OF ANY SUMS YOU HAVE PAID.

1.   **GRANT OF LICENSE:** In consideration of your payment of the license fee, which is part of the price you paid for this product, and your agreement to abide by the terms and conditions of this Agreement, the Company grants to you a nonexclusive right to use and display the copy of the enclosed software program (hereinafter the "SOFTWARE") on a single computer (i.e., with a single CPU) at a single location so long as you comply with the terms of this Agreement. The Company reserves all rights not expressly granted to you under this Agreement.

2.   **OWNERSHIP OF SOFTWARE:** You own only the magnetic or physical media (the enclosed disks) on which the SOFTWARE is recorded or fixed, but the Company retains all the rights, title, and ownership to the SOFTWARE recorded on the original disk copy(ies) and all subsequent copies of the SOFTWARE, regardless of the form or media on which the original or other copies may exist. This license is not a sale of the original SOFT-WARE or any copy to you.

3.   **COPY RESTRICTIONS:** This SOFTWARE and the accompanying printed materials and user manual (the "Documentation") are the subject of copyright. You may not copy the Documentation or the SOFTWARE, except that you may make a single copy of the SOFTWARE for backup or archival purposes only. You may be held legally responsible for any copying or copyright infringement which is caused or encouraged by your failure to abide by the terms of this restriction.

4.   **USE RESTRICTIONS:** You may not network the SOFTWARE or otherwise use it on more than one computer or computer terminal at the same time. You may physically transfer the SOFTWARE from one computer to another provided that the SOFTWARE is used on only one computer at a time. You may not distribute copies of the SOFTWARE or Documentation to others. You may not reverse engineer, disassemble, decompile, modify, adapt, translate, or create derivative works based on the SOFTWARE or the Documentation without the prior written consent of the Company.

5.   **TRANSFER RESTRICTIONS:** The enclosed SOFTWARE is licensed only to you and may not be transferred to anyone else without the prior written consent of the Company. Any unauthorized transfer of the SOFTWARE shall result in the immediate termination of this Agreement.

6.   **TERMINATION:** This license is effective until terminated. This license will terminate automatically without notice from the Company and become null and void if you fail to comply with any provisions or limitations of this license. Upon termination, you shall destroy the Documentation and all copies of the SOFTWARE. All provisions of this Agreement as to warranties, limitation of liability, remedies or damages, and our ownership rights shall survive termination.

7.   **MISCELLANEOUS:** This Agreement shall be construed in accordance with the laws of the United States of America and the State of New York and shall benefit the Company, its affiliates, and assignees.

8. **LIMITED WARRANTY AND DISCLAIMER OF WARRANTY:** The Company warrants that the SOFTWARE, when properly used in accordance with the Documentation, will operate in substantial conformity with the description of the SOFTWARE set forth in the Documentation. The Company does not warrant that the SOFTWARE will meet your requirements or that the operation of the SOFTWARE will be uninterrupted or error-free. The Company warrants that the media on which the SOFTWARE is delivered shall be free from defects in materials and workmanship under normal use for a period of thirty (30) days from the date of your purchase. Your only remedy and the Company's only obligation under these limited warranties is, at the Company's option, return of the warranted item for a refund of any amounts paid by you or replacement of the item. Any replacement of SOFTWARE or media under the warranties shall not extend the original warranty period. The limited warranty set forth above shall not apply to any SOFTWARE which the Company determines in good faith has been subject to misuse, neglect, improper installation, repair, alteration, or damage by you. EXCEPT FOR THE EXPRESSED WARRANTIES SET FORTH ABOVE, THE COMPANY DISCLAIMS ALL WARRANTIES, EXPRESS OR IMPLIED, INCLUDING WITHOUT LIMITATION THE IMPLIED WARRANTIES OF MERCHANTABILITY AND FITNESS FOR A PARTICULAR PURPOSE. EXCEPT FOR THE EXPRESS WARRANTY SET FORTH ABOVE, THE COMPANY DOES NOT WARRANT, GUARANTEE, OR MAKE ANY REPRESENTATION REGARDING THE USE OR THE RESULTS OF THE USE OF THE SOFTWARE IN TERMS OF ITS CORRECTNESS, ACCURACY, RELIABILITY, CURRENTNESS, OR OTHERWISE.

IN NO EVENT, SHALL THE COMPANY OR ITS EMPLOYEES, AGENTS, SUPPLIERS, OR CONTRACTORS BE LIABLE FOR ANY INCIDENTAL, INDIRECT, SPECIAL, OR CONSEQUENTIAL DAMAGES ARISING OUT OF OR IN CONNECTION WITH THE LICENSE GRANTED UNDER THIS AGREEMENT, OR FOR LOSS OF USE, LOSS OF DATA, LOSS OF INCOME OR PROFIT, OR OTHER LOSSES, SUSTAINED AS A RESULT OF INJURY TO ANY PERSON, OR LOSS OF OR DAMAGE TO PROPERTY, OR CLAIMS OF THIRD PARTIES, EVEN IF THE COMPANY OR AN AUTHORIZED REPRESENTATIVE OF THE COMPANY HAS BEEN ADVISED OF THE POSSIBILITY OF SUCH DAMAGES. IN NO EVENT SHALL LIABILITY OF THE COMPANY FOR DAMAGES WITH RESPECT TO THE SOFTWARE EXCEED THE AMOUNTS ACTUALLY PAID BY YOU, IF ANY, FOR THE SOFTWARE.

SOME JURISDICTIONS DO NOT ALLOW THE LIMITATION OF IMPLIED WARRANTIES OR LIABILITY FOR INCIDENTAL, INDIRECT, SPECIAL, OR CONSEQUENTIAL DAMAGES, SO THE ABOVE LIMITATIONS MAY NOT ALWAYS APPLY. THE WARRANTIES IN THIS AGREEMENT GIVE YOU SPECIFIC LEGAL RIGHTS AND YOU MAY ALSO HAVE OTHER RIGHTS WHICH VARY IN ACCORDANCE WITH LOCAL LAW.

ACKNOWLEDGMENT

YOU ACKNOWLEDGE THAT YOU HAVE READ THIS AGREEMENT, UNDERSTAND IT, AND AGREE TO BE BOUND BY ITS TERMS AND CONDITIONS. YOU ALSO AGREE THAT THIS AGREEMENT IS THE COMPLETE AND EXCLUSIVE STATEMENT OF THE AGREEMENT BETWEEN YOU AND THE COMPANY AND SUPERSEDES ALL PROPOSALS OR PRIOR AGREEMENTS, ORAL, OR WRITTEN, AND ANY OTHER COMMUNICATIONS BETWEEN YOU AND THE COMPANY OR ANY REPRESENTATIVE OF THE COMPANY RELATING TO THE SUBJECT MATTER OF THIS AGREEMENT.

Should you have any questions concerning this Agreement or if you wish to contact the Company for any reason, please contact in writing at the address below.

Robin Short
Prentice Hall PTR
One Lake Street
Upper Saddle River, New Jersey 07458